THE COMPLETE

LESBIAN & GAY PARENTING GUIDE

THE COMPLETE

LESBIAN & GAY
PARENTING GUIDE

Arlene Istar Lev, CSW

BERKLEY BOOKS, NEW YORK

THE BERKLEY PUBLISHING GROUP
Published by the Penguin Group
Penguin Group (USA) Inc.
375 Hudson Street, New York, New York 10014, USA
Penguin Group (Canada), 10 Alcorn Avenue, Toronto, Ontario M4V 3B2, Canada
(a division of Pearson Penguin Canada Inc.)
Penguin Books Ltd., 80 Strand, London WC2R 0RL, England
Penguin Group Ireland, 25 St. Stephen's Green, Dublin 2, Ireland (a division of Penguin Books Ltd.)
Penguin Group (Australia), 250 Camberwell Road, Camberwell, Victoria 3124, Australia
(a division of Pearson Australia Group Pty. Ltd.)
Penguin Books India Pvt. Ltd., 11 Community Centre, Panchsheel Park, New Delhi—110 017, India
Penguin Group (NZ), Cnr. Airborne and Rosedale Roads, Albany, Auckland 1310, New Zealand
(a division of Pearson New Zealand Ltd.)
Penguin Books (South Africa) (Pty.) Ltd., 24 Sturdee Avenue, Rosebank, Johannesburg 2196,
South Africa

Penguin Books Ltd., Registered Offices: 80 Strand, London WC2R 0RL, England

This is an original publication of The Berkley Publishing Group.

Copyright © 2004 by Arlene Istar Lev
Cover design by Steven Ferlauto
Cover photos by Digital Vision/Picture Quest, Creatas/PictureQuest
Text design by Julie Rogers

PRINTING HISTORY
Berkley trade paperback edition / November 2004

Library of Congress Cataloging-in-Publication Data

Lev, Arlene Istar.
   The complete lesbian & gay parenting guide / Arlene Istar Lev.—Berkley trade pbk. ed.
      p. cm.
   Includes bibliographical references and index
   ISBN 0-425-19197-4 (alk. paper)
   1. Gay parents—United States.   2. Parenting—United States.   3. Family—United States.
   I. Title: Complete lesbian and gay parenting guide.   II. Title.

HQ75.28.U6L48 2004
649'.1'08664—dc22
                                                              2004057080

PRINTED IN THE UNITED STATES OF AMERICA

10   9   8

For my handsome boys

Alternative families are not just about alternative ways of conceiving children . . . but LGBTs having children is about alternative relationships between donors and recipients, between biological and non-biological co-parents, and especially, the relationships between each of the above and children that come out of these arrangements.

JENIFER FIRESTONE, *ALTERNATIVE FAMILY MATTERS*

CONTENTS

Foreword

In her book, *The Complete Lesbian & Gay Parenting Guide,* Ari Istar Lev gracefully and forthrightly takes on a full exploration of how we, as lesbian, gay, bisexual, and transgender people, become parents, how we manage our relationships, and how we continue to celebrate and struggle as families. For all of us who are parenting, the common thread that we share is that it is the most difficult *and* most satisfying endeavor we have ever undertaken. Ms. Lev not only celebrates our successes as a community but examines struggles inherent to being human and therefore shared by our community as we engage in parenting and family-making.

It's been a long time since the first primer on parenting in the lesbian, gay, bisexual, and transgender community was published, and I'd like to be able to say that we, as a community, have experienced tremendous changes. In so many ways we have. And yet in the most basic and necessary way—the need to belong and be fully recognized, included and protected as equal members of our communities and country—we continue to struggle and strive to take our rightful place. As the executive director of the Family Pride Coalition, I work in that struggle every day. I'm proud of the gains we have made over the twenty-five years of representing the LGBT parenting community. Clearly, as we become more visible and take on the challenges of parenting side by side with our heterosexual counterparts, we gain greater recognition and foster the awareness that we are worthy and that our children are doing just fine according to all observable measures.

As the mother of two children, a son who is nineteen and in college and a daughter who is eight and in second grade, I can say firsthand that there is no magic prescription for parenting, as each child and each parenting situation creates new challenges and delights to explore and experience. What I do learn over and over again is that the power of community can never be overstated nor underestimated. Because no aspect of our family life can be taken for granted, our community continually sets the bar for intentionality in this thing we call parenting. And yet, there is no other endeavor less predictable than this. As a community we need to share our struggles and joys, and we need to find ways to learn together. This book offers an insightful overview of the elements and richness of our community as we strive to seek models where before there were none.

One of the beauties of LGBT parenting is the opportunity to create our families in ways that make sense to each of us personally. Without the models that often usher most families forward unquestioningly through the maze of raising children, we are forced to consider the impact of a full plate of options. I think that this nurtures in us a kind of thoughtfulness and togetherness that renders very positive results. I am continually amazed by our children and the adults that they become. There are no accidents here. They become as we are, woven from the models that we provide, and they learn through the richness of our struggle to not take respect, diversity, human dignity, and civil rights for granted and, according to the research, to view others with a greater degree of empathy than their peers. While there is much cause for pride and celebration, there are also realities to be reckoned with. Coupling and parenting are not always a picnic, and our community needs to relieve itself of the expectation of perfection and to examine the pitfalls of parenting as single parents, as couples, as daughters and sons, as employees, neighbors, and community members among all of the other facets of our human complexity. As pioneers, many of us feel the strain of setting an example for our own and other communities. Parenting is complicated enough. Parenting as a minority that enjoys very few protections and precious little support can sometimes feel nearly impossible.

When I came out, my son was five, and I remember writing that I felt as if the entire community was holding its collective breath, awaiting the first signs that this "experiment" with parenting would fail. I know from years of conversations with LGBT parents that we share a sense of parenting in a fishbowl. The strains of this are enough to challenge every single one of us from time to time. We are not superheroes nor should we hold ourselves, or allow others to hold us, to impossible standards. Ms. Lev openly challenges us to be honest about this struggle and to seek help when signs of its wear and tear become evident. She bravely and knowingly contributes truth to our ongoing struggle in her chapters on substance abuse, domestic violence, depression, divorce, and other challenges not particular to the LGBT parenting community but present in all communities, and therefore, part of our realities as parents and family. It is imperative that we recognize these realities and allow ourselves to address them honestly and compassionately for the well-being of ourselves and our families.

We need not be perfect. All we each need to be is the best parents we know how to be. And together as a community I see evidence that we are doing an admirable job. I celebrate you all, and I welcome you to continually question, to educate yourselves, and to find community to support you in this amazing and ever joyful journey of parenting.

Aimee Gelnaw, Executive Director of the Family Pride Coalition

Acknowledgments

As I make the final edits on this book I am amazed at how much the world has changed for LGBT families during the past few years. Although many of the couples who contributed to this book identified themselves as "married," few thought we would see the reality of *legal* gay marriage first in Canada and then throughout the United States. There is no doubt that our communities have come of age, and it is a heady time to be living!

I am aware, as all authors are, of the weaknesses of this book. As I ready it for publication, I find myself rewriting sections on surrogacy, on adoption, on support groups—because our community keeps changing and growing, and I keep learning. By the time this book is published, in just a few months, I am sure sections of it will be outdated, because we—LGBT families—are changing the world faster than the speed of light. I thank my agent, Jacky Sach, and the Penguin team for running with me to keep up with all of these changes.

In the last two years I have learned so much about the diversity of our communities, and I thank those who have patiently taught me: friends, colleagues, clients, and my online community of queer parents. As always, I thank my muses, the LesbianMoms Email Listserve, and Gay Adoption cyber network for endless support, advice, ideas, intellectual debates, and creative ideas. I honestly can't imagine parenting without you. I want to especially thank my readers—Lauren DeFilippis, Kathryn Laughon, Simone Ryals, Ruthie Bolden, and Gwendolyn Alden Dean—for their gracious and invaluable feedback, some of which I used, and the rest I'm still thinking about.

I am deeply indebted to my family for giving me the time necessary to complete this project; I am literally typing this as they all pack the car for our annual summer trek to Provincetown for Family Week, where we can blend in easily with other families like ours. Thank you, Sundance for all your support. Thank you, Shaiyah ("Which book is this?") and Eliezer ("I hate that stupid book")—you fill my heart with joy.

In the last week I have received three E-mails, one from a friend whose daughter has just come home from India after a two-year bureaucratic wait. They are dealing with all of the intensity of a three-year-old child, uprooted from her home and culture and trying to adapt to her new family. It is a joyful and awesome time for their family and for all of us who know what it is like to wait for a child, and then face the mixed emotions of realizing that you are now in it for life. The other E-mail is from another friend, a woman who reached out for support to me a year ago when she found out that her foster daughter would likely be adopted by a biological aunt. The couple entered the situation fairly sure this would become a permanent adoption, and after a year of legal advice and advocacy they have made the loving decision—with a wisdom reminiscent of King Solomon— to not drag this child through years of court battles but to let go of a child they thought was theirs forever. As this book is going to press, this lesbian family is spending the summer playing and enjoying this child, whom they will have to wave bye-bye to as the autumn leaves begin to fall. My heart breaks for this family, caught in the sharp snares of a dysfunctional adoption system in need of massive reforms. The last email is from another woman, whose family spends their days driving their handsome three-year-old son to chemotherapy appointments, and watching the ravishing effects of the poison that will hopefully save their son's life. I pray that the institutions in which our lives are embedded hold fast this sacred trust and remember how fragile we sometimes are. There are many more stories that need to be told as we build our lives on the edges of the American dream.

Introduction

When I was growing up in the 1960s in Brooklyn, New York, the idea of being a lesbian—which I was strongly suspecting I might be—was indescribably frightening. Lesbianism was absolutely *queer,* other, different, and marked me in shameful ways. There was simply no concept of being a lesbian *mother.* An oxymoron for sure, lesbian motherhood connoted an impossible hybrid, something akin to a flying boat, a bright shadow, or as the joke goes, military intelligence. There were clearly two paths ahead of me: one was of a heterosexual union—since I was a hippie this didn't necessarily imply legal marriage or suburban lawns—and the other path was a life of lesbian bars, clandestine sex, and social ostracism.

This choice weighed heavily on me. As I moved through my teenage years my passion for women became more, shall we say, acute, and my lifestyle choices felt less like an act of volition than an inner expression of authenticity. I followed my heart, because the other "choices" left me feeling dead. I came out as a lesbian, and images of myself with small children crowded around my long hippie skirts began to fade. I grew more comfortable hanging out with Amazonian warriors, reveling in our freedom as liberated dykes, and I left behind fantasies of motherhood. My childless state was a badge that differentiated me from my heterosexual friends, who seemed to accidentally get pregnant with even more frequency than I attended political demonstrations.

With few exceptions, in those days lesbians just didn't have babies. In some ways the exceptions just proved the rule, because lesbians who had babies virtually always had them while involved with men, often ex-husbands. Lesbians with children either had fought hard to retain custody of their children or fought hard to financially survive without support from the fathers. After all, how could a lesbian actually "get" a kid without either sleeping with or marrying a man, both heinous sins within the ethical code of burgeoning lesbian-feminist communities of the early 1970s. When I officially came out as a lesbian at twenty-one years old, I burned my diaphragm (literally; it smelled terrible). Not needing birth control *and* still being a sexual woman was a sign of ultimate liberation.

Then I met Sophie, a lesbian about a decade older than I, who had decided to get pregnant. The story as I remember it may not be true in the sense of being factual, for time has rendered fragile the ability to discern history from allegory from mythology. What I remember is that Sophie decided to have a baby with two male friends—yes, I said, two. I cannot remember if they were gay or straight, but I lean toward thinking they were gay. I do not know if she or anyone knew which one was the actual biological father. My memory is that she inseminated herself with both of their semen. I do clearly remember that afterward a bunch of dykes went into a backyard in Berkeley, California, and circled around her and chanted and howled at the moon. Sophie became the first lesbian I knew to take charge of her own fertility and make a baby. She actually got pregnant from this unorthodox approach and became a lesbian mother, and with this act brought together two paths that had seemed separate and opposite in my life. Robert Frost be damned, I didn't have to choose one road or the other, I *could,* or rather *I* could, become a lesbian mother!

Sophie's child is now old enough to become a parent; indeed he is about the same age today as the women who birthed the two babies I adopted. In the two decades that have passed since we circled around Sophie under that California full moon, and the day the judge in New Jersey, smiling, said to my partner and me, "You are both responsible for this child *forever,*" there has been a virtual conflagration of baby-making, baby-getting, baby-having, and baby-loving, not only among lesbians, but within all segments of the queer world.

I decided to check out the validity of my memory about Sophie's baby-making and, having access to the world at the tip of my tapping fingers, I E-mailed a cyber friend in the Bay Area and said, "I'm looking for a woman I haven't seen in about twenty years (except briefly at a conference about fifteen years ago). She lives in the Bay Area, and her name is Sophie Finegold." She E-mailed me back in about ten minutes, saying, "I think I know who you mean, I will send your query to a local Bay Area E-mail list I'm on." An hour later she had five responses in her E-mail box, one with Sophie's address and phone number, two with Sophie's E-mail, and three from more cautious people who said, "I'll tell Sophie you are looking for her." I E-mailed Sophie, and within less than four hours, there was Sophie's E-mail, saying that my memory held little truth.

For the dyke record, Sophie (who asked me to use a pseudonym, for good reason, since I obviously can't be trusted with a truthful story), lived with two men, one of whom is straight, one of whom is gay, both of whom are uncles to her son, and neither of whom were the donor. The donor was a friend of a friend of one of the uncles. By the way, this uncle who she lived with was also her ex-lover from before she came out, which makes this an excellent way to open a book on queer families. The donor did not know Sophie (although she knew who he was), which allowed some anonymity and legal protection for her family. They have since connected, and her son has since met his donor and has an adult relationship with him. This story—both my fantasized version and Sophie's truthful tale—still stands as LGBT parenting at its most essential queer best. And Sophie still stands as a pioneer.

The original title of this book, my working title, was *How Queer: Lesbian, Gay, Bisexual, and Transgender Parenting.* My publisher was concerned about marketing a book with the word *queer* in the title, and perhaps some of you who are reading this now would agree that you might be less likely to buy a book with the word *queer* in the title. I confess that I don't agree. I like the word *queer* a lot, so although I lost the battle for the title, I have retained the word in the text. There are a few reasons that I really like the word *queer*. First of all, it is just too cumbersome to keep saying "lesbian, gay, bisexual, and transgender," and queer is simply easy shorthand. But my real reason is not for convenience. It is because the phrases *gay parenting* or even *lesbian and gay parenting* do not do justice to the width and depth of the diversity within the LGBT community. My hope for this book is to be more than a primer or how-to book on mainstream gay and lesbian parenting, but rather a celebration of how very queer LGBT family-building really can be.

On the surface, L, G, B, *and* especially T people might not fit neatly under one banner; the differences between each of these groups, not to mention the individuals within these groups, may be more disparate than whatever it is that links us together. What exactly do lesbian, gay male, bisexual, and transgender people have in common that would justify this lumping together of identities and communities?

Indeed, what connects us may be related more to how we are seen and treated by the outside world than anything we inherently hold in common. When someone told Jenny Boylan (author of *She's Not There: A Life in Two Genders*) that transgender people don't have much in common with gay people, she poignantly responded, "Except for the fact that we get beaten up by the same people." Although I'm not sure that group identity should necessarily be formed by the prejudicial views of outsiders, I *am* sure that the best way to fight injustice is through the forming of broad coalitions with similar interests.

In terms of family-building strategies, the issues facing lesbians, gay men, bisexuals, and transgendered people are similar enough to warrant strong alliances and working partnerships. Like all coalition-building work, this means that the groups involved must work through their assumptions about one another and their prejudices toward one another. For all the discomfort of linking these distinct communities together, it is hoped that the overarching goal of unity and shared struggle will be advantageous in affording us all civil rights and securing safety for our families.

Lesbians and gay men are often linked together in their work toward common political goals and have also shared many shared social venues and community spaces. However, this unity has often been assumed more by the media than has functioned within neighborhoods, political groups, or social events; lesbians and gay men have, for the most part, built very different social and political communities, exemplified perhaps by comparing the San Francisco Castro Street neighborhood populated mostly by gay men, and the Michigan Women's Music Festival, a yearly summer lesbian gathering. But even that comparison is not fair, because not all gay men identify with the primarily white, middle-class, urban culture of Castro Street, just as most lesbians do not partake in the annual trek back to nature to live naked in women-only space. This is not to deny the positive working relationships between lesbian and gay men in national organizing, or the deep emotional ties between individuals, as well as the intimate bonds created between lesbians and gay men since the advent of the AIDS crisis. It is meant to acknowledge that there are areas of differences between gay men and lesbians that have often resulted in political, social, and cultural community-wide struggles. The ease with which "lesbian and gay" flows from many of our lips has not necessarily been reflected in the makeup of our dinner parties or political alliances.

Bisexual men and women have often felt as marginalized from the mainstream lesbian and gay movement as they have from heterosexual culture, and have often experienced the same harsh prejudice from gay people as they have from straight people. Bisexuals have been assumed to be promiscuous, closeted gay people who are afraid to come out by many lesbians and gay men, and have been accused of spreading HIV, "using" the gay community, and not being honest about who they really are. Of course, the truth is that bisexuals have been very clear about who they are, and that clarity has made some lesbians and gay men (as well as some heterosexuals) profoundly uncomfortable because the truth about bisexuality disrupts binary assumptions regarding the nature of sexual identity and attraction. Bisexual people can be monogamous as well as polyamorous, they can be closeted or out, and as capable of (or inept at) intimacy and long-term commitments as other queer people, or, for that matter, any group of people. Bisexuals who are involved in long-term gay or lesbian relationships may be assumed to be gay or may feel pressured to identify as gay. Bisexuals who are involved in long-term heterosexual relationships may be assumed to be not gay, or closeted, and although their identity and commitment to the gay community may remain important to them, this is rarely recognized. Bisexuals may or may not share similar cultural values with gay and lesbian people, depending on the individuals. Although the word *bisexual* has been added to the banners and letterheads of many queer organizations, the issues that concern bisexual people are often marginalized. When I refer to same-sex couples, even when I rely on the shorthand of using the terms *lesbian couples* or *gay couples,* I am aware—and want you, the reader, to be aware—that many of these relationships have members who are bisexually identified.

Even biphobic people will reluctantly admit that bisexuality is a stigmatized sexual orientation, whereas transgenderism and transsexuality appear, on the surface, to have very little to do with issues of sexual orientation, but rather address issues of gender identity and expression. Transsexuals are people who describe a profound discomfort with their biological bodies and desire to live within the social parameters of the "opposite" sex. Commonly transsexuals utilize medical treatments (hormonal therapy and surgeries) to enhance their comfort in their bodies and to best express their gender identity. Transgenderism describes a broader spectrum of gender identity conflicts and resolutions, including those who express gender dysphoria, those who express cross-gender behavior, and those who live in gender transgressive ways. Transgendered people may identify as transsexuals, cross-dressers, gender variants, gender benders, and they may or may not engage in medical interventions to change their biological bodies.

Why, you may well ask, would issues facing the transgender community be covered in the same book as issues relevant to gay, lesbian, and bisexual people? Well, the answer is that some transgendered people simply *are* gay, lesbian, and/or bisexual. Certainly, some postoperative transsexual people are involved with people of the same sex (even if some of these couples were heterosexually identified before transition). Additionally, many transgendered people who are not currently seeking body transformation are involved in same-sex relationships. Finally, many gay, lesbian, and bisexual people who may or may not identify as transgender are also gender transgressive, including lesbians who identify as butches, and gay men who identify (or who are identified) as sissies or nellies. There are no clear, distinct lines separating where lesbian, gay, and bisexual communities end and where transgenderism begins. Many of the issues that transgendered parents face are similar to issues that LGB people face, although there are profound differences, too.

I am choosing to use the word *queer* to encapsulate all the diverse identities that are expressed when one says "lesbian, gay, bisexual, and transgendered," which is not meant to assume that each of these groups share all that is important to them with the other groups, or that this coalition is without struggle. My goal is not to minimize our differences but rather to represent the breadth of issues we face.

The reality is that even using the expression LGBT does not necessarily do justice to the diversity of family forms within our communities. *Queer* is the best word I can find that includes those who are marginalized for sexual and gender-identity issues. Even though for some of us it is a harsh, negative term, I have come to see it as a playful term. It was not always so. Once upon a time, as I've told you, I grew up feeling very, very queer. Perhaps some young people growing up in the early years of the twenty-first century who are wondering if they may be gay, may be able to come to terms with their sexual orientation without ever feeling queer. Perhaps they are growing up in a hip neighborhood in San Francisco, Chicago, New York, or Paris. Perhaps their parents are progressive liberals who support gay rights and have gay friends, so they've had strong positive role models; perhaps their parents are themselves gay so they have always been raised with the wisdom in their bones that "gay is good." Perhaps.

My experience tells me that although lucky kids like this exist, few youths are free from the internal experience of feeling queer, in the most negative sense of the word. Even living in a hip neighborhood, even with liberal parents, even with gay parents. Heterosexuality, as "the" human expression of what is normal, ordinary, customary, typical, usual, expected, common, average, and standard, is everywhere. Gayness is still other, different, exotic, unusual, and well, queer. I am choosing to use the word *queer* because LGBT parenting is still an oxymoron in most places in the world, and even in most Western, First World countries, it is still unusual. Assumptively, most of you reading this book are gay parents, or parent wanna-bes, or friends of gay parents, or social workers and psychotherapists who care about gay parents and want to learn more about us. To us, gay parenting might not seem so queer. You might even say, "I know *lots* of gay parents," and indeed that may be true.

You need to trust me here . . . most people still think we are really an exotic species. Perhaps they even find us beautiful in the way my older son and I stare at the okapi in the African wildlife books. Delicate, gentle in a deerlike way, with the striped legs of a zebra ("a relative," my six-year-old says, "they are in the same family"), okapis live deep in the African jungles, hidden, exotic, and endangered. Mainstream culture may find us attractive, even exquisite. They may be comfortable sharing day care centers with us and recognize us as being members of the same general species, the same human family, but generally speaking, like most readers' relationship to the

African okapi, they will not do much to ensure our survival. Western civilization, at least in its postmodern forms, is built on pluralism, and with the exception of right-wing fundamentalists and conservative defenders of "family values," gay families are nominally accepted, but we are still considered odd and different, and our families are ultimately very fragile.

Now, some of you will say, "How does calling us queer help us to become more stable, more secure, more accepted within this diverse and pluralistic society?" Indeed, some of you will say, "Calling us queer *hurts* us; it reinforces what they say about us and makes us not only exotic but weird." I disagree. I disagree because frankly, I think they are right. We are exotic and frankly a bit weird. (Note: The word *weird* is said to derive from Wyrd and her sisters, the tree nymphs, whom the pagans knocked on wood to awaken. Invoking weirdness is to invite their protection.)

Perhaps I have now invoked your anger (not a good way to start a book, my agent reminds me), but let me explain. I know not all of us are weird. I know that much of the gay and lesbian parenting community, like most of the gay and lesbian community, like most of the folks in all of our neighborhoods, are just pretty regular people. We have nine-to-five jobs, manicured lawns, eat wholesome food, and spend too much money during the Christmas season. LGBT parents are no less exhausted at the 5 A.M. feeding, they are no less concerned when their child's fever registers at 104 degrees, and their couple relationships (including their sex lives) are no less challenged by the busyness of working and day care, dinner and laundry, and all of the complexities of family life. Lesbian moms and gay dads are as overwhelmed about money and as frightened about teenage substance abuse as any other parent. Gay parents need to balance housework and careers, find appropriate day care and good pediatricians. Single gay parents, like all single parents, need to turn to family or friends for help, or face these challenges alone. We are just regular folk, nothing particularly queer about us.

However, when examined through the lens of heterosexual coupling, marriage vows, and monogamous sexual intercourse, the world of gay and lesbian baby-making and baby-getting is a bizarre bacchanalian circus, whether baby-making involves homespun rituals using dry ice and needleless syringes or invasive biotechnology and petri dishes; whether baby-getting entails legalistic paperwork involving intrusive social workers and INS regulations, or the sudden thud of realization that some of the babies needing homes are fourteen-year-old veterans of the foster care system, who burn down the homes that are offered them. Of course it is not just LGBT people who utilize donor insemination, reproductive endocrinology, surrogacy, adoption, and foster care to expand their families, those are just the *primary* ways that we do. Within our communities, engaging in heterosexual intercourse to make our babies, particularly with a person we wanted to continue an ongoing lover relationship with, well *that* is often considered very queer.

For many people in the gay and lesbian community, the expansion of gay and lesbian parenting seems to be an incredibly conservative thing. "My Gawd," a friend yells, "you are living just like my parents did!" However, there is little about how we create our families that resembles the heterosexual norm. Whether by stepping outside the system (i.e., using sperm from a known donor and inseminating at home), or by pushing up against the system (i.e., insisting on your legal rights to have both of your names on the birth certificate), lesbian and gay parents, even the most regular folks among us, have challenged the face of family life in America. The cracks in the system are not mere fissures that will heal, but they are dismantling and ultimately reconstructing definitions and forms of the family. In other words, the conservative right may not be so wrong after all. The thesaurus tells me that one of the synonyms for *queer* is *remarkable*. Our queer families are very remarkable—significant and awesome—and leaving their mark on the very structure and function of family development.

I am not using the word *queer* just because *they* think we are queer, or even because I *know* that we are queer in that awesome kind of way; I am using the word *queer* because, if the truth be told, some of us *are* very queer. And I mean *very* queer. In many ways we do not live the way our parents did. Let's face it, when Sophie got pregnant with her two male friends twenty years ago, even I thought that was very weird (knock on wood). I mean my friends and I, all Amazon warriors who chanted at the moon goddess, laughed about it over tacos at lunch. Not laughing *at,* but laughing big, long belly laughs: Who did we dykes think we were making babies with turkey basters and gay men! We were disrupting the whole damn patriarchal system, and we knew it. (Of course, we weren't raising that baby, either; that is something Sophie and the uncles had to figure out how to do.) We knew it was weird, and queer, and depending on our families of origin, we either didn't mention this baby-making business to them or we timed the disclosure perfectly, knowing we would leave our parents, back in the urban ghettos and suburban tract houses of our childhood, howling at their own moons. As a friend's father said, "What a strange mixed-up world you are creating." Indeed.

I know this makes some of you defensive. We are not queer, not weird, but normal, average, usual. . . . We need to tell them how normal we are. These are some of the families I know; you decide how standard we are.

- Sally and her partner, Marianna, have four children, the oldest two from Marianna's past heterosexual marriage. They live part of the week with Sally and Marianna and part of the week with their father and his new wife. The younger two were conceived by Marianna using Sally's brother's semen and are twins. The twins refer to their donor daddy as Uncle Matt, but understand that he is biologically their father. Uncle Matt also has children of his own, which are cousins to all four of Sally and Marianna's children. The older children call Marianna Mommy, and they call Sally Mumu, a name they made up. They call their father Daddy, and his new wife by her first name. The twins refer to Marianna as Mommy and Sally as Mama.

- Bill and John were together for fifteen years when they decided to become parents. Both are white of European descent, and they used the foster-adopt system to bring home two African-American siblings, a four-year-old girl and her six-year-old brother. When the kids were six and eight years old respectively, they were freed for legal adoption, and after a sustained fight with the Department of Social Services, Bill was legally allowed to adopt the children that the two men are raising. The children refer to them as Poppa and Daddy.

- Jamie got pregnant as a single woman with unknown donor semen using a sperm bank. She is raising her son Teddi as a sole parent, with some help and support from a sister and her mother. Jamie is currently dating a woman, and is considering having another child at some point. Her son calls her Mom.

- Lisa and Lori were together for ten years and had three children together. They broke up, and both have since become involved with other women, whom they are each living with. The children spend time with each of their moms, who have made a commitment to remain in the neighborhood in order to keep the kids in the same schools. Lisa and her new partner are currently looking into adopting a child from Guatemala. Lori's new partner has two teenagers from a previous marriage who live with them full time. The children refer to Lisa as Mommy, and Lori as Ima; they refer to their mother's new partners by their first names but think of themselves as having four moms.

- Manuel and Gorge have two children from a surrogacy arrangement. Glenna birthed both children for the couple, the first time with Manuel's semen, and the second time with Gorge's, and remains a distant friend of the family. The children know who Glenna is and enjoy seeing her; they refer to her as their birth mom, but do not see her as a parental figure. Gorge is a stay-at-home parent, while Manuel supports the family financially. The children refer to them as Daddy and Papa.

- Jessica and Chris have been partners for ten years and have two children, a six-year-old son and a two-year-old daughter. Jessica birthed both children after getting pregnant through donor insemination with an unknown donor utilizing a sperm bank. Chris is a female-to-male transsexual who transitioned when their older child was two years old. Both children know about their father's history; they refer to their parents as Mommy and Daddy.

- Leanne has two adopted children, a daughter from China and a son from Vietnam, who are now teenagers. Her lover, Tiki, has been with her for five years now, and the kids refer to her by her first name and view her as a parent. Leanne is white, of European descent, and Tiki is black, of West Indian descent.

- Marti and her best friend, a gay man named Gary, chose to have their son Benjamin together as a couple. The three of them live together, and Benjamin refers to them as Momma and Poppa. Poppa has a boyfriend who Benjamin calls Uncle Pat. Marti and

Gary are not lovers, but did conceive Benjamin the old-fashioned way.

- Lucinda and Marcus are a white, unmarried couple and have been lovers for fifteen years. They have an open relationship and both identify as bisexual. They have four children; the two oldest Lucinda birthed, and the two youngest are biracial and were adopted. The children all know that Lucinda and Marcus have other lovers (although the adoption agency does not), some of whom are close family members. The kids refer to their parents by their first names.

- Kristy and John are a married couple who have two teenage children, conceived through sexual intercourse. John is bisexual, and monogamously committed to Kristy. John is active in a gay dad's group, and the children know that he is bisexual and have attended Gay Pride marches with their parents. John and Kristy have been married for more than twenty years, and the children call them Mom and Dad.

- Jacy lives alone with her five children, two that she birthed and three who are adopted; all call her Momma. Jacy is a single parent but lives within a large cooperative community in a progressive urban neighborhood. Her children are home schooled, a shared endeavor with four other families. Jacy works in the local food co-op three days a week, and works with all of the seventeen children involved in the cooperative school. Jacy has available to her many friends and neighbors who spend time with the children and help with parental and household tasks. Although Jacy is the only legal parent to her children, she has more help and assistance in parenting than most two-parent nuclear households.

- Rosie and Mishka have been lovers for thirty years. They have raised twelve children between them. The oldest children were conceived during Rosie's first marriage, and eight others were legally adopted by Rosie; the last three are fostered by the couple, although the legal paperwork is in Mishka's name. There are currently six children still at home, and they are considering more. Many of the children have physical or emotional disabilities, and some have significant health-related problems. The children call them Momma Rosie and Momma Mishka.

- Gayle and Maria have four children together. Two were birthed by Gayle, and two were birthed by Maria, using the same unknown donor through a sperm bank. They have been a family for twelve years, and their children refer to them as Mommy and Momma.

- Daphne has two children, ten and twelve years old, who live part of the time with her and part of the time with their biological mother. Daphne is a male-to-female transsexual and is the father of both children. Daphne's ex-wife is remarried. The children call their mother Mommy, their "father" Daphne, and their stepfather Pops.

- Gordon is a single gay father to Michael, who is five years old and who was adopted at birth. Gordon would like to adopt another child within the next few years. Michael calls Gordon Daddy.

- Janice had a child with her ex-lover Karen, and Jacky is now seven years old. Janice got pregnant with Steve, who is an active father in Jacky's life. Steve has been with his partner for more than twenty years, although Steve's partner is not a parent to Jacky. Jacky refers to her father as Daddy and his partner as Uncle Rob. Janice has a new lover, Becky, who is raising a friend's child. The friend is a heterosexual woman who has been unable to stop using drugs, so she asked Becky to take the child, a son named Patrick. This is an informal situation and has continued for over four years. Patrick, who is ten, refers to both women by their first names but calls Jacky his sister. Additionally, Karen has since become lovers with a man and has had two children in this marriage. Karen has remained active in Jacky's life, and her children and Jacky refer to each other as siblings. However, Janice and Becky do not have any relationship with Karen's family. Jacky refers to Janice as her mommy, to Karen as her aunt, and to Becky by her first name.

This list is certainly not all inclusive. If you don't see yourself in the list, hopefully you will recognize your unique family later in the book. This list is, however, a composite of some of the forms of family-building that are taking place in the LGBT community. This very queer notion—that lesbians could be moms together, that gay men could adopt children, that bisexuals could build stable families, that transgendered people could be wonderful parents—is a notion whose time has come. What has come to be called *alternative families* include a diverse range of people and family-building structures, some of which are not all that alternative, and some that are very queer indeed.

Some of our families—single parents, stepfamilies, adoptive families, foster families—are bell-curve normal, except that being same-sex couples makes us look unusual to outsiders. We live fairly conventional, mainstream lives, with the exception that our children have two daddies or two mommies. We are church-attending people with nine-to-five jobs—or often one stay-at-home parent—who see ourselves as average families, although, of course, sensitive to the fact we are not always perceived that way.

Other LGBT people are parenting outside of a normative nuclear family paradigm, having developed and nurtured diverse and unique family forms. In addition to the many children being raised in homes with two primary parents of the same sex, some of us have chosen to conceive and raise children together in opposite-sex partnerships but as out lesbians and gay men. Gay men are having biological children through surrogacy arrangements, and lesbians are using their lovers' eggs to produce children that are biologically related to both women. Lesbians and gay men are adopting children in unprecedented numbers, creating high percentages of interracial families through both domestic and international adoptions.

Some of our families may look very typical on the outside—gay men and lesbians parenting together, transgendered families who are, or appear to be, heterosexual—but are obviously more complex. Issues like non-monogamy and serial monogamy, as well as children living in multiple homes with several parents, are volatile issues in all family life today, not just queer-headed households.

Alternative family-building has been under criticism by the religiously orthodox and the politically conservative for destroying the traditional family and undermining moral values. Of course, any student of the family knows that it is not just LGBT people that are disrupting the old paradigm of family. Although queer families are perceived of as different in fundamental ways from other families, the truth is that families have changed dramatically in the past few decades, and our families just reflect that diversity. Family life in general is in a huge upheaval. The family in contemporary Western culture is dramatically different at the turn of this century, and in many ways our same-sex, alternative, and mixed-race families are increasingly common as the traditional home of *Father Knows Best* recedes in memory. In reality, *Father Knows Best* was never the norm for most Americans (nor were suburban homes with white picket fences), and I suspect most of us have figured out by now that Father simply did not always know best.

The nuclear family model of stay-at-home moms, fathers who are the sole financial support of the family, and the children of their biological union, is fading fast. For instance, only 25 percent of American households are nuclear families (married couples with children under eighteen), and only about 50 percent of children are being raised in traditional nuclear families. About 25 percent of children are being raised in single-parent homes, and this includes both never-married parents and those who have divorced. Approximately one in every twenty births is a mixed-race child, with over two million biracial children currently living in the U.S. There are over one million mixed-race marriages (i.e., legal, heterosexual unions).

However, creating radical new families has presented us with unique challenges, particularly regarding the way that family is often defined within the legal system. In most states and countries, same-sex couples are, by definition, not allowed to marry and therefore not perceived of as legal partners. In most states and countries, two people of the same sex cannot be on a child's birth certificate, and therefore the legal status of our children, as belonging equally to parents, is challenged.

Sadly, we often use these antiquated laws to hurt one another during custody disputes when partnerships dissolve. As important as it is to fight for legal recognition and increased civil rights, it is also important to recognize that the very complexity of our families is challenging to standard law procedures. In some families, donors are daddies, and in other families, they are not; in some families, parents are lovers, and in others, they are not. The law must come to recognize the diversity of family-building options and recognize the uniqueness of each of the structures we develop. However, it is also incumbent upon us to reflect carefully on the choices we make regarding our families, to recognize that we are building alternative structures, and to do so responsibly.

Children within Western cultures are being raised in many varied situations, including by single moms and dads, by grandparents, by stepparents, and of course by never-married parents. In reality, they always have been, but what has changed is the standard—more families don't fit the template than do. There are many complex forms that queer families are creating, whether we are living middle-class, suburban, churchgoing lives with our same-sex partner in the heartland, or living nonmonogamous, pagan, gender-bent lifestyles in San Francisco (or geographically vice versa). Our children attend public and private schools or are home schooled, and we attend the PTA meetings at their schools. Our children ride school buses in rural communities and attend day care centers in inner-city neighborhoods. We parent our children with ex-spouses and ex-lovers, with grandparents, aunts, and uncles, as well as current partners and friends. Our children may or may not look like us. Our children may have daddies, or donors, one mommy, one birth mother, and two stepparents; our children may or may not have role models of the opposite sex. Some of our families are multiracial, some of our families are formed by adoption or foster parenting, and some of our families maintain contact with our children's birth families. Whatever the nature of our families or the circumstances in which they were created, our families deserve legal protection and institutional sanction.

In many respects, queer families are no more or less different than most families, although LGBT families sometimes take tremendous pride in being different. It is precisely this sense of uniqueness that I want to celebrate by using the term *queer*. Although many of us have very average families, albeit same-sex ones, some of us have built families that are blatantly unusual either in our gender presentations, our family configurations, our mixed-racial makeup, or our lifestyle choices. *Queer* is not meant to disparage those less outrageous than it is to make sure those of us who are more outrageous are not left out, because ultimately, the queerer we appear to be, the more in danger we are; and the more in danger some of us are, the more endangered all of us are. Read that last sentence again.

It is far too easy for those of us who are white and middle class, living in suburban neighborhoods with manicured lawns on the outskirts of progressive cities, and receiving domestic partnership benefits to distance ourselves from those of us who are poor, or gender-bent, or living in less common family configurations. A white gay man says, "I am a totally normal person raising a kid. I don't want to have anything to do with bisexuals and transgendered people." Ultimately, what seems normal to him might not seem so normal to outsiders who view him first and foremost as a homosexual—and the same way he wants to distance himself from those he considers unusual, others may want to distance themselves from him—particularly when times get hard, and anyone reading the newspapers knows that times are getting harder.

I want to suggest a different solution for our LGBT communities than distancing ourselves from those who are queerer than we are. I want to hold our most fragile families at the center—lesbian moms fighting custody battles, transsexual parents fighting the adoption system, interracial gay dads fighting for joint custody, foster families trying to secure legal rights, and those of us with unusual or exceptional lifestyles. As long as the most vulnerable among us are without rights, the rest of us will always be in danger. The only way to secure our families is to validate the diversity of family-building options available.

I want to hold the most queer of our families at the center of our circle: stay-at-home butch moms and trans dads who birth their children; nonbiological lesbian moms who raise children for whom they are never legally recognized parents; gay men and lesbians who parent children together; transracial families who leave strangers on the street gaping because they can't make sense of what they are; disabled gay dads of gender-bent adolescents; and children living with four parents who are all their moms. We are forging ahead into what is truly new territory as we not only take our place alongside other families but diversify the landscape of schools, day care centers, and neighborhoods. It is hoped that we can do this respectfully, honoring our commitments to one another, and remembering that while our families are changing the world, our children will be changing us. We must rise to this occasion, preparing ourselves for the greatest adventure within an often hostile environment. As we make homes for our queer families, we must remember to hold the best interests of our children at the center of all our decision making.

Queer people are OUT, breaking new ground. We are building our families in the light of the day, as our people have never done before. Are we odd, unusual, and exotic? Are we curious, perplexing, or remarkable? Or are we merely setting new standards?

PART ONE

NOW THAT YOU'VE DECIDED TO BECOME A PARENT

CHAPTER ONE

• • •

"Alternative" Families

WHO COULD HAVE imagined that lesbian, gay, bisexual, and transgendered people would have become such a vibrant and visible part of mainstream Western culture? A mere thirty years ago homosexuality was a diagnosed mental illness, and homosexual people belonged to a furtive, underground community of outlaws, without any legal standing, political influence, or ways to protect our loved ones.

Thirty years later, in some parts of the United States, lesbian, gay, and bisexual people have secured antidiscrimination laws in housing and employment and domestic partnership rights. The concept of lesbian and gay marriage—which grants our families the same status and protection as heterosexual couples—is no longer just a pipe dream but is currently being debated in the highest courts. We have legally won the ability in some states to adopt our partner's birth children (sometimes before the child's actual birth) and to coadopt children together and be the legal parents on the birth certificate. According to a recent report, about 60 percent of the nation's adoption agencies now accept applications from gay and lesbian people.

The battles for civil rights is far from over; most states still blatantly discriminate against lesbian and gay people building families, and the legal and psychiatric status for transgendered people is only now beginning to change. However, gay and lesbian headed homes are no longer uncommon; it is estimated that the total number of children in the United States living with at least one gay parent ranges from six to fourteen million. Few of us could have imagined the rise of LGBT families as a recognized family form even a decade ago. It is undeniable that what was once a very queer idea, LGBT family-building, is now becoming a part of modern life in the twenty-first century.

Of course, LGBT family-building is not really a new idea. As long as there have been lesbian, gay, bisexual, and transgendered people, there have been LGBT parents. In other words, we have always been here. Social scientists and postmodern queer theorists argue that it is inaccurate to use modern labels in a historical context, and they would suggest that due to the power of language to construct identity that what we now call *gay parenting* is a contemporary idea. One cannot be something if there is no word to identify it. Indeed, the concept of homosexuality as a separate identity was first invented in the late nineteenth century, and it was only with the industrial revolution that people were able to move away from family farms, villages, and tribes and into urban centers where same-sex coupling became feasible. I remember a friend sharing her joy in first hearing about a bisexual gathering at a conference. She said, "I didn't know there was a name for people like me or a place where I could talk with others who had a similar experience." To create the place and the name, there needs to be a word, a way to recognize and distinguish one's identity; naming is always an act of empowerment.

Of course, people have always behaved homosexually and bisexually, and undoubtedly same-sex people fell in love and experienced intimacy since the dawn of human civilization. However, before the birth of the modern gay liberation movement thirty years ago, few LGBT people would have recognized their identity as gay, let alone felt pride in that identity. To couple the word *gay* with the word *parent* is a radical act first possible in contemporary Western culture, and it would not be possible without the gay pride movement of the past three decades. Nevertheless, and with all deference to queer theory and the social construction of family development, queer people—same-sex lovers and gender-variant people—have been rocking sick babies till the wee hours of the morning, changing noxious diapers, and trying to spoon-feed vegetables into resistant toddlers, whether or not they proudly proclaimed themselves as queer parents.

Indeed, it would have been very foolish for them to boldly proclaim their queerness, for throughout much of modern human history this would have been an open invitation for the state to remove their children from their home. Homosexuality and gender transgression were "naturally" seen as paradoxical to the definition of family. It is sometimes difficult for us, living in the United States in the early years of the twenty-first century, to realize the incredible stigma even a generation ago for alternative family forms like unwed mothers, or the rigid, draconian laws that forbade interracial marriages and frowned upon any independence for women in and out of heterosexual marriages. The idea of out lesbian and gay people having babies, forming families, and not only applying for but insisting on legal rights to parent children not biologically related to them is indeed a postmodern development. Within the last decade LGBT parenting possibilities have expanded in previously unimaginable ways, establishing our families as a viable and visible presence and challenging more traditional definitions of family. We are looking at nothing short of a revolution in family-building.

Revolutions may make certain social experiences possible, or at least nameable, but they do not necessarily make them safe or easy. The decision to become a parent is rarely a simple one for most lesbian, gay, bisexual, or transgendered people. For older people, there was simply no decision to be made: being gay had precluded being a parent. Or in other situations, being a parent precluded being gay. More than thirty years later, young people are coming out knowing that parenthood is possible for them because they see images of gay parents on television and in magazines. They are still left with many decisions about exactly how to become a parent and numerous fears about what their children, being raised on the slopes of the bell curve, will endure.

E-mail: I am 22 years old and live in the Midwest with my girlfriend who is 24. We are thinking of having a baby, but we have no idea where to begin. We live in a small town and no one knows we are gay except a few friends. I do not think our parents will accept this child, and I'm terrified that he or she will be tormented in school. Can you advise me?

In my role as Dear Ari, a nationally recognized columnist for LGBT parenting concerns, I receive at least one E-mail a month similar to the one above; they all tear my heart out. The options for this young couple are far superior to what was available to me at their ages, but they will need to find supportive physicians, procure sperm or battle ignorant adoption agencies, educate parents and day care systems, and perhaps find themselves without familial support. In the worst-case scenario, they will be victimized by hostile neighbors or bosses, without legal recourse or police protection. It is hard to not send back advice that simply reads: "Move."

But of course, moving may or may not protect them. Certainly, living in a larger city in the U.S. may provide them with easier access to reproductive services and supportive clinics that would barely blink an eye at a lesbian couple. They may find child care where they are not the only gay family; indeed, one friend in San Francisco says, shrugging, "I'm in a Lamaze class with *all* lesbians. It's not such a big deal." Of course it's not a big deal until you've sat in a Lamaze class with five heterosexual couples who are afraid to sit near you and an instructor who refers to "your friend" with a sneer while she continues to discuss the importance of fathers to the healthy development of children. If you are lucky enough to have access to gay-affirming institutions, it is no big deal, but if you don't—and most people don't—it is a huge deal. Big cities can offer some protections, but of course not everyone can afford to move, or even wants to, and lots of gay couples are finding ways to build families in the heartland or the Bible Belt and are left with numerous decisions on how to build and protect their fragile families.

HETEROSEXUAL MARRIAGE AND THE BEST INTERESTS OF THE CHILDREN

Lamaze classes for pregnant lesbian couples and shipping frozen sperm to small rural communities are contemporary adaptations for family-building. It is important to recognize, however, that LGBT parenting is not, in essence, *new*; it has always existed. What is certainly new, though, is the visible presence of our families and the fight for legal rights and social recognition.

Until recently, LGBT people who wanted to have children, had—with

Long Way Home
BY MELISSA HART

The policeman looked at Ms. Whitney and Mother standing in the doorway with their arms around each other. I saw something hateful flash in his eyes—something mean that I didn't understand at all.

"I'm sorry, miss," the policeman said to me, "but you have to go with your father. . . ."

I thought of all the times in the last month that I'd seen my mother cry. This was the worst. "Bye, Mother," I whispered.

And suddenly, we were being driven away, waving frantically at Mother from the back window of Daddy's car. She leaned sobbing against Ms. Whitney. "I'll see you soon, kids!" she cried. "We'll be together soon!"

"We'll be back!" I cried through my tears. I waved until Daddy turned the corner, and then she was gone.

I was nine years old when my father arrived at my mother's new house with the police and seized custody of my younger siblings and me. He was outraged that my mom had chosen a woman over him. Never mind that he abused her and would go on to abuse all three of his children. The court system believed him to be the more suitable parent because he was heterosexual and had a corporate job.

Twenty-three years later, my siblings and I still ache over losing our mother because of her sexuality. My sister resents her, believing she should have remained with our father for the sake of her children. I cringe every time I have to admit that my mom could have been more savvy in the divorce proceedings, hiding her love for a woman until she was ensured custody of us.

In my work as a gay rights activist, I still come across stories like mine—dramas in which a parent sues another, or in one case, children sue their parent, because of ignorance about homosexuality. When I speak at PFLAG meetings, I meet gay parents who have been sued by their spouses for child custody, due to ignorance and anger. I lecture at colleges and bookstores, as well, and so many parents come up to me afterward to tell me how my words have touched them because they, too, lost custody of their children or have friends to whom this occurred.

I long for the day when parents are evaluated only for their ability to create a loving and supportive household, which my mother did two weekends a month for us—all the time the court would allow. My siblings and I didn't lose her just once—we lost her over and over as we watched her drive away every other Sunday night, knowing we wouldn't see her again for ten days. Children simply should not be subjected to this kind of pain—pain that continues to rip me up inside and make me all the more determined to fight for parents like my mother.

Melissa Hart is the author of the memoir Long Way Home *(Windstorm Creative, 2000) from which the passage above is excerpted.*

very few exceptions—but one viable option: they became parents through some involvement in heterosexual coupling. Most commonly, these were people who married because, well, that's just what people *did* in those days. Dealing with coming out meant having clandestine sexual and romantic encounters with members of the same sex or leaving marriages and losing custody of their children. In such situations, it was often impossible to retain custody of their children following the dissolution of a heterosexual relationship or marriage.

Lesbian mothers were often deemed unfit, by virtue of nothing more than their lesbianism, although some women were able to retain custody by remaining closeted or by having cooperative ex-husbands. It was rare for fathers in general to retain custody of their children in those days (and still in these days), and near impossible for a known gay father to even be granted visitation. Only in the past twenty years did gay fathers and lesbian mothers immersed in heterosexual divorces begin to challenge the court system's homophobic stance that gay and lesbian parents were inherently flawed parents because of their sexuality. In recent years some more progressive courts have begun to grant custody to lesbian moms and gay dads, although heterosexist assumptions still plague these proceedings. Conservative and oppressive courts routinely still use archaic homophobic laws to disallow lesbians and gay men from retaining custody of their children.

The courts have held that homosexuality and transgenderism are not "in the best interests of children," and therefore simply being gay or being gender variant have been reason enough for parents to lose custody of their children. Although the court systems in some parts of the country have become more educated in understanding that sexual identity does not impact the quality of parenting, homophobic law still holds power in much of the United States, leaving lesbian, gay, bisexual, and transgendered people who have children from heterosexual unions afraid to initiate divorce proceedings or afraid to live openly with their same-sex spouses.

Although it is easy to imagine that situations like Melissa's family endured are ancient history, we must be cognizant of the prevalence of this kind of homophobia today. For example, in 2002, a lesbian mom lost custody of her children when the Alabama Supreme Court decided that the mother's homosexuality made her an unfit parent. Judge Roy Moore wrote a thirty-five-page opinion stating that homosexuality is "abhorrent, immoral, detestable, a crime against nature, and a violation of the laws of nature." In 2003, the ACLU became involved when a seven-year-old Louisiana boy was scolded and told *gay* was a "bad word," and forced to write, "I will never use the word 'gay' in school again," after he told a classmate that he had two gay moms.

In recent years many national professional organizations have taken a public stand in support of lesbian and gay families (although not necessarily families with transgendered parents). This includes public policy support from the American Psychological Association, the National Association of Social Workers, The Child Welfare League, the American Academy of Family Physicians, and the American Association of Pediatrics. These public policy statements, in addition to the advocacy within the LGBT community from national organizations like The Family Pride Coalition, COLAGE, GLAAD, the National Center for Lesbian Rights, The National Gay and Lesbian Task Force, and the Human Rights Campaign, are increasing positive outcomes within the legal system, as well as the changing the public view of LGBT families in the media.

Sexual orientation and gender identity should, of course, never be used to make judgments on custody and visitation, and despite decades of attempts, researchers have been unable to find any evidence that the children of LGBT people are harmed by being reared by queer parents. Custody decisions are always complex, but the courts must come to understand that severing a loving relationship between parent and child based solely on issues like gender expression and sexual orientation is never in the "best interest of the child."

So, despite numerous positive changes in the court system, LGBT parents who are leaving heterosexual marriages are always in a vulnerable position. Since the pressure to heterosexually couple is still very strong in Western society—despite the availability of other contemporary options—it is to be imagined that many people will continue to marry and have children before coming to terms with their sexuality and/or gender identity. Although many LGBT people are forming families after they are out, many children will continue to be born to families with a parent who will come out during their childhood or adolescence. One face of the LGBT community will always include families coping with the residuals of both coming out and divorce.

CHOOSING TO HAVE CHILDREN AND THE BEST INTERESTS OF THE CHILDREN

One of the more exciting developments in the past two decades has been the advent of lesbian and gay people choosing to have children as out gay people, both alone and in committed lesbian and gay partnerships. Through donor insemination, adoption, fostering, and surrogacy, the numbers of out and proud lesbian and gay families continue to rise. In the last few years some transgendered people, as out and proud trans people, have also chosen to begin families, seeking assistance from adoption agencies or choosing to have children through pregnancy. These new family forms are challenging many societal institutions such as the medical and judicial establishments, school systems, adoption agencies, and the media to address the needs of our families in a respectful and educated manner.

The concept of gay and lesbian parenting has introduced into the public forum questions about what really is in the best interests of the children. It is not only conservatives who raise these questions; often gay and lesbian people themselves wonder if they can be good parents, or if living in a gay/lesbian family will affect their children adversely. When lesbian and gay people become parents, it is, generally speaking, an active choice. Choosing children, whether we have children through birth, adoption, fostering, surrogacy or stepparenting, is something we must pursue and create in the face of judgment, misinformation, and often the lack of legal recognition for our families. Choosing to become a parent is not an easy decision. As with all major life decisions, this choice comes with both negative and positive consequences.

For some of us there has never been a question about wanting to become a parent; we have always known that we would. For others, perhaps we assumed that being gay precluded being a parent and have been surprised to see that parenting is a viable option. For all parents, gay and straight, parenting involves a lifelong commitment that brings with it responsibility, a reprioritizing of daily tasks, and a reevaluation of life goals and values. For most of us, it invites us to revisit our own childhoods and our relationship to our families of origin, as well as to assess the stability and functionality of our current intimate relationships.

It is a healthy process to evaluate your life to understand where children might fit in, and to decide how to bring children into your life. It can be worthwhile to examine your finances, your future plans including your career goals, as well as the communication patterns and commitment of your partner and friends. For some of us, this evaluation process will lead us to realize that children are not for us, and we can maintain a child-free life, knowing that we made a conscious and intentional decision. For others, despite obstacles, concerns, or fears, we may make the decision to pursue parenting.

"IT WILL CHANGE YOUR LIFE FOREVER"

This is the most common expression that one hears when querying friends and strangers on what becoming a parent will be like. Prospective parents often find this annoying and somewhat pompous. However, experienced parents might be sharing an intimate wisdom. When my son was a few weeks old, I hired a baby-sitter so that I could go to a conference. I met a woman there, an ex-student, who had heard that I had just adopted a child, and she said to me, "This will change your whole life." I remember saying to her, "Well, you know, I've lived a whole bunch of different lives already. This will just be one more change." Oh, the arrogance that was me. She assured me that this was different, that having children would change my life in ways I couldn't yet imagine. That it would change the meaning of life itself. Indeed, she was right. Over the next few weeks, months, and years, it was as if my whole life as I knew it, the entire screen of all my existence, had a huge hole cut out of the middle that was then filled with my son's needs, and the edges of that circle were left to me. Mostly I sleep on those edges today.

The truth is that there are few things that are as totally life altering as becoming a parent. It is, first of all, literally, forever. Secondly, although everyone expects to love their children, the overwhelming intensity of the parent/child bond often surprises most people. Parenting can be completely consuming in a way few other life experiences can be, especially when parenting infants and small children. It is these two qualities—forever, coupled with unbridled passionate commitment—that can be transformative for many people.

In addition to the emotional intensity of parenting, especially beginner parenting, there is an increase in the physical workload that can be burdensome and exhausting. New parents often comment that they simply cannot believe how many loads of dirty laundry an eight-pound infant can generate in a forty-eight-hour period. It is commonly understood that for each child added to the family the workload exponentially increases.

Most parents juggle the emotional and physical needs of parenting in addition to the demands of their work life, as well as the needs of their significant other, a creative life, political commitments, and socializing. It can be a daunting endeavor.

Despite all the vagaries of parenting, it is also full of unprecedented joys. Witnessing a child's first smile, hearing her first words, or watching him drive away in your car really is a life-changing experience. As exhausting as the 2 A.M. feeding or a screaming nightmare can be, feeling the trust of an infant looking at you, or a child clinging to you, or a large man with your eyes confiding in you can provide one with a sense of purpose and fulfillment. Parenting will change your life forever, and perhaps life as you knew it really is no more. However, as one lesbian mom said, "I realize now that I had no life before I had my babies; now I have a full life."

Solo Parenting

Many of us considering having children are single. Single gay and lesbian parenting is a valid life option and one with distinct advantages as well as unique challenges. Some of us are single because we simply haven't found the right person yet, and some of us are single by choice, preferring to not couple in a traditional manner. Some of us are in relationships with partners who are not interested in becoming parents, and others who are involved in intimate relationships may still choose to single parent. Sometimes lesbian and gay parents become single parents due to the death of a spouse; here the family must respond to the crisis of a traumatic loss as well as to the surviving parent's new role as single parent. In divorced families, even when custody is shared, each parent may function as a single parent when he or she is with the children.

Far too few of us realize that every person who makes a commitment to parent, even those with solid and loving partnerships, may end up as single parents. Every person choosing parenthood should examine the ques-

On My Own

The hard part of single parenting is that it takes so much more work than when you're partnered. If I want to run an errand, I have to call a friend, arrange a time, set up the house (meal or snack, things to drink, maybe clean up a bit), and then go through with it even if I don't feel like being apart from my son at that moment. Fortunately, I have a lot of friends who are willing to help out, but it would be nice to just say, "I'm walking to the corner store; back in five minutes," and then walk out the front door.

Sometimes I just don't feel like I fit anyone's mold—the other single mothers by choice (SMC) who are so often straight, the queer moms who are so often partnered, the queer moms who are so very often lesbian, the bi folks who so rarely are parents, the bi folks who are parents but are parenting with a person of the opposite sex and so seem like a regular straight family. Then at other times I feel like I fit in just fine in many places: when I share a question on my Internet bulletin board for parents whose babies were due the same month/year as mine, or I post on my lesbian and bi moms E-mail list and feel like I'm chatting with best friends who totally know me, or I trade baby-sitting and have a chat with another SMC and I feel like I totally get where she's coming from; her life is my life. So much of it is attitude and self-acceptance.

Still, I often feel at the edge of other moms' universes. As a queer mom, when I talk with heterosexual moms, many of whom are *so* straight, and I hear their "Plan A" stories, where they dated everyone they could to find a husband before they had children, I feel completely lost; I absolutely don't relate. I see straight-partnered moms with their husbands, and I can't help but reflect on how different our lives/families are, and feel so removed from that. I do sometimes wonder how straight women view me when I let slip about my female ex, etc. Do I shake up their world? Or in this queer mecca of San Francisco, is it just another mild data point for their own gaydar?

I'm aware of the differences I feel with other queer-mom friends, too—so many are partnered and face a different set of issues. They have so much more to deal with by being out—as in crossing off "Mother" and "Father" on forms and writing in "Parent" and "Parent"—or in not being out. I can't even imagine not being out, but yet in order to really be out as a bi mom, I have to advertise who I am by wearing T-shirts with queer themes and talking about my ex.

As a single mom by choice, the only things I really miss about not having a partner is the other set of arms to hold the baby while I shower and that other paycheck. And sometimes, I long for someone to drag over to the crib to gaze at the sleeping baby and agree with me that he's the most beautiful baby in the world. Yet I am often grateful that I don't have to share my wonderful boy with anyone else.

Jennie is a bisexual single mom to Graham, two years old, living in the San Francisco Bay Area.

tion, "Can I do this alone?" before becoming a parent. Conversely, every person choosing single parenthood should also examine the question, "If I choose to become a single parent, how will I integrate a partner into this family?"

It can be argued that in many ways heterosexual women have always functioned as single parents, since parenting was typically seen as a woman's primary responsibility. This is not meant to minimize the father's contribution to his children, financially or psychologically, or to disparage traditional heterosexual parenting patterns, but the fact remains that women have traditionally handled the daily tasks of parenting with little help from others. It might take a village to raise a child, but in our modern age, single mothers have often shouldered the burdens and witnessed the joys without a village to help them.

There are many benefits to solo parenting that are often overlooked in a world where *single parenting* is synonymous with *unplanned pregnancy* or *divorced family*. While it is true that single parents make up a significant number of families living in poverty, it is also true that single-parent homes can be carefully planned families. Many single people, heterosexual as well as gay and lesbian, are actively choosing to become parents; this is particularly true for people thirty-five and older, who are secure in professions, not involved in a significant relationship, who deeply desire to become a parent and are tired of waiting for a significant other with whom to share parenting. In fact, sometimes gay and lesbian single parents feel invisible as gay parents, appearing to blend into the mainstream in a way that same-sex couples cannot.

Single parents have the distinct advantage of not having to share decision making with anyone else. This eliminates some of the more difficult aspects of parenting, like different discipline styles or divergent values around whether it's okay to eat sweets before dinner or go to school in unmatched clothes. The difficulty this presents for single parents is that they don't have another parent to lean on in times of strife or illness. Often friends or other family can step in, but single parents must cope alone when school is unexpectedly closed or a child requires a sudden trip to the emergency room. Despite the challenges, single parenting is an option for all LGBT people, and sometimes the benefits can outweigh the negatives of balancing the intimacy of needs of couples with the overarching needs of growing children.

SAME-SEX COPARENTING

As gay and lesbian parenting becomes more commonplace, many couples are confronted with the inevitable question, "Should we become parents?" For gay and lesbian people who are absolutely clear that parenting is a path they desire, the question of partner ambivalence to parenting may become a major stumbling block to dating as well as a permanent commitment. Although it is, of course, possible to have a committed intimate relationship with an adult who is not sharing the parenting of a child, it can present certain obstacles regarding time, money, and energy, as well as life priorities.

When one partner is more committed to becoming a parent than his or her spouse, a decision may need to be made regarding the primacy of the relationship versus the desire for parenting. When a loved one deeply desires to become a parent, it can place immense pressure on a partner who is unsure. This is particularly true of lesbian couples where a biological clock may begin ticking loudly, and the couple may not feel they have indefinite time to process their emotions. Some people have chosen to end long-term relationships because their desire to parent was paramount, and the relationship could not accommodate this change. For others, their commitment to their relationship took primacy, and grieving for children they could not bring into their relationship became an integral part of their relationship process.

It is true that many people who enter parenthood with mixed emotions and ambivalence nonetheless become loving, committed, and involved parents. For some people, however, their fears about parenting do become reality, and despite everyone's assurance that once the baby arrived it would all just jell, these parents find themselves resistant to and resentful of the demands of children and family life. It is, therefore, important that partners who have ambivalence be allowed to fully examine their feelings about parenting in an honest and contemplative manner. It is equally important that the partner desiring parenting be allowed to express her often passionate baby hunger or his fears about losing his lover if he pursues parenting.

When partners feel differently about becoming parents, these issues are not easily resolved. Even when both partners desire children, they may not agree on how to bring children into their lives, the number of children they want to raise, the division of labor between the spouses, or how out to be

The "Other" Parent

Mary and I are, in practice, and in the eyes of our kids and everyone else we know, equal parents to both of our children, and have been since day one. We made the decision to adopt each of them together, we both provide financial, emotional, physical, and practical support. Although coparent adoption isn't an option in Virginia, we've hyphenated the kids' last names, and few people here even know that only one of us—me—has legal ties to the kids.

Mary earns, as a Realtor, about five times (in a bad year) what I make as a public school teacher. If something were to happen to her—and it's not just theoretical, since she was diagnosed with a slow-growing lymphoma several years ago—none of the rest of us would be eligible for social security or pension benefits, which means that, although we could survive, our standard of living would change drastically (i.e., we'd have to move from our house, for one thing).

If something were to happen to me, although I've indicated in my will that I want Mary to parent the kids (*and* we have a power of attorney reiterating that fact, *and* we have a coparenting agreement, *and* Mary claims Lucas on her tax return), my family of origin (and here I'm particularly worried about my fundamentalist brother and his nutso wife) could sue for custody of our kids and, here in Virginia, stand a decent chance of *winning*. Not that they want two more kids—especially two (gasp!) African-American kids—on top of the three they already have, but they might go for it just to "save" my kids from life in a lezzie household.

While having only one legal parent doesn't have any impact on my kids' day-to-day lives, it stands to have a great impact on them if something happens to one of their parents before they reach adulthood.

Kathy and Mary have been partners for twelve years and are parents to Lucas, age nine, who came home at two and a half, and Deja, age four, who came home at four months; they live in Charlottesville, Virginia.

with their children. In facing the important and sometimes staggering questions of whether to have children and how to do it, couples need and deserve support in learning to compromise and resolve differences. It is often useful to consider a support group for other wanna-be parents or couple counseling with a therapist trained in gay and lesbian family issues.

Parenting together as equal parents is the ideal for many LGBT couples. Some research has shown that lesbian couples who have children exhibit more egalitarian partnership patterns than heterosexual couples, in terms of both household chores and actual child-rearing practices. The term *coparenting* is often used to describe the process of equal parenting, although some find the term needlessly cumbersome. It is often true that the term *coparent* is used as a way to name the nonbiological parent in a way that some find offensive; the term is used here as an adjective to qualify a parenting strategy, not as a name to refer to the "other" parent.

Coparenting can sometimes be negatively impacted by the legal systems that do not support or encourage families headed by two same-sex parents. Although parents may want to, and intend to, be equal parents, when only one parent is legally endowed with the title of *parent,* it can create a hierarchy of power between the partners and a lack of stability for the children.

Although, LGBT parents work hard to minimize the impact of living without legal protections, this can weaken the foundation a family is building. Thankfully, more states are recognizing same-sex parents and allowing both parents to legally adopt their children, which minimizes some of the outside strain. This is true in families formed by pregnancy, surrogacy, and adoption. Currently, in some states, potentially adoptive parents are disqualified simply for being gay, which some couples deal with by applying to adopt as a "single" parent. However, in other states, being single automatically eliminates your chances of becoming an adoptive parent, an extreme way of rooting out potentially queer parents. All couples who choose to adopt internationally must remain closeted and apply as a single parent. It is important to not minimize the stress this places on a family that is *in their own minds* building a family together as coparents, but in the eyes of the government and/or the adoption agency, they must pretend to be just friends. Sometimes the nonadoptive parent, who is technically a roommate on the paperwork, is involved with the process as a supportive friend, which often means that he or she needs to coo at the new baby, pretending that it is *not* his or her child, while the new mom or dad gets all the attention. This can be enormously taxing on a family's emotional health during the intense throes of traveling to another country, meeting a child for the first time, dealing with governmental and legal entities, as well as mediating the different cultural practices of being in a foreign country.

Of course, these challenges can, and are, overcome daily in LGBT families. With or without legal protection and societal recognition, LGBT partners make serious, stable, and long-term commitments to one another. Couples work hard at the labor of parenting, negotiating differences, supporting one another, and developing daily routines that assist in the smooth functioning of family life. Coparenting is the dominant model of parenting in most First World countries, and LGBT people have also embraced this nuclear parenting paradigm and have successfully created homes where both parents share the role of heads of household.

Stepparenting

Sometimes LGBT people fall in love with others who already have children. Perhaps these children are from a previous heterosexual marriage, a previous lesbian or gay union, or perhaps this new partner has always been a single parent through birth or adoption. In any case, when you partner with a parent, you are not simply entering a relationship with your new lover but also with his or her children.

When the children are the product of a previous relationship, they may be living in more than one home and coping with the loss of their original family through divorce or due to death. In circumstances such as these, children may not be terribly accepting of a new person in their parent's life. Additionally, the new stepparent may have as much ambivalence about becoming a parent as the children have accepting a new parent. For some people a ready-made family is an ideal situation; however, integrating new members into any family is complex, especially if both partners have children from previous relationships.

Depending on the age of the children, your commitment to parenting, your partner's interest in your becoming a parent, and the role of other adults in the children's lives, your relationship can be one of a caring friend, the parents' partner, or a stepparent. Each role has responsibilities and challenges, and forming stepfamilies of any kind demands a high level of communication in navigating these challenges. For example, since single parents are used to having the final say over their children, they may encourage a new partner to be a more integral part of the family and yet balk at their first attempts at discipline. Or a partner's ex (particularly heterosexual ex-spouses) may resent the presence of a new parent in the children's lives and may undermine their role. Developing intimacy with children while forming a new lover relationship requires finding a proper balance. The most important thing to do is to understand that all stepfamilies take tremendous work as they are coping not only with the formation of this new family but the legacy of its previous constitution. When marrying into an established parent/child family, you are engaging in a situation that has

Blended Families

Jackie and I have a simple coparenting arrangement. We first started forming our family a scant six months ago, and we're still relatively new to each other, and new as a family—but we're not completely new to parenting. Our household consists of Jackie (computer geek extraordinaire), Catherine (me, the science nerd), and two girls (Connor, age six, and Lauren, age four). We came into this as two single moms with two only children, so our merger has some unique twists. Both children were conceived via unknown donor insemination, and we were both in relationships at the time our children were conceived. Both of our relationships fell apart within the child's first year; in each case, when the children were seven to eight months old, we became single moms. Both of our exes have maintained little to no contact with the children and do not participate in parenting in any significant sense of the word.

We both work full-time; neither of us is particularly butch or femme, and we share household and parenting responsibilities more or less equally. The girls attend private school. Jackie does the morning routine with them, and I do the evenings. Each of us is the biological and legal parent of only one kid; correspondingly, each of us has absolutely zero legal standing with the other kid. Second-parent adoption is not yet an option in our state, but in truth, we're not quite ready yet to take that step, although we both parent both of the children. Our coparenting agreement is based upon a commitment to building our family and our relationship; we share priorities and goals about the children's care and well-being. I think there's good balance between us: often, one's strength complements the other's weakness. This is likely to be our saving grace.

However, it's certainly difficult at times to navigate subtle differences. The girls, whom we've nicknamed Plague and Pestilence, are very different ("Mommy, am I Plague or is she?"). Lauren (the child I birthed) has certain habits that irritate the hell out of Jackie, but they don't even register on my radar. And vice versa. We've acknowledged that there are/will most likely be two sets of rules in some cases. The fact that they're such different children dictates that to a degree, but we've also come to understand that there are some things about which we feel so strongly that we retain some sort of primacy with respect to the child we bore. For example, Jackie is adamant that Connor's choice of clothing not be typically girly. I don't share those views; in fact, I find them rather restrictive. Lauren will be permitted to choose certain types of clothing, where Connor will not. There's a "no Barbie" rule in our house, but only because Jackie feels strongly about that, too—Lauren had three Barbies who mysteriously went on a long vacation (they were replaced with less offensive dolls, at my insistence that having a doll in and of itself wasn't a Bad Thing).

There are many compromises that we're learning to make, but we're also learning that it's possible to have absolutes. In our world, at least thus far, it isn't necessary that everything be fifty-fifty. We do try to hold the children's best interests as the primary goal, but we also acknowledge that the girls have different motivators, different personalities, and (gasp!) different parents. It's okay that they get different answers depending upon whom they approach, as long as we agree to support each other's position on big issues. (This is universal parenting stuff; it's got nothing to do with the fact that there are two moms involved.) Most of our issues have to do with stepfamily things—

boundaries, your kid/my kid, integrating different styles, etc. We're tackling them as we go along, with reasonably good progress so far. We remain committed to the idea that if we're careful, if we pay attention, we can make this work.

Catherine, partnered with Jackie, parents to Connor, age six, and Lauren, age four, lives in rural Delaware.

a history—often a long history. Despite the work and challenges entailed, stepfamilies can be healthy and successful and are a wonderful way to become a parent, even if it was not something you had originally planned for.

REALLY ALTERNATIVE FAMILY STRUCTURES

All of the family forms mentioned above—families formed by divorce, solo parenting, coparenting, and stepparenting—are family forms that are common in the mainstream heterosexual community. In addition to these family structures, LGBT people have adapted and created many other family configurations. Relationships between children and their known donors—who may be seen as uncles, parents, family friends, or acquaintances—are not unusual, although they require careful planning. When a biological father is named on a birth certificate, it creates a legal relationship to the child that may preclude a nonbiological parent from securing her legal rights. These open relationships are increasingly common among families formed by adoption and surrogacy, whereby the family maintains contact and connection with the biological family. Again, it is not just LGBT families that are choosing these open configurations, but many heterosexuals—single and married—are choosing known donor insemination and open adoption and surrogacy arrangements to form their families.

Increasingly, children are born into seemingly traditional heterosexual families that are nothing of the sort. Lesbians and gay men are joining together to form families and partnerships, developed solely around their parenting functions, and sometimes close friendships. They are commonly not lovers or sexual partners, but are forming families in which to parent children. They may plan pregnancies through donor insemination or sexual intercourse. Their reasons for these unique situations are varied. Perhaps they are single and simply desire to share parenting with a friend. Perhaps they feel most comfortable in a traditionally gendered parent-headed family, believing that it is best for children to have a mother and father. In some situations, it came about slowly over time, i.e., the donor became a close family friend and coparent, although this was not originally planned. In other situations, this evolved in tragic and painful ways, when donors sued for custody of children that they originally agreed not to parent. When donors win these cases, the biological parent may be forced to share parenting with a man with whom she had no interest in coparenting. This is one reason that decisions to have open donor agreements must be carefully thought out in advance.

However, lesbians and gay men are parenting together in greater numbers, challenging the simple assumption that a man and a woman together with a child is a heterosexual family. Lesbians and gay men are often coparents, perhaps living together in the same home, and actively engaged in parenting children together, but yet are not themselves a unit, but are single or involved in other gay sexual relationships.

Within the transgender community, parenting options can become more complicated but also more sophisticated. For those who are transitioning their sex, one of the important variables to examine are the future options for parenting and any grief or loss they may have about losing their reproductive capacities. Many male-to-female transsexuals are freezing their sperm so they can have biological children through insemination at a later date. Others have chosen to have their children before beginning the transition process or have delayed transitioning in order to ensure the successful pregnancy of a partner or spouse. Female-to-male transsexuals have sometimes chosen to give birth before transition, or in some cases, after transition. Surely, the presence of a bearded, pregnant man in a Lamaze class constitutes a new, rather queer family configuration!

Transgendered people have had difficulty securing placements through the adoption system. In more conservative states, they have been blatantly excluded (and since transgendered and transsexual people have no legal protections in most jurisdictions, they have no recourse). In more liberal ar-

As Queer As It Gets

I'm a queer woman, and a parent. My child has a daddy, but it's not from a heterosexual dalliance in my past or from a donor arrangement gone sour. My son has a father, a dad, because that's the way we planned it.

In the queer community, perhaps the most transgressive act a woman can do is to have a child with a man. I still have the replies archived from a lesbian mother's E-mail list when I announced that I planned to have a child with my closest friend, a queer man. I was a new member, and I was seeking input from others who'd taken a similar path. I received input, all right—ranging from "Why would you want to do that?" to dire warnings that if I went that route, a court might someday decide that this guy might actually be (gasp!) my child's father!

Which was precisely the point—I wanted him to be my child's father. Quite literally from the day I met him—a day we spent talking from breakfast until dusk about politics and books and science and our families, I knew this was someone I wanted in the life of my as yet unconceived child. Two years and a lot of discussions later, including time spent together poring over sperm bank "donor menus"—one of us (and I don't remember which) hit the duh moment. We realized that the easiest, cheapest way for us to achieve the goals of 1) me getting pregnant, and 2) him having a parentlike role in the life of my child was simply for him to *be* the child's other parent—genetically as well as socially.

I didn't go into this baby-making endeavor thinking that my future kid needed a daddy—not at all. In fact, as far back as I can remember, I always envisioned being a single mom—I wanted to be a single mom, I had no interest in competing with anyone for authority! But now, I'm so glad that's not how things turned out. I love being able to watch our son, and see his daddy's traits, such as his excellent spatial reasoning and mathematical skills, mirrored in him.

We're now about six years into this adventure—our son is turning five. Although we know of others who have chosen a similar path, we don't actually *know* any other families like ours. Some days it's difficult and lonely to have chosen the path we took to become parents and not having other people to bounce ideas off of—or even with whom to commiserate. Instead, we invent the rules as we go along, which has actually become a tremendous reward.

Ironically, the same confusion with which most people approach our family structure affords us a huge amount of flexibility, too. Since there's no ground swell of opposite-sex queers choosing to coparent, there are really no rules or expectations about how to do this. We've found great success in just doing what works for us and for our son. We're lucky in many ways: living where we do, there's not a huge gay establishment that could look askance at what we've done, but the area's progressive enough that there's no problem with preschool (where many of the teachers are alternative in various ways themselves), the neighbors (the lesbian couple next door is always glad to have the little guy out "helping" rake leaves), or even our coworkers, who may not understand fully how we've chosen to parent, or why, but who acknowledge that it seems to be working for us.

A few areas have been difficult: Dating has been a bit challenging, since people are confused by this ever-present opposite-sex, best friend coparent, who is not my lover. Although our families of origin are now accepting, when I first told my mother I was pregnant, she was insistent that we needed to get married so that other children would treat our child well; she was also concerned whether we were both fully committed to this undertaking.

The most difficult areas, ironically, have nothing to do with our gender or sexual orientation. We're a TV-free household, and despite the grandparents' best attempts, manage to keep licensed character commodities (Disney, Rugrats, etc.) absent from the household as well. I'm polyamorous, and we've had many discussions about people being independent and free, and that being in a relationship with someone doesn't make that person one's property.

Although it is certainly not always easy living differently from more typically structured families, at this point, I can't imagine parenting any other way.

Elaine coparents her son, Gregory, age five, with Wayne, in the Pacific northwest.

eas, they have been put through extensive evaluative home study processes, but run into endless red tape while waiting for an actual placement. This is an area of adoption law that will need serious reexamination in the coming decade.

Sadly, transgendered people have routinely lost custody of their children following their transition. The courts are extremely biased against transsexual parents. Even in more progressive cities, transphobia still reigns in situations where custody decisions are made following the dissolution of heterosexual marriages, following a transgender self-disclosure. This is true despite research showing that children do adjust to parental sex reassignments with minimal difficulties, and experts petitioning the courts to not disrupt families simply based on gender identity issues.

The issue of transgender parenting presents unique social dilemmas. It can be disconcerting when a child yells, "Mommy" in a store, and the person who answers has a deep voice and thick beard. School systems are unsure how to manage families with a transitioning spouse, and peer pressure for young people can be overwhelming while they are trying to acclimate to the gender reconfigurations in their family.

Another type of a family configuration is gay and lesbian families where the partners have divergent gender roles and/or expressions—

butch/femme lesbian couples, and gay male couples where gender is polarized in what many consider to be a typical heterosexual paradigm. It is interesting that so much of the research on lesbian parents has emphasized the equality of their parenting roles; it is unclear why this research has failed to reflect the lives of butch/femme couples whose parenting styles may be complementary but are not necessarily identical or parallel. In many ways, gendered relationship patterns with the LGBT community often succeed in making everyone uncomfortable. Other lesbians and gay men often accuse them of mimicking heterosexuals, and heterosexuals see them as feeble replicas.

Butch and femme identities have very little to do with heterosexual roles but are about how people experience their gender within the context of their sexual orientation. Within the lesbian community butch identity is a masculine identity within a female body, and femme identity is an expression of more traditional female sexuality for a female, which although it may sound like a "normal woman," in the context of lesbian communities, this can often be very queer. Gay men and others also use butch/femme language to describe their relationship to their gender and how they enjoy expressing it. Although the term *butch* can be used in many contexts, for many butches the word is not an adjective that modifies another word (i.e., butchy lesbian), but an identity construct in itself. Some butches identify more with the father role than the mother role, and many are somewhat torn about where they fit into any parenting model, feeling outside of the heterosexual world but yet not quite part of the lesbian models. Being butch can present unusual dilemmas when a female person with a masculine identity is doing a traditionally feminine task like birthing a baby.

Same-sex partnerships are often accused of lacking in opposite-sex role models for the children, but gendered same-sex relationships are viewed as giving children confusing ideas about gender. Despite the discomfort, children growing up in gendered same-sex families do not seem to have any greater concerns dealing with their gender identity or sexual orientation than do other children. However, children are often burdened with having to explain their unique family forms to their peers and teachers or even grandparents. If they are growing up in an open home, they will simply ask questions when they are confused. One little boy was getting dressed with his mom one morning. As he watched her put on her boxers, he said, "I'm

But Is It Natural?

One of my favorite things about being pregnant and butch was to be somewhere and be called sir, and then as they looked down toward my belly, the look of panic in their eyes. I once was at a lesbian mom/wanna-be mom picnic with my wife and was introduced to someone by the host. The woman I was meeting looked at me, looked at my belly, back up at my face, and then to the host and said, "But she is the bu—" The host quickly interrupted and said, "Yes she is, isn't that great!?" I guess not everyone is comfortable with pregnant people who don't shave.

My experience with pregnancy wasn't bad at all. My partner modified most of my boy clothes with panels and such so I could wear jeans (my jeans, not funny maternity jeans) until the very end, and I just bought bigger and bigger T-shirts as the pregnancy progressed. I had a great obstetrician that kept physical exams to a minimum and made that part of it as comfortable for me as she could. I really appreciated that.

There is, however, very little support for butches having babies. The support that I found was actually on the Internet because in my real life people just didn't know what to do with it in their heads. Most of my close friends were supportive, but toward the end when my belly popped out, even they started treating me a little femmy.

I was told by strangers and even a good friend that being a pregnant butch "just wasn't right." I say however a baby can get here and have a loving family is right. One friend of mine who is a femme once said, "What could be more studly than a butch having a baby?" Now, I have my body back and a wonderful daughter. Family is family, no matter how it begins or who brings the baby into the world.

10 Points for the Friends of Pregnant Butches

1. Don't open the door for her unless it is your habit together, especially if you are another butch!

2. When planning a baby shower, avoid the frills and cucumber sandwiches; make it more like a Superbowl party.

3. Don't even show her those funny maternity underwear!

4. Laugh with her when she comments on the recent growth of her chest (i.e., boobs) and how she would love to see those on someone else. Reassure her that they most likely will go back to normal again.

5. Don't talk about how the baby will come out. Truth is, she is painfully aware of what lies ahead, and the reminders serve no purpose but to make her uncomfortable.

6. Do joke about the size of her belly. . . . Size does matter, and she will likely brag about it.

7. Remind her that she is still *the* butch, in every way she ever was, and that some femmes find it quite studly.

8. Remember it's a baby coming into the world, a joyous occasion for anyone. Save personal discomforts that you may have about a butch bearing a child for yourself; after all, it's too late for her to change things now anyway.

9. Raging hormones and butches rarely mix well; be nice to the pregnant butch.

10. Let her hand out the cigars after the birth.

Anne Carvi, coparenting with her ex, mom to Zoe, age one, Columbus Ohio.

just checking. You *are* a woman, right?" Children like to be able to sort things out (as do most grown-ups), but learn to deal with the reality that some things, and people, are not easily sorted.

Other alternative family systems include many LGBT families that have multiple adult caregivers in addition to the biological or adoptive parents. This may include aunts or uncles, grandparents, and cousins, those who are genetically linked as well as those who are relatives by choice. It also may include their parents' ex-lovers, close friends, and new lovers, who may not be parents, but may be close, extended family members. This can evoke questions when the child says, "This is my Patty," thinking that she or he is explaining or defining the nature of the relationship. To the child, "my Patty" is no less familial than saying "my grandmother."

In addition to families with multiple caregivers, some of us have built large extended families through adoption.

It is, of course, not just LGBTs that have unique families. Single parents, gender-bending parents, divorced and stepparent families, foster families, transracial families, and even families where the parents are into kinky sex, all exist outside the queer community. Indeed, one of the ways that LGBT families often make connections and find support is with other alternative families who are heterosexual. It is, however, also true that the process of building an LGBT family requires creativity and resourcefulness.

Therefore, LGBT people who are forming families are not limited by pre-conceived notions regarding what makes a family and have available to them original and unique options for developing innovative family forms and structures that will work best.

OUR UNIQUE CONTRIBUTION

Some will argue that gay families are just like other families, and indeed in most ways we are. One lesbian mom suggested that her family was more normal than any other family in the neighborhood, and that actually the family next door was downright strange. I suggested that even though her family might be 100 percent "normal" (albeit there are two moms and no dads), I would hope that being a lesbian couple might heighten their awareness of difference, and perhaps *they* would be more tolerant of their very strange neighbors than other members of the community might be.

There are some unique traits of LGBT families in general, although as individuals we represent every part of the spectrum of human diversity. Although crossing all boundaries of rich and poor, old and young, representing orthodox religiosity and pagan New Age pan-spiritualism, as well as every ethnic, racial, and cultural group, LGBT people have also built communities that, by and large, embrace certain values.

LGBT communities offer a rich diversity of race/ethnicity, gender, and cultural expression. Many lesbians and gay men work in jobs or have hobbies that are not traditionally gendered (i.e., women can be carpenters and men can be artists), and children growing up in LGBT homes are often exposed to a greater range of options regarding gendered behavior. Although I have no statistics to back it up, it does appear that interracial relationships are relatively more common in LGBT communities, particularly in larger cities. Many children are being raised in mixed-race homes where the partners are from different ethnic or racial backgrounds, and/or are living in transracial families formed by adoption. Now certainly, there are also many heterosexual people who raise their children without sexist role expectations, and who are in mixed-race families, but it is common for LGBT people to appreciate and seek out diversity in neighborhoods, school settings, and playgrounds. Diversity, in identity as well as expression, is often valued in LGBT communities, though in reality we often fall short of our own vision.

When someone says LGBT families are alternative, it invokes the question of, "Alternative to *what?*" Of course, the answer is that LGBT families are alternative to the singular model of heterosexual, normatively gendered, single-race, opposite-sex, two-parent families that some will swear are the backbone of modern Western life. In reality, there are multiple models of family life available in First World industrial nations, as well as numerous more traditional familial configurations throughout the world, that continue to evolve through time. Throughout most of human history, people lived in tribes and extended family systems and were part of multi-generational household units; significant numbers of people still live in these traditional ways. The modern nuclear family is an aberrant family form and is far less common (and less functional) than most people acknowledge. The 2000 census has given us valuable information about the contemporary American family. For instance, in the past decade, there has been a 72 percent increase in the number of unmarried cohabiting partners, and women raising children without a husband present grew by 25 percent. The divorce rate for heterosexual couples is 45 percent for the first marriage and 60 percent for the second marriage, and most divorced people remarry. Only 40 percent of children grow up in homes with two biological parents. Despite the fears of some contemporary commentators about how gay marriage and gay parenting will destroy the American family, the traditional American family was a myth long before gay people came out and insisted on our rights to legally couple and raise families.

I'm not denying that LGBT families are alternative, but rather pointing out that LGBT people are not alone in being alternative. Innovative family forms have continued to evolve throughout Western society, and queer families are not the harbingers of that diversity but are merely another reflection of it. Being alternative to the mainstream expectations of the nuclear family model does offer LGBTs more freedom and opportunity to create our families outside of cultural limitations.

Alternative families and queer families represent not only diversity but also empowerment. LGBT family-building is not something that just happens, as is far too common among young heterosexuals who have not had the opportunity to consider whether they want to become parents, but are

Super-Sized Family

Katherine and I have been together for nineteen years and live in British Columbia. We started as a blended family. Katherine had a teenage daughter, Gina, and I had two children, Hope, age eight, and Ben, age six. When the youngest children hit their teens, I developed a case of premature empty-nest syndrome, and so we decided to add to our family through adoption. We now have eleven children and two grandchildren.

Our family is constantly in motion. Our oldest three children are now independent adults. Two of them live in the same community, and we see them often. Hope recently left her marriage and returned with her two daughters, Madeleine, age three, and Makenzie, age two, to live with us. Our sixteen-year-old, adopted at age five, is working full-time and going to school part-time. Delayne, age thirteen, adopted at age four, is being home schooled this year, as well as participating in a community band, cadets, and tai chi. Thomas, age twelve, adopted at age ten, is active in every sport available and trying to figure out how to balance athletics with academics. Connor, age eleven, adopted at age three, is also a sports enthusiast, and although he struggles with learning disabilities, he has an active social life and does his best at school. Ethan, age ten, adopted at age fourteen months, loves gymnastics and spends a lot of time at his computer writing stories. Rhiannon, age nine, adopted at age six, also has serious learning challenges but is a budding stage star and is active in a youth choir that performs all over the province. Recently, we added Kayla, age four, and Ian, age three, to our family, and they have formed a solid unit

with our granddaughters. These will be our last additions, but we have said that before!

Our family dynamics are different than those of a small family. Our children often forgo calling friends because there is always someone to play with at home. They have highly developed conflict-resolution skills and have learned to turn to family first for fun and help. But so many children means less parental attention, and so they have become independent in many ways. If they can reach the buttons on the washing machine, they do their own laundry, and they each learn to cook and clean better and younger than their friends. On the positive side, we seem to do more together as a family than others. We go swimming weekly, we go to beaches, parks, movies, and other places en masse. The older children never hesitate to pick up a crying baby or push a toddler on a swing, and my older boys are as good at changing diapers as any parent.

As for Katherine and me, we have learned that keeping our relationship passionate and fulfilling is vital to keeping our family stable. To do this, we create time to spend just the two of us, and time to spend with adult friends (other adoptive parents of large families). This type of family isn't for everyone, but it works well for us.

Brynne and Katherine, partners for nineteen years, have eleven children: Gina, age thirty-four, Hope, age twenty-six, Ben, age twenty-four, Dan, age sixteen, Delayne, age thirteen, Thomas, age twelve, Connor, age eleven, Ethan, age ten, Rhiannon, age nine, Kayla, age four, and Ian, age three; and two grandchildren, Madeleine, age three, and Makenzie, age two. They make their home in British Columbia, Canada.

thrust into parenthood as the logical next step. Family-building, as LGBT people practice it, is an active, creative, thoughtful process, raising questions about our abilities to parent as well as our rights to parent. LGBT people think about issues like pregnancy versus adoption, legal documentation, what names to call each parent, how roles will be divided up, and are aware upon entering parenting that they are falling down the proverbial rabbit hole and will never emerge the same. LGBT parenting is alternative because it involves choice and conscious action. Although it may be a sad proclamation about the state of most families, consciously choosing the form and structure of your family *is* a radical alternative.

Maybe someday LGBT families will raise nary an eyebrow. Maybe people will learn to not assume that everyone has a mother and a father, that all children look like their parents, that all mothers birthed their own babies, that all spouses are opposite sex, or are living in the sex in which they were born. Maybe someday society will not hold out heterosexual coupling as the norm, and therefore same-sex partnerships will not be the other. Judith Butler, in her book *Gender Trouble*, says, ". . . the original identity after which gender fashions itself is an imitation without an origin." Alternative families are only alternative if we assume an original, normative blueprint with which all else is compared. If we reject heterosexual, two-parent families as the original blueprint (and our brief sojourn through the sociological statistics about contemporary as well as historical families has demanded this rejection), then queer families are not so alternative. If there is no norm with which to compare it, then it is not an alternative, an imitation; but same-sex as well as opposite-sex parenting becomes possible within what is just an array of diverse choices for family life.

CHAPTER TWO

• • •

Paths to Parenting—
Family-Building Options

DECIDING TO BECOME a parent can be an arduous process for many LGBT people. Some people have delayed their coming out or avoided addressing their sexual or gender identity issues because they longed for children and feared being queer would disqualify them. For those reared in fundamentalist religious traditions, conservative, or emotionally repressive families, or with moral concerns regarding homosexuality or transgenderism, the choice to have children is complicated by the values of their upbringing regarding bringing children into an alternative family structure.

Others may feel comfortable being LGBT and are surprised to find issues surfacing when they begin to plan for a family. For some LGBT people, internalized homophobia/transphobia has a way of taking a seat—front row, center—when the idea of children is raised. Sometimes people are embarrassed to admit their concerns and are shocked at their intensity, thinking they had worked through self-doubt about their identity years before. The reality is that parenting brings most of us out into the mainstream world in new ways, having to face complex discussions with medical personnel, adoption specialists, and extended family members. For those of us who have always lived more immersed in the heterosexual world than the gay community, it may bring issues of our gayness into social discussions in a more intimate and potentially conflictual manner.

For all LGBT people, it is essential to resolve fears and concerns about your right to be an LGBT parent *before* you begin the process of planning your family. This does not mean you need to resolve every issue related to parenting—indeed you couldn't if you tried—it simply means you are comfortable being a lesbian mom, gay dad, bisexual or transgendered/transsexual parent, and understand that this will impact parenting in novel ways. You need to be comfortable knowing that being queer is compatible with parenting and that you are prepared to face the issues that present themselves. If you are an out LGBT person, you have probably already addressed these issues regarding your family of origin and your work life. If you have always been closeted—or perhaps just reserved and cautious—parenting may force you to be more out and visible than you've ever been. Parenting makes discretion more complicated, and you will have to face other people's judgments while embarking on this journey. The more comfortable you are with yourself, the easier it will be to address intrusive negative opinions.

Having made the decision to move forward means that you have examined your finances, discussed potential obstacles with partners or friends, told your parents of this decision, and considered how this will impact your career or job. You should be done soul-searching and have resolved major questions within your own heart before actually moving forward.

There are many paths to becoming a parent, and each one has its own built-in joys and challenges. It is important to remember that there is no one right way to become a parent. In fact, many families choose to utilize a different path with each child brought into the family. Parenting options are not, of course, different than they are for heterosexual parents, though LGBT parents are often more active participants in considering all the options available. LGBT people are, generally, unlikely to become parents without careful planning and conscious decision making on how they bring children into their lives, although it is important to acknowledge that sometimes parenting can just happen through an expected pregnancy, the death of a sibling who leaves young children without parents, or "inheriting" children because of a friend's addiction or mental illness. Being thrown into parenting can be overwhelming and intense, and much of the soul-searching alluded to above happens *after* the kids are fed and tucked into

bed. Obviously, the more prepared a person is for this life-changing journey, the better equipped you are to tackle the inevitable challenges that will
confront you. However, the truth is that no one, no matter how much
they've planned, is ever truly prepared, so don't feel bad about learning as
you go; honestly, we all do that.

PATH NUMBER ONE: PREGNANCY

Pregnancy is probably the most common way in which lesbians become
parents. Pregnancy is also a possible path for starting a family for gay male
couples through surrogacy or a coparenting agreement with a woman. For
lesbians and gay men, accidental pregnancy is obviously rare but is, of
course, possible. Lesbians can become pregnant through unwanted sex,
i.e., rape, and must then make difficult decisions regarding the continuation of the pregnancy. Gay men and lesbians can also sometimes find themselves involved, to their own surprise, with someone of the opposite sex,
and may be careless, or perhaps unlucky with birth control. Bisexual and
transgendered females involved with members of the opposite sex can, of
course, become unexpectedly pregnant. However, the vast majority of lesbian, gay, and bisexual people who have children through pregnancy have
made active and conscious choices about how to become pregnant.

Lesbian Couples Making Babies: Dads, Donors,
and Decisions

Lesbian couples who opt for pregnancy must make numerous decisions, including decisions about which woman will carry the baby, donor insemination versus sexual intercourse, anonymous donors versus having fathers
in their children's lives. Pregnancy always involves precautions regarding
HIV and other health risks. Additionally, the role and legal rights of a nonbiological parent, must be considered.

For some lesbian couples, the decision as to which partner will carry
the baby is simple; one wants to, and one does not. In other couples, both
partners want to get pregnant, often with the older partner or the one assumed to be less fertile going first. Although it is often assumed that all lesbians choose donor insemination to get pregnant, many lesbians, as well as

bisexual women, opt for sexual intercourse with men. Some women feel this is more natural, while others maintain it is important to them that the conception takes place in a sexually intimate manner. Others just feel that this will increase their chances of conceiving. The biological father may be a lover or a friend and may remain in the child's life as a dad, an uncle, or simply a donor, or he may have no further involvement in the child's life. The decision to have a known biological father raises important issues regarding the child's legal parentage. Choosing a known father, through sexual intercourse or donor insemination, is not a decision that should be made casually, as it can impact custody decisions later in the child's life.

For lesbians who are choosing donor insemination, the first question that arises is the use of a known versus an unknown donor. The term *donor insemination* and/or *alternative reproduction* are preferred over the term *artificial insemination* to remove the stigma of insemination as an unnatural or inauthentic form of reproduction. The question of known versus unknown donors is a complex issue. Known donors are seen by most judicial systems as fathers, and if a man chooses to pursue parental rights at a later date, this can create numerous legal problems for the couple, including potential court-mandated shared custody. Although legal donor agreements can be written before the pregnancy is pursued, they are rarely legally binding in a court of law. For this reason, many women choose anonymous donors or work with sperm banks as a protection against any future custody battles. However, using a known donor offers the benefit of more complete access to medical information, as well as an opportunity for the child to know his or her biological heritage and enjoy a wider extended family.

As already indicated, using an unknown donor may protect the family from any future custody problems. The difficulty with unknown donors is the limited access the child will have to information about his or her genetic heritage. Such information can be important for medical or psychological purposes. It is unclear as of yet whether some children conceived by anonymous donor insemination will feel some of the same concerns regarding their biological heritage that some children adopted in closed adoptions feel regarding their lack of access to information about their history. Adopted children vary in their interest in knowing their biological roots, and it can be assumed the children born from donor insemination will also have a variety of opinions regarding their closed records.

Some sperm banks have responded to these concerns and have devel-

Using a Known Donor, as Easy as 1, 2, 3 . . .

When Mindi and I talked about having a baby, we always knew that we had to find someone who was willing to be a sperm donor; we would never be able to pay for it otherwise. We asked three of our friends. One said no immediately, one disappeared and we have never seen nor heard from him again. When Mindi asked Adam, I was a little skeptical. I had only met him twice, and he was a former coworker of Mindi's and not a close friend. He told her that he would get back to us, and when he did three months later, he said yes. We were so nervous when we went out to dinner with Adam to discuss the details, Mindi spilled his fancy blue drink all over him. We discussed the details of our relationships and decided that Adam would remain a family friend but not a parent.

We weren't sure what proper sperm drop-off etiquette was, so the first time Adam came over we made a welcome sign for our door, and bought him a mum plant. We told Adam that he would have to bring his own magazine, as we had no idea what would work for him. We waited outside on the stoop for him to finish and call us back into the house. We said quick good-byes and got to making a baby. We had the speculum, little flashlight, baby medicine dropper, and the GladWare container that held the semen all lined up on the nightstand. We put on some soft music, but I got too nervous, and we had to shut it off. Mindi was so scared of hurting me, of spilling the semen, of doing something wrong, I don't think she breathed the whole time.

Two weeks later we found out that I was pregnant. We told all our friends, and a week later I miscarried.

We tried a second time, and bought Adam a candle.

The third time we tried to conceive was a snowy Friday night. We bought Adam Chinese food for dinner, and we stayed in the living room with the door closed while he was in the bedroom; it was too cold to wait outside. Adam left, and we got busy setting up our supplies.

The insemination went smoothly, and while I was lying in the bed with my feet up against the wall, the telephone rang. Our friends wanted to know if we wanted to go with them to synagogue. Mindi said, "Malkie has five more minutes to lie here, so pick us up in fifteen." We went to services, prayed for success and conception, and eight and a half months later, on September 13, 2001, two days after the Twin Towers fell, we had Micah. While the world felt like it was ending, our world was just beginning.

Mindi and Malkie, partners for five years, parents to Micah, age two, and Max, six weeks old, live in Brooklyn, New York.

oped a special program where anonymous donors can have information released to the child when the child becomes of age. For some people this is a wonderful midway solution between known and unknown donors. The donor will never be able to interfere with the raising of the child, and is potentially available to the child for purposes of medical or paternal lineage information. Another recent innnovation is the Donor Sibling Registry (http://www.donorsiblingregistry.com), which allows the children of donors who are being raised in different families to connect with one another. Parents and children over eighteen post information on the site based on their donor number, and many matches have been made. In some cases families have remained in touch, and donor siblings are developing relationships similar to those formed by birth siblings in adoptive families.

Many women inseminate at home, a process easily accomplished for women without fertility problems. This can be done in a number of ways. One way is with a known donor, a male friend or lover or a relative of the nonbiological mother. Using the sperm donated from a family member of a partner has the added benefit of making the child biologically related to both women. It is essential when utilizing semen from a known donor that everyone involved is clear about the expectations and responsibilities regarding sexually transmitted illnesses, genetic history, parenting roles, finances, and the relationship status of all involved. Since men have been known to change their minds about their relationship to children born from their donor semen, legal paperwork is strongly recommended, regardless of how close the relationship may be at the time of conception.

Another pregnancy option is to use an unknown donor. This can be accomplished in two ways. One is to use fresh semen that is anonymously transported by a friend. The donor in this case may not be known to the women but may be known to another person in their community. Sometimes the women know who the donor is, but the donor does not know who the women are. One benefit of inseminating at home with a known or unknown donor is that the cost for fresh semen is usually zero, although sometimes a small fee is paid to legally demonstrate the intentions of the donor and recipients. It is important to remember when inseminating informally (i.e. without a sperm bank) that the availability of DNA testing makes it easy for an unknown donor to become *known* very quickly.

Another option is to use a sperm bank and have the anonymous sperm shipped directly to your home. Some women prefer to inseminate in a physician's office, and in some states it may be difficult to work with a sperm bank if you are not affiliated with a physician. Also, women having difficulty conceiving can be monitored more thoroughly when working with a physician and will have access to many medical procedures that can-

Using an Unknown Donor: Thaw and Then Bake for Nine Months

My partner Betsy and I didn't have any trouble deciding to have a kid. We didn't have any trouble deciding on the timing—we had been together for five years and had bought a house the year before. The decision for me to carry the baby was easy; I wanted to, I had younger eggs, Betsy couldn't be pregnant (she has a heart condition) and didn't want to be anyway. We were set in jobs that allowed us financial stability and flexibility.

Deciding about the donor was a different story. Betsy really wanted to use a dear friend who is a swell guy in many ways—but after he cheated on his wife, began drinking more than I was comfortable with, and needed our place to stay in a crisis, we decided that an unknown donor just might be a better option.

We wanted to have our insemination experience be as inexpensive and basic as possible, so we decided to do at-home insemination. After some hours calling fertility clinics in our city, I discovered that one would store donor specimens (as they are so delicately called) free of charge while we were in the process of trying to conceive, and they didn't care if we inseminated at home. The sperm bank we wanted to work with was happy to ship specimens to the clinic all at once so we wouldn't have to pay (a lot) for shipping every cycle. And since all we had to do was call the clinic one day before insemination, we didn't have to worry about the timing of shipping either. All good, right? Yes, but now we had to pick a donor.

Betsy was thirty-seven and I was thirty-one at the time we were trying to conceive, but in our combined sixty-plus years of shopping experience, nothing—even buying a really excellent pair of cowboy boots in a trendy store in Berlin—had prepared us for shopping for a donor. This version of playing God (our baby *will* have dimples) was both unsettling and, to be honest, a little bit thrilling. The two-page profiles that the sperm bank had on their Web site free of charge (longer medical histories were available for a small fee) were surprisingly revealing. We wanted a donor that had some Italian heritage, like Betsy, and had the aforementioned dimples, but other than that, we were willing to be swayed by the personalities that these profiles revealed. We found we were really drawn to the guy who liked "fluffy cats," but were turned off by the donor who liked "the tiger." Many donors favored blue, though there was the occasional purple lover. Strangely enough, everyone seemed to like Italian food. In the end our favorite wasn't available, so we bought up the last six specimens of the number-two guy on our list, after reading his stellar family medical history and listening to a taped interview. Turns out he's pretty smart, a fantastic athlete, likes to read, and wants to travel to Africa, all of which only enhanced the green eyes and dimples.

So we had the stuff, now we just needed to figure out my body. We had been taking morning temperatures and peeing on the ovulation predictor sticks, so we felt we had a pretty good handle on things until someone suggested we buy a speculum and track what my cervix was doing. Planned Parenthood didn't have them for sale, but our local feminist sex toy store did, so we were in luck. Betsy found just the idea of a speculum gave her fits, so after some clumsy wangling of the speculum, flashlight, and mirror, I was able to monitor my cervix as well. And in the end, my cervix was the best indicator of my fertility.

During the first cycle we were set to inseminate we found ourselves with a busy social schedule during the days leading up to insemination day, which made us awkward dinner company at times. One night at a new friend's house I announced I was going to go pee on a stick and that I would be back in a minute. After determining that I was not quite ready to ovulate, I put the cap over the stick and returned to the dinner table. Completely forgetting my manners, I put the capped stick on the table to show Besty and our friend, who by then was turning green at the thought of my urine on her nice tablecloth. I quickly explained that the stick was *capped* and completely clean, but I don't think she's ever really forgiven me.

Anyway, insemination day did come, with my cervix open, good cervical fluid, temperatures right, etc., so I called the fertility clinic to explain I'd be in the next morning to get one of our specimens, which had shipped to them earlier. The very nice lab guy said they would thaw and count the specimen and have it ready at the appointed hour. The next morning, as Betsy was carefully arranging our fertility rocks (a story for another day) and pillows, I drove the fifteen minutes to the clinic and went to the lab. The lab guy was there, hunched over a textbook in which he had highlighted many passages about insemination, and explained with a very red face that the book said that after insemination I really had to have an orgasm to give the sperm the best chance of making it to the egg. I found it very touching that he had done extra research for the crazy lesbians inseminating at home, though I was probably redder than he by the end of the conversation. I fled with the specimen vial tucked into my bra and clutching a paper baggie containing a 1 cc syringe.

When I got home I was hustled into bed, Betsy filled the syringe with the sperm as if she'd been doing it her whole life, and, propped up on about six pillows, she squirted the little guys in. We then proceeded to follow the lab guy's instructions to the letter (though not without a bit of awkward fumbling—those damn pillows kept getting in the way).

Well, I felt every possible early pregnancy symptom during those two waiting weeks, but my period came right on time. This was a huge disappointment, even though we knew the odds were something like one in twelve. We tried three more times, and no luck. We had two specimens left, when we threw caution to the wind, inseminating two days in a row. The second day my cervix was really, really open (maybe we had been too early the other times?) and, using our last specimen, I got pregnant. Audrey was born six days early, with a short, relatively easy labor. Guess she was in a hurry to show off those adorable dimples.

Abigail Clay, partner to Elizabeth Streib for seven years, and parent of Audrey Eleanor Clay-Streib, age three, Seattle, Washington.

not be performed at home. Depending on one's insurance, these procedures can be covered by health insurance, though some insurers specify that single women (i.e., not legally married to a man) cannot use insurance for fertility purposes. There are some homophobic physicians that refuse to work with lesbians, but many other doctors are comfortable assisting lesbian couples. Some medical facilities insist on routine psychological screening before they will perform medical services; others only have this provision for lesbians and single women. Phone calls to local gynecologists/obstetricians, gay community centers, and sperm banks will help you find the most supportive medical personnel.

The costs for sperm when utilizing a sperm bank are about $200 for one vial of semen, plus the cost for shipping and maintaining it frozen until use whether you inseminate at home or at a physician's office, which can run another $400 or more. There will be additional costs for medical treatment when inseminating in a physician's office, and the cost of semen is not insurance reimbursable (can't imagine *why*), although some have claimed it as a health care related cost when filing taxes. Whether you are using semen from a known or unknown donor, it is essential that HIV testing be conducted.

Gay Male Couples Making Babies: Coparenting and Surrogacy Decisions

For gay men pursuing parenthood through pregnancy, a number of options are available. One option would be a coparenting arrangement with a woman (heterosexual or lesbian) who would become pregnant from his semen (through sexual intercourse or insemination), and they would agree to raise the child together as a family. It is becoming increasingly common for gay men and lesbians to make a family with each other this way, sometimes including each of their partners to create a four-parent family (though not all parents can be legally recognized).

Another option for gay men is a surrogacy arrangement. Surrogacy is the process whereby a woman carries a baby who will be raised by the gay couple. Surrogacy commonly involves a pregnancy created by the insemination of sperm from one (or both!) of the men into the surrogate, who carries the child for the couple so that the child is the biological offspring of the surrogate and one of the male partners. Other surrogacy arrangements are possible utilizing donor eggs and other assisted reproductive technologies.

Surrogacy is expensive, costing at least $20,000. Due to the exchange of large sums of money and the question of women's reproductive rights that may allow the woman to change her mind, surrogacy also involves complex legal and political concerns. Surrogacy can be pursued privately or through an agency, and it is always best to work with a competent attorney familiar with these arrangements. The couple choosing surrogacy can allow for a connection to the birth mother similar to an open adoption situation. Despite the cost and the legal and political issues that surrogacy may entail, it can be a wonderful way for gay men (at least those with some financial privilege) to become parents of their own biological children.

PATH NUMBER TWO: ADOPTION

Adoption is increasingly becoming a popular path to parenthood in our communities. For gay men, it is probably the most common path to parenting, and for lesbians it is increasing in prevalence. In part, this is due to changes in many state laws that now allow gay people to adopt, as well as a substantial increase in social workers and agencies willing to work with lesbian and gay families.

There are approximately five to six million adoptees in the U.S., and according to recent statistics nearly six of every ten Americans have had a "personal experience" with adoption (i.e., either they, a family member, or a close friend were adopted, adopted a child, or placed a child for adoption). One study estimated that in 1992, 126,951 children were adopted through international, foster care, private agency, independent and stepparent adoptions.

Adoption is the process of taking a child into one's family through legal means and raising this child as one's own. Adoption is a sacred family tradition that has been practiced throughout history. Often children are available for adoption because their birth parents are deceased or are unable to care for them. Adoptive parents are often unable to have children biologically or choose to adopt because they realize that there are children who need homes. There are a lot of myths and misinformation about adoption, leaving some people concerned that adoptive families are not as real as birth families. Although all children have birth (or biological) parents,

Surrogacy: Growing Generations

You might say that our family is about as cutting-edge and high-tech as you can get: two gay dads and three "test tube" babies. However, my partner of eighteen years, Marcellin Simard, and I see our three children (Malina, seven, Luc, five, and Harley, almost two) as beautiful, healthy, and typical kids. We created our three children with the help of wonderful surrogates and egg donors and the medical process of in vitro fertilization. Through the process of surrogacy, we were able to be full participants during the three pregnancies and were there in the delivery room for all three children (in fact, we were the first to hold them). We have no questions about our kids' prenatal care (the surrogates are pros at being pregnant) and the surrogacy process allowed us to create children with a biological connection to us (not that this should be important to anyone else).

We began exploring the process of creating a family back in 1990. We started by looking at adoptions—both domestic and international. In those days, it was difficult for gay couples to adopt newborns (which we wanted to do), and we faced a number of obstacles. The most significant one was that I would have had to masquerade as a single man (gay couples were not allowed to adopt back then). We would have had to lie to the social worker for our home study ("Marcellin's my roommate!") and we just didn't want to start out building our family on a foundation of falsehoods. We then looked at surrogacy and the IVF medical process. We were lucky in the beginning that a friend of mine agreed to donate her eggs, and a colleague of Marcellin's agreed to act as our gestational surrogate. We located an IVF doctor who was willing to work with us (again, back in the "dark ages," it wasn't easy finding professionals who would help a gay couple). A couple of years later, our daughter Malina was born. Thereafter, through several other surrogates and egg donors, our sons Luc and Harley were born.

Needless to say, I have learned a lot about the process of surrogacy. After Luc was born in 1998, I decided to devote my professional career to surrogacy (I was, at the time, a corporate attorney). I helped establish with Gail Taylor a surrogacy agency, Growing Generations, which has been dedicated to helping gay people create children through surrogacy. Growing Generations is now the second largest surrogacy agency in the world and has helped create over 220 babies for over 550 gay men and women around the world. As a result of the enormously gratifying success of Growing Generations, I have been able to assist my clients by drafting surrogacy and egg donations agreements and by obtaining prebirth parentage judgments so that my clients are declared as the legal parents while their surrogate is pregnant, and their names are placed directly on the birth certificate at the birth of their child. I now find myself in the fortunate position of being one of a handful of attorneys in this country specializing in the legal areas of assisted reproduction and family formation.

My life is busy but rewarding. I not only get to have three great kids in my life, but I also have the opportunity of sharing in the incredible experience of helping others create the family of their dreams.

Will Halm and his partner Marcellin Simard have been together eighteen years and are the parents of Malina, age seven, Luc, age five, and Harley Simard-Halm, age two. Growing Generations, in Los Angeles, California, can be reached at 323-965-7500, www.growinggenerations.com.

adoptive families are legal families, "real" families, and forever families. Adoption options include both domestic and international adoption.

The adoption system is complex and difficult to negotiate and requires patience and perseverance. However, for gay and lesbian people—single or coupled—it presents a positive and wonderful way to build a family. When considering adoption, numerous issues present immediately including: domestic versus international adoption, cost factors, infant or older child adoption, and how out to be with the agency or social worker. Many gay and lesbian couples are concerned that they will not be allowed to adopt because they are gay, and certainly this varies from state to state. Most states do not allow same-sex second-parent adoption, which means that only one parent will be allowed to legally adopt the child; consequently, the other parent will have no legal rights to the child.

Although adoption can be a first choice, for many people adoption begins because one desires having a child and for numerous reasons cannot simply biologically create one. For many adoptive parents, what starts out as a search for their own fulfillment becomes instead a desire to provide a home for children who do not have one. The initial desire for a healthy newborn can over time become a fierce commitment to an emotionally traumatized, physically challenged thirteen-year-old who desperately needs a loving home.

Domestic Adoption: Public, Private, and Agency Decisions

Domestic adoption means that the children needing homes are born and living in the United States and are available for adoption through a public agency or foster program, or a private agency or attorney in the U.S. Children are available for adoption from birth through adolescence. Domestically adopting a child from a public agency—especially through a foster-adopt program or adopting a child with special needs—is financially feasible for almost every family. In addition, the state will often pay a stipend to help support the child. It is also possible to adopt a newborn from a public agency, although the wait may be longer.

The cost of private agency adoptions can range from $5,000 to approximately $30,000, depending on the age or race or health of the child and the financial needs of the birth mother, as well as the fees of the particular agency or attorney involved. Although adoptions are usually finalized within months of the child's placement, this process can sometimes take longer. When adopting through a public agency—particularly when working with foster-adopt programs—the rehabilitation of the birth mother, the reunification of the birth family, or custody disputes can potentially disrupt the adoption. This time of waiting for finalization is often frightening to adoptive parents whose status as parents to the child they are raising is still legally unstable, and it is because of these fears that many choose international adoptions. However, it is possible to work with a public agency and only accept a placement of a child who is already freed for adoption.

International Adoption

For citizens of the U.S., international adoption means that the child is born in another country and becomes available for adoption by families in the United States. International adoption can be quicker than domestic adoption (once the paperwork is in order), and depending on the country with which one is working, the adoption can be completed within the first year of the child's life. International adoptions can be expensive and often involve traveling to another country—sometimes for an extended time—to pick up the child. The cost is rarely less than $10,000 and can be as high as $50,000. Different countries remain open or closed (meaning that a particular country is currently willing to place children for adoption in the United States) at different times, so placement options can fluctuate. Countries can also close in the middle of an adoption procedure, creating emotional pain and frustration for the potentially adoptive families, as well as the children involved. (Note: This use of the terms *open* and *closed* should not be confused with whether or not the adoption records are open or closed to the adoptive child.)

Currently, there are no countries that will knowingly place a child with

Adopting an Older Child

There are so many positive reasons to adopt an older child it was really the only option for us. I feel more comfortable with older kids, not babies. We both have active careers, and felt we needed a child that already knew how to go to the bathroom and feed himself. But the most important reason of all: once we viewed the thousands of tykes on the Internet, waiting for families, begging for families, it just tore us to shreds.

Our two-parent, same-sex couple adoption will be the first in Louisiana (New Orleans). At least that's what OCS (Office of Community Services) tells us. Our whole foster/adopt process with OCS has been nothing short of a nightmare on Elm Street. We've experienced about every emotion possible, had battles at almost every step, and we continue to fear what they (OCS) will or will not do in the coming months. We were originally given two photographs of children that they felt were good matches. Both were living in a group home. We spent the entire weekend trying to decide which one we would like to begin talking with. The hard part was knowing that we were actually making a decision to leave one child behind—talk about heart-wrenching! After a couple visits with Mark, age ten, we learned he was also visiting with another potential adoptive couple who is straight. Thus, the horror story begins.

Mark started alternating weekend visits between us and the other couple, who lived about an hour's drive from town. During all of this, we were constantly reminding Mark that it did not matter which family he chose, and that it was entirely up to him. All that we cared about was his happiness in his forever home. We told him that he could take all of the toys and belongings that he received from us to his new home. Of course, we were actually ripping our insides out—we wanted Mark with us so bad. The alternating weekend visits seemed to go on forever. We waited and waited, not so patiently, for the final decisions to be made.

Sometimes we were told that it would be Mark's decision that made the final choice in placement. Other times, we were told that OCS would make that decision, no matter what Mark's choice was. Misinformation ran rampant. We never knew what would happen. Thoughts crossed our minds relating to the idea that OCS may not be interested in placing a child in our home because of our sexuality. As it turned out, our social worker eased those worries quite well, as she explained that our sexuality had no bearing in her mind on the adoption finalization. Through several weekend visits we had already gotten the feeling that Mark wanted to choose our family. Of course, we worried that he could be telling the same things to the other family. We didn't know what to think or feel. Eventually, we were invited to a meeting with a couple of social workers and Mark. The meeting was to make sure that Mark was aware that we were a homosexual couple, and to be sure he did not have any problems with that. The meeting was a disaster. Here is a ten-year-old child, sitting in a large conference room, with us on one side of him and two social workers on the other. The table was long and wide, and the room was sterile. The atmosphere was entirely too intimidating for Mark, and everyone could tell he was extremely nervous. He replied to questions with the shortest answers possible. Needless to say, he understood who we are, and made the statement that if he had to choose, he would want to live with us. Mark moved in a week later, following a good-bye visit to the other interested family. We ended up with Mark, but not without some rough times.

Mark's education had been erratic and wasteful. In fact, education at his last school (while living at the group home) consisted of watching movies. We've now got him in a private school, where he has homework in every class, every night of the week. This is a huge adjustment for him. Yeah, we are getting some resistance, and homework has caused some tears, but we are getting through it. We just keep our expectations high, and he is jumping.

We also decided early on to take our son off of all medications they were giving him; he appears to be fine without the meds, for that matter is doing better than he was with the meds. Now we have to find a physician who can verify that our son, in fact, doesn't need the meds, in order to provide the court enough evidence that we know what we are doing and that Mark is doing well. Perhaps all children in the system are just routinely medicated, but clearly Mark does not need these meds.

Postplacement services with OCS has been awful. Our required monthly visits may just be a phone call to schedule a home visit that never happens. OCS is a horribly overburdened office, with children everywhere waiting for a home. The social workers are extremely overworked and underpaid. We expect things to fall into the cracks, and they do. We try to stay on top of everything, but it does require phone calls, meetings, and patience. Through it all we found new friends, experienced all kinds of emotions, stood up to ignorance, and learned more than we anticipated. What makes it all worthwhile, of course, is our new son.

Todd Parker, and Chuck Diehl, partners for eight years, are parents to Mark, age twelve, and live in New Orleans, Louisiana.

a lesbian, gay or bisexual person. This has at least two consequences for gay men and lesbians choosing to adopt in this manner. One is that they must be closeted in the procedures. The other is that international adoption means only one parent will be able to adopt the child initially. Most lesbian and gay families choose one partner to be the legally adoptive parent, while the other parent plays a supportive role until the child is securely home in the United States. A second-parent adoption can be initiated later if the state you live in allows this, although it is best to have another social worker or agency complete the second home study, or it could raise questions about

The Perfect Fit

I am a forty-three-year-old white, lesbian-identified bisexual, and my husband, PJ, is a forty-eight-year-old transgendered female to male, and has been living as male for three years. Although the first question most people want to ask is, "Are you still a lesbian?" PJ's transition has not been a serious threat to my sense of identity. The short answer is, "Yes, I am"—most people don't want the long and nuanced answer—"and PJ is my soul mate." There was a brief adjustment period when I worried that I would not be accepted in any community, but those worries have never come true and, over time, I came to enjoy being able to transcend so many artificially constructed social boundaries.

PJ and I have wanted kids since we got together. Before PJ's transition, we both tried donor insemination, but our eggs are aging. When each of us had tried four to six times, we let it go and began to look at adoption. We began to investigate Waiting Children (older children, often needing adoptive families because of severe abuse and neglect in their birth families). The county social workers basically panicked when PJ outed himself on the application.

The interview with them was very painful. They played good cop bad cop and confused me with an air of patronizing protectiveness: "We just want you to know what you are up against." They maneuvered the discussion so that I found myself volunteering to take a break and revisit the possibility in six months. That way they could not be accused of roadblocking us in a state where a Human Rights Amendment protects us. They put us on a six-month

hold, citing technicalities that were clearly stall tactics. Furthermore, nothing they said assured us that we would be acceptable as candidates to them after that set-back.

PJ knew to be angry right away and confronted them with the fact that what is in his pants is and should be as much a mystery to the world as what sits in anyone else's pants. But I went numb and became confused and doubtful. When they left our momentarily immaculate house, I curled up on our carefully made bed and felt like I had just watched someone die. For a few days, I wanted to give up on kids and plan vacations to Europe or get a time-share in Manhattan and become collectors of Broadway musical experiences. But PJ stayed grounded until I came around. He is my rock.

One day an E-mail crossed our computers about an intersex baby in Kolkata, India, who also needed a forever home. The baby was born with ambiguous genitalia, deemed a girl, but thankfully has thus far been untouched by surgeons. Quite serendipitously, it turned out that we live just a couple of blocks from a lesbian couple who have adopted two children from the same orphanage. They hooked us up with a queer-friendly agency and a wonderful social worker who is not one bit scared of us. We got our home study done in language that does not out PJ as transgendered. Just three and a half months after learning of Asha's need for progressive parents who are comfortable with rearing an intersex child, all our paperwork is currently en route to India. If we had cooperated with the time line set for us by the first social workers we met, we would be back at the drawing board right now.

Asha is intersex and waiting alongside children who have disabilities, in a high-quality orphanage. This child is well loved, with no signs of attachment disorder, developmental delay, disability, or medical problems. Asha was passed over by both heterosexual and gay and lesbian prospective parents. We know this because we have talked to some of the people who decided not to consider adopting Asha. Asha should have been snatched up in the first year of life. The social workers who passed on us should have jumped at the chance to place children with us. But gender assignment is the most important social aspect in a world where there are only two choices. There is a phobic, sometimes even violent reaction to those who diverge. I fear for our child's emotional and physical safety. But what parent does not?

Sue and PJ have been together since 1997, and are parents to Asha, age three. They live in Minneapolis, MN.

withholding information for the first home study and potentially disrupt the adoption. It is important to note that the effort of being closeted throughout the process can be extremely stressful for many families.

For families with a transgendered parent, building our families can be extremely challenging. The world of lesbian and gay parenting are light-years ahead of the challenges facing preadoptive families where one or both partners are transgendered or transsexual. Many families who are able have chosen conception, even if they would've preferred to adopt, because of the endless frustration and red tape within the adoption community. In some families, a biological female partner chose to get pregnant with donor semen, and in other families an already transitioned female-to-male partner has chosen to carry a child, essentially being simultaneously a birth mother and father to the child! Others, however, have persisted in the adoption process.

Open and Confidential Adoptions

Open adoption means that the adoptive parents know who the birth parents (or mother) are and that contact can be maintained between the two families. When adopting an infant through a private agency, the adoptive family can often meet with the birth mother before the child is born. The amount of contact between birth parents and adoptive parents can vary, depending on the wishes of the adoptive families, as well as those of the birth parents. Open adoption does not ever mean that the biological parents have legal rights to the child. Adoption, by definition, means that the biological parents' legal rights are terminated, always and completely, and except in very, very bizarre situations (usually caused by legal loopholes, errors in paperwork, etc.), adoptions are permanent and forever. Despite the large media focus on disrupted adoptions, the chances of an adoption being reversed are probably less common than children being removed from their birth parents' homes for reasons of neglect or abuse.

Open adoption does not necessarily mean that birth parents will have contact with your family or have an ongoing relationship with the children. It means that the adoptive parents have information about the birth parents, including their whereabouts, so contact can be established if that is in the best interests of your family. Open adoption means that you, the legal parents of the child, can make decisions about the kind of contact you want with the birth family (obviously they have a say in this, too, if, for instance, you want frequent contact and they do not). Legally, the decision for contact rests with the adoptive parents in an open adoption, although emotionally this can be more complicated, of course.

Contact with the child's biological family (not just parents) can consist of letters, phone contact, or spending time together in person. Sometimes the birth parents are "aunts and uncles" to the children, in other words, a part of their lives; more commonly, they are names and faces that are talked about and perhaps occasionally talked to on the phone. Often the contact is only through a third party, like the original agency, so the birth parents do not know where the adoptive family lives.

One benefit of open adoption is that you can have access to medical information. This can sometimes be lifesaving if the child has developed certain medical problems where donor tissue must come from a close family relative.

In confidential (sometimes referred to as "closed") adoptions, the adoptive families have little or no information about the birth parents, and the birth parents have little or no information about the adoptive families. Adoption paperwork is always sealed and legally inaccessible in both open and confidential adoptions; however, in closed adoptions it is not possible to make contact with the family to gather information if it is desired at some later point in the child's life. Issues regarding open versus confidential adoptions are controversial in the adoption community, where adoptive parents' desire to protect their children and/or the birth parents' desire for anonymity can conflict with the adoptees desire to have more information about their genetic heritage. (Confidentiality in records was not originally developed to impede adoptees from accessing their own history, but rather to protect them from intrusive outsiders.) Confidential adoption processes protect the adoptive parents from any legal repercussions or unwanted social contact from the birth parents, and some adoptive parents avoid domestic adoption, which is more commonly open, for this reason, although it is also possible to adopt domestically in a confidential adoption.

The relationship between birth parents and adoptive parents is often perceived of as adversarial. Adoptive parents are often fearful of birth families, perceiving them as potentially invasive and pushing for more contact than the adoptive family desires, or even extorting them for money. Although certainly these situations are possible, they are far from the norm. Birth parents, in my experience, tend to be grateful to adoptive families and appreciative of the contact they are allowed. They are often sad and somewhat guilty for having placed a child for adoption, and the ongoing contact, watching their birth child grow up loved and healthy, serves to be a healing salve for them. Undoubtedly, open adoptions can be emotionally complex situations, in part because adoptive parents feel protective toward their children's exposure to some of the difficulties their birth parents may face, including poverty, illness, or substance addiction. In some cases they may be angry or judgmental of the conditions of the birth parents' lives. It is also true that some birth parents are manipulative and intrusive, and their ongoing presence in a child's life can be damaging. This is particularly true when a birth parent is a substance abuser.

Although international adoption and confidential domestic adoption are often chosen in order to protect adoptive families from any perceived interference from birth parents, i.e., as a way to strengthen and protect the family, some adopted children experience these closed adoptions as an additional loss. Some adopted children have a strong, unremitting desire to have information about their biological roots, and being cut off from access to this information can be a lifelong challenge. Some international adoptees have been successful in searching for birth families, but this is not common. Sadly, policy that was created to protect children and their adoptive families, as well as birth parents who do not desire contact, has in some situations created another set of hurdles for some adopted children.

Whatever decisions birth parents, adoptive parents, and state record departments make about the availability of information and the accessibility of contact, the child—who will eventually become an adult—will ultimately be the one most impacted. As society moves toward open records, many adoptees are seeking out their biological family and longing for more information and contact with their countries of origin. Although the desire on the part of adoptive parents for closed adoptions is understandable, it might be something important for society as well as individual families to revisit as we consider what is in the best interests of the child. Remember, the adoptive family always determines the kind of contact between a birth parent and a child who is adopted; it is only as open as the adoptive parents decree, so there is really little to fear.

Regardless of whether you are adopting domestically or internationally, or choosing an open or confidential adoption (or even whether you have the choice), it is essential that adoptive parents remember that adopted children *always* have biological roots, and some children are profoundly emotionally connected to their birth families and their history. Adoptive children always have a history that we do not, indeed cannot, share with them, and they have the right to as much contact as can be safely provided. They essentially have two family trees and need our support and encouragement if searching for their birth families is important to them. For some children, this will be irrelevant to their lives; they simply don't care that they were adopted. For other children, it will a central organizing principle of their identity; this has nothing to do with whether your kids love you or honor you *as* their parents. It is just how it is for them and should be respected as any other experience or journey that our children find salient. Adoption is not a historical fact but an ongoing facet of identity, and must be respected as just that.

Foster parenting is another option for those who are unwilling or unable to make a permanent adoption plan for a child; there are many children who are in need of temporary homes. Children in need of permanent families may have been removed from their families due to neglect or abuse and have not been freed for adoption. Some foster children have long histories of living with addictions, domestic violence, mental illness, and neglect of basic daily needs. There is no doubt that they may be challenging to

Child-Centered Adoption Practices
BY MICHAEL COLBERG, JD, CSW

LGBT adoptive parenting has come of age. Although the debate regarding whether we should be allowed to adopt continues, the truth is that LGBT-parented families have, in many ways, become mainstream. Our families are written about, filmed, and studied. More and more agencies are training their staffs to work with LGBT preadoptive couples. We have come a long way.

When my partner and I began the adoption process fifteen years ago, we were hard-pressed to find an agency or attorney who would work with us. This was before openly LGBT adoptive parenting was common or accepted. We, in effect, had to advocate for ourselves. We were forced to figure out how to adopt from outside the traditional loop. In doing so, we had an opportunity to learn about the essential nature of adoption. I learned that the word *adoption* describes the ongoing relationships that result from moving a child from one family, his or her biological or birth family, into another family, his or her adoptive family. *Being adopted is not an event but an ongoing process.* By the time that we became parents, we understood not only that adoption is a lifelong process but also how important it is for a child to know and honor who they are in the fullest sense of the term—valuing both their biological and adoptive heritages.

Society generally still thinks of adoption as an event, as merely a means of becoming a family. It does not understand the ongoing nature of adoptive relationships and the unique developmental challenges present for those touched by adoption. Moving a child out of and away from his or her biological family and into a new adoptive family is an event that will be understood in different ways at different stages of development. As the implications of this move are not understood or respected by the population at large, the developmental challenges present for adoptive families are not expected or acknowledged. Our families are expected to act as if they are like families formed biologically, and differences are often looked upon as problems. We, as LGBT adoptive parents, are particularly well-suited to remedy this situation.

Our community has a long history of having been an invisible minority group. We were generally raised to be members of the straight community and had to work hard to make our differences known. Not only have we come forward and made ourselves visible, we have, as a community, made major contributions in many areas of society, and we took a leadership position as we showed society how best to organize itself to meet the AIDS crisis. This acceptance of difference is crucial to our children's well-being.

When LGBT adoptive parents are not educated about adoption, they may feel that they are doing something wrong when their child wrestles with feelings stemming from their being adopted. It is only when we understand the true and complex nature of adoption that we can make use of our experience, be with our children as they express their feelings, and help them to feel proud of who they are in the world—just like we have learned to do.

There are important similarities between the experiences of adoptees and those had by members of the LGBT community. Neither LGBT persons nor adoptees are socialized into their minority status by their parents. Neither adoptees nor members of the LGBT community are commonly parented by members of their own minority group. LGBT people typically have heterosexual parents, and adoptive parents are generally not adoptees themselves. Neither the LGBT community nor the adoption community have the same civil rights as those enjoyed by the population at large. We can become especially skilled mentors for our children when we utilize the experience we had making sense of how to value the heritages that come from our families of origin and the heritages that come from the LGBT community.

To prepare for becoming parents, my partner and I needed to learn about how adoption impacts an adoptee and all of his or her parents throughout their lives. We learned first about being adopted and then about what parenting through adoption required. We came to a place where our understanding was *child-centered*. One of the dangers present in becoming mainstream is that we are now being invited to join a placement system that focuses on getting a child and often ignores what it means to be a good adoptive parent. This means that the gay and lesbian community runs the risk of succumbing to society's insistence that we make gay and lesbian parented adoption a gay rights issue rather than about the children and their needs. Child-centered adoption means parenting from a perspective that identifies, respects, and focuses on a child's need to integrate all of their heritages and find value in their adoptive and genetic heritages—at the same time.

We must acknowledge that being LGBT is not equally important for all LGBT persons. Neither is it equally important to all LGBT parented adoptees. Nor does it hold the same degree of importance for an individual at various times in their life. There are other layers of diversity including, but not limited to, race, ethnicity, religion, intelligence, economic situation, emotional maturity of the parents, the family's geographic location, the form of the adoption, the nature of the parents' and of the child's larger community. We need to learn how to identify and address whatever layer of diversity is important in our children's lives at any given point in time. Sometimes being adopted is more important than having same-sex parents or being of a different race than parents, and sometimes having same-sex parents is the focus. It is not always easy to distinguish what is going on.

My daughter, who was nine at the time, came home a couple of years ago saying that she hated having gay parents. I asked her why, and she said that she hated having to explain the whole thing all of the time. She also said that, even after she explained that she had two dads, kids would ask her which of us was her real dad. By this time, crying and in my lap, she told me that she would have to tell them that neither of us were her real dad. Her sadness was, at that moment, about being adopted, not about having gay dads. I sat with her, and we both felt the sadness of not having a biological connection, and then she got up and went back to her life. This could only happen because I had an awareness of the nature of adoption. Understanding the similarities between her struggles and my own made me realize that I could use my coming out experiences to help me gain empathy for my daughter's feelings about being adopted.

No longer should we discuss whether or not we should be parents. The proof of our viability will come when we raise healthy human beings who have much to offer society at large. When we take the time to understand the ongoing nature of adoption, we can use the wisdom we have gained from having been an invisible mi-nority and help our children to be proud of who they are and able to explore and value what it means to be an adopted person. Once again, the LGBT community can take a leadership role as we help our children appreciate both sameness and difference and as we assist society to expand its understanding of what it truly means to be a member of a family formed through adoption.

Michael Colberg, JD, CSW, and his partner, Gene Parseghian, have been together for twenty-five years and are the parents of Rachel Colberg-Parseghian, age fourteen. Michael works as an individual, couple, and family therapist. He specializes in adoption and has offices in New York City and in Dutchess County, New York. You may reach him at m.colberg@relatedbychoice.com.

rear, even (or especially) for short periods of time, but they are also desperate for loving, stable, and safe homes and consistent medical care and education. Some foster children are eventually released for adoption and can become a permanent adopted child.

Parenting foster children is not a part-time activity. Foster children often need enormous amounts of attention, and parenting strategies that involve therapeutic skill. It can also be extremely difficult to devote yourself to a child and have him or her returned to the family of origin, especially if you are concerned about whether the parent has been sufficiently rehabilitated. Watching scared, medically fragile, and traumatized children blossom into laughing, healthy, and secure ones can be an emotionally fulfilling, albeit a time-limited, parenting option.

White Parents and Children of Color: The Need for Cultural Responsibility

Many of the children in need of adoption and foster care in the United States are children of color, particularly African-American, Latino, and biracial children. Ideally, placing children in homes where they will see their color and culture reflected presents an excellent opportunity for LGBT people of color to expand their families, as well as offer homes for children in need. There are, however, more children of color needing placement than homes available within their own cultures.

Transracial adoption is a way to offer homes to children of color by white adoptive parents. This is a controversial issue that has been the subject of numerous public policy debates. Remember, we live in a country where it was *illegal* for people to marry across racial lines until the 1967 Loving versus the State of Virginia decision. Families are thought of, by nature, as comprising people of the same race. Racist policies have been challenged in this country, ensuring that our buses are integrated and our schools are integrated but family constellation is only minimally regulated by social policy. Biracial people—people born from parents of different races—are still seen as exotic and different.

The number of transracial adoptions in the U.S. is not known. In 1972, the National Association of Black Social Workers issued a position paper opposing transracial adoption, based on a belief that children raised in white homes would be robbed of their culture and communities. In-race adoption became the preferred approach to adoption. Unfortunately, this often meant that many children were simply not adopted and lived out their childhoods in foster care and group homes, never knowing the security of a "forever family."

The concerns voiced by black social workers about the integration of the children's cultural identity are certainly legitimate concerns, but research has not validated them. It is true that transracially adoptive children feel uncomfortable with their physical features and feel awkward among people of their own racial backgrounds. However, the research has shown that children raised transracially are well-adjusted and have healthy self-esteem. The social policy dilemma regarding transracial adoption has been: how well-adjusted can children be who express racial identity concerns and conversely, how well-adjusted can any child be living without a family?

In the early 1990s, policy changes were instituted that prohibit states and agencies from using discriminatory practices in adoption and foster care placements. The passage of the Multiethnic Placement Act (MEPA) in 1994, and the Interethnic Adoption Provisions (IEP) that followed in 1996, forbids agencies from denying or delaying placement of a child for adoption *solely* on the basis of race or national origin. Agencies now cannot even consider race, culture, or ethnicity as a factor in decisions to delay or deny a foster or adoptive placement (or they risk losing federal funding). Its proponents believe the policy to be critical in ensuring that the thousands of African American children in foster care waiting for adoptive families will be adopted. Opponents are concerned that trans-racial adoption is only a partial solution and detracts attention from more pressing problems affecting children of color and their families. The actual impact of these changes in adoption policy will be revealed as these new procedures are implemented.

Due to the complexities of racism, children of color are often available for placement at reduced financial costs, since they are officially considered harder to place, and some agencies have specialized programs focusing on the placement of children of color. In the last decade, more children of color are currently being placed in white homes, offering them stable families. However, the issue of the maintenance of their cultural heritage has yet to be fully addressed in public policy or adoption processes. Many white families assume that it is enough to love their adoptive child and raise them without prejudice, not realizing that it is an emotional handicap for a child of color living within a racist society to lack a positive sense of their racial identity, as well as skills to recognize and combat institutional racism. Sometimes when asked about racial issues, white preadoptive parents are insulted or defensive that these issues are being raised by agencies and social workers, assuming racism on the part of the interviewer. In reality, social workers and adoption specialists are attempting to discuss the complex issues of transracial adoption with families that may not really understand the implications involved in raising children of color.

Transracial adoption in the United States includes primarily two groups of children: the domestic adoption of African-American and Latino children, and the international adoption of Asian (Vietnamese, Chinese, Korean, and Indian), South American (Guatemalan, Peruvian, and Columbian), and Eastern European (Russian and Romanian) children. The adoptive parents are most often white, and the children are generally of color, although some adoptions are technically transcultural versus transracial (i.e., adoptions from Eastern Europe to Euro-American parents). Parents who are of color also adopt children of color, and children of color are sometimes adopted by parents who are of color but from different racial or ethnic backgrounds than themselves, and occasionally, white children are also adopted by families of color.

Since many gay and lesbian families are choosing transracial adoption, the faces of our community are increasingly filled with multiracial families. Many transracial adoptions also take place internationally, bringing children from completely different cultural settings into the United States. This is yet one more way that LGBT families are challenging traditional notions of family.

Race is, of course, an invented idea, invented by white racist male scientists at the turn of the last century to rank people into groups, deeming who were worthy and who were inferior. White people, particularly those who were Christian and from northern Europe (as well as male) were considered better human stock than those who were Asian, African, Jewish, or other non-Aryan peoples. All human beings are from the same human race, although we differ in the textures of our hair, the color of our skin, the features of our faces and physiques, the languages we speak, the spiritual beliefs and practices we follow, and the habits and values of our cultural traditions. These differences are in some ways extremely superficial and in other ways determine our core experiences of being alive and a member of our collective society. But despite the fact that race as a scientific category is a falsehood, *racism* is, sadly, a universal legacy.

People of color who are critical of transracial adoption often say, "What can white people offer these children? Can they offer to sing to them in their own language, can they teach them about their heritage, the strength of their people? How can a white person teach a child of color how to survive?" These are important points, not merely ideologically but contemplatively. White people adopting transracially need to be able to respond to these questions, not to win political arguments but because their children themselves may ask them the same questions someday.

It is sadly true that many white families are often poorly prepared for the challenges of transracial parenting. Some white families are surprised by the level of racism levied at people of color until they become an adoptive parent of a child of color. Some white parents seek out lighter skinned children in their (often misplaced) attempts to avoid blatant racism. Sometimes white parents say, "Race doesn't matter. I'm raising my child to be an American. I'm raising my child to not see or think about race." They believe they are doing their children a favor by raising them to be color-blind; however, in a color-sighted society, blindness is not a blessing but a liability. The system has neglected these children's needs by not insisting that adoptive parents be educated about race and racism before placing the children.

However, white parents can become educated about the racial and cultural needs of their adopted children and can commit to raising them with a sense of pride in their heritage. Children of color often have different hair and skin needs than white people, and sometimes, different health considerations to be aware of. Holiday celebrations, cultural rituals, food from their ethnic heritage all assist the child in learning to incorporate their identities into their families. It is not an easy responsibility, and as Jana Wolff, a white mom who adopted an African-American son, has said, "Becoming black is an inside job . . . [my son's] evolution into a proud black man will occur largely outside the walls of our home . . . well beyond the reach of my loving white arms." Jana Wolff is recognizing her limitations as a transracially adoptive mother and the challenge of raising a child to embrace an identity within a culture that their parents will always be, what she refers to as a "tourist."

Despite these very real challenges, the reality of contemporary American society is that thousands of children of color are living in foster care and group homes and are in desperate need of permanent homes and loving families. White parents may not do it perfectly, probably will not do it perfectly, but they can be taught about cultural diversity and can learn about the child's heritage. They can learn to speak the child's birth language and incorporate the child's culture into their own.

They cannot, however, do this alone. People of color are often angry when white parents turn to them as role models and for support, but the truth is that there is a generation of children—African-American, Hispanic, and Asian—who are being raised within loving white homes with parents that lack some of the skills necessary to raise their children to be comfortable within their cultures of origin. White parents need the skills, experience, and support of families of color to help raise these children to survive in an often hostile society.

Adoption is mired in a long history of colonialism, imperialism, and racism, and the children needing homes today are the inheritors of our collective human past. In transracial adoption, there is not simply the inability of the birth parent to raise the child, but the legacies of racism and poverty that have left these children homeless and unwanted. I once heard an analogy made about the numbers of children of color in the adoption system to the impact of industrial pollution in our rivers. The factories upstream, in this case the history of racism, poverty, and imperialism, have polluted the rivers downstream, impacting the lives of so many children now in need of homes. Surely we need to stop the factories from polluting and examine the political and economic situations that re-create the conditions of poverty and abuse. However, blaming institutions and political systems for the evils that have caused so many children to need to be adopted does not help to solve the daily struggles for these children who need homes. If you will, those who live downstream from factories that pollute the waters must work to not only stop the polluting but also clean up the rivers in our own neighborhoods. Rearing abandoned, neglected, and abused children is an act that must transcend the complex color barriers in our society. Communities of color and families formed by adoption must work together toward the goal of raising these children in safe, loving, and culturally informed homes. This is an act that Hindus call karma yoga, and the Jews call *tikkun olan*—spiritual work to repair the world.

Transracial adoption, like all adoption, is born of loss and wounding. A child does not have a family and needs one. Once a child is adopted transracially, it is not only the child who is living within a different culture but the parents themselves who have adopted the child's culture. Transracial adoption is ultimately about healing; it can be a bridge transcending the xenophobic history that has separated families and cultures.

Children of color being raised in white families may well feel differently about white people than other people of color do; after all, it is white faces that they see when they are tucked in at night, white hands that rock their owies away. Parents raising children of color may also feel differently about people of color and communities of color. Some people of color do warmly embrace transracially adoptive families, recognizing them as tribal relatives, albeit ones with some strange customs. When white parents of children of color see young boys on street corners late at night, they do not see the same potential danger that some white people might see. They see the faces of their sons under those hooded sweatshirts. When your child is the target of racist violence, your allies become other people of color; what better alliance can there be against racism than one where white people and people of color are working together for the safety and future of their children?

A Big Multiracial Lesbian Family

It all started with a dream—a dream that I wasn't sure was possible until I actually began the process to adopt in 1996. I had two biological sons who were both older teenagers, and I was ready for more children. It started with two failed adoptions, and then Jasmine came home at two weeks old. I was instantly and hopelessly in love with this beautiful, tiny creature. She was the beginning of a wonderful and fulfilling journey.

Two years later, Caleb came home. A year after that, Jules and Joey came home. Two more years passed, and Shawna and Devon arrived. The house is now full of children between the ages of two and five years of age. We plan to adopt two more children, and that will fill our house and our van. Why so many children so close together? It just happened that way, so we moved with the tide. And we wouldn't change a single thing.

Our family is a blend of African American, Asian, American Indian, and Caucasian. Two children came home with cleft lip and palate, one has mild cerebral palsy, one was prenatally exposed to cocaine, two are biological siblings. Judy and I are so blessed to share our lives with these wonderful children. We laugh, we cry. They have such character and strength and teach us far more than we'll ever be able to teach them.

I have to say that our experience with transracial/transcultural adoption has been positive for the most part. However, we're just entering the school years with Jasmine now in kindergarten. I recently visited her class just to observe, and as I entered the room and introduced myself, a small black boy blurted out, "*She* has a *white* mamma!" I think it may be time for the first adoption discussion at school.

My extended family has been slow to warm to the idea of such a diverse family. For this reason, we have grown a family of choice, so that the children have cousins, aunts, and uncles who are interested in and participate in their lives. We also have a local LGBT parent group where they meet families who are similar, and different, than theirs. We answer their questions candidly, with age-appropriate information. The time is coming when the questions will be more difficult to answer, but we keep our hearts and minds open and teach them to do the same.

My partner, Judy, and I are never idle. Laundry is never finished, someone is always hungry or needs to be held or kissed or tucked into bed. There are doctors' appointments, parent/teacher conferences, and speech/physical therapies to attend. We attend cultural festivals, read tons of books, hike in the woods, make handprint stones, braid hair, Band-Aid knees, and watch funny movies. Ultimately, we're like any other family. We work, play, fuss, argue, and make up. We laugh, tell bad jokes, and kiss each other good night. Judy and I watch our children grow, and our hearts fill with boundless love—because they are proud children of color, proud of themselves and of each other.

Libby Rice, who is Caucasian and American Indian, has lived with her partner, Judy Pitts, who is Cau-

casian, for the past two years, and they are parents to Jasmine, age five, Shawna, age four, and Devon, age three, who are African-American; Julian, age five and Joey age four, who are Cambodian; and Caleb, age three, who is African-American, Caucasian, and American Indian; they live in Atlanta, Georgia.

Since many LGBT families are choosing transracial adoption, the faces of our community are increasingly filled with multiracial families. This is yet one more way that gay and lesbian families represent a progressive and inclusive model for social change.

In advocating for transracial families, a number of factors must be taken into account. First and foremost, all children deserve loving homes. We must look at what has caused this overload of children of color in foster care, including the racist social policies that have contributed to it. We must look carefully at issues of poverty that make children of color available for adoption, domestically and internationally. There is an underutilization of families of color as potential adoptive parents, and this must become an outreach focus for adoption professionals. Ideally, social services should be in place to help keep birth families together, assist them in reunification when possible, and to involve the support of extended family during times of crisis. When it is not possible for children to remain in their birth families, permanency decisions for children should be made quickly, and preference should be given so that children can remain in similar racial, cultural, ethnic, and geographic communities. However, children should not languish in foster care or orphanages who need homes, when homes are available, regardless of the potential difficulties involved in transracial adoption.

When a child is adopted into the family, he or she arrives with the legacy of their birth culture. It is necessary to maintain an identity with his or her racial and ethnic community to assist in building healthy, positive self-esteem. This can be accomplished through books, travel, and studying historical figures and knowledge about the culture of origin. Most importantly, children need flesh-and-blood role models and relationships with people who physically look like them or are from the same cultural background. This impacts decisions a family might make about schooling, neighborhood, religious affiliation, and/or child care centers. If the family does not currently have people of color in their lives, in addition to examining why and how this has come to be, it is important to be willing to seek out new friendships and explore new social venues. If you feel resistance to this, it is worth carefully looking into your prejudices before you invite a child into your home.

HOME STUDIES: THE KEY TO ADOPTING

Whether you are considering a domestic or international adoption, fostering or private adoption, an open or closed adoption, an infant or older child, or an out or closeted adoption, the path to adoption involves certain steps.

First of all, you must find a social worker, agency, facilitator, or attorney best suited to your purposes. Working with an agency or attorney can be expensive, so choose who you will work with carefully, and do not be afraid to ask questions about their placement history, costs, and the time it will take to place a child with you. Always carefully examine an agency's history of successful placements as well as pending legal problems. Make sure that the adoption experts you chose to work with are comfortable with LGBT families and will advocate for you.

Adoptions hinge on one indispensable item: the home study, which can be done through a public or private agency, or a private social worker. Home studies are clinical assessments that involve anywhere from one to three long visits with a social worker with at least one of these taking place in your home. The actual approach and regulations for the home study vary from state to state and agency to agency. Home studies involve extensive documentation, more for international adoptions than domestic. You will need copies of your birth certificate, marriage and divorce paperwork, proof of income, savings, investments, and mortgages. You will need a criminal background check, including fingerprinting, and documentation showing that you have not been found guilty of child abuse, neglect, or criminal charges. Additionally, you will need a medical clearance showing that you are in good health and references from three to five people. Finally, you will need an extraordinary memory and the ability to reiterate your entire childhood history, including your grandparents' discipline strategies, your educational background, and the name and address of every home you've ever lived in.

Home studies often feel invasive and are designed to actually be invasive. You are, after all, being examined for your worth as a prospective parent, a procedure that is, of course, not required of families who birth children. Although the paperwork may be tedious and there's the fear that your home, finances, relationship, or lifestyle might not be acceptable, most social workers are not looking to disqualify potential adoptive parents. They are generally supportive advocates for families. It is therefore best if you can be out and honest with the social worker about your lives (although in some states this may not be possible), so that she or he can determine how to best present your family in the written paperwork. Depending on where you live, and the social worker involved in the case, having a criminal history, a substance abuse history, a current mental health problem that is being treated, or a serious medical illness that is in remission or under treatment, will *not* prevent an adoption from taking place, although it may make the extensive evaluative process even longer. Private home studies range from $500 to $2,000, and many times home studies are included in an agency's services.

Finally, remember that a successful adoption depends on persistence and effort. You must be a proactive advocate for your own family. Surf the Web, read adoption books, join adoption groups and LISTSERVs, contact attorneys, promote your family, and let everyone know that you are ready to expand your family through adoption. Be aware that social workers often need to be pursued; agencies need to be contacted again and again. Adoption can be a frustrating bureaucratic process involving lost paperwork, disappointing leads, and newly painted but empty nurseries, not to mention endless communication with agencies, social workers, and attorneys with a hurry up and wait attitude. Nonetheless, be assured that adoption is a wonderful way to build a family, and there is no shortage of children patiently awaiting your persistence.

Whatever path you choose to build your family, this is also a time of many fears, much excitement, anticipation, and often frustration as you look forward to an unknown future. Some of us are lucky enough to get pregnant on the first try, have lovely pregnancies, easy adoptions, and enter parenting with gentleness and ease. Some of us slog through the baby-getting process, feeling as if we are in a dark room, groping with hands outstretched, and wondering if the low sounds we are hearing are a baby whimpering for us or just our own hollow breath echoing in the silence. All of us parent wanna-bes are full of dreams of the miracle to be.

• • •

CHAPTER THREE

Roadblocks on the
Family-Building Path

SOMETIMES THE FANTASY of building a family is not as easily attained as you had hoped. Perhaps we long for a partner to share this journey with but are unable to find one; or worse, perhaps the partner that we have and adore is ambivalent about—or even dead-set against—having children. Perhaps we are struggling financially and wondering if we will ever feel materially stable enough to begin a family. Some of us are deeply involved in recovery from addiction and childhood abuse issues, or struggle with mental health issues like depression or bipolar disorder, and we wonder if we will ever be emotionally stable enough to have children, although we long to be parents.

Sometimes we wait for everything to be right and realize that this will never happen. Some people decide to forgo having children, realizing that their mental stability is indeed prohibitive or their recovery from addiction too unsteady. Other times we accept that financial stability may remain elusive, but it really is okay to have the kids share a room and buy clothes at Sally's Boutique and Targée (i.e., The Salvation Army and Target). And as all parents finally come to accept, we may not be perfect—indeed, we will not be perfect. No matter how hard we try, we will not have all of our psychological issues fully worked out, we will not have all our duckies in a row. However, we can come to the realization that we are mostly okay and as ready as we ever will be. Sometimes, we have to make sacrifices to move forward.

> Larry had been with his partner for almost fifteen years, and their relationship, although not perfect, was happy. Except for one small thing. Larry wanted to be a dad, and Marcus did not. Larry waited patiently, then later cajoled and begged, and finally they invested in therapy, but ultimately the issues never changed. Larry wanted to be a dad, and Marcus did not. Larry made one of the bravest and scariest decisions of his life: he ended his relationship with Marcus to pursue his dream of becoming a dad.

Despite all of our queer soul-searching—some say that LGBT people are the most prepared parents in the world—things do not always turn out the way we would like. Pregnancy may be hard to achieve, adoption may remain elusive, and the families we end up creating may not look like the one of our childhood fantasies.

WHEN THE BEST MADE PLANS FAIL: INFERTILITY AND PREGNANCY LOSS

The growth of the lesbian baby boom has given many women the sense that once they resolve their own concerns about becoming parents, all they need to do is decide on a method of insemination, and pregnancy will be easily accomplished. The reality is that infertility is very common, affecting at least one in six heterosexual couples, and many believe there is a rise in both male and female infertility problems. Perhaps this is related to the ecological crisis our planet is currently facing, although even a brief overview of the Hebrew Scriptures will reveal infertility struggles to be one of the major difficulties facing women in biblical times.

Infertility is not just a lesbian issue, although within the LGBT community lesbians have been impacted by infertility perhaps more than any other group. However, it is not just lesbians who can be impacted by infertility. Bisexuals are often placed in a double bind, living betwixt and

Waiting Is the Hardest Part: Trying to Conceive

I remember thinking that any woman who wanted a child as profoundly as we did could achieve that goal. Now I believe that any woman who wants a child can achieve that goal, but it is completely unlikely that your child will come to be created and delivered to you in the distinctive manner that you plan for or expect. That happens only to a chance few, and it was quickly clear that I was not a member of that lucky minority.

Over two years and twenty-four cycles of multiple inseminations, I revised my philosophy. Pregnancy didn't necessarily come to women who were planful, perhaps even obsessively prepared. Being ready to parent, good karma, incense and candles, being open to our future child—none of these cerebral invitations influenced the timely union of egg and sperm within my body. As we revised our plan, changed our pros and cons, renegotiated our previous decisions, I asked myself again and again: Which is more important, the outcome or the process?

Our initial scenario: vaginal insemination done at home, done by my partner, Phyllis, in a warm, personal setting where together we would create our family. We are very skeptical of the medical community and wanted to avoid medical intervention at all costs. We wanted to use a known donor or ID release donor—someone who could/would be specifically identifiable to our child to be.

This would be a financially viable solution, where our costs were to be minimized by our own involvement in the process. After all, heterosexual couples don't have to pay $500 a month to get pregnant. Why should we? Liberally, we mentally allowed ourselves six months, and at the outside (but unlikely) a year to become pregnant.

Our successful scenario: twenty-four cycles later, intrauterine insemination in the physician's office, using frozen sperm from an anonymous donor from an East Coast sperm bank. My lesbian physician was sick the day I ovulated; her office called to cancel the insemination. I ended up lugging a huge tank insulating one tiny vial of semen to the unknown office of an unknown male doctor—someone Phyllis had located who was willing to do my intrauterine insemination, although we had never met and he had no direct referral from my doctor. I was taking Clomid, we had spent about $6,000 at this point, and it was the only insemination in the last two years that Phyllis could not attend. Very, very, very different from the process to pregnancy that we had so carefully planned.

In between that beginning and end, we used a known donor who we later found out had a zero sperm count (this was not a fun conversation, either); we used two lesbian friends as go-betweens with local donors; we used a local doctor who had one fresh donor and a homophobic staff; we used a lesbian OB-GYN; we used two sperm banks; vaginal, intracervical, and intrauterine insemination; I had blood tests, an HSG, an endometrial biopsy, what seemed like a million postcoital examinations, and took fertility medicines. Each failed cycle meant a reevaluation of our process, and often, an escalation of medical intervention and costs. Frustratingly, there was no identifiable reason for my continuing failure to conceive.

Over those two years, we were on the emotional roller-coaster ride of our lives—two weeks to ride the car to the top of that steep hill, and two weeks to come careening down to the bottom—never stopping to get off. I never, ever would have thought that the day would return when I could get my period unexpectedly, arriving as a complete surprise. My personal body alert level could not have been higher. Who knew that my body had so many twinges, blurps, and glitches—any of which could have been impending signs of either ovulation, conception, or menstruation—and none of which I felt confident of identifying accurately. The longer it took to become pregnant, the more I second-guessed my body, my intuition, my feelings. It is difficult to put into words how deeply this process intervened in our relationship. In some ways, it was as if we had become a threesome: me, Phyllis, and getting pregnant.

People asking if I was pregnant made me feel angry at their insensitivity. I was physically unable to be in the company of pregnant women. I was extremely judgmental of every tired or frustrated mother, silently admonishing what I saw as their lack of appreciation for the gift of children in their lives. I didn't want to see used condoms littering the grounds of the campus where I worked when I was paying premium prices for semen. My perspective was that men seemed to be recklessly dumping semen everywhere, thoughtless of the consequences—unless they knew you wanted it. Now that I

wanted it, it was comparable to plutonium. Government controlled and regulated, tested, divided, frozen, thawed, washed, and counted—a minuscule vial with an excessive price. Each time my period arrived, I ate my emotions into a deep and bitter silence. I gained more weight in the two years it took me to become pregnant than in the time I was pregnant. And the pregnancy weight is gone, but twenty pounds of the getting-pregnant weight still remains. It is a daily reminder of my struggle, begun ten years ago.

About eighteen months into the process, Phyllis offered to begin trying to become pregnant. I've heard from many well-meaning folks about how lucky we were to be in this circumstance, because we had the opportunity to use her reproductive system as our backup plan. However generous her offer, however well-meaning those people who suggested our luck at dual reproductive systems, it felt a lot more like dueling reproductive systems. Our plan was for *me* to become pregnant. I could not picture her potential pregnancy as anything other than a reminder of my reproductive failure. We struggled forth, continuing our efforts at achieving my pregnancy, tabling the issue for some time in the future. A time I didn't ever want to see.

Here's a piece of advice: don't buy pregnancy test kits every month. As soon as I heard that some women could get their periods throughout their entire pregnancy, I was doomed. Not to be gross, but I could be bleeding down my leg and convinced I was pregnant, all because someone had the nerve to tell me this tidbit of information. For about six months in a row, I went to a local contraceptive clinic to turn in a urine sample for a free pregnancy test. I know they thought I was a sex worker. Who else would wonder if they were pregnant each month? Finally, the pressure of dropping that sample off to Thelma each month was too great, and I did tests at home. Whose great idea was it to put two pregnancy tests in a package? Gee, I still have one for next time. . . . When your period is at least three full days later than your longest cycle, go get a blood test. Waiting is the hardest part.

Don't believe the karma crap. Not getting pregnant has nothing to do with whether or not you are a good person. Time and time again, I took solace in the fact that young women were getting accidentally, unwittingly pregnant in the backseats of cars, or at high school football games, or at wild parties. These women had not become pregnant because they had put out the proper karma and they were telling the universe that they were ready to bear and raise a child.

Each month as I waited to inseminate and then waited to see if this would be the right time, I created a retrospective history to explain the potential outcomes. If I didn't get pregnant that month, it was because I'd had trouble with the ovulation test kit, or because work was so stressful that month, or because the thermometer had broken. The month I got pregnant, it was because I went backpacking for five days the week before I ovulated (the lots-of-healthy-exercise-helped theory), or because the male doctor provided the testosterone boost needed to kick start

my system or to kick start those sperm, or because I ate all of those yams to increase my fertility.

The yams. You really start getting desperate. People make well-meaning, offhanded remarks about enhancing fertility, and suddenly you're trying things and ingesting foods you would have never imagined. Eat a yam every day, and you'll get pregnant. I drank an herbal fertility tea made of licorice root and something else strange. Can you believe I've forgotten? I probably drank a gallon a day. Strange-tasting stuff, but who cared? Then there was the month we drove around looking for crowded sports bars postinsemination, looking to get that testosterone rush, which another well-meaning acquaintance suggested was absolutely necessary for conception. Male pheromones or something odd like that, and I was ready to sniff male air immediately—if it would get me pregnant.

Rationally, nothing was different the month I got pregnant. My period was three days late, but I told myself I had miscounted the days, that I was setting myself up for yet another profound disappointment. I could feel my cramps arriving as they had each month for two years. I went for the blood test alone; I didn't want Phyllis to think that I was obsessing about pregnancy testing again. I had a tampon in my pocket as I waited for the test results in the doctor's office. The nurse looked out the door anxiously and invited me into a little consultation room so she could, I assumed, tell me the negative results and let me grieve a little more privately. While I didn't really believe I was pregnant, I didn't want to not believe it, either.

"You're pregnant!" the nurse said, showing me the blue dot on the white background. "A blue dot means you're pregnant!" I'd spent many months of this battle with this woman, and she expected immediate celebration. I wanted to believe her but, to be perfectly honest, I was in complete denial. "I can't be pregnant," I blurted out. She asked: "What do you think happens when you mix sperm with an egg?" I replied confidently, "Nothing happens, no one knows that better than me."

It took about four months into our pregnancy for me to be able to wipe without inspecting the toilet paper for the inevitable start of my period. About the same time, my abdomen began to swell, and shortly thereafter, that sweet and tiny miracle would knock on my uterus, as if to say, "I'm really here—believe it!"

Maybe it's because I began this process as a graduate student, but I have kept each excruciating detail of our path to pregnancy in chronological order in a bulging three-ring notebook. Twenty-four cycles of temperature charting, ovulation test kits, doctors' bills, hospital bills, sperm bank information packets, profile sheets on individual donor possibilities, prescription receipts, notes of questions I carried to appointments. Each and every item a reminder of how precious our gift and how difficult our process. And I know

that we are among the lucky ones after all, because we are rewarded every day by Keegan's songs, smiles, and surprises.

And as we contemplate the potential expansion of our family, considering changing our "absolutely only one" thoughts to "maybe two?" I know that a big consideration on my part is thinking about walking that pathway to pregnancy again. Did we discover the magical combination of medical intervention that engineered our pregnancy, or was it just luck? Do I need to plan monthly, preovulatory backpacking trips? Will the process go quickly or take two years again—or longer—or perhaps not work at all? Those questions can't be answered, and of course they are only one facet of our thoughts on this issue.

I just keep telling myself: I believe a woman who wants a child can achieve that goal, but it is completely unlikely that your child will come to be created and delivered to you in the distinctive manner that you plan for or expect.

Kelly McCormick and Phyl Gorman, partners for twenty-one years, are parents to son Keegan, eleven, in Columbus, Ohio. Find Kelly at www.momazons.org. She is a longtime lesbian moms' activist and the creator of Hearts and Hands, a "new arrivals" book designed to celebrate diverse families and our wonderful children.

between both the privileges of the heterosexual world and the oppression directed toward the gay community. A bisexual woman struggling with infertility may feel additional pressure to have sex with a man, even if she is in a monogamous lesbian relationship. She may be willing to have sex with a man, which might increase her chances of getting pregnant, but her lover may feel threatened by this. A bisexual woman who is involved with a man may feel somewhat invisible in a fertility support group, with either only lesbians or only heterosexual women. Gay men who are offering to be sperm donors or gay men who are choosing to parent with a lesbian woman can also be impacted by infertility, either their own or the woman's. This can be an issue in surrogacy situations as well. In a relationship where one (or both) partners are transgender, unexpected infertility can be an additional issue, impacting both family-building and transition. Among transgender people it is becoming increasingly common for people to postpone beginning hormonal therapy until they have had children, so fertility itself (not necessarily infertility per se) can therefore become an additional stress impacting not only the desire for children but also the timing of transition.

Infertility increases exponentially as women age. Since many lesbian women are first considering parenting in their thirties or forties, getting pregnant may not prove as simple as they often had hoped. It is not uncommon to hear a thirty-year-old woman say that she will have children in another ten years or so. In reality, chances of successful pregnancies, particularly without medical intervention, decline rapidly over the age of thirty-five, and even more rapidly after forty. Many women are confident that they will be able to have children later in life and are gambling with their biological clock, unaware that they are risking their reproductive potential. Pregnancy is truly a miracle of timing, and time may be the one thing that aging women do not have. As one woman said, "My biological clock is ticking so loud, I can hardly hear anything else."

Women in general have been postponing pregnancy due to later marriages and commitment to their careers; lesbians have also been impacted by this trend and additionally many have spent their most fertile years dealing with coming to terms with their sexual identity. Since the technological advances of reproductive medicine in the last few decades, many women are consciously postponing pregnancy, depending on these medical advances to push their biological clock. Women say, "First I will complete law school, and then I think we will start trying." There are many good reasons to have children later in life: job security, greater maturity, and increased patience. However, many women are unaware of the realities of potential infertility and may have a false sense of confidence. For instance, they may say, "Oh I have four friends who got pregnant at forty-one," which,

Waiting Is the Hardest Part: The Transition Decision

I was thirty years old when I decided to proceed with transitioning from male to female. I had only been married for a few years, and as expected, this was a terrible blow to my spouse and our marriage. For the next several years it was not clear we would stay married, let alone have children. Thankfully, we have managed to do both.

We had always hoped to have children, and this did not change, given our new circumstances. However, we thought long and hard about whether this was something that would be okay for our future children. Not because we felt that there was anything wrong or shameful with me/us but because we were concerned about how society might treat our kids. We also had concerns about how my situation might make our children view their own gender . . . especially if we had a boy. How could we make sure that he would be comfortable and proud of being a man when I had decided it was not the right path for me? Would he feel like there was something wrong with being a boy? There were also practical questions like what would our children call me? How was I going to transition if having kids meant I could not start on hormones until we were done? I am not sure we have found the answers to all our concerns, but we ultimately felt that most parents have to face their own equally difficult questions and that we at least were approaching parenthood recognizing some of the obstacles we would have to face. I hope that whatever difficulties my being transgendered might present my children, that the courage and strength I have shown to accept who I really am, and to

live my life openly in an often hostile society, might be an example to them to be true to themselves and accepting of others. I also hope that my spouse and I serve as an example to them of love and commitment in what many would think an impossible situation.

Our decision to stay married and have children has had a huge impact on how I have been able to proceed with transitioning. It has made me go much slower than I would have, for my spouse, and because we wanted children, meaning I could not start hormones until we had our family. We were not interested in artificial insemination, adoption, etc., as long as we were physically capable of having children together. I was also certain that I wanted my children to know me only as female . . . to keep things as simple as possible for them. Luckily, I have been able to proceed to living full time without the benefit of hormones. I am still planning on banking sperm before starting hormones, so that should we desire more children in the future, that will remain an option for us.

I am currently a stay-at-home parent and have been living full-time as a woman for close to a year now. My daughter is now a year and a half old and is truly a miracle. When I think of how close my life was to one without children, I see the miracle even more clearly. My spouse, who also works in the medical profession and continues to work full time, is early into her second pregnancy, and I plan on starting hormones soon. In the short time I have been a parent, all the issues my transitioning has created have not occupied nearly as much of our time and energy as the everyday events that having children presents to all parents (diaper changing, cleaning, cooking, bathing, bedtime, etc.). As for what challenges my gender status may pose for us as a family in the future, we will just have to wait and see.

Erica Rea, M.D., and her spouse Abigail Rea, Ph.D., have been married for eight years and are parents to Cecelia, age two, and they are expecting their second child, a son. They currently reside in New Hampshire.

although true, may mask the reality that many more women who tried, with the help of advanced medical procedures and at the cost of thousands of dollars, were not successful. Success stories make much better press ("Woman 48, Pregnant with Twins Thanks to the Brilliance of Medical Doctor") than the repeated failed attempts of women struggling with infertility "(Woman, 35, Has Ectopic Pregnancy, Following 6 Years of Infertility Treatments, 2 In Vitro Cycles, and Spending $16,000").

It is not uncommon for lesbians experiencing infertility to begin considering options they had previously disallowed. This may include working with anonymous donors, agreeing to certain medical procedures—either diagnostic or curative—and utilizing fertility-enhancing hormones to increase their potential to get pregnant. These procedures can be physically invasive (potentially retraumatizing for sexual abuse survivors), costly in terms of money, time, and energy, as well as psychologically stressful.

For some women, their attempts at getting pregnant may be successful; maintaining the pregnancy, however, may prove more difficult. Miscarriages, ectopic pregnancies, stillborn children, and severe pregnancy complications resulting in pregnancy loss or termination are physically and emotionally draining. Lesbians struggling with infertility and/or pregnancy loss often feel scared and isolated.

Infertility and pregnancy loss are topics rarely spoken of in the lesbian community, and the impact of infertility treatments can be stressful on couple relationships. Friends and family can be surprisingly insensitive, medical procedures painful and invasive, and baby hunger all consuming. Finding a competent reproductive endocrinologist (RE) is essential, as is developing a support network to cope with the ups and downs of the reproductive cycle, the sense of loss and failure when things don't work out, as well as the potentiality of bringing children into your family in a different manner.

Many women worry about their ability to conceive and wonder if they are even capable of getting pregnant. Usually these fears are dismissed by loved ones, who point out the plethora of baby carriages in the park and express excitement about a new baby. It is very important, whether or not your fertility concerns turn out to be substantive or not, that you be allowed to voice these concerns and receive support for your feelings. Some concerns may be rational, and perhaps related to stories that you've heard other women have gone through, or your own family history of fertility.

All the women in my family have had miscarriages. I don't think I could survive that after waiting so long to have a baby.

Other concerns might be less rational, but nonetheless will feel just as real.

I've just never felt like I could get pregnant; I have always known that this would be really hard.

Not all women experience fear and apprehensions about getting pregnant. You may have always assumed that you can and will get pregnant whenever you are ready to begin trying. Perhaps you have even begun decorating the nursery and planning for your maternity leave.

We decided we wanted to have a Christmas baby, so we began inseminating in April, hoping for a Capricorn. That was three years ago! Now we'd be thrilled to have a baby any time of the year.

Fertility, as has been said, is compromised by the age of forty. This, of course, does not mean that it is impossible to get pregnant after age forty—forty is not a magical number—but starting in the mid-thirties, it does become more difficult for many women to become pregnant. Given the high rates of infertility, it is realistic to be concerned about fertility as you age. Fertility and reproductive medicine (like the reality of parenting itself) is plagued with unknowns and many possible outcomes. Unexpected infertility can be surprising and shocking. For women who come from large extended families, there may have been no preparation for someone struggling to conceive. Many women experience feeling defective or broken.

Some women, especially those who come from very homophobic backgrounds, may believe that this is punishment for being lesbians. Sometimes these negative views are reinforced by medical personnel in subtle and not so subtle ways. Doctors might say, "Well, if you were a heterosexual couple, I'd tell you to go home and have a lot of sex now, but all we have is this one vial of semen." The underlying message is that if you were doing this the normal way, then you wouldn't be having the problems you have.

Although it is important to have a good support system, friends may become as invested in your conception as you are, and become another source of pressure. They may repeatedly ask, "Are you pregnant? Did it work?" making the woman who is struggling feel like a failure. One woman said, "I ended up taking care of other people's sadness over my infertility, more than anyone took care of me." The opposite reaction is also possible whereby friends can minimize your concerns. They may try to encourage you by saying, "I'm sure this time is *it*," or "Lots of women don't get pregnant for many, many months." Or sometimes they just forget what is the most important thing in your life. One woman mentioned to a friend who knew she was trying to get pregnant, "I just got my period." The friend responded, "Oh, I know, me, too. And I have such cramps." This left the woman feeling invisible and disconnected.

The reality is that even under ideal circumstances, many women do take a while to get pregnant. The literature recommends that women do not even see a fertility doctor (unless there is already a known fertility problem) until they have been trying for at least one year. For women who are older than thirty-five, they suggest you begin having fertility testing at about six months. Even though you may not have started out with many fears, a few months or even years into the process, you may have now developed rather intricate ones. It is important before attempting pregnancy that you spend some time evaluating your fears about fertility and pregnancy.

> Marianna was very concerned about going to a physician to help her get
> pregnant; the procedures were frightening for her as an incest survivor.
> She tried to work with the medical team, but after a few months decided
> the treatments were too invasive, and she decided she couldn't continue
> trying to get pregnant.

Waiting Is the Hardest Part: A Journey Through Genetics

Approaching our sixth anniversary as a couple, and our second wedding anniversary, we began the process of becoming parents. Hope had always felt strongly about using a known donor since her parents are both Holocaust survivors, and there was little information about her extended family that had died. She wanted her child to have access to information—to not have to struggle with the unanswerable questions she has dealt with for much of her life. Although I was a bit uneasy about using a known donor, fearing the complications of a third party in our baby-making, we began asking our friends at our *chavurah* (monthly gathering of friends who celebrate *Shabbat* together) to help identify a candidate. We specified that we'd prefer a non-Jewish donor, as we knew it would be safer genetically. However, we have very few non-Jewish friends as we both work and socialize in the Jewish community; our first prospective donor said no, and the second said yes!

Max and I have known each other for almost twenty years. He held one of the *chuppah* (canopy) poles at our wedding and was as close to a brother as either one of us would ever have; we consider him family. We spent hours talking with him about the parameters of our relationship, and what both he and we wanted from the arrangement. After a few months of discussing the details, we grew comfortable about having "Uncle Max" in a special role in our family. We set a date for insemination. We had our lawyer draw up an agreement to declare our intent to have me adopt the child and to have Max terminate his parental rights.

And we went to the gynecologist for a checkup, and advice on genetic testing. The gynecologist submitted Hope's blood samples to a specialized lab that does a Jewish panel, testing for twelve genetic diseases that are common in Jews from eastern European ancestry. It took a few weeks to get the results, and we hadn't really thought much of the process, other than wanting to move forward soon. A few weeks later, we received a call from the gynecologist's office, informing us that Hope is a carrier for Canavan disease.

We were upset and disappointed that we would have to postpone the date for our first insemination in order to make time for Max to get tested. We offered to pay for the test. He said he'd look into it. We waited a couple of weeks, on pins and needles, fearful that he was reconsidering his offer to be our donor. He went to his physician for the testing, and we went ahead with our planning, revising our insemination schedule, and even E-mailed him a two-day window we wanted to reserve for the next month's ovulation. We got a call from him a few days later, and he didn't sound so happy.

Max: "I've got bad news."
Melanie: "Canavan?"
Max: "Yep. But not just Canavan. Tay-Sachs, too."
Melanie: "Oy."
Max: "Yeah, I said to the doctor, 'So it looks like I'm just a genetic cesspool.'"
Melanie: "Oh, don't say that. You can still do this. Uuh. Just not with us, I guess."

We were back to square one. We had gotten so far with Max, in terms of being open to a new family picture that would include a known donor, in terms of using a very close friend, risking our friendship, dealing with my nonbio mom feelings of jealousy that Max could do something to produce my future child that I could not. And with a simple test, it felt like all that work went down the drain.

With some distance from the phone call, we were able to gain perspective. We reminded ourselves of the privilege we have to do so much to prevent a genetic disease from producing a child destined to die before their tenth birthday. We've asked Max if he'll consider no less of a role in our family than what we had agreed upon if he had been the donor. We have a new donor, and we still have Uncle Max.

Melanie Levav and her partner of six years, Hope, are the proud parents of Aaron Charles (Aharon Shalom in Hebrew), who came screaming into the world on October 30, 2003. They live in Brooklyn, New York.

Infertility is a painful and emotionally draining medical experience, on par with other medical experiences that are far more life threatening. The analogy to cancer treatments may seem hyperbole, but the invasive medical procedures, the impact of office visits and drug schedules on daily life, as well as the emotional investment in a cure make the similarity obvious. Although infertility is not life threatening, it psychologically can feel that way, especially if having biological offspring is seen as the survival of your genetic history. This is not an irrelevant issue for those who are only children or come from families that are the survivors of calamities. Sometimes it is our very genetics that compromise our fertility.

Often people who have not experienced infertility are unaware of how overwhelming and totally absorbing it can be. It is, first of all, expensive. Even with excellent medical coverage, the medical costs are staggering. Fertility drugs, in vitro fertilization, and donor egg retrieval can easily bring monthly costs over $10,000, making these options accessible only to women of some financial privilege. Having good insurance can make this journey less expensive but still involves the constant hassles with managed care for coverage. Claims are often rejected, money that should be reimbursed can take months, and in some cases treatments are refused. Some women have said that dealing with managed care is a second full-time job. It is not unusual for families struggling with infertility to spend tens of thousands of dollars and go deep into debt, trying to conceive. Obviously these costs are less painful if a successful pregnancy results, and they can be devastating when it does not.

Even when women are able to conceive, there is no guarantee that they will be able to successfully maintain a pregnancy. Pregnancy loss, miscarriage, and fetal death can happen at any time during the pregnancy. Miscarriages early in pregnancy are fairly common—about 30 percent of pregnancies, by some estimates, end in miscarriage, sometimes very early in the pregnancy. Many more fertile eggs never implant in the womb, and the woman might not have known that she was pregnant. As pregnancy progresses, the risk of miscarriage decreases. Miscarriages are common; approximately a third of women will experience at least one miscarriage, and the likelihood of miscarriage increases after a first miscarriage and also as women age.

Losing a pregnancy or finding out that a baby you are carrying has died is devastating. Sometimes medical experts as well as family members can try to push the woman who recently lost a baby to try to get pregnant again quickly. When you lose a baby it is not, however, *another* baby that you want, it is the one that you lost. Grieving the loss of the baby—or in some cases a multiple pregnancy—is not something that is gotten through quickly or easily; it can be a lifelong loss. The memories and hopes for the baby can remain with you, and the child you were not able to raise is a permanent part of your heart.

Shifting gears from joyful anticipation of having a baby to facing the realities of infertility and the potential of never being able to conceive or give birth to a healthy baby is a stressful process. Numerous emotional issues surface when dealing with infertility, including isolation, depression, rage, feeling broken or damaged, and relationship strain. Of course, not everyone has the same reaction, and some women do take these losses in stride. However, for women who are coping with intense feelings about infertility, it can be very isolating.

It is especially difficult to be around others who have children or are pregnant. Often women begin to consciously withdraw, retreating within themselves. Single women in particular can struggle with isolation. Even if you have lots of supportive friends, they may become tired of the fertility process or just not as sensitive to the daily ups and downs as a partner might be (or that you might fantasize a partner might be).

I just began to want to stay home all the time. I dropped out of my course at the university, stopped being active in the local gay democratic club, and started coming in to work later every day. I just wanted to be in my room and be where it was quiet and read or watch TV. I hated socializing with friends that I used to really enjoy.

Isolation is different from needing privacy and discretion about your fertility process. It is always acceptable for you to remain private about your treatments and decisions, and it is nobody's business how you are conceiving. It is also healthy to spend time alone with yourself, to retreat and heal while coping with infertility. However, if you find that you are spending inordinate amounts of time sleeping, not eating well, feeling annoyed at everyone and hopeless toward yourself, you may have developed a clinical depression.

I was so depressed that I just couldn't get out of bed to go to work. I knew that if I missed any more time, I would lose my job, and I knew that if lost my job, I would lose my health insurance, which would, of course, end any chance of my getting pregnant. This really should have motivated me to go to work, but I just couldn't.

Many women experiencing infertility also begin to feel intense rage and hostility toward others. It might be directed at the medical personnel, pregnant women, friends who are parents, a partner, or anyone within eyesight. This can be exacerbated by the use of fertility hormones, which often increase the intensity of emotions.

It just seemed that everywhere I went there were pregnant women. Even at the damn doctor's office. Why couldn't he figure out another time to see me than when all the pregnant women were coming in? Did he think this was going to encourage me? I was so pissed at him for his insensitivity that I blew up at him and his receptionist. They didn't know what hit them.

One of the complications regarding rage is that medical personnel *are* sometimes insensitive, discussing your "case" in public hallways, telling you procedures don't hurt (or "shouldn't") when they do, or being unavailable for procedures during your most fertile time. However, even if medical personnel lack compassion, it does not mean that you are coping with their bad behavior in a socially acceptable manner. Yelling at your partner or boss can potentially threaten these relationships, even if you are right. The first step is to be honest about the fact that you are having difficulty managing your emotions. Depression, which can manifest as sadness, fury, or a critical irritability, must be addressed, and a therapist knowledgeable about both infertility and depression can be very helpful.

Sometimes it is necessary to take a medication break for hormonal treatments; however, this also prolongs your fertility process and can increase the ticking of your biological clock. The power of hormones on your emotions should not be underestimated. It is true that not everyone responds with the same intensity, but for those who do, it can be an emotional roller coaster. The underbelly of most rage is incredible sadness, loss, and pain. Let yourself grieve.

Many women struggling with infertility feel that there is something wrong with them, that they are broken, damaged, or somehow different from other women; you may feel shame that you cannot simply get pregnant. For lesbians, unresolved issues related to their own sexual identity can intensify this feeling. If you are still harboring concerns over whether or not lesbians should have children, or whether a lesbian family is a good place to raise children, or if donor insemination is normal, infertility might bring all these issues to a head.

> My body feels surreal and not my own since I've begun this process. I keep waiting for them to find something that will prove I am an alien. I just don't feel like a woman anymore. I mean, what is more natural than being able to get pregnant?

Being poked and prodded by doctors unfortunately reinforces the feeling of being broken. The doctors are searching for a way to label your disorder so that they can cure or fix you. Do not allow the search for treatment to become an obsession. Women's bodies have too long been at the mercy of outside judgments of what is normal or abnormal. Resist the temptation to regard your body as bad or sick; she is really just doing the best she can.

The impact of infertility on lesbian relationships has hardly been discussed in the literature on lesbian relationships. Perhaps because parenting is new in the lesbian community, struggling with fertility is still a taboo topic. As in heterosexual relationships, infertility brings up feelings of inadequacy, anger, disappointment, and fear for lesbian couples. Whereas male partners might feel concerned that it is their fault she is not getting pregnant (even if this has been ruled out), lesbian partners can also feel helpless, wishing that they could do something to help the lover conceive. A sense of feeling impotent may set in, feeling like they are completely outside of this complex process. For butch and/or FTM partners, this can feel like one more assault to their masculinity.

Sometimes there is sadness that they cannot biologically father the child and other times there is an assumption that they would want to birth a child if their partner's conception fails. Medical personnel and family members often ignore partners' needs, and sometimes their role within the relationship may be undefined. Sometimes they are asked to not be present for inseminations or even fertility consultations, or in very homophobic communities, they may need to remain completely invisible while the lover pretends to be in a heterosexual marriage.

Fertility impacts on the couple relationship in many ways. There is, first of all, simply the stress of going through this monthly roller coaster, which both partners experience, though only one may receive support.

> Trying to get pregnant nearly wrecked our relationship. We thought that having a child together would just bring us closer. I always felt as if she was angry with me for not getting pregnant quicker, although she denied this. She said that I became impossible to live with, but I didn't really see any changes in my behavior, except that I was very sad. It is the hardest time in the thirteen years we've been together.

Couples need to continue talking to one another. Issues about when to stop trying, start pursuing adoption, or having the other partner try to get pregnant can often become volatile issues within the partnership. The context of how decisions are made regarding the financial cost of infertility and adoption can become complex issues as they would in any marriage. One of the unique issues of lesbian parenting is that there are often two wombs that can potentially carry the baby. This does not mean that there are not emotional or other relational issues that determine which womb is the one chosen to carry the baby. There is, of course, no guarantee that the other womb will not also have fertility problems.

Perhaps the woman struggling with infertility does not yet feel ready to stop trying, but her partner really wants to try herself. The one coping with infertility may feel that her partner is competing with her, and this can be further exacerbated if her partner is able to conceive quickly. Stories abound in the lesbian community of couples where the older partner tried for years to get pregnant, and her lover got pregnant on the first try. Or in one case, both got pregnant at the same time, and certainly two pregnant women and two new babies at the same time can introduce strain (as well as joy) into a marriage!

Given the emotional upheaval described above, how does one know when to stop? Especially since most women who try to get pregnant succeed, and many women with infertility problems are able to eventually succeed. Some women, however, are simply unsuccessful at conceiving or being able to carry a child to term, even when physicians can find no known reason for their infertility.

As Cherie Pies says, "It's best to assume you can become pregnant until you discover you cannot." However, at what point do you decide that you cannot? How many months or years go by? How many different sperm donors, or injectable drugs, or medical doctors, do you try before you say, "I cannot become pregnant." In order to make this decision, a number of variables need to be examined. Are you able to accept that you cannot conceive? Are you stopping because someone else wants you to, or because you believe that you've given it all you've got? Some doctors will tell you that it is your decision to stop when you are ready, even if they believe that your chances of conceiving are very low. Are you able to live with the reality that there may always be the miracle baby within you? That for the rest of your life you will hear those miracle stories of women who got pregnant beyond anyone's wildest dreams, and you will wonder, *Could that have been me?* Can you afford to continue? Many couples are deeply in debt, and to continue will increase their debt. Will you try some other way to have children? Stopping is ultimately an act of surrender, of accepting not the impossible but the improbable, and learning to live with that loss. For women who want to have children but do not consider adoption an option, stopping will ultimately mean not becoming parents. The loss for these women and their families is compounded, and needs to be addressed as an issue of profound grief.

If you are in a relationship where your partner will pursue pregnancy, you need to examine how this will feel to you if she conceives easily. Will you be able to be a supportive partner during her conception, pregnancy, and delivery? Will you be able to consider the child your own? Can you balance your pain with this other joy?

When dealing with infertility, it is necessary to develop some coping strategies. Here are some suggestions to help you get though this challenging time.

- If you are having unexpected infertility problems, the most important thing to do is gather information. The field of reproductive endocrinology continues to grow as advances in technology increase. There is a plethora of medical procedures that can often indicate precisely what the difficulties conceiving are, and in many cases they are able to correct the problems in order to make conception possible. The importance of medical information cannot be minimized.

- Find an infertility support group. This can be a local chapter of Resolve, or it can be a more informal group. Although the majority of women in these groups may be heterosexual, do not assume that they will be rejecting or homophobic toward you. Call the group facilitator and ask her if they've had other lesbians in the group, and how she would assist your successful integration into the group. If you live in a metropolitan area, there may be groups especially for lesbians struggling with infertility. You can ask your physician for a therapist who specializes in infertility and see if he or she is perhaps willing to start a group, or if there are other women, or lesbians, in his or her medical practice that might be interested in starting an informal group.

- Check out the Internet. The Internet has abundant resources and private E-mail lists for infertility and pregnancy loss. Some of these are specifically geared toward lesbians. Some medical doctors are also on-line offering advice, and Web sites are chock-full of useful information, but the greatest gift of Internet access is the wealth of emotional support from other lesbians who are experiencing infertility.

- Find safe places to vent. You have a right to be angry and sad that you are having trouble conceiving. Find someone who is especially good at being present for someone else's feelings without giving advice. (Note: not everyone is good at this.) Ask them if they are willing to listen to you when you feel like you are going to pop a cork. Pound a pillow, scream in the car with the windows shut, exercise with vigor, knead dough, chop wood, and stay away from loved ones when you feel like you are not safe to be around. Find people who will let you cry for as long as you like without trying to cheer you up.

- Find inspiration and reflection through reading. Many women have struggled with fertility, and writings about infertility go back to biblical sources, such as Hannah, who wept at the steps of the temple in Jerusalem, begging God for a child. Turn to the writings of women who have felt this way, and accept that these experiences are part of what "natural" women experience. Read the words of women who have dealt with other assaults to their definition of womanhood, particularly women who have had hysterectomies and mastectomies. If you feel your womanhood threatened by infertility, write down all the ways that you are a *real* woman. Read the list out loud. Read it again. Realize that your ability to nurture a child has nothing to do with biology.

- Work on your internalized homophobia. If your infertility is feeling connected to your lesbianism, this is important information for you about how you really feel about being a lesbian. Use this as an opportunity to houseclean more of those old messages about your worth as a human being. Realize that your sexuality is not merely about your ability to reproduce. Being a lesbian is a fine way to be human, and a wonderful way to be a parent. Look at your body naked in the mirror. Honor her for how hard she is trying. Forgive her for letting you down.

- Acknowledge that the infertility is hard for both partners. This needs to be said verbally and repeated often. This is not to minimize the pain of the woman undergoing infertility treatments, but to respect the difficulty of being a loved one witnessing this process and living with its consequences. Partners may feel very cut off by the withdrawal, and yet be recipients of the rage. Their pain is often unacknowledged, since they are technically not the one experiencing the infertility. Develop a support system for the partner. This is essential, whether it is a therapist, a support group, family members, other partners of lesbians trying to get pregnant, or on-line supports. Do not minimize your need for support and fall into the trap of having to be the "strong one." Honor the relationship, and develop a healthy respect for what you do share together, and a strong memory for all you love about one another.

- Sexuality is an area that can become particularly affected by infertility treatments. When a woman is having her body poked at by medical instruments and injected daily with hormones, she just might not be feeling as sexually connected. During periods of coping with infertility, the sexual contact between lovers, or the interest in pursuing a new sexual relationship for those who are single, might diminish. If you have a lover, spend intimate time together, even if it is not sexual. If you don't have a lover, find close friends who will hold you.

- Working with a therapist who is skilled in lesbian family issues can be very helpful. It is important to find a therapist who is knowledgeable in issues related to fertility, couples issues, and LGBT people, and perhaps adoption issues if this is an option for you. This may not be easy to find, and a good therapist who is willing to spend time learning can be valuable also.

- Spend time doing things not connected to fertility issues. Whether you are coupled or single, or for that matter, waiting to adopt, try to fill your life with meaningful activities. Go away for the weekend, even if you can't afford it, read poetry, finish your dissertation, paint your house, collect baseball cards, reread old letters from ex-lovers, get a new haircut. Enjoy doing all the things you won't have the time to do if you succeed in having children.

ADOPTION AND THE WAITING GAME

Adoption issues have been covered in the previous chapter; however, it is worth noting the specific issues that impact people waiting for a child to be placed in their home. Whether you are seeking a private or public adoption, through an international or domestic agency or attorney, paperwork and waiting are the names of the game in the adoption world. Many people begin to question the agency they are working with and feel discriminated against for being gay, being single, or not being wealthy. Although it is certainly possible that you are being discriminated against, it is also true that waiting for an adoption placement can be a long wait for heterosexual, married, and wealthy people.

The following letter was written on an adoption LISTSERV to a list member who wrote of feeling frustrated by the endless wait for an adoption placement. Although it is written for preadoptive couples, it may also be useful to those trying to conceive, as well as those who are single, with small adaptations.

As tempting as it is to end this section with uplifting stories of successful pregnancies and adoptions, I will refrain from that. The pain of infertility is not always alleviated by successful pregnancies. Adoption is never a "cure" for infertility but an alternative way to build a family. For some people, a successful adoption is followed by unsuccessful placements, disrupted adoptions, and painfully long waits for the right placement. For many women and their loved ones, infertility is a hollow place that one learns to live with. I want to honor these empty places by not rushing to fill them with success stories.

The roadblocks in this chapter may be disheartening, and perhaps you experienced infertility or an adoption wait, or even a miscarriage that you have not found quite as devastating as I described here. I respect that we are all different in how we experience life's disappointments. For many people these experiences have been life-altering, and my purpose here has been to honor the impact infertility and other roadblocks can have on our families. Facing disappointment and losses, whatever the outcome, can make our families stronger. It is actually an excellent preparation for the ups and downs, disappointments and joys of parenting.

Waiting Is the Hardest Part: Adoption

Dear Patiently Waiting,

If you haven't already done it, make a list of at least fifty things that you want to do without the benefit of children around—fifty things as a couple. Feel free to throw in an additional twenty-five or so for you as individuals. Think big, think small, think trips, think nice restaurants, think time with folks who don't care for kids, think hobbies, think sex (trust me on this one! Nothing stops enjoyment of that great position or technique or spiritual intimacy or whatever during sex like the wail of a child or the gurgle of vomiting over the baby monitor), think exercise, think books, think things late in the evening, think faith community or spiritual exploration, think . . .

Now, start doing them. Do them well, and if you enjoy them, do them again if finances and other considerations permit. Don't feel guilty that you are enjoying them so much. In fact, pat yourself on the back for being so clever to do them now!

Arms still aching from the emptiness of not holding your child? Folks encouraging you to spend time with other kids, and doing that just makes it worse, but you still want to spend time with kids? Spend some time baby-sitting kids, not just babies, with special needs. ADHD not under medical control. Autism. Blindness. CP, especially severe. Nonverbal, nonambulatory MR. Whatever.

It will give you something to think and talk about other than waiting while you're waiting. It may point you to a calling. It may teach you what referral you might need to turn down. It may help you down the road when your own beautiful child turns out to have a little condition or need you couldn't foresee.

Last, appreciate the days of longing for your child. Perhaps your child will come from a birth family that did not appreciate the gift of a child. But more likely the birth mother or father or grandparent or sibling or someone misses that child daily. Your days of longing can help you respect in a new way whatever part, be it total or minor, the birth mother or parents had in making the adoption plan, even if they were unfit parents in other ways.

Grace has been partnered with Margie for thirteen years. They are parents to Jeannette, age seventeen, and Clare, age ten, and live in North Carolina.

• • •

CHAPTER FOUR

The Realities of Parenting

WHEN PARENTS GATHER together for a rare cup of hot coffee, or an even rarer evening out without children, a common refrain that is heard is, "Having kids totally changes your life." Indeed, many parents will attest to the fact that parenting is life shifting in a more dramatic and forever way than any other event or circumstance in the adult life cycle. Certainly, other experiences can be intense and transformative—new career, relocation, permanent partnership, illness—but parenting has a way of shifting the ground you are standing on and making you question and reevaluate the basic value and meaning of life itself. Wow! That sure does sound dramatic!

The first thing to understand about parenting is that there is no way to prepare for it. I know that most of us will try anyway—reading child development books, decorating the nursery, and discussing discipline strategies months in advance. LGBT parents might be the most prepared parents in the world, since coming to parenthood was not assumed but an active choice. However, all the preparedness in the world still leaves new parents emotionally raw and psychologically blindsided to the realities of parenting.

Of course, some LGBT people come out long after the decision to parent was made. For people leaving heterosexual marriages, it can be a difficult transition for their children, who are now becoming part of a gay family. In these situations it is not LGBT identity that is shaken up by parenting, but parenting that is impacted by the developing LGBT identity. Perhaps a lesbian or bisexual woman became pregnant young, or perhaps a gay man or transwoman had children in a heterosexual marriage years before coming to terms with their sexuality and/or gender identity. Coming out issues are faced and addressed while managing day-to-day parenting responsibilities.

It is not uncommon for LGBT people in this position to wonder if coming out will harm their children. It is important to know that all the research that has been done on LGBT families—and this is an area that is well-researched—has shown that although this can be a tumultuous time in family life, children who are stable and well-loved are able to adapt to parental disclosures with minimal setbacks. However, one of the realities of parenting for these families is that they may have to address high levels of internalized homophobia, as well as the emotionality of shame and stigma. After all, the parents are probably coping with numerous issues themselves in *their* coming out—their own fears, prejudices, confusions—and these are experienced and projected onto the children in the family.

It is one thing to have a parent who is LGBT and is comfortable with their identity helping their teenager deal with peer harassment; it is an entirely other thing when parents themselves have few skills to address these issues and yet are the ones who are supposed to be teaching these skills to their children. Of course, parenting is all about thinking on your feet and being a leader when you might only be a few feet ahead of your child in terms of knowledge or experience. The issue for parents who come out after having children is not so much dealing with the realities of *parenting* but the realities of being a queer parent in a homophobic world.

Parents who are leaving long-term (or not so long-term) heterosexual marriages to pursue increased authenticity in their sexual or gender expression sometimes feel guilty that they are dragging their children through this coming-out process. Even if you are not feeling guilty yourself, there may be people invested in making you feel guilty! Those parents who have been single for a long time can still surprise their children if they become involved in a gay or lesbian relationship. Coming out as transgendered can often confuse and frighten children, especially teens. After all, most kids want to fit in more than anything else, and having LGBT parents does not bode well for fitting in.

Sometimes, however, our kids surprise us. When one woman came out to her almost adult children, they said, "We thought you came out about ten years ago. You mean you weren't involved sexually with all those women friends you were hanging out with?" In that case, the mom was literally the last one to know. For those of you reading this who came out after your children were already voting members of your family, remember that your honesty, directness, and growth in your own personhood will be one of the lived lessons of your children's growing years. If you don't come out to them, they may end up doing it for you, as one mom learned when her sixteen-year-old son crawled into bed next to her while she was reading, and said, "What'cha reading, Mom? A book on how to be a lesbian?" The more you can be yourself and model living with dignity, the more you will encourage your children to be fully themselves also.

THE INTRUSION OF REALITY

For LGBT people who are out and beginning families, there are two realities of parenting that may be different from what you expected. The first is that the act of parenting may impact you in ways that are unexpected or more intense than you had imagined. The second is that your child may not be who you expected.

Parenting will change your life in predictable ways: you will have less time for friends, hobbies, and sleep; you will have less energy for work, relationships, and sex; and you will have less money for everything. Parenting will also change your life in ways that are less predictable. Some parents find that their values become a bit less liberal on issues like school uniforms, teenage drinking, curfews, and premarital sex. You may have thought your sister was too strict when she wouldn't let her seven-year-old ride her bicycle across the street, or your neighbor was rigid when she wouldn't let her fifteen-year-old go to a concert, but now that the child is yours, you may discover to your own surprise that thirty seems young to allow your "baby" to begin dating. Most parents find themselves more protective than they had envisioned themselves. Particularly those who grew up streetwise may find that it is hard to allow their kids onto the streets in order to toughen up and have the experiences that might make them wise. You may find yourself thinking that having street-stupid kids might not be such a bad idea after all!

Sometimes the arrival of our child or children surprises us. Perhaps you were sure that you were having a girl child; perhaps the sonogram even said you were. And there you are, the mothers of a bouncing baby boy, wondering how to parent a male child. Rationally you knew that you had a 50 percent chance of having a son, but somehow the task of raising a male person in what had been a women-centered home may feel daunting. Issues that you might have minimized before, i.e., how to balance feminism with assuring his stable self-esteem as a man-child, challenges basic political and personal beliefs about gender, child development, and the meaning of maleness.

Perhaps you've had a vision of the kind of parent you wanted to be—kind, compassionate, attentive—and then you find angry voices coming out of your mouth, sounding much like your own parents. "Do you know what time it is?" a father screams at his two-year-old, who has, of course, no idea what time *is*. "I'll give you something to cry about," a mom yells at her five-year-old who is throwing a temper tantrum because she can't have a second ice-cream cone. Exhausted and ashamed, parenting does not always bring out our finest traits but sometimes gives us a frightening glimpse into our own parents' failures, as well as an insider's view of how some of the evils of the world can actually happen. A father who worked as a child advocate for abused children shared this at his daughter's year-old birthday:

> I never understood how anyone could hit, beat, or shake a helpless newborn infant until I had a two-month-old baby who screamed for ten to fifteen hours a day from colic. I suddenly understood how parents threw infants against walls and off balconies. Thank God that I have good coping skills and a supportive family, but I can see how a parent who is stressed and without supports can resort to the unthinkable. It is not an understanding I ever wanted to have, but I am a wiser man today for surviving this past year without hurting a child whom I dearly love.

Colic deserves a few paragraphs of its own. Some newborn babies are colicky; it's a fact. Colic is not like anything else in the world. Some people say that colic is about indigestion, and recommend numerous ways to eliminate gas in the baby's abdomen, from antigas drops to special bottles. One woman recommended using a dowel to squeeze all the air out of the milk bottle before feeding; another recommended placing the baby on top of a clothes dryer on his belly and allowing the vibrations to ease the belly pains. Others don't think colic is about gas at all, but rather about hypersensitive nervous systems, perhaps in babies born prematurely or who are just very sensitive to outside stimulus.

This is what colic looks like: it usually starts in the late evening, when the baby gets fussy and starts crying. She will then start to cry loudly, turning red, flailing her hands and legs, and turning beet red from the intensity of her wails. She will do this whether or not she is held or rocked. She pushes her body away from you, resisting any attempt at comfort, and screams. The screams can last anywhere from an hour or two to as long as ten hours or more. The baby usually repeats these screaming episodes on a regular basis starting at two weeks, and it can last for six months. However, babies are unique, and some can do it for most of a twenty-four-hour period, some only do it for a few days or weeks and then stop, and others, well, with some babies you can watch the seasons change out your window, while you rock, sing, soothe, and try to ease the urge to shake or pinch the baby.

It is a natural tendency to want to stop what is hurting your child, and some people have had great results changing formula, burping in certain positions, using white noise in the background, sleeping with or cuddling the child, and other parents have found that no matter what they did to ease the colic, their baby screamed and screamed and screamed. At the pediatrician for the third time in a week, a dad asks, "How do I know that there is not something really wrong? Maybe it's her appendix. How would I know?" The physician assures the dad that it is just colic and that if the baby becomes very very quiet and inactive, *then* he should worry.

Colic is not to be trifled with; the level of exhaustion caused by lack of sleep and intense baby caregiving can be overwhelming, even for the bravest of souls. One of the great challenges of colic is that you are offering endless comfort to an infant who generally does not appear to be receiving any of the comfort. When most of us think about the joys of parenting, we imagine the relief a little one feels when being scooped up by supportive, caring arms when we have a boo-boo. Colicky babies do not

Surviving Colic
BY ARLENE ISTAR LEV

We were warned that two children meant more than twice the work. We are told that having two children "really" made you a family, in a different way than just being two parents and one child. We were told that we were now two against two, and we would be irrevocably turning the balance against ourselves.

I thought I was prepared. I longed for a baby to hold and rock and cuddle. I was so hungry for another baby, a hunger that only those of us obsessed with wanting children can understand. I had waited a long time, and I thought I was prepared psychologically, financially, and emotionally to open my arms and heart to this new child.

Then came the colic. Oh, I had heard about colic. I had read articles and books about the difficulties of managing colicky babies. I confess to having thought it all sounded a bit overdone. After all, babies cry, some babies cry a lot, right? I had read about how having a colicky baby can make new parents feel inadequate, since the child is so difficult to comfort. I thought that perhaps that was true for first-time parents, but I had already been through infancy once with my older son and thought I was more confident than that. I had heard how sleep deprivation can make you so exhausted you begin to feel like you are losing your mind. I had thought, *Been there, done that,* the first time around. I had thought I was prepared, but oh, one is never prepared for colic.

There is no way to explain the daily exhaustion caused by a shrieking child who will simply not be comforted. My plans with this little one to work from home for the first few months, as I had done with my older boy, became impossible. We hired a friend to jiggle the baby for a few hours a day, so I could attend to my work. My partner and I shared the night feedings and night pacing, depending on who had more responsibility at work the next day. We bought white noise machines and invested in homeopathic chamomile. The laundry piled up around us, as did the dishes. The man at the Chinese take-out restaurant answered the phone, saying, "And how are you tonight?" Our older boy began to take off his socks at night and fold them neatly to wear the next day, knowing that there would likely not be clean laundry.

Although on some level you know that others have survived this, the isolation is overwhelming, and you become too exhausted to do anything other than survive. From two weeks of age, lasting well into his fifth month, my infant son screamed. He screamed for most of every day. He hardly ever slept; his naps lasted about twenty minutes. He insisted on being held all the time and relentlessly screamed any time you put him down for a minute. Going to the bathroom became a luxury I could ill afford. He woke up at the sound of a light switch two rooms away. His little body refused every formula on the market, except for stuff that cost $20 a can. He pushed his body away from our comforting hands. And he screamed and screamed and screamed.

I was so exhausted I found myself

nearly falling asleep while driving, not to mention the difficulty of sitting with my clients. I would take catnaps while the microwave heated up my lunch. I gave up all nonessentials like haircuts, dusting, and balancing the checkbook. I rocked and held and got accustomed to saying, "I am sorry, I just cannot meet that deadline. Honest, I'm not usually like this." I called my partner at work, interrupting important business meetings, bawling into the telephone, "I can't do this. It was a mistake. You must come home now." To her credit, she often did.

My love life consisted of one thing: having someone to hand the baby to who I trusted would not hurt him; something I did not fully believe with anyone else, given the loud, unending nature of his yelling. Although my relationship became less than satisfactory, for the first time in my adult life, I had no interest in discussing it. Having no communication, no private time together, seemed like a fine way to live; I appreciated for the first time my partner's ability to avoid dealing with difficult issues.

Every attempt we made for a few adult hours together was thwarted by sickness—either the baby's, one of us, or the baby-sitters. It became a joke that just offering to stay with our son might render one incapacitated for days with strange strains of the flu. The one time we got away for an overnight, we spent the first three hours comforting the baby-sitter on the phone while the baby screamed in her arms. Then we slept for ten hours straight. As unbelievable as it may sound, the only thing we wanted to do when we finally woke up was go to Toys "R" Us and buy presents for our children.

We have survived. He is now a happy, talkative, crawling baby nearing his first birthday. He has a funny sense of humor, eats regular food, cuddles, allows himself to be held, and joy of all joy, sleeps for at least eight hours most nights. We are beginning to catch up on our sleep, have gotten our much grayer hair cut, and even folded the laundry. We have survived colic, and I will never again underestimate the power of a screaming infant to completely immobilize two radical dykes.

This was previously printed online at www.lesbiaNation.com and in CommUnity News, *Albany, NY.*

seem to be comforted at all by the efforts at parental love, or if they are comforted it is a brief hiatus before the wailing resumes. Many parents, particularly new parents, find themselves feeling inadequate, imagining that it is their lousy parenting skills that are causing the distress. Even the most skilled parents are undone by colic. When a first child is colicky, a second child who is not may seem like the easiest baby in the world. When a second child is colicky, after an easy first child, the parents may find themselves questioning why they decided to have a second child.

The good news is that colic does end—usually within a few months, definitely within the first year. One woman suggests that babies who are colicky "get all their crying out in the beginning," and hardly tantrum during toddlerhood. Parental anecdotes are not scientific data, but if the fantasy of a postcolic latency period can help you hold on, then this one ranks as a useful rope to hang on to. However, colicky babies can sometimes be high-maintenance toddlers, and yes, sigh, high-maintenance teenagers, too. Remember, it's not about you; it's just one of those parenting things, that may not be what you bargained for. But get used to it. Lots of parenting is like that.

Colic is, of course, not the only trying health issue a new family can face. For many parents, one of the difficulties of new parenting is how hard it is to talk about the intense feelings of anger, rage, exhaustion, disappointment, and depression that sometimes accompany parenting. Recently, I visited two new moms. One of them had a ten-month-old child, and the other one had an eight-month-old child. One of the moms said to me, "I've had trouble bonding with her. I know that I love her, but it is an abstract feeling, not visceral the way I thought it would be. Loving has come slowly to me. Mostly she feels like a stranger still, someone I have to take care of, and whom I enjoy, but I know there is more to parenting than what I feel so far." The other mother said, "From the moment I saw her, the maternal urge was intense and fierce, a rising mama lion kind of love. I knew I would kill for this child, that nothing mattered in the world more than her." The second mother was the parent of the eight-month-old, whom she had adopted at two months old; the first mother had birthed her daughter in an underwater home birth. Despite the hype about maternal instinct, parents—men and women, adoptive and biological—each bond with their children within their own time frames. For some parents it is immediate, for most parents it grows more slowly, and feeling truly connected and bonded can not only take a while, but can ebb and flow month by month.

Feelings of love and bonding can also vary from child to child, even within the same "litter" for those who have birthed or adopted multiples. Often children who are harder to parent—children who are colicky, children with special needs, children who have difficulty sleeping through the night, or trouble keeping food down—can also be harder to bond with, invoking guilt in the parent who is aware of how much the child needs them but is feeling stretched to their limits. The images on television commercials of the new mom humming softly, cuddling a sweetly sleeping infant from her rocking chair might actually look more like this: a parent awakening predawn on less than four hours of sleep to a howling infant covered in diarrhea and spit up and the realization that all the onesies have been cleaned, but are still wet in the washing machine. These more truthful images might not sell fabric softner, but it would help parents feel less isolated with the challenges of parenting. Parents often wonder if the chaos in their lives is a reflection of their competence as parents, when in reality it is just part of the nature of parenting. All new parents have moments like the ones above.

It's been said before, but babies don't come with instructions. Perhaps closer to the truth is that they don't come with the right instructions. There are, of course, people with free advice. Mothers—it really is mothers who do this in my experience, not fathers—tend to have an endless supply of advice. Walking down the street, the first woman stops me to say that my son is cold and should be wearing a sweater. The second woman says he's too hot; I should take off his socks. Magazines, books, and television commercials bombard you with opinions about baby food, diapers, and try to sell you 10,000 "necessary" items, as if babies have always had, and couldn't live without, plastic carriers, bouncy seats, binky clips, and Elmo silverware. One woman, who is committed to a lifestyle of "voluntary simplicity and sustainable living" was shocked the first time she looked through a baby catalogue and realized how much junk she could buy; she was even more surprised when after looking through it for an hour, she decided that she really did *need* many of the items. Her solution was to recycle the catalogue. It is true, though, that there is no shortage of things available to buy for your child and people telling you that most of them are essential to raising babies.

What is harder to find, though, are actual instructions on how to make the things you have work. My first baby carrier was propped in an upright position until a father of four came to visit and showed me that the baby carrier could be easily moved into a number of positions, some easier for carrying, or sleeping, and others easier for feeding. Installing the car seat into the car for the first time can create hypertension, if you haven't had previous experience (and as I learned with baby number two, even if you have). Most parents are installing a car seat for the first time as they leave the hospital or the adoption agency, holding a tiny baby while nurses and

Bringing the Babies Home

When Angela and Linda adopted their daughters, ages twenty-six months and ten months, they were thrilled but a bit overwhelmed. Linda says: "We were originally setting out to adopt an infant but had not had any success. On a Wednesday, we got a call asking if we would be interested in an infant and her toddler-aged sister. We hadn't really thought about a toddler too much, but we immediately said yes. We ran out and did some quick emergency shopping at Wal-Mart for some car seats and other essentials that we were missing. We had some infant clothes, a crib, etc., but we didn't have anything that would be for a two-year-old. We talked to the foster mom that night, and she gave us a little bit of information about the girls, but she didn't know much, as she had only had the girls for a day herself! We hopped on a plane Friday morning. They were in our arms that afternoon (less than forty hours after the initial call).

The foster mom came to the hotel with them. We spent an hour or so of getting to know you (including how to make formula, what they would eat for breakfast), then realized that there was a *long* list of things that we needed but didn't have. The foster mom agreed to accompany us to the store to give us a little bit more support. We get out to the parking lot and realize that we have to figure out how to get those car seats fastened securely. The foster mom came to the rescue and ended up doing most of it herself while we were holding the girls, who had just woken up from naps. Panic started to set in. How were we supposed to take care of these precious girls when we can't even get the car seats in without help? We all went to Kmart to buy diapers and stuff (foster mom had to remind us we would need wipes), and then she left during the shopping trip. It felt like we were never going to get out of there. By the time we finished up, we were exhausted.

We had sworn that we would not have *our* children eating junky fast food, but we were too exhausted to even be able to think about going to a grocery store. We ended up going to Burger King (hanging head in shame). It felt like we were admitting that we couldn't handle parenthood. I have never cried so hard. After wanting to be a mom and have children for so long, I was terrified. I told Angie we had to give them back because we had no clue what to do and whatever we were supposed to do, we obviously couldn't. Of course that first night Mykeisha fell in the bathroom and busted her lip open, Mikaila kept trying to stick her fingers in the electrical outlets, and we were so tired we could hardly stand.

We tried to get the girls to go to bed at seven because we were soooo tired. As soon as we started talking to them about going to bed, Mykeisha freaked out and started howling for her mommy. She also realized, at that point, that the foster mom was gone. She would not go anywhere near the bed. All that crying upset Mikaila, who proceeded to add to the cacophony. Some small corner of my mind told me that one day I would want to remember this, so I took out a camera to take a picture, and Mykeisha immediately stopped crying and posed for the camera. Jackpot! I had her get in bed to pose for another picture. Angie read her a book we bought at Kmart, and she finally fell asleep. Mikaila was still crying, of course. It took several hours of walking the floor until she finally exhausted herself and went to sleep. Angie and I collapsed into bed; finally we could rest. Of course Mikaila did not sleep through the night. She woke up several times, but at least she would go back to sleep if we gave her a bottle.

The next morning we once again broke our rules about what we would never do with our children. We plopped them down in front of the television (at least it was PBS). We had to figure out how to entertain two small children who seemed to have boundless energy in a hotel room with very few toys/books for two weeks. We visited every park/playground and kids' museum in the area. We let them watch more TV in those two weeks than we ever thought possible.

And feeding them! It was a good thing Mykeisha could talk, because the next day she had to remind us it was time for lunch. Those were the hardest two weeks of my life. It took us a month before we figured out how to eat at the same time as them and seven months before we were able to sit at the dinner table together. Eleven months later, I figured out how to shower when home alone with the girls. (Until then, I had to shower late at night after everyone went to bed.)

Of course, even when we finally got the girls home, we still had quite a bit of adjusting to do. Almost every night Mykeisha would wake up crying. One night, about a week after we got home, Mykeisha woke up crying and woke Mikaila up, who immediately joined her sister in howling. We thought that perhaps the closet was scaring Mykeisha, so we decided to move her bed. In moving her bed we knocked the phone over. We didn't realize it at the time, but the phone had a button that was programmed to call 911, and when the phone fell, that button was hit. We just picked up the phone and hung it back up. The 911 operator tried to call us back, but we had turned the ringer off before we went to bed so we could get some sleep. Both kids were still screaming when I noticed a car pull into our driveway and stay there with the lights on. Angie went to check it out. She looked out the window and saw two people with flashlights walking around the house, and she yelled for me to call 911.

I couldn't hear her over the noise of the kids. Finally one of the men came to the front door, and she was able to see that it was the police. They insisted on coming in to make sure that everyone was okay and no one was holding a gun to our heads. They walked around the house and peeked in the bedroom where the kids were screaming. Mykeisha saw them and froze in terror. The police saw that everything was okay and left. Poor Mykeisha must have thought that they were coming to get her, because she immediately got back into bed, quiet as a mouse, and hasn't woken us up crying since. It took us quite a while to get her over her fear of police after that night!

> It got a little better over time, and now I know their cries and behaviors, as we close our first year together, but I still can't believe we survived.
>
> *Angela and Linda, parents to Mykeisha, age three, Mikaila, age two, and Spencer, three months old, live in the rural South.*

social workers are watching (often not helping due to legal constraints). Some parents have expressed the irrational fear that some professional will repossess the child if they are not exhibiting proficiency in car seat installation. Given the fact that most car seats are not installed properly according to the National Highway Transportation Safety Administration, perhaps your blood pressure should be raised over this issue.

Once my baby-sitter got the baby into his car seat, but when she had to close the stroller, she couldn't figure out how to find the mechanism to unlock it so it would fold like an umbrella; otherwise it was too bulky to fit into her car. After a frustrating twenty minutes, she flagged down a car with a baby seat visible in the backseat, figuring they would know how to unlock the stroller, and indeed, they did. High chairs, attachable table chairs, the sides of cribs, and even the complexity of snapping on baby outfits can be daunting for those who are not dexterous or mechanically inclined; for those who are spatially challenged, it can be a disaster. Most parents simply learn by the seat of their pants.

New parents have a million questions about the right way to do things. What formula is the best? How do I clean an umbilical cord? Should I immunize? Should I cosleep with my infant? When should we start solid food? Is it better to have a schedule for food or feed on demand? Of course, I have numerous opinions about all of these things, but the bottom line is that every parent struggles with making the best decisions he or she can for their little ones, and there is no right or wrong answer to the above questions. It depends on the baby, the parent, and your own rhythms, timing, and values. Some babies are never breast-fed, and others are breast-fed till seven—yes seven. Although breast milk is undeniably the best food for a newborn, babies who are not breast-fed for health reasons or due to unavailability of breast milk also thrive in loving homes. Some babies start solid food at only a few months old, and others mostly live on breast milk till they are talking. Children are incredibly adaptable, and parents each have to find their own way, sorting through the voluminous opinions available to find workable solutions that fit their own styles and goals for their family.

I was on-line at our local food co-op when my older son was an infant. I was buying organic pureed vegetarian baby food, which was triple the price of the mainstream brands. I felt very good about the healthy choices I was making for my son, who was always a good eater and could consume more than a few of those jars in one day; I was buying a case or two. The woman checking me out said, "Oh, you are the one buying all the baby food." *All?* I knew I was buying a hefty amount, but all? The woman looked at me intensely as if striving to make an assessment. "Most people who shop here make their own baby food," she said with more than a hint of judgment. I was clearly a deficient parent for allowing jarred baby food. I wondered if all those other people were also growing all their own organic veggies, and hand-sewing their baby's clothes. I was pretty sure they weren't a full-time working-out-of-the-house single parent, as I was. A week later, I was sitting with some moms, who commented on the weird food I was feeding my baby, and gasped when they saw the price. Spooning chicken with rice and sugar into their eight-month-old baby's mouth, they laughed at me for spending so much money on organic food.

Parenting is all about making decisions for you and your child that fit your values and lifestyle. In most things, you may find yourself falling smack in the middle of an issue. I would not feed my infant meat or sugar, but I also could not see spending my precious time with him cooking; store-bought organic food felt like a fine compromise, as shocking as it seemed to be for both the purists and those for whom chicken and stars *was* the healthy choice. In other issues you will find yourself on one side or the other— Diaper Genie: spawn of the devil or gift of the gods? Wherever you fall on any issue, remember there will be many people with strong opinions about how else you should do things, what would be healthier for your child, better for the environment, or just plain *obviously* a more logical decision.

Perhaps none of this has been a struggle for you. Maybe car seats were easily secured, formula decisions a no-brainer, and perhaps you found new parenting blissful and exactly the way you'd imagined it. Perhaps you had a marvelous birthing experience, bonded instantaneously with your child, who slept through the night at two months old, rarely cried, and ate food effortlessly. Perhaps you and your lover resumed your active and kinky sex life within weeks of the birth and moved with ease and delight through all the stages of parenting. Sadly, you might also be the only parents with enough time on your hands to read this book. I say, *"Mazel tov"*—but please be gentle with those of us who are less together or less lucky. It is only fair to acknowledge that some people do find the transition to parenting a fairly simple series of gentle changes. However, some of us are really knocked for a loop, even if we longed to be parents for a decade or more, and our lives are never quite the same again.

Parenting and Time

The most important thing to realize is that parenting is not a part-time job. Whether you are planning on parenting solo, with a partner, or with a tribe, parenting is very time intensive. Children have needs, lots and lots of needs, and babies need round-the-clock care. Even sleeping babies need to be checked up on often. Newborn babies need to be fed every few hours, and then burped, and then changed, and then after a short nap, they are ready to start in again. They do this day and night, and in the middle of the hot dinner you just put on the table. My mother-in-law jests that when her children were small, she didn't get to have a hot cup of coffee for fifteen years. I can still see the sharp looks of the handsomely dressed gay men sitting at the table next to us at the Lobster Pot in Provincetown, while our dinners got cold in front of us, and we tried to manage the bawling infant and the toddler who was throwing a tantrum on the floor.

In addition to the actual care that babies need, there is also the mess that they create. You might think a dependent sleeping baby might not actually be able to generate a lot of mess, but most babies need to be changed a number of times a day, between leaking diapers, dripping bottles, spit-up, and drool. Our first child needed to have a bib twenty-four hours a day to catch the voluminous drool that poured from his mouth; this meant we had to own about forty bibs or do a laundry every few hours. Once children begin eating solid food, you will find carrots in their ears, mashed potatoes in their hair, and thighs stained with red strawberries. Baths are a frequent event and often require two adults to manage the relationship between hard porcelain tub and slippery, wet baby flesh. A friend with a newborn recently said, "I couldn't understand why everyone kept buying me onesies. How many did they think I needed? Now, six weeks into this, I realize I need every single one of them."

Parents who are home full-time with babies will tell you that they live in a netherworld. Day and night become meaningless, life is divided up by naps, quick meals, and how many loads of laundry have been completed. For those who try to parent while continuing to work outside of the home, or maintain professional careers, the need for competent baby-sitters who you trust becomes an all-consuming obsession, while you sit in business meetings knowing the laundry is growing taller at home, and fearful you will miss the baby's first steps. Baby-sitters notoriously cancel or don't show just in time for the most important business meeting of your life, confronting you head-on with the utter inane simplicity of a statement like, "My children are more important than anything else in the world."

For some people, new baby time is the best time in the whole world. It is a time where nothing exists but baby, and it is filled with the getting to know yous and endless moments of loving, intimate exchange. Some parents will tell you that having a new baby is so great that as each baby grows, they long for another to take its place. Babies smell sweet (at least when properly bathed). They are adorable, with their eyes tenderly tracking your every move. They laugh and smile and giggle and sometimes belly-laugh deeply and warmly. For them you are the center of the universe, and in their eyes you begin to think that you are worthy and beautiful and powerful. Like little monkey babies (our closest animal relatives) they mold into your body, and as they grow they cling to you, small extensions of your soul, safe and secure in your arms. Having a baby dependent on you can give you a sense of purpose and fulfillment, knowing that serving their needs is essential for their survival.

Other parents are clear that this is a time to be gotten through. Like slogging through mud season in Vermont, pushing a broken-down car uphill, surviving food poisoning, new baby time is nothing short of hell. One woman said, "I felt completely trapped. If the baby cried one more time, had one more leaking poopy diaper, and sucked my cracked nipples one more minute, I was going to go postal. By the time my partner came home, I was in tears. I would literally shove the baby at her, while she was walking in the door, yelling, 'We made a mistake, I'm sorry, I just can't do this.' Gratefully, he grew up to be a really cute toddler who speaks in almost full sentences. It took me a while to remember why I wanted to have children, though."

It is important that you know now one of the great ugly truths about parenting. You will likely lose some friends. You might lose long-term friends. Friends who you thought would be there forever are suddenly nowhere to be found. Friends who swore that they would be there to baby-sit seem to have numerous other commitments while you are desperately seeking an hour break. Sometimes friends who are accustomed to long, intimate conversations can't adapt to the short "mommy conversations" that parenting demands, constantly shifting your attention for kids' interruptions. They may call in the middle of the dinner hour, not understanding the level of chaos that family life creates while food is being prepared and devoured and then cleaned up. Other friends demand spontaneity, wanting to go for a hike, a beer, or a weekend out, not realizing the level of planning that an outing can take. Many, many friends will resent the constant cancellations due to childhood sicknesses or canceled baby-sitters. The first few years of a child's life you are likely to miss birthdays, holidays, weddings, and once-in-a-lifetime conferences because the baby's needs simply come first.

Since friends may or may not show up as they offered, it is crucial to make careful preparations if you plan to be a single parent. You will need backup plans, sitters you trust, and as many friends and family members as are offering to help. Sometimes those who become the biggest helpers are not the people who you would've thought would be *there* for you. You may find your social circles dramatically shifting.

Having a new baby is not the time to remodel your house, finish your dissertation, or reconnect with your lover, although many people have done exactly those things. The baby will take over most of your time, and your job is to surrender to this process. On the edges of the baby's time, like a big circle cut in the field of your life, *that* is what is left for you. There you can watch a movie, call a friend, or do another load of laundry. Probably you will want to sleep. Probably you will want to sleep more than you've ever wanted to do anything in your whole life.

The Mystery Child

Many, many years ago I read a short story about a woman who had a lot of children. She said that in the family she came from everyone had blue eyes and hated breakfast. Now she is in the kitchen early in the morning with a gaggle of small children with large round brown eyes, clamoring for sausages, eggs, cereal, and seconds. She said, "I have no idea who they are."

Sometimes our children will be strangers to us. This may seem more obvious for those who are adopting, but it can be equally true for birth parents. Sometimes the stranger aspect is physical: How did this light/dark, tall/short, fat/thin child wind up in my care? Sometimes it is more of a personality issue. You have two left feet and your daughter is a star athlete. You are tone deaf and your son has a beautiful singing voice. You are shy and withdrawn, and both of your children are outgoing and theatrical. Perhaps more frightening for some of us, the femmy-est daughters seem to be born from the butchiest of women, and true macho men from the nelliest of queens. Think of it as a cultural exchange program.

Perhaps the differences are not that superficial. Maybe when you decided to adopt internationally, you hadn't fully thought of what it meant to have a dark brown child, or one with clearly Asian eyes, yelling "Daddy," in a crowded supermarket. And perhaps it means nothing at all, except that you feel surprised inside, and fear other judgments if you admit to the feeling. What if you are feeling profoundly uncomfortable with it, and others are indeed judgmental? What if the child you are rearing looks like a stranger to you, and you are not sure how to love him or her? Again, this happens to birth parents as well as adoptive ones. Sometimes a nonbiological parent will feel different from the rest of the family, and will struggle with admitting this to their partner. Nothing is more important than honesty to oneself and to loved ones (though not necessarily to the child) about these feelings. Chances are that others have felt this way, too. It can be an opportunity to compare features and personality traits and recognize the beauty in all the different ways we look. In families where differences are pronounced, coping with the stares and confusion of real strangers is a necessary task. The more comfortable each member of the family is talking about differences, the easier it will be to address outsiders.

This is particularly true parenting children with visible disabilities. Blindness, cerebral palsy, use of a wheelchair, speech impediments, braces, cleft palate, and use of sign language can mark a child as different. Friends and family are often uncomfortable when seeing the baby for the first time or meeting an older adopted child with obvious disabilities. What do they say? Should they acknowledge the difference? And most importantly, how

Not the Way I Thought It Would Be: Sue's Story

My former partner and I became foster parents specifically for babies with HIV. Over the course of three months we had a total of four foster placements, and only Eric was infected. One child stayed with us for two days, one for four weeks, and one child, Liam, stayed with us for thirteen months. Eric and Liam are twenty-seven days apart and arrived in our home around two weeks apart. We asked to adopt both Eric, who was HIV positive, and Liam, who was healthy except for asthma, but were told we couldn't adopt Liam because he is black. Eric is black, too, but I suppose they thought he would die before he could realize he had lesbian moms who were white and Puerto Rican.

We knew when Eric came home to us that he was HIV antibody positive, and when he was three months old, they were able to culture the virus from his blood. This meant he wasn't going to be one of the fortunate babies that could sero-revert. We believed he wouldn't live to see his first birthday.

At twelve months old, he started on AZT, the only drug at the time being tested on children. Although some people had severe side effects, Eric did not. He received his actual AIDS diagnosis when he was one and a half years old. We were told that people only lived two years past diagnosis. Every time we would go to the doctor, we would ask what his life expectancy was, but it soon became clear that Eric was going to outlive any predictions. Eric had things he still wanted to do.

My ex and I broke up when Eric was five years old, although we have continued coparenting. Eric is now fifteen years old. He is, in so many ways, a typical teenaged boy. He enjoys skateboarding and bike riding, and is a video game fanatic. He also loves going to the movies. If he hears part of a soundtrack, he can immediately identify the movie it is from. Eric's main interest, these days, is girls. He wants to have sex, get married, and adopt babies (in that order). I have been teaching Eric about personal safety and mutual responsibility since he started asking questions about sex at the age of five. There are some who feel that I have provided him with too much information, but I am convinced that, because of the knowledge, he is better equipped to make responsible choices.

People often comment on how wonderful I am to "parent someone else's sick kid" although they try to say it in a nicer way. The truth is, I had no idea what I was getting into. He tricked us. I expected to have some semblance of a baby hospice. Then, when they comment on how long I've "kept him alive," I reply jokingly, "I can't kill him!" In all seriousness, I am blessed to have been given the privilege of being Eric's mother. His presence has enriched my life in ways I couldn't begin to explain. True, it's not the way I thought it would be. It's better!

Sue is the mama of Eric, age fifteen, and Julian, age, two, in Stockton, California.

do *you* as a parent feel about this child? Parenting children with special needs is complex and challenging. One of the realities of parenthood is that anyone can become the parent of a child with disabilities; all of us are, of course, only temporarily able-bodied ourselves. Although adoptive parents who seek special needs kids may receive special training and at least have some idea of what parenting their child may mean, many parents are thrust into the world of parenting a disabled child through an unforeseen event, experience, or accident.

Most people would not make the choice that their child should have a disability, and it is commonly followed by grief, loss, anger, and sadness. Accepting a child's physical limitations or growing accustomed to a physical difference, learning how to care for the child's disability, and developing the skills necessary to communicate together are challenges that are additional to those of daily parenting. In some measure, though, one of the hardest obstacles for some parents to overcome is the shock that this different child is actually theirs.

Sometimes it is just the reality of *being* a parent that shocks and surprises us. "Come on, boys," my partner yells to our sons, and I find myself thinking, "Boys? Sons? How did I become the parent of two boys?"

Children are a mystery in many ways, in terms of who they are and who they become under our care. One friend of mine says, "Parents of one child always assume that the child is the way she or he is because of their parenting (for better or worse). But parents of more than one child have a new respect for genetics, karma, personality, and realize how very powerless they are in determining the kind of person their children will be." This does not mean that we can't or shouldn't try to give them the tools we think will help them become productive and happy adults, nor does it mean that we can't harm children by blatantly cruel or inhumane parenting. What it does mean is to a large extent they arrive as mysteries, unknown humans, who reveal themselves to us over time, and our job is to be able to show up and meet their emerging selves with openness, warmth, and welcome.

Who they will be and how we will mold them may turn out to be a very different journey than the one we entered into when planning a family. Most parents I speak with say that parenting is really nothing like what they thought it would be.

It is amazing all the fantasies we have about parenting: the daily joy of watching them grow, the intimacy of parent and child, and our images of how attentive, caring, and attuned to their needs we will be. Of course, we all also have the other fantasies, the fears that we will be awful parents, or for some of us, that we will be just like our own parents. The truth, of course, lies somewhere in the middle. We will have a unique and special relationship with our children, deep intimacies, and we will mostly be good, loving parents. It is also true that there are times we will feel like horrible parents, times we might even be horrible parents due to our own fatigue, illness, financial problems, or relationship woes, and for better or worse, we will see our own parents mirrored in our behaviors, at the same time that we see our parenting skills and faults in a new light.

WHAT AM I GETTING INTO?

If you've read this far, you've either decided that I really hate my kids, I wasn't cut out for this parenting thing, or that maybe this was a really bad idea and you should back out now. I really, really love my kids, honest. Just ask them and they'll tell you. The question of whether I was cut out for this parenting thing is fifty-fifty. I admit to still having fantasies of a loft in the Village, or a cottage at the Cape, with no smelly diapers, and a night's sleep without the sounds of Winnie-the Pooh singing ABC songs through a static-filled intercom twelve inches from my ear. I admit I miss long phone conversations with friends, without interruptions, and long for the freedom of not always having some part of my consciousness aware at all times about where my boys are (11:45, lunch at the day care, probably safe; 3 o'clock, and the big kids are going to the park, crossing the big street, murmur small prayer, hope the barely-out-of-their-teens child care staff is paying attention).

But that is only part of the story. The other part is I can no longer imagine living a life without children, as much as I would enjoy a good night's sleep. My children are a part of me, as much as my arms and legs; my life is entwined with their needs and dreams. I do not dream alone anymore.

Perhaps you are thinking, *And what's in this for me? No sleep, exhaustion, being broke, twenty-four-hour-a-day care—Why would I want to do this?* As I wrote that sentence, the door of my study opened for the twentieth time today (it's about noon). My older son stuck his head in the door, just his head, and gave me a tooth-filled grin (upper front teeth just came in, crooked, will cost about $3,000 before we are done). Just a big,

Look At Me, Way Up High, Suddenly, I'm Flying

It pays to be prepared, but not as much as one would think. The first mistake I made was not buying Christopher his own airplane ticket. Given how cramped the seating was, the tight space made things worse when Christopher was on my lap, because he wanted to grab the hair of the people sitting in front of me or the clothes of the people sitting next to me. It turns out that although I was worried about traveling with Caleb, he was a prince for most of the journey. My baby, Christopher, who turned a year old during the trip, had a full-blown toddler tantrum each time he was denied his own way, and he hated being confined to a small area for hours. First, he pulled over a cup of coffee belonging to the passenger sitting next to us and drenched both the passenger and me. Then he screamed his head off when I changed his diaper in the very cramped airplane bathroom, making the task even more difficult. I literally had to pee with him in my arms because he cried whenever I put him down. When he finally fell asleep my relief was unparalleled. If I buy him his own seat, we will take up an entire row, and this won't be as much of a problem. Definitely his own seat next time. Definitely!

Other than the seating, the flight attendants were all kind and efficient. We were allowed to preboard first, and the double stroller was always checked at the door of the plane just before we entered and waiting for us when we emerged at the next destination. I did have to remove the kids from the stroller, and the baby and I got the once-over with the metal detector (even had to remove my shoes), still, we made it through from ticket counter to gate in an hour or less. My only complaint about the airports was the lack of skycaps to assist with bringing the bags inside. They were there, just not when I needed them, and the cabbie was a real butthead and dropped us off in the middle lane rather than the lane closest to the curb. This meant I had to push the double stroller with four bags and two kids across an uncertain street. Fortunately, a kind stranger assisted by pulling the big duffel bag inside, though I never took my eyes off of them.

I took a cab from the airport to the first hotel, and when I arrived I learned that the school had switched us to another hotel, but the desk clerk at the old hotel had no idea where we were supposed to be staying. I finally found out that we had been booked at a hotel three blocks way. Three blocks, with a cold wind blowing, two children, and luggage! When I did arrive at the hotel, all I wanted to do was crash. My mom graciously took the kids for the weekend—this is the same woman I worried would never accept adopted grandchildren—and the best part was that I got to take three showers and a bath this past weekend *and* use the bathroom without any kids around. Little slices of heaven for a single parent. The best thing to happen this weekend was that I now know that I can travel with the kids by myself. There are some things I can do to make it easier next time, but it is doable. This trip also confirmed something else that's been on my mind. I really do want to start the adoption process again; I think I want a daughter.

Michael is a single, black, adoptive dad to biracial sons, Caleb, three, and Christopher, twenty-one months, in Fullerton, California.

wide grin, followed by a small, grunty giggle. He closed the door and headed back to his world, full of Pokémon, a toy guitar that he is building out of a shoebox and string, and a new cash register with a plastic credit card. He doesn't quite get that he is supposed to be collecting money from everyone, so he has been walking around paying *for* my lunch, shoes, and laundry for the past three days. He just wanted to check up on me, make sure I'm where I'm supposed to be, make sure that his world is stable and sane and predictable. He wanted to see my face, because for him my face is his home base and is a touchstone for making sense of this crazy world. Maybe that's not enough for you to deal with the realities of parenting; for me, it is enough. Over and over and over again, each day, I make this soul connection to other little humans that makes all else I do complete and full and meaningful.

Another way to view this parenting thing is kind of a survivalist obstacles course. Some like skydiving, some like white-water rafting, some like winter camping, and well, others just like parenting.

The realities of parenting are not all negative; the reality of parenting is generally extremely positive, and most LGBT parents will tell you that it was the best thing they ever did. But the idyllic images on television and most LGBT parenting books (or even mainstream parenting books) do not describe the challenges, difficulties, disappointments, and yes, I will say it again, exhaustion, inherent in new parenting. I fear this leaves many new parents isolated with their negative and fearful thoughts. Perhaps Irma Bombeck's wisdom is more applicable than Martha Stewart's and deserves reprints in queer newspapers. Dan Savage is the queer community's answer to Irma, with just a bit of Marquis de Sade thrown in for good measure.

One last note about reality: homophobia is alive and well and is a force to be contended with. Perhaps you live in a big-city gay ghetto, and all the queers are walking down the street with baby carriages, and you are thinking that being a queer parent is really no longer a big deal. You might be rudely awakened by the reality of homophobic America when you tell your extended family about your pregnancy, move to the suburbs, interview pediatricians, or sit through your first adoption home study. One of the most surprising rejections for some of us are the judgments of other LGBT people who think that having children is selfish or that it isn't fair to our children. Homophobia does not always come from the outside, but sometimes from within our own ranks.

Don't Kid Yourself
BY DAN SAVAGE

There were at least four or five at every bookstore I read at during my tour: a smiling couple who would look at me, smile a little broader, and tell me that my book—sometimes on its own, sometimes in cahoots with Jesse Greene's *The Velveteen Father*—had inspired them. They were going to adopt, too, or get a lesbian friend pregnant.

"Isn't it great?" they would say. "We're going to be dads, too!"

Most of the time I would smile right back and say, "Hey, that's great." And most of the time I meant it. But there were a few times—a few dozen—when I didn't mean it, when what I really wanted to say was, "You two don't look like parent material to me."

Take, for instance, the very young couple in Chicago who, reeking of cigarette smoke, cheerfully informed me that they'd already knocked up a lesbian friend. They were going to be dads in less than six months. "Hey, that's great," I said. But I was thinking, *You guys are too young and too smelly to be parents.*

We chatted for a minute, and then I stuck my foot in it.

"You two do realize," I said, trying to sound upbeat and helpful, "that once you have a baby you will *have* to quit smoking. Smoking is bad for babies, sudden infant death syndrome, asthma, slows their growth—stuff like that. Quit now."

Their smiles disappeared. One told me that his parents smoked, and it didn't kill him; the other told me it wasn't any of my business if they smoked or not. They were right, of course, but since they had just told me my book inspired them to have kids, well, I felt it was partly my doing, if not my business, that gave me the right to put in my two cents about the smoking issue.

There were other couples who reeked of smoke at my readings who told me they were having kids, and they were young guys in leather pants who looked as if they hadn't slept in a week and guys who told me they were going to adopt in order to "prove to the Republicans that we're just as good as they are." And in Portland a woman told me she was going to adopt with her girlfriend, a girlfriend who wasn't with her at the reading because "she's not out."

Having been burned by the smoker's rights advocates in Chicago at the beginning of the book tour, I didn't offer any friendly or helpful criticisms to the smokers I met in other cities, nor to the meth addicts, political activists, or partners of closet cases who told me they wanted to be parents.

Until now.

Look, guys, just because we can do something—like say, get your whole arm up someone's ass, stay up for nine days straight with the help of chems, or adopt a kid—doesn't mean we should or that we all should. And when it comes to babies, gay people should not lightly discard the one advantage we have over straight people. We don't have babies by accident. Two men can't get drunk one night and adopt; no lesbian has ever awoken from a long weekend's debauch to find a receipt from a sperm bank in her pocket.

Straight people, on the other hand, are always getting pregnant by accident, often with disastrous consequences. Too many straight people who aren't ready for kids—they're too young or too selfish—fall down drunk and get up pregnant. People who didn't plan for kids or never really wanted them make the worst parents; it's their children who may wind up abused and neglected and who may ultimately make their way into the foster care system—a potential tragedy for everyone involved.

But even while we homos fall down drunk at slightly higher rates than heteros, we almost never get up pregnant. Kids are something we have to think about and plan for, and so far most of the gay parents I know were fit and responsible and *ready* and had already given up cigarettes and leather pants and partying. They were out, and they were having kids because they wanted to be parents, not because they wanted to prove something to George W. Bush, or Lynne Cheney. In other words, they had kids for all the right reasons.

But now . . . I worry. I fear that the bad Madonna movie (*The Next Best Thing*), the serious book (*The Velveteen Father*), and the wiseass book (my book *The Kid*) are inspiring some impressionable gay people to make or adopt babies for all the wrong reasons. I worry about a wave of "accidental" gay pregnancies—gay and lesbian couples having kids because it seems like

the thing to do. Or, worse yet, having kids because people like me and my close personal friend Madonna make kids look . . . glamorous.

Kids aren't glamorous, though. They're hard work, they puke all over everything, and day or night, their needs come first. "Projectile vomiting" and "explosive diarrhea" are not exaggerations but terrifying understatements. What's worse, unless you happen to be Madonna and can afford to hire a live-in nanny, a baby pretty much kills your sex life. It's ironic that the religious right opposes both gay sex and gay adoption because, in my experience, nothing puts a stop to gay sex faster than a gay adoption.

Of course, I don't want to discourage gay or lesbian couples who want kids and are ready for them from adopting or getting pregnant. But there's no rush, folks. If you're still at a point in your life where you like cigarettes more than kids, you're not ready. If you still like going out more than you like staying home, you're not ready. If you're under thirty, you're not ready. If your partner is a closet case, she's not ready.

And if all you've read about kids is my book, you're definitely not ready.

This article was first published in out *magazine in October 2000, and is published with permission from Dan Savage, author of* The Kid: What Happened after My Boyfriend and I Decided to Go Get Pregnant.

On the other hand, those of you who are living in the Bible Belt and expect to find physicians rejecting, adoption agencies unwelcoming, families who will fight you in court for custody of your children, and crosses burning on your lawn may be surprised at the baby showers and social acceptance that your family engenders now that you look more like the average American family. In other words, there is simply no way to know for sure how parenting will impact your family, your community, or your job. Those of us who expect support may find ourselves alone, and those of us who expect rejection may find ourselves warmly accepted.

Whatever our fantasies are about what parenting will be like, it will probably be something else entirely. Whatever our fantasies are about who our children will be, they will likely surprise us. Even if they have Uncle Joe's nose, or Grandma's love of nature, even if they are a "chip off the ol' block" (even if the block was a grafted branch of the family tree), they will be their own persons, with their own needs, desires, experiences, and challenges. Kahlil Gibran said, "Our children are not our children, they are the sons and daughters of life longing for itself. They come through you, but not from you. . . . " As much as we feel connected to our children, and they are a part of us, they are also completely separate souls entrusted to our care. In other words, the fewer expectations you have, the easier it will be to let them become themselves and watch their growth with openness and awe.

PART TWO

BUILDING HEALTHY FAMILIES

CHAPTER FIVE

• • •

Queer Family Life Cycles

THIS CHAPTER MAY be more academic than the others, so if that is not your cup of tea, feel free to skip it. It seems important, though, in a book on LGBT parenting, to look at family-building within a larger context of what experts know about families in general. Social scientists, sociologists, and family therapists have continued to define, study, and examine what it means to be family. As gay marriage and gay adoption and queer families become part of the larger social discourse, it seems relevant to increase our knowledge of the social institutions we are embracing.

Families are social institutions that are structurally organized and embedded in a complex matrix of publicly recognized customs that are socially endorsed. Coupling has rituals, from dating through commitment, acknowledged with public functions like weddings, as well as private romantic vows. In the days before gay people openly had commitment ceremonies and legal marriages on the steps of San Francisco city hall, I was complaining to a friend about how heterosexual marriage was socially recognized and that heterosexual couples receive wedding gifts to help them furnish their new home that I, then single and living alone, would have to purchase myself. My friend sent me a food blender in the mail (this was long before Ellen DeGeneres made toaster ovens a famous lesbian coming out gift), honoring the life ritual of my being single and having my own apartment, with the same intentionality that a friend might recognize a marriage ceremony. Many of us learned as LGBT people to live outside of the social rituals, laughing in the face of heterosexual marriages and reveling in our very queer freedoms.

In more recent years, LGBT people are having commitment ceremonies, recognized in many situations by religious institutions, in-laws, and even employers at major corporations who offer insurance coverage for domestic partners. Gay marriage has become an item of public debate and civil disobedience. Parents of gay adults put pressure on them *not* to go straight but to settle down and find someone—a gay partner—and start a family. Gay marriage has become big business, while gay people search for cake toppings with two grooms and insist upon honeymoon suites in hotels where they once hid their coupled status by arriving separately and pretending to be business partners. Vermont was the first state to take the bold step of recognizing our relationships as equal to heterosexual relationships through a process of civil unions, unwilling to confer that powerful term *marriage* onto our relationships. Then, of course, Massachusetts decreed that it was unconstitutional to not allow gays to marry. Unless you've been living a very sheltered life, the gay marriage issue has been front page center in the U.S. news for nearly a year. By having our unions civilized, we became a bit more mainstreamed, and these changes have not gone unnoticed by the media, as well as within the political discourse of our own communities and nation.

Some within our communities have questioned whether commitment ceremonies and wedding vows are buying into a romantic dream that should have lost its glitter and luster a long time ago. Any intelligent person who is paying attention would notice the obvious flaws of the marriage institution. Heterosexual unions are rarely forever, despite the hype, and equality between marriage partners, despite forty years of feminism, is still an elusive goal. Marriage and the traditional family has its roots, after all, in patriarchy and in male ownership of land, children, women, and cows. Transforming these roots into viable, supportive, equalitarian family life has been a long-range process. For many LGBT people (as well as for some heterosexuals) marriage represented a kind of prison, and being free of that structure turned out to be one of the great secrets of coming out queer. Why should LGBT people buy into a failing institution?

In the early days of the gay liberation movement, LGBT people (as well as many heterosexuals) were attempting new models of relationships, from freer attitudes toward sexual expression, to open relationships, to a kind of serial monogamy, whereby when the spark had died partners gracefully separated, became friends, and moved on. Gay liberation was exactly that—liberating—and we were free of the strictures of heterosexual marriage, as well as the tyranny of parenting. Some old-time queers are still scratching their heads; how did we get from there to here?

Some will say that we have sold out or settled down, and others will say that we have grown up. I suspect it is a bit of each. I think that many people discovered that sexual freedoms were a bit more complex to manage than they had thought, and that the desire for emotional security and permanency was stronger than they had imagined (as elusive as it may remain). Some LGBT people began to discover that the old-fashioned customs—weddings, marriage vows, home ownership, and parenting—looked more and more appealing. Other LGBT people had always found it appealing and never had illusions about wanting anything but a traditional marriage. Certainly long-term coupling has always existed among LGBT people, and the fantasy of wanting forever relationships has always been a part of queer folklore, long before we were able to publicly declare our relationships. The gay liberation movement brought with it not only a greater diversity of lifestyle choices and an ending of the need to hide our love and sexuality, but it also brought with it a realization of how homophobic institutions invalidate our partnerships and make security and permanency difficult to establish and maintain. However we came to this place, as individuals and as a community, the desire for stable commitments and legal marriages that secure our families has become a goal for many LGBT people, and perhaps *the* goal for the first decade of the twenty-first century.

Whatever feelings one may have about traditional heterosexual marriages, or gay lifestyles, the desire for human intimacy, commitment, and security is universal, even if the structures we create to house our relations are diverse. However, in the process of building more permanent unions, many of us found that without institutional support, we were often left without health insurance, inheritances, and even being locked out of decision making during emergency medical procedures. We also began to discover that there were benefits to being included in certain social institutions, and that being excluded from them made us more financially vulnerable as well as less emotionally secure in the lives we were building.

It is also true that many of our families do not in any way mirror heterosexual unions; some of us have eschewed any attempts to mimic marriage ceremonies, and others boldly live in open partnerships, pursuing polyfidelity in their intimate relationships. Some LGBT people (as well as some heterosexuals) have successfully created multiparent families. However, LGBT parenting, whether traditionally structured or postmodernly fashioned, like all human relationships, exists within certain socially constructed parameters. Family life, straight or bent, moves through predictable stages and developmental processes, life cycle passages that unfold in time.

Passages Through Time

Psychological theory has defined human development as taking place teleologically, unfolding through an intrinsic and natural process, internally prompted within each person, and moving through time. This process has been considered universal, the same throughout the world regardless of gender, race, class, or culture, as well as intrapersonal, existing within, literally inside of, human beings. Developmental psychologists refer to this as epigenetic, a predetermined unfolding of a pattern or sequence that underlies all human development. Although everyone recognizes that human development is affected by things outside of the individual, like nutrition, poverty, and death of a parent, development has been considered mostly an inside job, taking place largely within one's own psyche. After all, even children living in poverty, experiencing neglect and sexual abuse, will learn to talk, walk, and feed themselves in almost all situations. Poor parenting may interfere with the timing of language acquisition, but the basic blueprint for language acquisition is considered inborn. Think of it as a foundation and structure for a house versus the interior decorating and landscaping.

Developmental life cycle theories—from the psychosexual theories of Sigmund Freud to the psychosocial models of Erik Erikson, from the complex object relations analyses of Margaret Mahler, to the popular self-help concepts of Gail Sheehy—impact the ways we each experience our own movement through the stages of our lives, as well as the way we perceive our children's growth. Those of us who have studied basic college psychology have come to accept Jean Piaget's descriptions of the cognitive developmental processes of young children, Lawrence Kohlberg's view of moral development, and Howard Gardner's vision of the multiple kinds of intelligence our children express. Even those of us for whom these names make you raise your eyebrows and shrug would be surprised how much of these ideas are part of popular culture. Ideas about infant attachment, adolescent rebellion, midlife crisis, even gender role acquisition, derive from the developmental concepts originated from these brilliant theorists

For a long time, developmental theories only focused on children's development, but modern psychology has remedied this with stage models that move through the entire life cycle. Flaws have been noted in these models; for instance, the majority of the research on human development has been done on limited samples of people (usually white, middle-class males) and some of their theories are blatantly biased (Piaget studied his own children; Kohlberg believed that girls could not reach higher levels of moral development).

One area in particular that has been addressed by feminists is the limitations in traditional theories regarding female development. Carol Gilligan examined the ways that male developmental theorists subsumed women into their models, ignoring the unique ways that women develop differently from men. According to Gilligan, women have traditionally valued caring, attachment, and cooperation, whereas men have traditionally valued autonomy and independence; based on a male model, women appeared dependent and underdeveloped rather then relational and connected. Stage models have also assumed that all human development takes place in an age-graded manner—infants must develop trust, children like to play, and old people contemplate their lives—that ignores the need for trust, play, and contemplation throughout the life cycle.

Additional to the above criticisms, stage models also suffer, nearly universally, from one great error: they minimize the role and position of the family in the development of human beings throughout the life cycle. All theorists, of course, acknowledge the importance of families and parenting, but they are seen generally as addenda to this epigenetic process. Parents can mess up one's development; abusive parents can nearly destroy us, but with good enough parenting, we will all unfold according to our potential. Mothers are particularly held responsible for these processes. It is not so much that this position is wrong, as it is limited.

Psychological studies of LGB development have also been viewed as a teleological process and as unfolding intrinsically within individuals. Coming out models have been very useful in describing the process of internalizing a positive self-image of an identity that has been socially stigmatized. There have been numerous models developed, the most popular being Vivienne Cass's, but Eli Coleman, Richard Troiden, and others have created similar stage theories. All of these models, despite a difference in nomenclature, show the person moving through a series of developmental stages from an early awareness and confusion about sexual identity to a mature integration and synthesis within the larger construct of self, emphasizing milestone events and developmental tasks.

Lesbian and gay people do not necessarily move through the stages in a neat order or at the same pace, and because people come out at different stages of the life cycle, it interacts with other developmental issues within the life cycle. Vivienne Cass has recognized in her later work that this coming out model is a product of modern Western culture, and that lesbian and gay identity might be experienced differently in other places in the world and throughout different historical epochs. Sexual identity development in this sense is not an intrinsic process like walking, but is impacted by the environmental conditions and sociopolitical climate.

Bisexual identity development has often been relegated to a stage in the gay or lesbian coming out process until Martin Weinberg, Colin Williams, and Douglas Pryor developed a model for examining the specific stages of bisexual coming out. Since bisexual identity can remain fluid, bisexual people can often maintain a greater flexibility in their sexual behavior, expression, and identity. The stages they outlined are: Initial Confusion, Finding and Applying the Label and Settling into an Identity, and Continued Uncertainty. Their last stage does not mean that bisexuals are confused, but rather that they remain open to changes in partner choice and fluctuations in the direction of their sexual orientation throughout their life. Fritz Klein has outlined the complexity of bisexual identity and become a fierce advocate for the recognition of bisexual people within the lesbian and gay community.

Examination of transgender identity development is in its infancy. Until recently, virtually all examinations of transgender and transsexual iden-

Vivienne Cass's Lesbian and Gay Coming Out Model

Identity Confusion: Occurs when a person begins to realize that he or she may relate to and/or identify themselves with being gay or lesbian; "Who am I?"

Comparison: Occurs when a person questions what these feelings mean and begins to rationalize and examine the possibility of being gay or lesbian.

Identity Tolerance: Occurs when a person comes to accept the probability that he or she is gay or lesbian.

Identity Acceptance: Occurs when a person begins to accept rather than tolerate the idea that they are gay or lesbian, often by connecting with other lesbian and gay people.

Identity Pride: Occurs when a person immerses themselves in the lesbian and gay community and culture and identifies with it. Sometimes rejection of the straight world accompanies this stage.

Identity Synthesis: Occurs when a person develops an internalized lesbian or gay identity and experiences themselves as whole; sexual identity becomes fully integrated into the personality structure.

Cass, V. C. (1979). "Homosexuality Identity Formation: A Theoretical Model." *Journal of Homosexuality 4* (3), 219–235.

tity have been through a lens of pathology. Gender variance has been seen as a problem within normative development, a failure to develop proper gender associations, and people who express nonnormative genders have been labeled mentally ill. A number of researchers, clinicians, and transgender activists have recently challenged this pathologizing of diverse gender expressions. I have proposed a developmental model for examining the coming out process for gender variant people published in my recent book *Transgender Emergence*. Transgender emergence is a six-stage process involving Awareness, Seeking Information/Reaching Out, Disclosure to Significant Others, Exploration—Identity and Self-labeling, Exploration—Transition Issues/Possible Body Modification, and Integration—Acceptance and Posttransition Issues. This stage model allows for a normative healthy developmental process for transgendered and transsexual people. Unlike most stage models, I tried to position transgender emergence as an internal experience occurring within a larger social and familial environment.

Most coming out developmental stage models, as well as most general psychological developmental theories, focus on the intrinsic and intrapsychic processes involved with moving from one stage to another, and therefore they downplay the role, context, and impact of larger systems, families, and communities as people mature through the life cycle.

Families and communities are like ecological niches. One cannot merely eliminate annoying bees without impacting the development of various flowers, which will in turn affect the food supply for the birds. Families in particular are interdependent and entwined together; family therapist Murray Bowen referred to this as the "undifferentiated family ego mass"— expanding on the idea that egos exist *within* individuals to the idea that one unified ego is also shared among the collective members of a family. We are not merely related to one another, but we live within one another. We hear our mother's voices *inside* of our heads; her voice forms our conscience. We often choose partners who resemble our parents—physically or in personality—and we model our parenting on how we were raised, consciously, unconsciously, or reactively ("I will *not* be like they were").

Virginia Satir, a social worker and family therapist, used to demonstrate this theory by asking family members to tie a rope around their waists and would then tie the ropes together in the center, forming a hub with spokes. She would then ask them to imagine what would happen when the phone rings, and of course, the fourteen-year old teenager would sprint toward the phone, dragging the entire family with him or her. Although in the real world, where we are not tied with physical ropes and would therefore not be literally dragged, we are only psychically dragged; perhaps one parent who is waiting for a phone call would feel annoyed, and the other is nervous about when homework will get done or concerned about the influence of the friend who keeps calling. Although the parents may appear to be focused on the television show they are watching, their energy is actually absorbed in their daughter's departure to the hall closet, while she chats with her girlfriend or (horrors of horrors) her boyfriend.

Families have a common emotional life, even though we are individuals with our own experiences. Virtually all human beings live in families (and certainly we were all born into them), and families have a sense of collective history as well as a vision of a shared future. Each stage of the life cycle outlined by the developmental theorists above (as well as the coming out stages outlined) does not happen independently to or within an individual, but numerous life cycles are acting interdependently with one another, creating multiple transactions within a matrix of what has been called the family life cycle. Betty Carter and Monica McGoldrick have created a six-stage model for envisioning the family life cycle that examines the multigenerational context of families—patterns, subsystems, and boundaries—that is embedded within the larger sociopolitical culture and the environment in which individual development takes place. Each stage has certain developmental tasks, key principles, or emotional processes that must be resolved. First I will outline the stages, and then I will address some specific concerns for LGBT people in this model and discuss the particular tasks LGBT people must resolve as we move through normative family-building.

Like all developmental models, the family life cycle is a general overview of a complex interaction of developmental and interpersonal transactions and is adaptable for each person's unique movement through life. These stages are not necessarily linear and are impacted by other sociopolitical and identity issues. Of course, not all people couple, and not all couples have children, not all people have children after they couple, and not everybody leaves home. Some people deal with the disability and death of their parents while they are still small children themselves; some people adopt adolescents and skip the stage of having young children; some partners marry across generational lines so that one is leaving home while the other is dealing with maturational issues. This general overview is not meant to rigidify these stages but allows flexible adaptation within a general model of family development.

How do LGBTs fit into this family life cycle model? Suzanne Slater has questioned this model's relevancy for lesbian families. According to Slater, child-rearing is not the raison d'être for lesbian families, the couple relationship is more central to the development of lesbian identity, and lesbians build extended families through friendship networks. She is certainly correct that many LGBTs have built secure extended families outside of their family of origin *and* without rearing a younger generation. Kath Weston has described the complexity of alternative family structures and the importance of our families of choice in building solid adult identities and communities. It is important to acknowledge that queer identity has developed outside of the hetero-patriarchal process of baby-making as the cen-

The Family Life Cycle

Leaving Home: Single Young Adults: Young people must accept emotional and financial responsibility for themselves, which means they must differentiate themselves from their family of origin, develop intimate peer relationships, and establish themselves in the world of work.

The Joining of Families Through Marriage: The New Couple: Coupling requires commitment to a new relational system, as well as realigning the relationships with the family of origin and friends to include the new spouse.

Families with Young Children: Having children means accepting new members into the system; adjusting the couple system to make space for the children including balancing child-rearing, household tasks, and finances; and realigning with extended family into new roles as parents and grandparents.

Families with Adolescents: Families with teens must increase the flexibility of family boundaries to permit children's independence and grandparents' aging processes, as well as focusing on midlife and career issues.

Launching Children and Moving On: At this stage, families must accept a multitude of exits from and entries into the family system, including developing adult relationships with children, renegotiating the couple dyad, and welcoming children's partners, in-laws, and grandchildren.

Families in Later Life: In the later stages of family life, people must accept the shifting of generational roles, accepting changes in health and death of loved ones, and supporting the middle generation's central role in the family.

Adapted from: Betty Carter and Monica McGoldrick (eds.) (1999). *The Expanded Family Life Cycle: Individual, Family, and Social Perspectives.* Third Edition. Allyn and Bacon/Boston, MA.

tral role in identity formation. This is especially important for women, for whom making babies has been seen as the single most important fulfilling activity of our lives. Indeed, it was long believed that allowing women to vote and work outside of the home would destroy their capacity to not only nurture children but to actually physically reproduce them!

From Slater and Weston's perspective, looking at LGBT families through a family life cycle lens ignores the alternative family structures that we have built to nurture queer people. LGBT people do not learn the values and norms of queer culture (generally) from their families of origin but must seek out community to foster this development. Often left out of the life cycle events and rituals of our families of origin, we have developed alternative rituals and unique language with which to describe our families and identify the relationships that are important to us. Both authors acknowledge the gayby boom, and each devotes one chapter to families with children. However, as much as I share their desire to develop ways of examining queer culture outside of the normative structure of mainstream society and traditional psychological theories, I am left feeling after reading these books that LGBT parenting is some aberration in queer life. I do not think this is their intention, but somehow family-building seems a footnote, an addendum, to what would otherwise be complete life cycle experiences.

Certainly one of the great joys of LGBT life has been the freedom to step outside of the assumptions and pressures of child-rearing. Indeed, one of the greatest values of feminism and queer life in the past four decades has been the ability to actualize a life outside of the defined parameters of our families, our culture, and others' limited descriptions of our identity. It is a long-known queer fact that the heterosexual world likes to borrow our hairstyles and fashion sense. I can only hope that our alternative ideas of family also spread far and wide. I would like to live in a world where no one assumes that all girl children will want to have babies, that all boy children will seek a female mate, and where relationship models include polyfidelity and remaining single as valid life style choices.

However, it is worth questioning whether the child-free lifestyles of the LGBT community have been free choices, or if they have been set by the external limitations of a hetero-patriarchal culture. Perhaps contemplating whether one wants to become a parent is a normative developmental process for all people—men and women—during their reproductive and middle years—a normative developmental process that was stolen, hidden, or barred from most LGBT people until this past decade. I respect the criticisms levied at the family life cycle model for not fully integrating the life cycle processes of single people and people who choose to live child-free, as well as many LGBT people's experiences. However, the LGB coming out models, as well as Slater's lesbian family life cycle, do not seem to fully integrate LGBT parenting as a normative process of LGBT identity development.

Joan Laird also notes the lack of attention that has been paid to the relationship we have with our family of origin as adults. Although the LGBT community has developed our own rituals and culture, we also are a part of the traditional communities around us and share in many social experiences with our extended families of origin. Although these relationships have sometimes been painful—we have felt cut out and cut off, we have felt misunderstood and been judged—most of us still retain contact and intimacy with the families that reared us. Those of us who seek to build families with children often return to those models for ideas, inspiration, and support, as well as critical reevaluation.

LGBT Family Development

For LGBT people who have often felt pushed out of our families and have sometimes been actually physically thrown out of our families, the idea that we are connected to our families through time can be disturbing. For those of us who come from dysfunctional, abusive, violent, and addictive families and have worked hard to distance ourselves from the pain of our childhoods, hearing that our families are still a part of us can be frightening. For adopted people, the questions may arise: Which family are we talking about? Who is my family? LGBT people have rarely grown up in families with other LGBT people. Few LGBT people have queer parents, and in order to become gay, in order to express our gendered and sexual selves, we needed to move away from our families, emerge from their perceptions of who we were. Coming out has often meant, not only coming out *to* our families, but also coming out *of* our families.

Recently I was teaching a social work course, and when we began the section on sexual identity development (conveniently sandwiched between adolescent development and adult coupling), one student said, "My brother is gay. He never told anyone in the family, and I guess I was too stupid to figure it out, even though he lived in San Francisco. Now he is coming home for the holidays for the first time, I'm not sure how we should be with him. It's been twenty-five years." Although my student was focused on how she felt about her brother and how the family would deal with him, I found myself thinking about this near-forty-year-old man who had lived away from family for his entire adult life; it wasn't only that he didn't know his nieces and nephews, but they did not know anything about his life. Presumably he has had lovers, relationships, friends, and social and political commitments. For example, living in San Francisco for the duration of the

AIDS crisis, it is reasonable to assume he has been impacted by the epidemic with questions about his own HIV status, as well as those he's been lovers with, as well as the loss of many friends. What has it been like to live through grief like this without having family to share it with?

Experiences like these are all too common for LGBT people. Many of us, perhaps far too many of us, have moved away from our families, have been rejected by our families, have little in common with our families, are tired of being judged by our families; indeed, we don't really see ourselves as related to our families, except through obligation and duty. Of course, that is not true for everyone. Some of us have always been close to our families, live in the same town, have had our partners warmly welcomed into the fold, and feel very comfortable being ourselves around them. Others of us may not have close relationships with family members but remain in contact, spending holidays and social occasions with them. Commonly, our partners are accepted, but little is said about who they are or what they mean to us. We visit, talk, and everyone is friendly, but as a gay colleague, a therapist, shared with me once, "Ed and I have been together for twenty years, and my mother has never asked me about him, and I've never thought it was important to tell her. I suppose she knows I'm gay, but the word has never been said."

Some of you reading this may find that shocking. Trust me, many others will not be sure why I'm mentioning it; that is, after all, just the way it is in some families. I will take a firm stance and say that it is not healthy for us as LGBT people, nor healthy for our families, to be cut off from our families of origin or to have our identities and experiences silenced within the larger family. That does not mean that every family relationship can be rewarding or meaningful or that every familial bond is worth reconnection. Sometimes the severing of bonds may be necessary; indeed, sometimes it is a historical fact and difficult to repair; but even if one cannot address the actual people who have been cut off, dealing with the ghosts that still live within our families and reside in our psyches is necessary for our own actualization.

Our relationships with our families of origin and the ancestral thread (birth and adoptive) that has brought us to this place in our lives are critical to our very definition of self. We cannot simply sever these connections without causing harm to our entire organism. Surely we can amputate our limbs or eliminate the bee from an ecological niche, but not without consequences to our body or the environment. Like phantom limbs, cutoffs in families form ghostlike aches: the whole system suffers, because individual family members are only parts of a larger system. Certainly this is true for LGBT people without children, but those of us who choose to bring children into our lives are irrevocably thrust into engagement with the legacies of our past (physically or psychologically) as well as reflections about the nascent and enigmatic future revealing itself in our children's eyes.

We all know that we are deeply impacted by our parents, but we often construct our nuclear families as if we were independent players instead of extensions of our ancestors moving through time. We tend to examine our daughter's unfolding from infancy to toddlerhood as separate from the development of our own process being the parents of a newborn to parents of a child. We do not contemplate how our parents' reaction to our becoming parents impacts how we actually parent our children.

LGBT people are bicultural—having one foot in the dominant heteronormative system and the other foot in our unique queer cultures. For some people our involvement in queer cultural life may be minimal, with our lives focused within our families of origins, our work life, and the mainstream community. For others of us, our lives are embedded in queer community networks, with only brief forays into the mainstream community. All of us, however, live with one foot in each of these worlds, balancing the unique issues that are part of LGBT life with the general issues of being human within a human family. This is even more true now that our right to marry and have families has become part of a national public policy debate. LGBT people negotiating normal developmental issues and issues like coming out and/or transitioning sex can impact life's developmental tasks, as well as impact our maturational processes in building families of our own. Utilizing Carter and McGoldrick's model outlined above, each stage is briefly examined for the specific challenges and tasks that an LGBT person might need to address.

Leaving Home: Single Young Adults: Certainly leaving home is a challenging issue for all young adults, but it can be an especially challenging time for LGBT people, as many of us are dealing with issues of developing sexual and gender identity that are in conflict with our parents' dreams. This can impact our ability to differentiate from our family of origin in a healthy manner, or their ability to develop a functional adult-adult relationship with us. It might impact our social networks and our work and career decisions, as well as our ability to establish financial independence. It is no accident that, according to the research, so many LGBT teens and young adults are homeless, suicidal, addicted to substances, and struggling with the basic skills of daily living. Fitting in with mainstream culture, finding LGBT support systems, defining a functioning sense of self, dating, and establishing healthy relationships with our families of origin are formidable tasks for LGBT youth. This often has created a developmental lag, whereby the tasks of adolescence are actually not resolved until well into adulthood.

The Joining of Families through Marriage: The New Couple: Families join through marriage when couples form permanent partnerships, but sadly for many LGBT people, their families do not even know that they are queer and have no wishes or interest in hearing about their lives or meeting their partners. Many transgendered people fear they will never be able to find a partner if they are honest about themselves; many gay people believe that gay relationships by their very nature are transitory. In order to effectively join another family, in-laws need to be welcoming; for couples to effectively become a part of their extended families, both of their families of origin must want them to join. Many LGBT people develop their couple relationship outside of their family's knowledge and experience only rejection and isolation for partnering.

Recently Joseph Nicolosi, the author of the book, *A Parent's Guide to Preventing Homosexuality,* was interviewed on Christian radio. He explicitly said that parents should *not* allow (!) their adult children to bring home a same-sex lover for Thanksgiving. According to Nicolosi, this would send a message to other children that homosexuality is acceptable. Nicolosi said that families should not tell their children they will love them unconditionally, but should strongly iterate their disapproval of homosexuality. He sent this message out three weeks before the Thanksgiving holidays. The damage this kind of message will incur, especially for those of us who come from religiously fundamentalist backgrounds, who had received at least a modicum of respect by being allowed to bring their lovers home, is exponential. It is a normal part of human development to bring one's partner home and for families to expand through coupling.

Any time families are joined by marriage, beliefs about family life are called into question; these issues are complex, especially when marriages cross racial, religious and class lines. All new couples struggle with rules about housekeeping, money, privacy, food choices, and the frequency of contact with their family of origin and friends. For LGBTs, these processes are complicated by differing levels of being out, the public presentation of being a couple, the lack of legal protections for our families, and our in-laws' respect and acknowledgment of our families. For transgendered people, this stage is often accomplished as long as they remain closeted about who they are, or in some cases, who they *were*. Families often explode when the history or revelation of gender identity is exposed.

Families with Young Children: Many people reading this book are in this stage of family development, and adults are focused on the care and tending of newborns. This means that solo parents need to develop adult supports for this huge responsibility, and couples need to adjust their relationship to adapt to new parenting responsibilities. Sometimes families that have rejected LGBT children reach out during this stage; the presence of grandchildren can often have the power to ameliorate old pain and disappointment.

When LGBT people step into this stage, they are stepping out of numerous preconceived messages about who queer people are and should be. The societal image of queer people is that we are childless, and this is true both within and outside of the LGBT community, the gayby boom notwithstanding. To paraphrase psychotherapist Cheryl Munzio, parenthood has never been part of the story we've heard or told ourselves about being lesbian, gay, bisexual, or transgendered. This means that we are, at one and the same time, becoming more queer—a queer gay person, if you will—and less queer, more hetero-normative, average, expectable, a breeder. Often new LGBT parents have a sense of vulnerability, surprised that someone is "letting" them do this, and fear that somehow they will wake up from this wonderful dream. Parents of older children are coping with being out in the school system and dealing with their children's friends and *their* parents' reactions to their family.

Families with Adolescents: The next stage is families with adolescents, which means that in addition to managing one of the most difficult stages of parenting—having your children begin to move out of the nest and encounter real dangers in the outside world—we are also managing our children's developing sexual and gender identities. All children of LGBT people will need to manage their emerging sexualities within the context of having queer parents. They will worry about pleasing us if they are straight; they will feel confused if they suspect they are gay. Although it may be surprising, some gay kids of gay parents fear coming out to the parents, in part because no teen wants to be like their parents. Although it sounds like the script for a good sit-com, it can be a terribly isolating experience for some youth. Of course, being gay doesn't mean they will be the same kind of gay, either. One gay teen was embarrassed by her leather dyke mom; she was a kind of preppy collegiate type.

Sometimes LGBT parents are confused or ashamed when their child is gay, fearful that that society will blame them for their kids' sexuality. Our kids need to manage their relationships to their peers and deal with outing or not outing their parents, which of course outs them, too. Sadly, LGB parents may not be any better skilled at coping with transgender identity in their children than heterosexual parents. In fact, they may feel overly responsible for their child's gender identity, erroneously thinking that their being gay somehow made their kid trans. Certainly they are aware that others will feel that way.

Transgender parents worry about how their gender expressions will impact their children. Most LGBT parents, regardless of their children's sexual or gender identities are more than a bit ambivalent toward their children's budding sexuality. As one mom said, "Smelly teen boys at my house was not what I had in mind when I had a daughter, but I'd rather them be at my house, where I can keep my eye on them, than anywhere else."

Launching Children and Moving On: When children leave home, LGBT parents need to begin to create adult relationships with their children, as well as welcome new partners and in-laws. Generally, by this stage of family life, everyone is fairly well adapted to coping with LGBT issues, but often in-laws are mortified that their child is marrying into a queer family, and issues about weddings and other family gatherings can be very stressful. Sometimes children do not want to invite a parent's partner to their wedding, especially if the parent came out later in life and the child has not really integrated their parent's sexuality into their lives. Often LGBT people who have managed the previous stages have close relationships with their own in-laws as they are aging, and many people have sweet stories to tell of a dying mother or father who told their partner to take care of their child or admitted that they felt the partner had become like their own child. This is, of course, how it should be; in-laws should become family. It is not just couples who partner, but families who join.

Families in Later Life: Finally, as we move into later life, generational roles change. For those of us who have grandchildren, we develop new relationships with our children as they potentially become parents, as well as fulfilling the time-honored role of grandparent. Too often elderly LGBTs have died lonely and severed from family. Let us hope that thirty years into gay liberation, and as we learn to heal familial bonds, that LGBT old people will remain integrated into their families, their life wisdom accepted, and their frailties gently tended. There is also the possibility that, as the baby boomers age, LGBT people who have children will have resources and support for our final stage of life that those who are childless may not have available. We should look carefully at this dynamic over the next few decades, making sure that all LGBTs are cared for in the later years.

Family systems psychological theory teaches us that families struggle most when moving from one developmental stage to another. For LGBT people, these developmental junctures are potentially more problematic because of the additional environmental impact of oppression and stigma. The life cycle tasks can become increasingly complex when we are moving through normative stages of development like settling into being a couple, having new babies or young children at home, or watching children begin to mature and leave the nest, due to the added complications of societal homophobia.

As If That Weren't Enough! The Impact of Other Identities

LGBT people are, of course, not simply queer, but we also have complex identities vis-à-vis our race, ethnicity, culture, religion, class, or disability status. Each of these identities has its own life cycle pathway, and its own process of identity development. Within the dominant white, middle-class, able-bodied, Christian culture, those of us who are minorities, including people of color, people living in poverty, people living with disabilities, or those who are of a nondominant religion, are dealing with additional issues of not only outside oppression but also self-actualization. These identities may be more central to our sense of self and more in need of daily negotiation than our sexual or gender identities. Certainly the interaction of these parts of self are complicated, and in this context we are not merely bicultural but often tricultural and more.

An entire book could easily be written examining the complex interface of issues of race/ethnicity, religion, class, and disability within the context of LGBT family-building and identity development. Too often the research and discussion about LGBT families has described white, middle-class, and primarily lesbian families, leaving the stories of, for example, poor lesbians, black gay dads, bisexual disabled men, and transgendered parents of color untold. Narratives left untold, unpublished, become hidden, and the people unable to tell their stories become invisible, not only to others but often to themselves.

People of color often feel torn between what seems to be a mostly white LGBT community on one hand, and their traditional communities that may or may not be warmly accepting of their identities. Moving back and forth from families that may sustain them if they remain closeted to LGBT social associations that may, consciously or unconsciously, want to whitewash them, people who come from communities of strong cultural and ethnic roots, including many people of color and immigrants, often feel a need to compartmentalize their various identities. Hopefully, these rifts will heal as more communities of color become more accepting of LGBT members and the LGBT community continues to expand in its diversity and visions of inclusion.

For those people with disabilities, the daily tasks of living often take precedence over other issues of identity. Managing pain, staying financially solvent, organizing caregivers, and retaining independence become the primary focus more than issues of sexual orientation, gender expression, or racial and ethnic identities. However, these issues entwine with one another when, for example, a disabled transgendered male depends on the open-mindedness of his caregivers to help him (cross)dress. When people with disabilities are parenting, there are all of the struggles inherent in living with a disability in a world that disparages those who "need," while at the same time being responsible to care for children who also need you.

Throughout this book are woven the intricacies of identity development: LGBT identity within a larger context of family life cycle development, while incorporating the complexities of other identity issues. It is ultimately a shell skimming the surface of very deep waters, and for all the narratives told that have been previously hidden, there are many more stories that will remain invisible. However, below are three stories about family life. The first is a lesbian couple moving into the stage of having young

The Unexpected

I have always wanted to have children, and when I was thirty-eight, with my biological clock ticking, I discussed it with my partner. Rachel was about to turn fifty and had already coparented a child who was at that time almost twenty-five. However, to my surprise and pleasure, knowing how much I wanted this, she agreed. The day our first shipment of semen arrived was the same day that Rachel was diagnosed with breast cancer. We couldn't even look at the tank and put it out on the back porch. I knew that I could not be there for Rachel's cancer treatments if we moved ahead with the insemination, so we postponed getting pregnant. We spent the next year focusing on Rachel's radiation and chemotherapy.

By the time we starting trying again, I was forty. We were told by our doctor that because of my age I had about a 12 percent chance of getting pregnant and carrying a child to term. I did conceive and spent a month on bed rest in my first trimester due to some terrifying bleeding that was the result of a torn membrane. We then discovered that we were carrying twins!

We began looking for a larger house, although the situation at my job was deteriorating. I was six months and one day pregnant when I was told that I would be losing my job in two weeks. The medical director of the agency saw me in the hall later that day, and on hearing I was only six months pregnant, prophetically said, "You look like you're about to deliver!"

I woke up at 4:45 the next morning, still steaming about what happened at work. I felt as if the babies had dropped and got up to go to the bathroom when I suddenly felt a rush of water. I didn't realize at first that my water had broken, and then I called for Rachel in a panic. We called the doctor and were told to meet him at the hospital. I grabbed a dress and threw it on and with a towel between my legs ran out to the car and lay down in the backseat. I began to have contractions in the car. I was glad I couldn't see the speedometer, because I knew Rachel was driving really fast, and I was already scared out of my mind that I was in labor so early.

I got to the hospital, and the doctor arrived a few minutes later. I was 90 percent effaced and 8 cm dilated. They gave me two drugs—one to help the babies' lungs develop and one to stop the labor. It was 7:30 in the morning. The goal was to either stop the labor or to try to go at least twenty-four hours until delivery because the lung medicine was better taken when in the womb and could only be given every twelve hours. The medication to stop the labor made it hard to breathe, which panicked me further. It quickly became clear that I was probably going to deliver at least one baby some time in the twenty-four-hour period, since she was already headed for the birth canal. I was moved by ambulance to another hospital, because the hospital where I wanted to deliver couldn't care for babies born earlier than thirty-two weeks. My doctor did not have privileges at the other hospital, so I was now in medical crisis with a birthing team whom I didn't know. So much for the planned birth experience!

They did not allow Rachel to go into

the ambulance with me. She went to get her car while I waited for the ambulance and came back announcing that she had a flat tire! Someone at the hospital helped her change the tire, and we then remembered that we had a house closing scheduled for 9:30 that morning. Rachel got on the phone, calling friends and family, asking them to pray and also calling our Realtor to let her know we wouldn't be at the walk-through or the closing and arranging for her to be our proxy. Rachel ran home to get the paperwork, and she stepped right into a pile of dog shit waiting for her at the door.

I arrived at the hospital, afraid Rachel would never find me (on a good day, Rachel is not so good with directions) but she came into the room shortly after I got there. At about 9:20, the Realtor arrived and had me signing papers in between contractions while Rachel was frantically searching the hospital for a notary. My room was like a business office, and although they tried to explain to me what I was signing, I really didn't care, I could have signed away my life.

The doctor, the one I just met, remained patient for a while with all the shenanigans but eventually had to remind them this was a high-risk situation, and she needed to do her job. For hours they monitored my contractions. At about 3:00, they realized that they couldn't stop my labor and stopped giving me the drugs to halt it. They moved me into a delivery room. It was much bigger and filled with machines, lights, and people. I saw Rachel's attention being drawn away from me with all the stimulation. I told her to come stand by my head and look directly at me.

I told her she had to just look at me until the babies were born, and she did.

After a short while they told me it was time to push. I had to ask them to teach me how as we hadn't gotten that far in childbirth classes yet. They gave me directions and asked me to hold it for ten seconds. Rachel counted for me loudly and emphatically—she was a great coach. Sophie was born at 4:28 and let out a little cry. I didn't even get to see her. They put her in an isolette in the back of the room. Rachel was still right by my head. I had to tell her to go make sure Sophie was okay. She did and came back, and then it was time to start pushing again. As I was pushing, Sasha's water broke (they were in separate sacs), and she pretty much surfed out at 4:38. She didn't make a sound, and I was worried. I didn't get to see her either.

We were very lucky to not only have an incredible NICU (neonatal intensive care unit), but also to live in a progressive community that was able to recognize a lesbian family. As soon as the girls were born, the nurses slapped a "Mother" bracelet on my arm and a "Father" bracelet on Rachel's, and she was treated like every other dad or mom at the NICU. Her parents were treated as grandparents, and her sister and brother-in-law were acknowledged as the family they are.

I remember the neonatologist coming in to my room a few hours after the harrowing birth experience. At the time I was sure his visit was obligatory. Why else would anyone put me through this at such a time? I can only vaguely remember the content of his speech—it had something to do with all the possible things that can go wrong when babies are born so early. It all sounded so tragically unreal. As he was speaking, I remember my eyes glazing over and his voice turning into a blur as I thought to myself, *I can't deal with this now; they're alive—we'll worry about this later if it happens.* And through the next two and a half months that they spent in the NICU, my focus continued to remain on their survival as there were numerous touch-and-go moments.

I'm not sure if we were in denial during those moments or if there is something about the way the doctors tell you when something is awry that does not really allow for emotional responses. They tell you the facts—for example: "We're having a hard time keeping Sophie's blood pressure up," and then they tell you what they are doing to try to remedy the situation. I don't ever remember them telling us she might not survive. It was only months later, when we were about to bring them home, that we heard the nurses reminiscing about how scared they were that night and how they didn't know if she was going to make it. Maybe we were ignorant—but in some ways, I'm glad we were.

As it was, I would live at the hospital every day from about 8 or 9 A.M. until 10 P.M. or later, and then wake up every night at 3:30 A.M. to call in to the NICU so I could go back to sleep knowing they were still alive. While at the hospital I would pump my breasts so the girls could have breast milk. We were unable to hold them for the first two to three weeks. Our only communication with them was through portholes of their isolettes. We

would sit for hours watching their oximeters; if they went below 90, they were not getting enough oxygen. We became addicted to those machines. There were numerous times they dipped below the magic number, and we would panic. Somehow the nurses could tell when it was real and when it was the machine. We learned to tell, too, but in the beginning, the sound of those alarms would send me into a panic. Friends and family would come to visit us at the hospital and were a great support. The nurses and doctors at the NICU quickly became our second family. I learned that I had to give up my need to know everything, because I just couldn't learn all the medical issues overnight, and I learned to trust their wisdom.

Our girls were so tiny—just over two pounds each and thirteen and a half inches long. Their skin was so thin you could see right through it. They were so fragile and hooked up to so many machines and tubes and IVs. Because of the lights used to treat the jaundice, they had masks covering their eyes. They took preemie-sized diapers and cut them in half at first. Sasha was hooked up to a special type of respirator that did the breathing for her. Sophie was on a regular respirator. After about twenty-four hours, they decided Sophie needed the same kind of respirator as Sasha—except there were none to be had anywhere. They decided to give her Sasha's. What if they both really needed it? How do you decide who gets it? Again, we had to trust. We also got to know two other families at the NICU quite well. They both had babies born at twenty-five to twenty-six weeks and were under two pounds. We shared all their scares and triumphs as well as our own. Over two and a half years later we were reunited when one of the families had her daughter at the same preschool as ours. She, too, has cerebral palsy, like Sophie.

Today our girls are five years old and in kindergarten. I can look back and see what the neonatologist felt obligated to warn me about. I'm glad that my survival instincts told me not to listen. If I had just listened to his words, I would only have known the seemingly tragic possibilities and none of the gifts of who they are. Sophie has spastic diplegia, cerebral palsy, and walks with a walker (although recently she announced after some wild dancing to some '80s disco tunes, "Mommy I don't feel like I have cerebral palsy anymore," and walked for two days without her walker). Sasha has developmental delays, which to her means that she falls more than other kids and she also has a hearing loss for which she will be getting a hearing aid. They both have asthma and have been hospitalized for breathing problems, pneumonia, bronchiolitis, and dehydration for a total of eight times each over the course of three winters. We are known in the ER of our local hospital as well as on the pediatric floor. Some of these hospitalizations were life-threatening. We have both taken off time from our jobs to be in the hospital with them, spending nights on those oh-so-comfortable chairbeds sometimes for eight to ten nights in a month. The hospital staff, upon having one admitted, would start taking bets on how long until the other one arrived; the winner usually

guessed two to three days later. We also see allergists, physiatrists, developmental pediatricians, audiologists and ENTs on a regular basis. Sasha has had CT scans, numerous X rays, RespiGam treatments, an MRI, and an operation when she was less than two months old. We have dealt with PTs OTs, speech therapists, special education teachers, and social workers as well. Thankfully, Rachel and I are social workers and know how to advocate to ensure our children get equal access to their entitlements.

Conversations with Rachel often go like this: "Did Sophie (or Sasha) get her nebbie (nebulizer treatment) yet?" "Did you give them their allergy pills yet?" "Do you know where Sophie's special shoes (braces) are?" This may sound dreary, but to us, it is just our life. Of course there have been times when we were so tired that we fought and blamed each other for our pain and exhaustion. When I have been totally exhausted, I suppose I have given in to moments of "Why me?" but it is never all of (or even a small part of) how I feel about who they are. I have learned how precious and sacred life is. I know how strong people can be, as not only Rachel and I have had to find strength when we thought there was none left, but my children are so strong and tough. The girls teach me to slow down on a daily basis. They are also sooo silly and remind me that life is never so serious that you should forget to sometimes wear your underwear on your head.

We have little time for political action on a large scale anymore. In the days BC (before children) we marched on Washington, New York, and every place else for gay rights, women's right to choose, and many other causes. Now we mostly march to bed at the end of a long day. Our political statement is mostly being visible. I have become aware that my family is very visible, and people recognize us. It's kind of hard to miss adorable twin girls (one with a walker) with two moms as we make our way through the world. Some people when I first meet them have told me that they have been watching the girls grow up as they drive past us on our busy street while we are waiting for the bus out front every morning for the past two and a half years. I have always believed it important to live your life with integrity and some semblance of grace, but I never realized how many people were watching.

Barbara Rio (aka River) and her partner of thireen years, Rachel Donik, are both social workers living in upstate New York with their twin five-year-old daughters, Sophie and Sasha.

children and how the best made plans for when we will have babies and what our families will look like do not always turn out the way we'd imagined. The second story is from a black disabled lesbian mom rearing a son in a racist culture and negotiating the stages of children leaving the nest, and the third is about a Latina lesbian adoptive family negotiating the multifaceted aspects of race, culture, and identity as they embark on the parenting journey.

LGBT people are not exempt from any of the life issues that impact all families: infertility, miscarriages, illness, or leaking roofs. Although most people do not want to think about having a child with a disability, the reality is that anyone who chooses to parent confronts this possibility. Pathos, humor, terror, absurdity, and contentment are all interwoven into the following narrative, as a family learns the value of courage and adaptation when they decide to have a baby.

Premature birth and disabilities can impact the family's development into parenting. Other areas that impact family life cycle development are issues involving race, ethnicity, culture, and class differences, as we try to raise our children in a racist and homophobic world. For LGBT people of color raising children, awareness of the multiple issues impacting their children's lives is never far from their consciousness.

Having regular, ongoing relationships with people from all backgrounds is a vital component in identity development for all of our children living in a multicultural world. It is not enough to simply raise your child without prejudice. Children of color need to develop skills in managing the

Finding Balance

So much has happened in these eighteen years since Patrick's birth. The fact that it has not always been easy is an understatement. I knew about the vulnerability of the black male, especially those being raised in single-parent households. It scared me. My arms of protection would only reach so far. Looking at my baby, I could not bear him becoming a crime or incarceration statistic. I did not want Patrick to become bitter, hating white people or being intimidated by them. I did not want him to resent me because I was lesbian or to feel that my choice to live my truth took anything away from him.

As Patrick shed his boyish size and voice, I noticed the negative responses to him as a black male. There was no doubt about our blackness, but my lesbian identity was not visible. Patrick seemed to take my sexual identity in relative stride. I feel that it was due in part to the immense diversity in our lives. We had friends who were from various religions, nationalities, sexual identities, and family structures. We talked about it. In most cases I allowed him to choose to tell his friends or not. When Patrick was in an elementary school group for children from single-parent households, he decided not to disclose my sexual identity. He said that being the only person of color in the group was enough to deal with. His decision saddened me. He had to choose because of me.

When Patrick was about nine years old, he asked me if I thought that I would ever get married again. When I looked at him with what must have been surprise, he quickly added, "Not to a man of course, to a woman! I just want you to be happy and have somebody because I have to go out into the world myself."

Patrick was eleven when my relationship with Diane became serious. I made it clear to Diane, as my potential partner, that my child and I were a package deal. He developed a relationship with her for himself. Diane and I went to the school open house together. We both sat at Patrick's desk and met other parents. We both went to the school play and took pictures. Many times it was Diane who responded to the calls from the school nurse, since my work schedule was not as flexible as hers. Patrick and I were a part of her family. Within our family, we were in a cocoon, supported and protected; but the outside world was not always so kind. Someone once scratched "Dyke" in the maroon exterior of my car.

When Diane and I ended our relationship, two years into it, I was left once again a single mother. Although my journey as a mother has been a trying one, nothing challenged my parenting like becoming disabled. Although I have only known about my disability for the past six years, its symptoms affected me over the past sixteen. I have multiple sclerosis and sarcoidosis.

Last week as Patrick and I traveled on the handicap bus, a four-foot-eleven-inch tall, slightly built, elderly white woman boarded. Even with her cane, she seemed a bit unsteady. I sat in the front of the bus in my wheelchair, wondering what this woman's reaction would be to my six-foot-tall, 270-pound., Afro and goatee-sporting, hip-hop-clothing-wearing son sitting in the seat with a CD player on his ears, bopping his shoulders. A few moments later, I heard Patrick and the woman laughing and talking. They did so the entire trip. As the woman left the bus at her stop, she put her hand on my shoulder and said to me, "You have a wonderful son. Have a good day." I smiled.

Today, I remind myself that my multiple roles coupled with motherhood get jug-gled right along with all of the everyday is-sues. Clearly this mothering thing is a continuing work. I am committed to being present throughout and feel blessed for the opportunity.

Deborah Williams-Muhammad is a black, lesbian, disabled, single, mother, artist, activist, and entre-preneur, residing in Albany, New York. Her son Patrick is eighteen years old.

reality of racism in their lives, as well as having the opportunity to be in so-cial environments that assist them in adjusting to living a bicultural life. White children need to understand racism, the privileges that they have simply because they were born white, as well as developing skills to unlearn racism so they effectively address issues that may come up in the school yard. For transracially adopted children, moving among people that share their racial heritage with ease is as important as the security they have at home. These parts of self must become integrated, or they may have diffi-culty feeling comfortable in their bodies.

For LGBT people involved in interracial or cross-ethnic relationships, white LGBT people raising children of color, and those of us living in mul-tiracial families, open conversation about racial differences and their polit-ical meaning is essential to healthy development. Children definitely notice differences and recognize the makeup of your family and social circles. They are aware of whether you have friends of other races, or whether you have judgments of people from other class backgrounds. They are con-scious of who you find attractive, when you flinch in public places, and which neighborhoods you avoid driving through.

Race and racism are complex subjects, and for families that are cross-ing so many social rules, there is often a sensitivity or defensiveness toward the questions from outsiders. Sometimes the complexities of our children's lives are misinterpreted because we are under constant scrutiny from oth-ers. The adopted Asian child who hates Asian food or the black child who hates cornrows may be expressing deep cultural conflicts or might merely be expressing personal tastes, or like all children, might simply be express-

The Complexity of Identity
BY JUANA MARÍA RODRÍGUEZ, PH.D.

My son is Latino, as am I. In the parlance of the adoption community, this is not a transracial adoption. Yet, my son's birth mother is from Oaxaca, Mexico, and is of Mayan descent. I was born in Cuba, and my partner is from Puerto Rico. Like most Caribbean people we have both African and Spanish ancestry, yet in Latin America we would both be considered white, unlike my son, who whether he is here or there, will invariably be classified as Indio, or Indian. These three countries share the same colonial language, Spanish, but the differences in history, culture, politics, music, food, and folklore are vast, differences that in many ways remain invisible to dominant Anglo society.

In the United States, the adoption of Native American children falls under the Indian Child Welfare Act, which grants tribes jurisdiction over the placement of any child custody proceeding involving an Indian child. My son is a North American Indian, yet because his tribal affiliations are south of the U.S. border, his ethnic status in the U.S. is Hispanic, not Native American.

But the significance of racial categories to the discourse of adoption is about more than semantics; oftentimes it is about money, and always it is about racial politics. Many agencies working in domestic adoption charge higher fees for the placement of children that are white, Latino, or Asian, in other words *not* African-American. Here Latino, Asian, and white fall under the same fee structure. Those wishing to adopt African-American children, deemed the hardest to place, are given financial incentives to do so. Some white prospective parents express the feeling that Latinos and Asians, whether adopted domestically or internationally, are more easily assimilated than African-Americans into white families and communities. In my own conversations with adoption agency administrators I have tried to sort out how they come to determine what racial category children fall into, what fee structure would an Afro-Cuban or Afro-Dominican child fall under? What about children that are of mixed race? Does the one-drop rule apply? (In fact it does.) What do these arcane and archaic systems of categorization tell us about how we as a society continue to view race, and how we assign value to children? How do they complicate how we might categorize transracial adoption?

As the discourse of adoption enters the public sphere, the importance of race, and the ways it is used to modify constructions of gender, become more understated and insidious. The media often like to depict battles between birth mothers and adoptive mothers; invariably the adoptive mother is presented as white, economically privileged, and articulate, while the birth mother is most often of color, poor, and undereducated. Good mother vs. bad mother, a battle mediated by lawyers, judges, and public opinion that pits women against women. These two worlds, and the cultures they often represent, are seen as separate and unequal, and usually it is a judge who must step in to decide who is the real mother, because under the logic of hetero-normativity, there can only be one "real" mother.

My experience with adoption has been quite different. Ours is an open adoption, which means his birth mother selected us, a Latina lesbian family, to raise her son. It also means that, even though my partner and I will have sole legal guardianship and custody, our son and his birth mother will have access to each other through pictures, letters, and visits. Although we are all Latinas, the realities of our son's birth mom are quite different from our own; she is nineteen, has been living and working illegally in the United States for four years, and earns $4 an hour cleaning hotel rooms. I am forty-three and work as a college professor. My partner and I own our own home. Although neither of us was born in this country, we are both U.S. citizens. We are out queers. The differences and similarities between our political, economic, and family circumstances can only be understood within the framework of transnational migration patterns, U.S. labor practices, Latin American sexual politics, international trade agreements like NAFTA, and the political and social histories of our countries of origin.

One of the questions I get most frequently when I tell people that my son is adopted is, "Where is he from?" the assumption being that because he is brown, he is foreign. The reality is that my son was born in Atlantic City, New Jersey. Today, Latinos are 12.5 percent of the U.S. population and growing (the youthfulness of this population also means that it is growing at a much faster rate than the rest of the population). My son will be part of this new generation of U.S. born Latinos, raised in a multicultural, multiracial, multiethnic household, community, and nation. He will also know that in addition to being Latino, he is also Oaxacan. That means that in addition to teaching him about the rich cultural traditions of our Caribbean island cultures, and my own spanglisized experiences of coming of age in the United States, I also get to enrich my life by learning, teaching, and sharing as much as I can about his ancestral traditions and culture. Whatever I think I already know about Mexican, Oaxacan, and Mayan culture will never be quite enough, and ultimately what I can provide him is not a re-creation of his authentic past, but the knowledge to create a meaningful self-identity that will allow for all the complications and contradictions of his life: Mayan, Cuban, Foreign, Oaxacan, American, Mexican, Boricua, Native, Queer, Adopted.

Juana María Rodríguez, Ph.D., and partner Frances Grau Brull have been together six years, and are parents of Mateo Alexis Grau Rodríguez, in Philadelphia, Pennsylvania.

ing a passing idea that might fluctuate like the weather. But, within a racist culture, our children's actions are dissected for meaning, and parents are torn between protecting children from overt racism on one hand and developing a solid identity on the other.

Questions of race and identity development are not only questions for white parents raising children of color, but for all parents raising children in a multicultural world, and certainly all parents adopting children. The newborn baby sleeping in his crib carries his ethnic heritage, the legacy of his birth family. Even if he is years away from understanding the meaning of color, or blood, or kin, his parents must water and tend carefully the branches of their grafted family trees.

As LGBT people embrace parenting in larger numbers and are building viable families, we are able to weave together many threads of experience. We can incorporate all we've learned building safe alternative extended networks within LGBT communities that embrace lovers, ex-lovers, and friends in permanent long-term families. We can include our families of origin, extending intergenerationally to grandparents and outward to cousins and extended members of our families, honoring cultural, ethnic, and familiar rituals that have history. And we can create new rituals that fully embrace all we are. Rearing children means we are continuing our ancestors' passage through time; we are building a future where LGBT people are a visible part of the family tree as progenitors of the next generation.

• • •

CHAPTER SIX

Couples, Families,
and Support Systems

AS THE NOW popular African proverb reminds us, "It takes a village to raise a child," and although this adage has become almost cliché at this point, the truth is that it really does take a village to raise a child, not to mention raising more than one child. For lesbian and gay prospective parents, this aphorism awakens the questions: Where is my village? Who will support me in this endeavor? Most of us do not live in villages but live in small—or large—cities, rural areas, or in the vast expanse of suburbia. LGBT people have worked hard to build viable communities, cyber villages, and alternative family structures, sometimes to replace families that rejected or abandoned us, and sometimes just because it feels good.

Many of us have come to see the limitations of our own utopian ideals: families that we've created, communities that we nurtured, often fall prey to turmoil, conflict, political disagreements, or simply move on. Coping with chronic or terminal illness; dealing with job loss, financial devastation, and poverty; or ending a long-term relationship can sometimes leave us alone, feeling like our village has become a proverbial ghost town. There are few of us who by the time we hit adulthood are not smarting from the sting of lost love, disappointment in friendships, and the dissolution of LGBT communities where we thought we had built a safe and solid foundation. Some of us, of course, never had a queer community, either because we have lived too far from city centers that have nurtured these communities, or because we simply haven't yet connected with them. Some of us were always leery of queer communities, perhaps due to our own internalized homophobia, or perhaps we had insight into the potential disappointment that might follow.

Nonetheless, by the time most of us consider having children, we are painfully aware of how much we need to rely on others and the limitations of our own support systems. Despite our commitments and pronouncements to stay together till death do us part, we would have to be wearing blinders to not see how frequently families break apart—queer and straight. Although we might have friends who are excited about our insemination attempts, or who may root for us during home studies, few of us have friends who will financially support us so that we can stay at home with our children or who will assist us in paying adoption costs. Many people may be thrilled we are having children and may love the actual children themselves, but the daily task of feeding, bathing, toenail clipping (more time consuming than you might imagine), diaper replenishment and the subsequent refuse removal, will fall to the parent or parents, while village life continues on outside your front door.

Some of you who are reading this are saying, "Well, what do you expect? That's how it is, that's always how it's been, that's how my mom and dad did it." Perhaps you are even feeling that you would want it no other way; you don't want a village to raise your children, you really want to do it within the confines and comfort of nuclear family life. Others of you who are reading this are shaking your heads. "That may be true for you, but I have really good friends, a mom who is always there for me, and my kid has, or will have, tons of aunts and uncles and extended family. I can't imagine doing this alone."

Of course there will be a spectrum of ways that we envision what parenting will be like for us, as well as a continuum of village support that each of us finds available, desires to utilize, or is able to maintain. Within this spectrum it is important to be aware that you will often need more help than you ever dreamed of, and it will often not be available to you. I know that this sounds depressing, but it is the experience of parents everywhere, perhaps not all the time, but over the years of parenting, both of these truths usually come home to roost at some point.

Before I was a mom, I had once gotten very ill. I was running a high fever, had lost my voice completely, and was sleeping twenty out of twenty-four hours a day, barely able to pee the dog. Since I was single and without a person who thought it was their job to take care of me, I made about twenty phone calls to find someone who could pick up some medication for me at the pharmacy. I discovered that dear friends had other priorities—jobs to attend to, lovers and children that needed rides—and although many offered to do it, by the time I actually had the medicine in hand it had been nearly twenty-four lonely and sick hours. It was a frightening experience, since I had been inseminating at home for many months and planning on being a single parent. The limitations of my village became abundantly clear.

I called a friend of mine, a heterosexual woman who had raised four children; she was not someone who lived in, or particularly believed in, the idea of community; she'd raised her kids mostly on her own. I said, "What do you do when you have a little one around, and you are as sick as I am?" She laughed. "Well, you do the best you can. You lower your expectations way past any place you ever thought you would. You survive." She then told me of the time she was sick, her husband was out of town, and she was home with a four-year-old and a two-year-old. She had fallen asleep on the couch, in a deep delirium type of sleep, and woke up suddenly, terrified. Where were the babies? She found them in front of the television, eating peanut butter out of the jar with their fingers. They must have climbed up on a chair and into the kitchen cupboard to get the jar of peanut butter, and then figured out how to open it. The television, living room rug, and their hair were covered in peanut butter. When she walked into the room, they looked up casually and said, "Can you get the jelly?" She said it was not the way she usually served lunch, and she was damn glad all the chemicals were safely baby-proofed. Sometimes you just do the best you can.

Support comes in many ways that we least expect it. Although the bulk of this chapter is about support through partners, friends, family, and groups designed to be supportive, sometimes we find support from the most unlikely sources.

As we talked about in the last chapter, the realities of parenting are not

Being Neighborly

Annabelle was five days old when she came to live with my partner and me in our home on a small farm in Tennessee. Our little girl is two now, and every moment with her has been a wonderful gift. My partner, Suzanne, and I lived together for seven years before we adopted our daughter. There is a ten-year difference in our ages; I was forty-three and Suzanne was thirty-three when Annabelle arrived. We had a difficult time making a decision about having a child, because Suzanne hadn't been around small children very much. Finally, I just did it; fortunately, Suzanne turned out to feel just as grateful for the outcome.

Pete lived across from our barn, and helped build it when he was a boy (long enough in the past that we needed to replace a few boards and windows due to the passage of time). He and I knew each other, but not well, before Annabelle arrived. As we were anticipating our daughter's birth, we tried to prepare Pete and other friends for her arrival. Once, my father asked whether Pete was supportive of our plans, and of course I said that he was. My father said, "Are you sure Pete knows your daughter is going to be black?" I assured him that Pete knew. "You had better remind him; you can't afford to get sideways with Pete, because he's mighty good to you!" Of course, I reminded Pete, who said color "don't make no difference from one person to the next."

Pete offered to feed our livestock and dogs while I traveled up North to pick up the baby. On our first morning back, Pete was at my front door at 5:00 A.M. with all the eggs he'd gathered while I was gone,

and with arms open wide to welcome our little child. Even though Pete had not attended church in about six decades (he's in his eighties), he did attend Annabelle's baptism at the Episcopal church.

Pete and Annabelle seem to have little in common: Annabelle is African-American, and without having been adopted might have grown up in inner-city Chicago. Pete is Caucasian (as are Suzanne and I). He is also a veteran, a trapper, an herbalist, a marksman, and an Appalachian. From that first morning until our family moved to the city a few months ago, Pete continued to care for our animals every day. He came by before dawn each morning to give Annabelle her breakfast, and he carried her down the steps while I packed the car with briefcase and baby bag. Annabelle went from that first sweet smile at Pete, over the top of the bottle he was feeding her, to jumping up and down exclaiming "Pete! Pete!" when he appeared on the front porch in the morning.

We really want Annabelle and any future children of color in our family to have opportunities to learn about their own ethnic heritage, and that is much easier to accomplish in a larger city, deeper in the South, so we decided to move to Alabama. Now that we live in the city, Annabelle is no longer the only child of color in her day care center; in fact, Caucasian children are the minority in her class. Also, like most major Southern cities, our new home has a significant percentage of people of color in leadership roles: one of the positive aspects of living here. These factors were highly influential in our decision to move here.

To be fair, though, I must admit that I have never noticed anyone being overtly racist or homophobic toward my family, regardless of whether we lived in a rural or urban area. Suzanne and I realize that the issues surrounding our family are complex, however. To that end, we have made a point to educate ourselves as much as possible through books, friendships, the Internet, and as many resources as we can find. Just as we did before moving, we try to keep Annabelle safe, and we try to surround ourselves with accepting and supportive friends of all races.

Back in Tennessee, we would hear that Pete had been talking about us around town: "That baby has the best two mothers in the state of Tennessee!" Pete cared for our family in a way that most people might only imagine a neighbor would do. His love and loyalty defied stereotypes. I am reminded, with gratitude, of the opportunity we have to defy others' stereotypes, as well. We hope to take Annabelle back to Chicago to bring home a baby brother or sister as soon as we can.

Cornelia Welch Watson, partner to Suzanne, is mother to Annabelle, age two, in Huntsville, Alabama.

always the way you envision them or want them to be. The best laid plans for how couples will share the housework, or how Grandma will do day care, or how a partner will stay home with the children, can quickly disintegrate when someone becomes ill and unable to work. For many LGBT people who are starting families, the first line of support is their couple relationship itself. For those who are building two-parent families, the establishment of a strong, healthy couple foundation is the key to the strength of the family.

Couples: Building a Family Together

Same-sex parents who choose to have children together are often without models for how to successfully parent together. The models that we have been raised with of heterosexual life may not be relevant to the families we are creating, or for those of us who are comfortable with that model, it may be challenging to reconfigure it within an alternative family structure.

Research has consistently shown that lesbians and gay men tend to model their couple relationships on a more egalitarian model then heterosexual couples have traditionally done. After all, LGBT people can rarely just follow the prescribed gender roles of their heterosexual parents. In the families we were raised in, Dad may have taken out the garbage and Mom may have baked all the birthday cakes, but in LGBT homes, even if we wanted to merely be on autopilot regarding role divisions, exactly who is the dad who should take out the garbage and what distinguishes one mom's role from the other mom's role? Generally speaking, LGBT couples have to work out the details of their division of labor, their roles and choices, with some kind of direct communication and consciousness about how they want to run their lives.

For some couples, these issues are simple and clear. Household tasks are divided by who likes to do certain things, who is good at doing other things, and it seems to work out easily: Mary does the cooking and cleaning; Louise does the bills and outside chores. In other families, the couple works hard to share all of the tasks, even if one is better at certain tasks or enjoys them more: Bob cooks on Monday, Wednesday, and Saturday; Mike cooks on Tuesday, Thursday, and Sunday, and they eat out on Friday evenings, both of them realizing that Monday, Wednesday, and Saturday meals are not of the same quality as Tuesday, Thursday, and Sunday meals. In some families, roles are easily divided up but are also easily negotiated and reevaluated; for other couples, roles can be firm and inflexible, i.e., Janet is responsible for household tasks, and Rae is responsible for car maintenance. For some, butch/femme couple roles tend to be divided in a traditional manner, with the butch handling more of the Daddy tasks, and the femme handling more of the Mommy tasks. This might mean that the butch works outside of the home for money, while the femme is a stay-at-home mom. However, in my experience, even if the roles are clearly divided on gender lines, this is rarely rigid, and there are many areas of functional overlap in terms of household and parenting tasks.

Sometimes there is resistance by one partner about doing certain tasks, due to social expectations or personal experiences. Although Lucy loves to cook and take care of the home, after twenty years in a heterosexual marriage where she was expected to do these tasks, she insists on having Annemarie share them. For Juan, who was born a female, he takes tremendous pride in doing traditional male tasks and is reluctant to share them with his boyfriend Mike; Juan is very resistant to doing traditional female tasks, but luckily, Mike does not mind.

Research has also shown that maintaining egalitarian divisions of labor is often more of an ideal than a reality, for both heterosexual and LGBT couples, once children arrive, although research has also shown that lesbians are doing a better job than heterosexual couples at maintaining peer marriages. All families struggle with issues of the division of household labor, as well as employment and child care responsibilities. The simple truth is that it is very easy to fall back on traditional marriage and family patterns once children arrive. For that matter, it is damn hard to *not* fall back into those patterns. Recent research shows that nearly a quarter of gay male couples who are parenting have one parent who is a stay-at-home dad, and the other who works to support the family. Maybe Father really does know best?

Many couples enter into parenting with a strong commitment to be equal parents, peers in all the decisions and daily tasks, and many couples have been able to succeed at this goal. However, the realities of daily parenting often mean that one parent is staying at home with a newborn infant, and/or is the only parent breast-feeding, and/or is the one who is available for pickup and drop-off to day care, and therefore can become the preferred parent (from the child's perspective), the more skilled parent, or simply the more available parent. The other parent may find himself feeling jealous of their bonding, left out of a love affair between his partner and their child, and depending on the dynamic between the couple, it is easy for one parent to become viewed as the competent one, while the other one takes the role of the traditional father—a support and baby-sitter, rather than a full-time parent. This pattern can become even more complex if the full-time parent is also the biological parent or the only legal adoptive parent, as the other parent's status is continually questioned by the outside world.

Many lesbian couples in particular seem to minimize the differences between biological and nonbiological parents. For some couples this may indeed be an accurate perception of how they see themselves—as equal, peer parents, where the role of biology is minimally relevant to their daily lives. One couple refuses to answer any questions regarding which one of them birthed the children to purposely avoid any focus from outsiders. Another woman with five adopted and two birth children answers the question, "Which ones are yours?" (the language people often use when they mean which ones did you birth) by scratching her head and looking at her multiethnic band of kids and saying, "I can't remember." Minimizing the importance of biological heritage can be an important step in understanding how little biology has to do with parental love or family ties.

Although couples often desire to minimize the importance of biology as part of their way to foster a sense of equal parentage, the role of biology in parenting has a long social history, and few of us are able to completely sever the importance of this role or identity. Some might argue that perhaps it shouldn't be severed at all. Certainly, biological parentage raises important questions about the difference between donors and fathers, as well as issues in open and closed adoptions. But it also raises questions about power dynamics between biological parents and nonbiological parents, especially in states where second-parent adoptions are not allowed.

Although some couples hold it as an ideal to minimize the differences between the biological parent and the nonbiological parent, these differences can sometimes become pronounced. In some families it becomes a taboo subject to acknowledge differences. Recognizing the power differential between parents where one is legally recognized as a parent, either through biology or adoptive status, and the other parent who is a legal nonentity, is the first step to resolving them. There are some differences that are more clear-cut, like breast-feeding and the reality and intimacy of pregnancy between mother and child.

Maria says:

> I found myself so jealous when Lisa was breast-feeding. It was a bond I didn't have, couldn't have, with my child. Lisa was able to satisfy her, take care of her, in a way I was unable to do. Their relationship became warm and intimate, and by the time I came home from work, the baby was already falling asleep for the night. When I tried to talk with Lisa, she said I was being silly, but she couldn't really understand what I felt like as the nonbiological parent trying to bond with my child.

Maria was, of course, not being silly but was expressing her frustration trying to be parent to a child she did not birth, was not biologically related to, and was not home to bond with five days a week. Perhaps this was in her head, perhaps this was the nature of being a parent who worked out of the home, perhaps there were subtle things that Lisa did that imparted a message that she was not an equal parent but a number-two parent. Although some nonbiological parents do not ever feel this sense of difference, many do, and it is important to break down the taboo about discussing this within your family. Talking about it will not create divisions that are not already there but will acknowledge those that already exist. If couples acknowledge these issues, they will be less defensive and more communicative and therefore more able to actually address the issues; conscious decision making about how to balance these differences takes commitment, awareness, and respect.

It is interesting to note that when couples break up, it is commonly the biological (or legal) parent who retains physical custody of the child/ren. This seems to be true even in planned LGBT families, where the intention was always to coparent and be equal parents. This seems to be less often true when second-parent adoptions have been completed (in the states, provinces, and countries that allow this), although we do not yet have any studies researching this phenomenon. Although we try to minimize the impact of not having legal custody of our children, it can erode our own sense of entitlement, and during the chaos and disillusionment of divorce and custody battles, biological and legal parenthood suddenly becomes a means to wield power. I suspect that sometimes this is because the biological element was always more important to the birth mother than she was willing or able to acknowledge, although of course she might simply be wielding her power to ensure legal custody.

We need to begin to address these issues in our relationships, to ask serious questions about the nature of our family, the roles of family members, and the expectations we each have of one another. It is easy to make assumptions about what it means to share parenting, or be financially dependent on a spouse while one is a stay-at-home parent, but it is best to examine these issues in depth. What does it mean to coparent, to be equal parents? In some lesbian custody cases, the biological mother has tried to win sole custody saying she didn't know that having a second-parent adoption would mean that she lost the privilege of being able to take her child in the event of a breakup. Many in the community have scoffed at this. How could she not know what adoption meant? Underlying the legal battles here are psychological issues. Many biological mothers (and some fathers) have a sense of ownership toward their progeny; it may not be politically correct to admit this, but pretending that one doesn't feel this way will not eliminate the feelings or the dynamics that potentially evolve from that.

There is less harm done to children by acknowledging different levels of parenting responsibilities than to pretend things are equal, only to realize later how profound the differences really are. One family formed when one mom had two teenagers; the other woman wanted to get pregnant and start a family. After long negotiations, they decided that they would have the baby, but that the biological mother would be the primary parent. She would do the midnight feedings, the PTA meetings, and deal with the laundry and mess. The other parent became a dear friend, an aunt of sorts, though she ended up doing a bit more laundry and cuddling than she had planned (after all, she fell in love with her partner's daughter), but was never a full-time parent. In some ways, this is no different from the division of labor that many heterosexual couples have, although heterosexual couples would still identify themselves as parents, even if the mother did most of the work, physically and emotionally. In this family, they discussed and planned for a new model and language that would work for their family.

When one member of a couple is more committed or interested in parenting, people often push the couple to go ahead, assuming that once the child is here, the more reluctant member will fall so in love that they will want to be a full-time parent. This is a dangerous assumption to make for the birth mother, who may unexpectedly find herself functioning as a single parent. Although roles can and do change throughout the life cycle of any family, establishing parenting commitments and defining the language and roles of the parents is important to the creation of a stable family unit.

The bottom line is that there is no blueprint for how parenting roles should be. Some couples do parent equally (and apparently according to the research, many lesbian couples seem to function well with a peer parenting system). Other couples have distinct differences in their roles. Yet other couples start out with assumptions about the way they want it to be but find that their plans are not turning out the way they wanted. One mother wanted to continue her high-powered professional job following the birth of her daughter, and after months of exhaustion and depression, realized she wanted to be a stay-at-home mother. Her partner was furious, since her lover's income was their mainstay, and now the burden of the finances would be falling on her head. Having the baby not only changed every aspect of their lives but impacted their financial status in dramatic and unexpected ways.

Sometimes women who are stay-at-home moms feel invisible. They are not seen as productive members of society, and perhaps their lover is unable to comprehend how hard the work is staying home with little babies and maintaining a relatively clean house. As the one making the milk, she may feel less important than the one making the money. It is very important for couples who have divided up their lives into stay-at-home parents and working-out-of-the-house parents, that both jobs are valued and appreciated. It is also important to continue evaluating the roles you chose. It may have seemed like a wonderful idea to stay home alone with the triplets, but the reality of it may be more than you imagined. Day care, or a mother's helper, may be a better solution.

Each of us is different, and our relationships with our children will reflect these differences. We may bond quickly with one child and not another. We may feel jealous of how our partner is with the baby, wanting to have that connectedness to the baby, or perhaps just wishing our partner was that connected with us. You may find that your spouse is not as careful as you are about baby-proofing, or more committed to home schooling than you'd ever imagined. As you start to parent together, there will be much you will continue to learn about one another. Assume that you will find differences in your opinions and parenting styles; it will be easier to accept when you do.

Due to biased and homophobic laws, many of us live in families where the legal rights of both parents are not honored. In blended families, where a spouse was formerly heterosexually married, there may be an ex-wife or ex-husband that has legal custody, rendering the stepparent a legal nonentity. The importance of legal recognition of our families will be the topic of the next chapter, but it is important to acknowledge here that the first step in protecting our families is to develop honest and clear communication with our partner regarding our intentions in coparenting and about emotions that arise during parenting that may challenge our intentions.

Despite good intentions, sometimes relationship dynamics change. In one family, the stay-at-home parent became essentially a single parent, which was acknowledged by both partners. When the relationship split up, the coparent retained contact, but no custody, of the children. The change in legal status reflected what was the actual reality of their relationship, despite their intentions at the beginning of the relationship. In other situations, however, if both parents do not have legal rights, the legal parent can render the nonlegal parent invisible and disrupt a parenting relationship, *regardless* of the actual relationship between parent and child. In this situation, the legal parent is using the homophobic court system to pull rank over her partner. In some of these situations, if the legal parent had been able to admit to her sense of exclusive rights to the child in the beginning of the parenting process—i.e., not just state coparenting intentions, but honestly admitted her resistance to sharing equal parental status—the nonlegal parent could have entered into the relationship more knowledgeable about potential outcomes. It is also true that acknowledging and discussing these issues could have potentially shifted the sense of entitlement for the legal parent. Biological and legal parents will not be able to do the psychological work they need to do to truly share parenting—particularly in jurisdictions without legal protections—unless it becomes acceptable for couples to discuss these issues and acknowledge potential differences. Couples enter parenting agreements assuming that they have equal status, defiant that the courts do not recognize them, defensive that anyone would dare see a same-sex couple as anything less than any other married couple. Yet legal differences and biological differences are real, and to ignore how these can impact the psychology of parenting is to ignore the proverbial elephant in the living room.

The first step in building a support system for couples who are parenting together is to create an honest, strong communication for the couple. Parenting will bring with it many difficult issues that are hard to discuss; roles, expectations, assumptions, and division of labor are areas that all families need to address. LGBT families have the ability to address them consciously, so we can create family models that work for us, not against us.

Going Solo: With a Little Help from My Friends

The one difference between single parents and those who have children in a committed couple relationship is that single people absolutely *know* that they need support in order to thrive as parents. Their support system might include their parents or siblings, close friends, or a tightly woven network of day care providers, baby-sitters, and nannies. Sometimes single parents help support one another, sharing child care and even eating together one night a week. Those who plan to become single parents are, by and large, well-educated, somewhat financially secure, independent people who are not waiting for Mr. or Ms. Right. Perhaps they would prefer to be in a successful, long-term relationship in which to begin their family, but they have clearly made the decision that they are not willing to wait for a partner to be a parent. Becoming a single parent by choice can give you plenty of opportunity to make arrangements for the care of your child, although like all parents find out, it doesn't take much to upset the applecart. It is not a decision for the faint of heart, and many choose to forgo parenting entirely, because the thought of single parenting is simply too frightening.

Single parents are clear about what they want: they want a baby (or perhaps a child). They must figure out how to expand their family (pregnancy, surrogacy, adoption), and how to support the child (or children) solely on their own resources. This means having a work environment that is supportive to parents, having a stable income, and being willing to walk through the medical and/or social work appointments on their own. In a world where babies are thought to enter the world through couple relationships, going it alone, especially as an out LGBT person, can be challenging.

One of the paradoxes of single queer parenting is the invisibility. When completing an international adoption home study, you can simply say, "Yes, I'm single," and completely avoid the whole red flag of homosexuality and homophobia. Although some countries are prejudicial toward single people (particularly single males), all countries are biased toward LGBT people. Being single leaves you many parenting options available, without the fear of lying that would mean committing perjury and potentially disrupt your adoption. Invisibility can limit the direct, hostile affects of homophobia and transphobia, and can make blending into mainstream culture—day care settings, pediatrician's waiting rooms—easier. This is no little thing, since being a visible queer parent can sometimes make life's little tasks a formidable event.

Invisibility is a double-edged sword, of course. First of all, LGBT people with children often don't recognize that you are family, and they don't understand when you are waving at them and smiling in a ridiculous manner, that you are trying to connect. This can be isolating, particularly when you have no one to share the daily ups and downs of parenting. Single parenting means that you are the one person making all the decisions

---

Like a Fish Out of Water

I am a single lesbian, although I have been at various times in a committed relationship with a man (when my daughters were born), and in a committed relationship with another woman that recently ended. In general, I have not felt very welcomed or supported in the local LGB community at any time. I don't know how much of this is just me, and how much is because I don't fit the mold very well. I think of the mold as a lesbian in a relationship with another lesbian who decide to have kids together. My kids are older, being eleven and thirteen, than the current crop of kids with LGB parents here in town. Also, parents with kids older than eight just might not feel welcome. Maybe this has a lot to do with the fact that this is a small LGB community. I'm not aware of any other single lesbian moms who are active in our local LGB parenting group, I know of some single lesbian moms here in town, but they aren't part of the parenting group. I suspect pretty much due to the fact that they feel like fish out of water, being the odd one out. This can turn into a vicious cycle.

Laura, mom to Heather, thirteen, and Rachel, eleven, lives in Southern California.

---

regarding your child's care, and are the one ultimately responsible—when you are sick, tired, and emotionally distraught. Many single parents experience bouts of feeling overwhelmed with managing a work life and a child, without any help with household chores, finances, and of course, the endless needs of children. More importantly, there is generally no one else who loves your child with the same care and intensity, and few people are as interested as you are in every coo the baby makes, or every drawing the four-year-old brings home. Some single parents complain that it is harder not having anyone to share the joy with than the heartache. Single parents can sometimes feel disconnected from the wider LGBT parenting community, which may be perceived as a coupled community.

Sometimes parents are thrust into single parenthood due to the untimely death of a spouse, a divorce, or abandonment. Having to rearrange your life, develop child care networks and support systems, while still managing housework, finances, and job responsibilities, in addition to the grief, loss, and anger you are experiencing over the changes in your life, is overwhelming. Not just your own grief, loss, and anger, of course, but the child's. Sometimes it is difficult to find the support you need.

Single parenting is no longer an unusual or aberrant lifestyle. Since 1970, the number of children living in a single-parent family has doubled.

In fact, statistics from 1992 indicate that single-parent families represent 30 percent of U.S. households. Based on current trends, there are predictions that upwards of 70 percent of children born since 1980 will spend some time living in a single-parent home before their eighteenth birthday. If you choose to become a single parent, you will not be alone. If you wind up becoming a single parent, there are others who have gone before you. Even if you are coparenting with an ex, chances are that when the children are with you, you are still basically functioning as a single parent.

Single parents struggle with numerous issues, including being the sole financial support of the family, having very little time for one's self, and still needing to meet their own needs for intimacy and sexuality. Dating can be a challenging obstacle for those who are single parents. Having children can be a turnoff for some potential dates, as well as a major turn-on for others, who may long to become intimate very quickly in order to be a part of their romanticized view of home and hearth. Additionally, dating means managing child care arrangements as well as others' judgments of you for daring to have a social and sexual life, particularly toward a new parent who is single.

Decisions also need to be made regarding how much exposure your children will have to the people you are dating. Will you allow a lover to sleep over? How many dating partners is it acceptable to have your child witness? Even if you are comfortable having many lovers, how do you manage how your child explains that in a public school setting? An innocent child's remarks can bring social services to your door in a flash, and although having more than one same-sex partner may be a minor issue in your mind, it might represent perversity and depravity to those who have the power to disrupt your family forever.

We also need to be aware of our children's desire to have a normal-appearing home. What is to you a casual dating relationship may represent hope for a two-parent family for them. How we share our dating and sexuality with our children also impacts how they see intimacy and their own emerging sexual selves. Whatever values we impart to them are always being assessed and compared to the images of heterosexual marriages reflected in the media and their classrooms. Children are sometimes zealous in accepting new lovers as "Daddy," long before you might be considering elevating a date to a spouse. Children can also, conversely, be intolerant, jealous, and judgmental of those you date. Growing up in a single-parent

Choosing Our Children, First Priority

My very busy boy with the huge brown eyes was adopted at age seven and a half. He had both love and hardship in his first family and came to me as a confused, traumatized child. I entered parenting with much thought and preparation about the challenges I knew we would face: parenting a child of another race and culture and parenting a child who had faced many losses. My son's terminally ill first mother and I poured energy and love into helping him make the transition. His despair, confusion, and sheer rage, however, overwhelmed our household. My then-partner had grown children and did not really want to parent again. She supported me, however, in my desire to be a mom, and said she would be a support person, an auntie to my boy.

Had my son been a cute little helpless baby, this might have worked. The lovable but scared, raging, and extremely hyperactive little boy in our household took its toll on our relationship. I loved reading him stories at night, being in awe of his nonstop antics and, on the occasions he slowed down enough to allow it, snuggling him on my lap. At the same time I was covered with bruises from his physical assaults, in despair about replacing the windows, doors, and furniture he had broken, and was utterly exhausted from living twenty-four/seven with such a troubled child.

My partner just could not or would not adjust to our vastly changed lives. While I took him to therapists, visited special-ed teachers, and implemented various parenting strategies, she simply withdrew. She was angry, blamed me, blamed him, seemed to have forgotten all of her social work training, and left me feeling completely alone.

For my part, I felt and do feel like my commitment to my son simply had to outweigh my commitment to her. He was a seriously emotionally disturbed child, alone in the world, and I was his mom. She could move on with her life without me and I without her, but at age eight, he could not make it alone. Painful though it was, my decision was to parent my son, even if it cost me the relationship.

Our relationship did end. For me, parenting actually became easier, as I did not have to struggle with her in addition to meeting my son's needs. She has chosen to have virtually no contact with him, which makes my life easier but was one more abandonment for him.

I found little support in the LGBT community in parenting my son. The public face of our queer parenting seems to be about inseminations, adopted babies, two mommies or daddies making a happy family. Although our community has taken in a disproportionate share of older adopted troubled children, the stresses that brings are seldom part of our parenting discussions. Certainly there is little discussion of the toll such parenting takes on relationships.

I found most of my support in a network of adoptive and foster parents. Many, if not most, are very different in outlook, political philosophy, and lifestyle. Many are fundamentalist Christians, active in antiabortion politics, to the right of the political spectrum. I agree with them on very little except the love of our children and the belief that we can make a difference in their lives. And yet these have been the people who offered concrete suggestions, read the late-night E-mails, and listened to the anger and despair without judgment.

The queer community would not or could not acknowledge the reality of parenting a very difficult child. The foster/adoptive parent community has not been a place that could support me as a lesbian, as a woman whose long-term relationship ended, as a parent in a queer family. Much of my parenting journey has been lonely.

These days our lives are much less bleak, and my son is a very different child. Eight years later, much therapy, radically different parenting, and my son's own choice to manage his anger differently have changed our lives. He is a high school student who enjoys school, plays in the band, and is as pleasant daily as most seventeen-year-olds. He is not an easy person, and he still has difficult moments, but I am very proud of him and have hopes for him to be a productive adult. Two other children, one adopted as an infant, and one, adopted at age six, have, joined our family, and I now have a girlfriend who supports my parenting, and I feel like I can support others parenting challenging children.

My hope for our queer community is that we can acknowledge and support the many different kinds of parenting we do. I hope that in our desire to appear as successful parents to the world at large, we don't overlook those parents who struggle, who need support, and who are still very much a part of our queer community.

Estel Clares lives with her seventeen-year-old son and almost seven- and six-year-old daughters. Her three children joined the family through adoption; all were transracial adoptions, two U.S. and one international, and they live in a Midwestern city.

home often means that they are accustomed to your availability and are not used to being displaced while you share a bed or a deep laugh with someone else.

Ultimately, being a single parent means knowing in your bones that you are *enough*. Donald Winnicott spoke about the good-enough mother, meaning that although no parent is perfect, children do not actually need perfect parents. What they need are parents who are good enough, who take care of them with love and tenderness, and respond to their basic needs for shelter, food, warmth, in addition to being present for their emotional needs. Not 100 percent of the time, and not always with four stars, but consistently as best as they can. Being a single parent means knowing that you can be enough for your child. And you can be, but paradoxically, you can't do it alone.

Building Support Systems

As Bob the Builder says, "Can we build it? Yes, we can!!" It is best to start building early on, before children, but it is never too late to build support systems. The first place to start building a support system for those who are coupled is with your intimate partner. This includes taking time for long walks, long talks, about your parenting philosophies, your fantasies about having children, and how you see parenting together actually working. You may be surprised to find that your partner is strongly opposed to adoption, or desires a very large family, or harbors uncommon butch desires to breast-feed.

Talk about logistical things like who can get maternity leave from work, how much you are willing to spend on infertility treatments, and how having a criminal history might impact adoption choices. Think about how pregnancy will impact sobriety or how parenting will impact getting to 12-step meetings. Think about your sleep patterns, bad habits, and your relationship to your own parents. It is not a bad idea to see a therapist for preparenting counseling, although if you are adopting, your social worker can also take this role. No matter how much you think and talk about these issues, parenting will still hit you like a ton of bricks, but in the early weeks, months, and years, having had those conversations will give you a good base to start with, even if how you feel about many of the answers will have changed.

Do not assume that because you have a partner, you will not need other support. Probably the gravest mistake couples make is seeing each other as their sole support in parenting. Sadly, this often happens even if it is not your desire or plan. Given the isolation of nuclear families, even those of us who really want to be part of supportive communities find ourselves isolated with our partners. At least when people plan on being single parents, they are commonly strongly committed to finding supportive friends and encouraging involvement from their families of origin. However, the advice below applies to both single parents and those who are parenting together.

You will need to think about long-term issues when you plan on having children. Although none of us likes to think about dying, we need to have wills to protect our children financially, but even more importantly to designate guardians for our children. If we are single, this is essential, but couples often forget that horrors can happen whereby both parents are killed together in a car accident. Some gay people have become parents because they were the designated guardians of a sibling's children, when the sibling and his or her spouse died, leaving young children without either parent. One friend of mine is the designated guardian for both of her siblings' children. It was an honor at first, but then she realized that if something should happen to both of her siblings (unlikely but not impossible) she and her husband would be responsible for a collectivity of seven children, in addition to her own! I kindly did not ask her to be our children's guardian, despite the unlikely event that all of the parents involved would come to a sudden demise.

Guardians are often godparents for children, not just someone who we leave our kids to if we should die but someone who is intimately involved in their lives. A guardian can be a parent's sibling or close friend, but whatever the familial relationship is, they are commonly thought of as aunts and uncles and remain an important part of the child's extended family.

It is important to spell out, through carefully delineated conversations, the kind of relationships you hope your close friends will have with your children. It may seem obvious to you that your best friend will remember your kid's birthday and be available for school plays, but she may be content with visiting a few times a year with outrageously expensive, inappropriate toys. You may assume that your friends will adapt to your having a newborn and just start to hang out at your house more, but they may continue to socialize nightly at queer bars, where your child is unwelcome, even if you somehow thought a smoke-filled bar with loud music was okay for the baby. Alternatively, some friends may have a sense that your child is community property, and may assume that it is okay for them to take her on long walks, or have an equal vote in his food choices, and may feel insulted by your sudden control. People who are not parents may have little understanding of how your life will change with children; they may be oblivious to the changes, or they may be unsympathetic. Friends who are already parents may have much less time for you than either you or they hoped for.

Talk carefully with your friends about issues around baby-sitting, as well as emotional availability for support. Few things are more important to new parents than having a close friend to vent to, who will not call Child

Finding Support Where You Can

When I decided to adopt as a single gay man, I sought out support in a number of ways. My parents are deceased, but my cousins have been supportive from the start of the adoption process. Many of them wrote letters of recommendation for me when I decided to adopt my son from Guatemala. My two closest girl cousins were with me almost constantly in those first difficult months, and I still count on them for advice, invitations to family gatherings, and an occasional life-saving baby-sitting or picking Jose Antonio up at school.

My neighbors were the big surprise. My neighborhood is straight and quite working-class. I never expected the tremendous support that we've received. Starting from the big welcome-home shower they threw when Jose Antonio came back from Guatemala, they've been constantly present, helpful, and interested. My street is sort of like Mayberry: there are benches out front, and people gather on them when nothing special is happening, just to chat and socialize. This has been a great release for me, to be able to go out and have a bunch of people, kids for Jose Antonio to play with when he has nothing in particular to do (and he's driving me nuts in the house!).

When I first adopted, there wasn't much of a gay parents' support network in this area—odd, considering the huge gay population of the area (south Florida). Little by little, it's been developing, first by means of a gathering sponsored by the Family Pride Coalition and then by means of kids' parties and such among people who met each other there. It's been nice,

but not what I really consider a support network. I suppose it's like other aspects of gay life, that you can find yourself in a room full of gay people and have nothing in common with most of them except your sexuality. When I go to these gatherings, I often find myself with people I don't feel much in common with aside from our kids. I guess it's always hard to find kindred spirits. It also seems like the same urge for fabulousness that characterizes other aspects of gay male life is very present here: lots of bragging about homes and furnishings and kids, including fortunes spent on surrogacy, etc. I suppose this sounds very reverse-snobby, and maybe it is, but another gay dad friend of mine pretty much shares my impressions.

When I first started the adoption process, my agent referred me to a male couple on the west coast of Florida who were about six weeks ahead of me with the whole adoption process. We got quite friendly over the phone, and they helped me enormously with all the required bureaucracy. After both our babies arrived, we started exchanging visits. The boys have become extremely close, and they talk about each other all the time in between visits. We are making a concerted effort for these boys to have each other in their lives. The minute the kids see each other, they grab onto each other and tear off to do mischief. On one visit, they immediately disappeared into Jose Antonio's room. We heard lots of banging in there, but it sounded safe, so we didn't pay much attention. When we finally went in, we saw that the boys had taken down every single one of Jose Antonio's toys. They were literally swimming in toys, dozens and dozens of toys. We all marvel at how closely the boys have bonded, since they only see each other once every couple of months.

One of the most important people in my dad life is my ex-lover. We had broken up long before Jose Antonio's arrival, but Luis was incredibly touched by the baby and asked to be a forever part of his life. I was more than happy to oblige. So he became Uncle Luis, and he helps me immensely with everything. Jose Antonio adores him, too. Along with my cousins, he's the most important part of my support system.

My friends have been good, but I just can't do much with them anymore. I can't go on regular trips to the movies, our pre-vious favorite activity, and adult-type social dinners are a problem, too. I have a lot of theater friends (I'm a professional actor as well as a high school teacher), but I can no longer perform, nor can I attend many of the theater social gatherings. It's easier for me just to hang out with other people with kids (mostly straight), so my social life has changed considerably.

I only had one set of gay friends who've partially dropped me because of the baby. They're a couple of men who've been together for fifty years. I think they find my decision to adopt somewhat bizarre, and I feel like I've moved down a few rungs on their list of folks they must see. All my other friends have been great.

Warren Julecrist, single dad to Jose Antonio, age two and a half, Hollywood, Florida.

Protective Services when you discuss fantasies of throwing the baby over the balcony if she doesn't stop crying. Close friends who you can vent to are also important because they hopefully know you well enough to sense when you are not venting and actually in deep trouble and *need* outside support. Parents need people in their lives to bitch and complain to, they need people who will not judge the piles of laundry, or who express care when we decide we simply cannot continue to work a nine-to-six job and leave the twins with the baby-sitter, even if it means an uncertain financial future.

Look carefully at your social networks and determine who is a good listener, who is a good baby-sitter, who is able to respond in a crisis, and sit and talk with each of these people and see if they are willing to be part of your extended support network. Your mom may be willing to make food but not baby-sit, your sister may be willing to clean your bathroom but not change diapers, your friend John may be available to drive you to a pediatrician, but not emotionally available to hear your fears about your child's fever. Pick people carefully so you know who will feed the cat, who will put

Dykes To Watch Out For by Alison Bechdel

Grandmother or Just Close Friend of the Family?

Although Amanda and I have been together for over eight years now, Amanda's mom, Wanda, has only recently accepted Xavier and me as Amanda's family. Wanda refused to go to our wedding and refers to our dog, Pierre, which Amanda had before we ever got together, as her only grandchild. She was always polite to our faces, but at Christmas Amanda would get a card saying "For my daughter," while Xave and I would get a generic one. She does not buy Xave birthday gifts, nor does she attend his performances, games,

etc. For the first time last year, our Christmas card Wanda sent was written to her daughter and her family. About the middle of last year, Amanda talked to her mom about accepting Xave and me as her family, and Xave as her grandson. Although she is definitely not anywhere as active in Xavier's life as my mom, things have definitely improved.

Brenda Kreiger, partner to Amanda Woods for eight years, parents to Xavier Kreiger, age eleven, lives in southern Indiana.

---

together the crib, and who will spend hours playing peekaboo so you can finish the report that will pay for diapers and baby food for the next month.

As bell hooks reminds us, child-rearing is a responsibility that can be shared with many grown-ups, and commonly children in black communities are raised with this extended community-based experience. In a nuclear family world, this kind of child-rearing is revolutionary, because it takes the pressure off mothers and other primary caregivers. It also means that children are being influenced by many other people, which can complicate our parenting plan but give our children a much wider view of the outside world.

For most of us, intimate support comes from a mixture of our own nuclear and extended families (meaning ourselves and our partners) and our friendship network, some of who may be long-term friends or ex-lovers, and other more recent additions. Nuclear family members may be surprisingly supportive once they get over the fact that you are actually doing this. Some families remain downright hostile, but for most parents, having babies is something they always expected you to do anyway, and it may be the most normal thing you've ever done. Despite the controversial politic of being accepted for breeding, it is often a welcome feeling after living as an outlaw to find your family warmly accepting. Many parents have an initial negative response, more so for gay men than for lesbians (homophobia and sexism being what they are). But once pregnancy has been attained, or an actual child adopted, even the more reluctant parents find themselves cooing at the child.

In families formed through transracial adoption, or in mixed-race families, there may be discomfort ranging from blatant racism ("*That* child will never be a grandchild of mine!") to more subtle distress about how "dark" the child is, or how she can show a picture to coworkers and explain who the child is. Some families have difficulty accepting a grandchild who is not biologically related to them and are less welcoming to a child that a partner birthed or that was adopted than a child of their own biological progeny. With some families this just takes time, as well as education and language regarding how to talk about adoption, queer families, or racial issues. Some LGBT people find that their parents and extended family become their main supporters, despite other issues they may have between them. In other families, the relationship can be strained, although they continue to be supportive in terms of child care and financial support. Our children often develop deep bonds with our parents, even when our own relationships with them remain tense.

Do not easily discard parental offers of support, even if you feel that they are rejecting of your life choices, and are only willing to be supportive because you are doing something they understand, i.e., producing grandchildren. On the other hand, do not throw all caution to the wind. Sometimes parents will appear to have a total about-face when you decide to have children, expressing support and excitement, and leave you unprepared for the continuing judgment and criticism levied at your lifestyle or parenting practices. Parenting may bring you closer to your parents but will probably not change deeply seated opinions about homosexuality, gender presentation, or other alternative lifestyle issues. Children often become a means of communication between the generations, bypassing other political, social, religious differences, and suddenly you may find that your mom, who was completely unavailable to you while you struggled with coming out, is the person willing to discuss poopy diapers for hours on end, bless her soul.

Regardless of whether your lover is supportive and your family is making baby preparations, you should make use of other available built-in social support groups within our communities. Not every community has support groups, of course, but many do, including Baby Maybe groups, gay dads groups (sometimes called Pop Luck Clubs), or mixed gay parenting groups. For a list of resources on already existing groups, please see appendix B. Organized groups like these can be sources of information on pregnancy, schools, and child development. They can be places to find emotional support to talk about children's health, emotional problems, or difficulties in your couple relationship since having children. They can offer resources within the community for gay-sensitive pediatricians, great local parks, or free children's events. They can also sometimes offer advocacy regarding LGBT education within the school system, or pro bono legal advice for those battling custody issues. They can also offer support space for children to be around other LGBT families and organized support groups for older teens, who although they think they do not need it, may need others more than they realize.

Even if LGBT-specific groups are not available, you may be able to find mommy support groups, or play groups, that are friendly and inviting to you, even if the majority of the members are heterosexual in nuclear families. Do not easily discard the support and attention of straight people. Some of them are very comfortable with gay people, and many of them have long experience with parenting and know a lot about how to be supportive to new parents. Many LGBT people will tell you that the majority of their support system is not other LGBT people but heterosexual families who have shown stick-to-itiveness through the ups and downs of daily family life. Some straight people have really done their homework regarding LGBT people, and are not only comfortable but sophisticated in their understanding of some of our more unique experiences.

Although not every city or town has resources for LGBT parents, in the computer age support is available to all of us, even those living in the outback, even those living in the boonies. The on-line world has allowed for the creation of many alternative communities, for those who are, or appear to be, different from the mainstream communities around them. Jewish yogis, those building polygamous relationships, and bodybuilders who like to garden—there is an Internet community brimming with life out there. Indeed, the transgender community has come of age on the Net, finding support and like-minded others. The LGBT parenting community is booming on-line, as we stretch our border to include Israeli lesbian moms, gay dads in South America, closeted Arab moms questioning their sexuality, and FTM transmen who are birthing their own babies.

Gathering, Guiding, Growing

As more and more lesbians and gay men begin the journey to parenthood, some questions remain the same: Will I be a good parent? Is my existing support system going to be enough? Will my kids be teased for having two moms? Two dads? Does my state provide any legal protections for me or for my partner? How do the schools in my area deal with alternative families?

Sometimes the questions can be overwhelming, and then for those LGBT parents in more isolated areas, the answers are too often vague or nonexistent. That's why the work of the Family Pride Coalition is so important. Family Pride is the oldest and only national nonprofit organization solely dedicated to education, advocacy, and programming efforts for LGBT parents and their families.

Gathering Our Families: Because many LGBT parents live in areas outside the gay urban meccas—where there are no gay and lesbian community centers, restaurants, or bookstores—one of the most important components of the work of the Family Pride Coalition is assisting parents in making connections with other families in their communities. There are nearly two hundred local parenting groups all across the country, and the Family Pride Coalition can help interested parents or prospective parents organize a local parenting group if none exists.

The Family Pride Coalition also provides information and referrals regarding adoption, surrogacy, donor insemination, and more to parents and those considering parenthood. Family Pride also offers technical assistance to those interested in making community organizations and events—such as community centers and Pride celebrations—more family friendly.

LGBT parents can also connect with other families like their own through Family Week events. Family Weeks—in Saugatuck, Michigan, and Provincetown, Massachusetts—are among the most popular offerings of the Family Pride Coalition, with hundreds of families participating each year. Parents can also take advantage of events like Family Pride Camp, Boogie on the Beach, Dads and Kids in the Desert, and family programming during Gay Days at Disney for vacation fun with their children.

"As the number of LGBT-headed families continues to increase, it is important that we create more and more places for LGBT parents and their children to gather together to learn, grow, and develop a sense of community with other families," said Aimee Gelnaw, executive director of the Family Pride Coalition. "We are committed to providing such places, and know that the families who attend these activities will be empowered and inspired by each other then and throughout the year."

Guiding for Our Families: Through its education and advocacy programs, the Family Pride Coalition works to promote safety and equality for LGBT parents and their children. Eventually, school becomes a central part of life for both parents and their children. The Family Pride Coalition is committed to making schools and curriculums more inclusive, and to promoting protections for all our children—both those with LGBT parents and LGBT youth—from discrimination and harassment in school. Through its education and advocacy programs, the Family Pride Coalition works to promote safety and equality for LGBT parents and their children.

The Family Pride Coalition also works to educate the general public about LGBT parents, by promoting positive and accurate images of our families by providing a consistent and passionate voice for full equal rights and protections for LGBT families. In partnership with other local, state, and national organizations, the Family Pride Coalition works to combat attempts to ban LGBT people from becoming adoptive or foster parents.

Growing with Our Families: As the number of LGBT families continues to grow, so must the Family Pride Coalition. As the needs of LGBT parents and their families evolve, the Family Pride Coalition will remain vigilant in the fight for LGBT families. With ongoing community support, the

Family Pride Coalition will continue to support underserved and isolated families of LGBT parents by building communities and affirming families at the local level. In cities and schools, in statehouses and houses of worship, the Family Pride Coalition will work to ensure LGBT families are included, celebrated, and protected.

Our community—LGBT parents, those considering parenthood, and our friends, families, and allies—have a stake in the future of LGBT families. Together, LGBT parents will dismantle the homophobia that too often impacts their own—and their children's—sense of well-being and pride in their families. The Family Pride Coalition is dedicated to serving *all* the families in our community.

This article was written by Corri Planck, Washington, D.C. For more information, or to become a member of the Family Pride Coalition, call, write, or E-mail to: Family Pride Coalition, PO Box 65327, Washington, DC 20035; 202-331-5015; 202-331-0080 (fax): info@familypride.org; www.familypride.org.

Whether you are seeking information on diapering a newborn or gay friendly churches, whether you are seeking information on donor insemination or how to hide sex toys from children, there are on-line communities full of connection, humor, and a space to vent from the exhaustion of parenting. See appendix C for a list of on-line resources.

Single, coupled, part of an extended family system who embrace you, or living alone in rural Montana, all of us need people around us to help us cope with stressful times. Starting a new family *is* a stressful time, and during the long haul of raising children, stressful times will come again and again. Plan carefully in the beginning who will be there for you and then prepare to reevaluate your support system over time. Many new parents discover that their house is full of friends and family in the first few months, but six months later it's hard to find someone to take a walk with you and your baby. We all live immensely busy lives, and the rhythm of baby tending does not often fit in with people's work, family, and school lives. You may want to talk with someone during the day when everyone is at work; they may want to talk with you after 11 P.M. when you are nearly comatose.

As best as you can (and it will be harder than you can imagine), try to take care of your adult needs to have some alone time, some time for creativity, some time for friends, and some time for intimacy, long talks, and sex. The stronger your support system, the less sleep-deprived you will be, and the more patient, loving, and attentive you will be able to be to your child. Tribal life had some major benefits over contemporary Western life in terms of caring for its members. As much as you are able to borrow from this model to create, utilize, and develop a tribal support system that will protect and nurture a place for your family to grow and sustain itself, you should do so.

In traditional South Asian Indian culture, where children were traditionally raised in large, extended families within small villages, the people worshiped the goddesses Lakshmi, Saraswati, Durga, and Kali. These powerful female deities, representing wealth, abundance, beauty, knowledge, courage, and power, all had between six and ten arms. This was not simply artistic rendering; they were all mother-goddesses and needed all their hands to complete their busy jobs of running the universe and caring for their 10,000 children. The message is clear: even the gods need more than two hands to manage their children.

CHAPTER SEVEN

Protecting Our Families:
Matters of Hearts and Courts

DR. GLENN MIYA and his partner, elementary school teacher Steven Llanusa have been together for sixteen years, live in Claremont, California, and parent three children. Before the judge decreed the adoption of their sons official, he reminded them, "Remember you will now be legal parents. In the event of a separation you will be required to provide child support." Glenn muttered to Steven, "Amazing! We have all the benefits of divorce without the benefits of marriage." This is, indeed, exactly the situation for many of us as LGBT parents; we sometimes have no legal rights to our children at all.

The relationship between queer folk and the legal system has always been a stressful one. From the days, not so long ago, when police raided gay and cross-dressing bars, hauled us off to jail, and published our names in the paper, to the more recent days when a lesbian mom lost custody of a child she had raised for thirteen years after her partner, the child's biological parent, died in a car accident—lost custody to the grandparents who were known child abusers—we have been at the mercy of judicial systems that do not understand our needs.

LGBT families are fragile. I know that we don't like to really look at this demon in the eyes—like our children, we sleep with the lights on and repeat the mantra over and over again, "There are no monsters under the bed"—but the truth is that we are stalked by some mighty powerful foes. Although LGBT families are growing in numbers and becoming increasingly more visible all the time, our families are still very vulnerable to societal bigotry and homophobic laws.

As I prepared to write this chapter, something I've been avoiding for most of the past week, I read an op-ed piece in *Newsweek* magazine. Dated September 16, 2002, Scott Sherman wrote a "My Turn" column called "If Our Son Is Happy, What Else Matters?" Scott tells the story of how he and his partner adopted their son Sasha, who was a medically fragile infant. Sasha was so neglected in the orphanage where he had lived until the age of seventeen months that he was diagnosed with institutional autism. Due to a congenital condition impeding his ability to walk, Sasha often stumbles and falls and, like many small children, has the bumps and bruises to illustrate his tenacity and persistence. However, unlike most American families, Sasha's dads became the focus of an investigation by the state's Child Protective Services due to concerns about their potential abuse of their son. As Scott says, "Done for the right reasons, that's the smart thing to do." However, Scott and his partner are suspicious that the report was not made for good reasons—i.e., concerns for Sasha's safety—but because some homophobic person thought that having two dads in and of itself was a sign of abuse.

Two loving parents, who have nurtured a small, sick child who is eating (and therefore growing), laughing, talking, and engaging affectionately with others, are accused of hurting, harming, and abusing him, all because some people believe that by merely *being gay* they are a danger to their child and therefore capable of heinous crimes needing state intervention. This story is not an isolated one. LGBT parents often fear the intervention of Social Services, not because their parenting is problematic but because they are under the scrutiny of judgmental and biased neighbors.

When my older son was a toddler, he was in a kiddie pool with a neighbor's child. Suddenly the two children, one male and one female, one black and one white, pulled off their bathing suits and took off running up the driveway and down the streets, parents in hot pursuit. I was highly conscious of who might be watching, fearful of the scornful eye of a neighbor who might see my naked son's body as a sign of some kind of perverted lesbian sex ritual. I realized that the other parent running beside me, my son's friend's mom, a heterosexual white woman parenting a child she had birthed, was laughing. She scooped up her daughter, tickling her, oblivious to toddler nudity, concerned only with protecting her child from cars. As I rushed to get my naked son back in the safety of the backyard kiddie pool, I shared with her my fears. At first she looked at me as if I was paranoid, overprotective, and a bit crazy. As we talked, she became sensitized to the many complex issues that ruled our family's lives: racial differences, homophobia, and the approval of judges to regard us as a worthy family. I became aware for the first time that not all parents worry about how they are perceived by the neighbors, that parental "ownership" of children is simply taken for granted by some more privileged parents. As many LGBT parents, we are aware that state authorities, unsympathetic social workers, callous judges, irate exes, and even disapproving grandparents can make our lives a veritable hell.

The basic rights of parents are not automatically assumed for many LGBT families. Being LGBT and fighting for custody after the breakup of a heterosexual marriage puts one at a definite disadvantage, since many judges will render you an unfit parent simply for being LGB or T. When lesbian families are formed through pregnancy, the nonbiological parent is automatically legally invisible. Families are often at the mercy of the changing intentions of known sperm donors whose biological contribution can become more important in custody decisions than the actual parent who has been raising the child. When couples are adopting children internationally, only one parent is officially able to move through the complex legal process, and even when adopting domestically in most states in the U.S., the adoption paperwork is done in only one parent's name. In foster-parented families, children are often returned to abusive family situations after years of living with a foster family that would love to adopt them; sometimes the birth family only becomes involved when they realize that the child is being reared by queers and they want to "save" them from this fate.

LGBT families have mostly been outlaws in the legal system. Becoming in-laws to one another involves fighting long-drawn-out legal battles so that the judicial system will recognize the alternative structures of our families. Lesbian and gay people who are birthing and adopting children are challenging the legal system to develop a more inclusive understanding of what is in "the best interests of the children." In a country where gay and lesbian marriages are not yet legal, and where most states do not allow for same-sex second-parent adoptions, children are often being raised in lesbian and gay families where only one parent is legally recognized. A nonlegal parent does not have basic legal authority to consent for (or refuse) medical care or have the child covered under his or her medical policy. She or he has no legal right to parent the child if the legal parent(s) becomes incapacitated, *no matter how long she or he has been parenting the child.* Furthermore, without a will, the child has no legal rights of inheritance. Heterosexual couples who birth or adopt a child are *automatically* considered to be the legal parents of that child, and both remain legal parents unless a court terminates one or both of their legal rights. This places our families in jeopardy and forces us to take measures to protect our families from homophobic legal systems that do not understand the structures or needs of our families.

Legal Documentation: Protecting Our Families within a Heterosexist System

Lesbian and gay families are challenging the legal system to recognize and support our various and unique family constellations. In a world where biological paternal rights have been sacrosanct, asking a judge to understand that a nonbiological partner who is raising a child is a parent, whereas the sperm donor is not, challenges the very roots of sexist and homophobic law. Our communities are challenging these laws in numerous ways.

First of all, same-sex second-parent adoptions—where both parents' names are on the child's birth certificate and they are both recognized as legal parents—are becoming increasingly common. Though available in only a few states, second-parent adoptions can be completed whether the child is a birth child or an adoptive one to the legal parent, as long as there are no other legal parents involved (i.e., a biological father). Furthermore, second-parent adoptions are sometimes recognized as binding in other states and countries when parents relocate. Secondly, the questions of psychological parenting are being raised in many custody disputes, whereby when the gay or lesbian couple break up, the nonlegal or nonbiological parent is still being recognized by law as a parent deserving of the privileges of custody and visitation.

Additionally, in a few states—California, Colorado, and Massachusetts—attorneys have utilized the Uniform Parentage Act, whereby lesbian and gay parents are able to file a Petition to Establish Parental Relations, which legally recognizes both parents before the birth of the child. Initially this was done in situations whereby one mother donated her egg for a child that the other mother carried, but in some counties of California, women have been able to have both mothers' names on the birth certificate at the time of the birth. Gay dads utilizing a surrogacy arrangement have also used the Uniform Parentage Act to establish legal parentage. This precedent has also been set in Vancouver, British Columbia, whereby both mothers' names are placed on the birth certificate at the time of the child's birth, with no additional fees incurred, making the idea of a second-parent adoption obsolete. These are exciting legal changes, although the status and permanency of these legal decisions are still in flux. Each law enacted and/or interpreted in our favor further protects our children and the security of our families.

Due to the nature of what is essentially a heterosexist legal system, our families are not just the victims of bias but are essentially misunderstood. For instance, Chris Hernandez, a respected Alabama teacher, had a daughter while in a heterosexual marriage that was in the process of being dissolved when the child was born. The infant was five days old when the mother and her lesbian partner moved in together. The father had minimal contact with the infant and provided little support for the baby. He would occasionally visit the child for half an hour, and did not do any overnights until she was two years old, and they were then infrequent. At about this same time, the courts ordered the father to pay child support, and this was deducted from his paycheck. He continued to badger the mother to return to court and request that he pay her directly, although they both knew she would never see this money unless it was removed directly from his paycheck. Despite his being legally required to maintain his daughter's health insurance, he had her removed from his policy.

When this child was six years old, the mother and her partner had a second daughter together. Meanwhile, the father had remarried a woman and was requesting increased visitation with his daughter. His new wife engaged in abusive and inappropriate discussions with the daughter about her mother and berated their family with harassing slurs and vulgar language. The woman was arrested and convicted for this behavior. The father retaliated and filed false charges against the mother and had her arrested at her place of employment. The case went to court, and the charges were proven to be false and were dismissed by the judge.

The father and his new wife had decided that his daughter should not be living in a lesbian household, so he decided to pursue full custody, claiming the mother was unfit. The child's court-ordered psychiatrist found the mother to be fit and in a healthy relationship with a loving family environment provided for the young children. The court-ordered guardian ad litem (child's attorney) found the mother to be the best parent and concluded the child should remain with the mother. The child's principal and teachers also concluded the mother was a well-respected parent and thought of highly at her Roman Catholic private school. In fact, everyone called to testify against the mother turned out to be good witnesses to her moral character. The husband's new wife was the most hostile witness. Although it was not pursued or proven, she lied under oath. She was definitely detrimental to his case. The father also insisted the child testify, and the judge allowed the testimony of the six-year-old to be taken in her chambers. The child denied the allegations of the father and his new wife and requested to continue living in the only two-parent home she had ever known.

Despite all this, the father still managed to win joint custody, and the judge decreed that the lesbian mother and her partner could not continue living together in the same house, or she would lose custody of her child! The couple sold the home they loved and had lived in for five years and bought adjoining town houses at a huge financial expense; they lived in this fragmented manner for a number of years to maintain their family.

The father has since been arrested twice and convicted of harassment toward the mother, and a restraining order was granted against the father. In the sixteen months following the court decision, he appealed the decision and has exercised his right to visitation only four times. He has since divorced his second wife and moved out of state and barely maintains contact with his daughter. This family has suffered enormously because, in the eyes of the court, biological parentage is worth more than an actual functioning parent when the relationship is identified as lesbian.

Chris Hernandez faced a potentially devastating loss; however, she chose to face homophobia with honesty and integrity and is able to look her daughter in the face with pride. These are Chris's words: *"I will not tell a lie or deny my love for any member of my family, even when society says lies are acceptable. Lies do not help the oppressed, and I will stand up for what is right! My child has learned to be honest and be accepting of differences. My parents are heterosexual, and I am a lesbian. I did not learn to be a lesbian from my parents, I learned from them to be honest and to believe in myself. The moral values that I am teaching and will continue to teach my children will be honesty, integrity, courtesy, diligence, perseverance, and the ability to think for themselves. Adversity does not mean we are weak; it is simply an opportunity to show the world we can and will endure, and in the end we will thrive and be successful."* Chris and her partner have since become parents to twins, William and Casey, and with their daughters are all finally united under one roof.

Chris is fighting a battle with an antiquated justice system in the U.S. South; a system that does not recognize our families but relies on traditional definitions of family that ultimately make our families suffer. Perhaps some of us expect this kind of blatant homophobia in Alabama. However, these situations do not only happen in conservative Alabama, but in liberal New York.

When Siobhan Hinckley and her partner Anita decided to have a family, they used a friend as a donor. It was always an open relationship between all parties, and they had written up contracts outlining the nature of their relationships. The donor and his partner were to have no financial responsibilities to the children, and Anita and Siobhan would function as the children's parents. The donor and his partner saw the kids frequently and functioned as important people to them. This arrangement worked out fine until Siobhan and Anita broke up.

Suddenly, the donor did not recognize Anita as a parent anymore, and the donor sued for joint custody and increased visitation of the children. Even in a state that recognizes gay and lesbian families, that has second-parent adoption, and allows lesbians and gay men to adopt as couples, Anita was seen as a legal nonentity, despite five years of parenting and all of the emotional, physical, and financial responsibility for the raising of the children. The donor won increased visitation with the children, and Anita's role as their parent was erased. Throughout the legal proceedings, the court ignored psychologists' and therapists' recommendations to maintain the lesbian family system that had nurtured, created, and reared the children. Defaulting to biology, the courts ignored the contracts.

These stories—painful, confusing, and extremely financially expen-

Unfit to Parent: Denise's Story

Late in 1997, when I could no longer stand the guilt of my transgenderism, I took the scary step of coming out to my wife. At first she seemed okay with it, and I thought that I was lucky to have this much support. As time went on, she became more and more argumentative, began throwing my "T" condition in my face at every disagreement, calling me a transvestite in front of my child. She then began to take every opportunity to belittle me and make me wrong for just about everything that she didn't like or that didn't go her way. All this was always in front of my child, so I was sure to look extra bad in front of him. Any time there was an issue with my child's behavior, she would be in direct conflict with my opinion on how to deal with his misbehavior.

My son was six years old at the time and had learned that he could play one parent against the other as a result of observing our constant conflict. This only made matters worse as my child's behavior continued to deteriorate. This of course angered me, which of course delighted my wife because she could now say how verbally abusive I was. It seemed as if every time I said anything, I was accused of being abusive. By this time my son had pretty much been alienated from me, which again played right into her hands. Little did I realize that all this time she was setting me up for just what happened next.

I was not allowed to do anything alone with my child without her supervision, and, of course, when I objected, she would threaten to leave me. She would accuse me of being a transvestite and a child abuser, and she made sure that my son knew just how awful I was. I was not even allowed to put him to bed at night. By this time someone (I believe it was her mother) had called Child Protective Services, who interviewed me separately on two occasions; ultimately the investigator saw what was going on and ruled the charges unfounded.

While all of this was going on, we agreed to get some counseling. We went together to a referral service provided through my job. She outed me to the counselor, and I could see in the counselor's eyes that she now thought I was some sort of hideous monster. The counselor referred each of us to different therapists, and the therapist I was referred to specialized in working with men with sexual disorders. I still don't know why we weren't sent to the same therapist who could help us at least try to resolve what seemed to be a hopeless situation.

In mid-February of 1998, I came home from work one evening and found the house stripped clean of my son and her. She even took the cat, who was *my* cat. Shortly after that, I received a restraining order from Family Court barring me from absolutely any and all contact with my son or her. Even by writing. She then contacted the Child Protective Services with a falsely enhanced complaint against me, accusing me of being a child molester, and that's a sure winner in a custody battle. Well, it worked for her. It cost me almost $10,000 to disprove it, and the court barred me anyway from contact with my child.

The court recommended I be mandated into treatment as a child abuser by a court-sanctioned therapist or institution as a precautionary measure before I would even be considered for visitation rights to my child. The ex, of course, got full custody, and I got screwed. When I agreed to see the approved therapist, I found out that before he could counsel me, I had to freely admit that I was a child molester. I AM NOT A CHILD MOLESTER, I NEVER WAS, AND WILL NOT BE FORCED TO ADMIT SUCH CRAP!!!!! As a result I have had absolutely no contact with my child in almost five years. I feel I probably will never have contact with him again.

I found myself emotionally destroyed and financially devastated (I paid the lawyer the equivalent of the cost of a brand-new BMW Z3 roadster, just like the one he showed up in after the divorce was finalized). On top of all of this I was diagnosed with cancer and spent eight months on chemotherapy starting in March of 1998. By this time I began to realize that all I had was me to rely on, and I wanted to do it as a woman. So, based on this realization, I decided to go forward with my transition. I realize that I have lost my child, but in spite of this I am finally the person I really always was, and I am delighted to be just that!!!

Denise, parent to Stephen, age eleven, Charlton, New York.

sive—are descriptive of a court system that does not recognize the structure and identities of our families. Despite contracts outlining our intentions, the biological ties are often still honored over the functional day-to-day relationships that we have carefully constructed. In a curious twist of legal tomfoolery, the exception to this rule is when a transgendered or transsexual biological parent files for custody of children who are biologically and legally theirs; suddenly they are seen as unfit parents, and the courts must intercede to protect the children. LGBT parents are very vulnerable in the judicial system.

Given the fragility of our families, and what is at stake in a court of law, how do we protect our families? Clearly, as Denise's situation exemplifies, we need to educate courts, attorneys, therapists, and other professionals about our families so our sexual and gender identities cannot be used by angry exes in the courts. Additionally, we need to fight like hell for the legal right to marry our chosen spouses, and for the government to recognize these marriages as legally binding contracts. The world watched as thousands of people were married in San Francisco; New Paltz, New York; and Portland, Oregon, in 2004, but it is unclear what the impact on public policy these acts of love and civil disobedience will have on federal law. Whether these marriages will be honored or not—and by whom—is an issue that will continue unraveling as this book goes to press. Surely, no one could have imagined a decade ago that we would see civil unions or gay marriage happen in our lifetimes. Yet the events of the past few years might be a harbinger of far-reaching changes in the recognition and legal security of LGBT people, making many of the other suggestions listed below unnecessary.

However, given the ambiguity and oscillation of the current status of gay marriage, in order to protect our families, certain legal documentation is recommended. This paperwork is expensive to file, involving attorney's fees, and it is also incredibly time-consuming. They are, however, necessary, essential to the basic legal protection of our familial relationships. Most of us would never consider having front doors without locks or putting our infants in cars without car seats; legal documentations are safety measures of equal importance. It is also important to realize that none of these measures are foolproof, especially when we are often dealing with fools. Laws differ from state to state, and county to county and are enforceable differently from one judge to another. Nightmares can still happen, even with proper paperwork, but it does offer at least a modicum of protection and in some situations creates secure legal firewalls.

Even when we are living in states that do not grant second-parent adoption rights, there is much that we can do to secure our families. It is essential for lesbian and gay families to have wills, power of attorney, guardianship, coparenting agreements, and other legal paperwork that recognizes nonbiological/nonadoptive parents. Custodial parents must make provisions for the children by clearly labeling the other parent in their will. Families considering donor inseminations should complete known-donor contracts. Noncustodial parents should always carry paperwork giving them permission to make emergency medical decisions regarding their child.

It is especially critical for LGBT people to know that if legal paperwork is not established, domestic partners will in all likelihood not be recognized as legal next of kin, and the hospitals and courts will look to the closest biological family member to make health care decisions. If an LGBT person becomes ill or dies, decisions about financial assets and the living arrangements of children will not be respected unless they are legally documented. There is, unfortunately, no guarantee that these documents will be recognized legally, but it sends the courts a clear message of intent regarding your definition of family. It is obvious that having an attorney well versed in gay and lesbian legal issues is essential. This paperwork is far too important to put off completing, to do yourself (unless you have a solid legal background), or to have done by a lawyer without prior experience in lesbian and gay families.

Second-Parent Adoption Second-parent adoption extends legal parental rights to a nonbiological or nonadoptive coparent without the first parent relinquishing custody of the child. This can only be done if there is no other legal parent (i.e., a biological father named on the birth certificate) unless they legally sign away their parental rights. Commonly, one must have an attorney file for this with the courts, following approval by a social worker, who will often have to complete a home study; the sex of the two parents is not taken into consideration when completing a second-parent adoption. The second parent is a legally adoptive parent who has the same rights (and responsibilities) in custody and visitation agreements.

At the time of this writing, eight states (California, Connecticut, Illinois, Massachusetts, New Jersey, New York, Pennsylvania, and Vermont) and the District of Columbia have approved second-parent adoptions, and in nineteen other states certain judges have approved same-sex second-parent adoptions, but they are not yet the official law of the land. If you live in a state where same-sex second-parent adoptions are granted, do not hesitate to complete this process. In Siobhan Hinckley's situation above, if they had filed for a second-parent adoption in New York State, and the donor had surrendered his legal rights, he would never have been able to later file for custody, and Anita could have never been declared a legal nonentity. Since the courts had decreed that Siobhan and the donor share joint custody, Anita has no legal claim to the children. Her visitation with the children depends on whether the legal parents will share their time. She also has no legal responsibility to financially support them. Second-parent adoptions are the greatest protection currently available to us in the U.S. to secure our families.

Some parents have expressed frustration and annoyance at having to complete this expensive and intrusive legal process, when our families should be valid from conception onward. Of course, our intentions to parent together *should* be what the courts recognize, and both parents' names *should* be placed on the birth certificate at the time it is filed, but we are still far away from such universal liberal interpretations. Given the size of the boulder that Sisyphus is pushing up the mountain, second-parent adoption processes can be a moving and sacred affirmation. Second-parent adoptions can serve to not only secure the second parent's legal right to the child/ren, but also is an opportunity for a family to honor the adoptive process for a nonbiological child. Like a naming ritual or a commitment ceremony, the act of formalizing a coparenting agreement can be more than legal; it can be a spiritual enactment of family building.

Coparenting Agreements A coparenting agreement is a document that explains the rights and responsibilities of each parent and can be created before a child enters the family, as well as at any time afterward. Coparenting agreements are vital when second-parent adoptions are not available, but they also can be instrumental in assisting all couples in identifying their values, beliefs, and hopes for parenting together. My vision is that LGBTs will lead the way for heterosexuals to begin to think through their intentions more carefully before beginning their families; another small but significant contribution we can bring to the wider society. Coparenting agreements can be very helpful to assist in custody-related decisions should a couple split up and can serve to protect the rights of a nonbiological/nonadoptive parent.

In a coparenting agreement process, each partner can outline their parental intentions and their joint commitments to the child. The legal parent can outline his or her intentions should s/he die, or regarding guardianship and decision making in his or her absence. It is also useful to plan out custody decisions in the event that the couple relationship has a shorter duration than the parenting agreement. The process of developing this kind of contract can be emotionally stressful; you may find out that your partner holds values and opinions that surprise you. It is best to hash all that out *before* there is a child present who will be impacted by this process.

Domestic Partnership Registration and Civil Unions Some localities have domestic partnership registration, which has few direct legal or financial benefits but can establish your intentions to be viewed as a family. Domestic partnership registration may be useful documentation to assist in applying for spousal health insurance benefits, as well as proof of your relationship status if it is ever questioned in a court of law. If questions arise about a parent's right to a guardianship, custody, visitation, psychological parenting status, or the nature of the relationship to the legal parent, domestic partnership registration can often solidify the often legally amorphous nature of LGBT relationships.

Civil unions are available at this time only in Vermont, and although couples from any state can be civilly unionized in Vermont, it does not carry any legal weight in any other state (yet!). Civil unions offer same-sex couples the closest thing to a legal marriage, including the same legal protections, recognition, benefits, and responsibilities within the state of Vermont, although it does not confer any federal recognition or protection. Couples in the other forty-nine states can travel to Vermont, have a "wedding" with a justice of the peace (mandated to perform civil unions, regardless of their personal values about same-sex relationships), or have a ceremony within a religious institution that will honor their union. Many small businesses in Vermont specialize in making these civil unions a magnificent event, and gay and lesbian weddings have become part of the Vermont tourist industry.

Both domestic partnership registration and civil union legislation are steps toward legal recognition of our families. If these opportunities are available to you, they may serve you well in a courtroom someday if you ever need to justify the nature of your familial commitments.

Domestic Partnership Contracts Even if domestic partnership registration and civil unions are not available in your state, county, or city, you can develop a domestic partnership contract, which will outline your intentions as a couple regarding finances, inheritance, and joint property. This is a legally binding contractual process and can serve to solidify your commitments and responsibilities to each other that a legal marriage would've automatically conferred. These contracts are not uniformly enforced, and laws differ from locality to locality, so it essential that your contracts are written up by an attorney who is knowledgeable about both contractual agreements and the current status of LGBT law.

Sperm Donor Contracts Sperm donor contacts are only necessary when you are using a known sperm donor, and the insemination is being done without the assistance of a physician. When you buy sperm from a sperm bank, the donor has already relinquished his legal rights to any children born through insemination. When women engage in alternative baby-making arrangements, including having intercourse with a close male friend or

Choosing a Known Donor: Simone's Story

Like parenting, having a known donor presented unanticipated complexities, but overall it has worked out very well in our situation. It is inaccurate to say that it was a choice so much as a matter of economic necessity. Throughout six years spent on the quest for conception, there had been numerous donors of both the frozen and fresh variety. Ultimately, it seemed silly to be spending a fortune on a commodity also offered free, especially since it didn't look like the dream of getting pregnant was very likely.

I placed an ad in the local gay bar magazines, and was glad I had the foresight to rent a post office box once the responses arrived. One fellow in prison noted he'd be getting out soon and wanted a threesome. Another sent nude photographs. What the gentleman who wrote in crayon on paper towels was trying to convey has yet to be deciphered. He was politely sent packing along with the rest of them. Finally, a seemingly sane man wrote.

He said his life was filled with friends and family, work and studies. He did not want to parent, but wanted to help a lesbian couple and see some part of himself live on. In no time, contracts were notarized, baby medicine droppers purchased for at-home self-inseminations, and our monthly meetings were scheduled. Within a year, my daughter was conceived. Three years later, he helped in the creation of my son.

At first, I was terrified he'd want a large role in their lives. True to his word, he is completely nonintrusive. Seeing him on birthdays and special occasions is always a joyous event. Now that I've had time to get to know him better and to appreciate daily the selfless gifts he's given, it seems silly to fear him loving them. The children, now four and six, know that he helped make them and how. I hope they can one day appreciate all that entails.

Not all of the lesbian moms I know have fared as well with their known donors. In some cases, the results have been disastrous—a step away from a rape victim having to share custody of a resulting child. A stranger, or even a friend, enters into your life to help make a baby, and then breaks his word and wants to share in that baby's life, and by definition your own.

Recently, I was asked what I would do differently in light of such travesties. Honestly, not a thing. Contracts are subject to the whims of the judicial system. People change their minds. I don't demonize known donors whose feelings are unexpected once they see their own eyes staring back at them from a bassinet, nor do I have anything against men wanting to parent when that's the planned arrangement.

What I do find despicable is people not living up to their word, and courts that cling to the misguided notion that genetic paternity—or maternity, for that matter—is so vital to the well-being of the child that it overrides the expressed intents of parties to an agreement. There is an inherent risk to having a known donor that is unavoidable until the courts uniformly recognize that a deal is a deal.

Simone Ryals, mama to Suzannah, age seven, and Caden, age four, lives in south Florida.

Choosing a Known Donor: Rita's Story

When I got pregnant, I was in a six-year lesbian relationship, and we were coparenting my partner's two young children. Both children had a known donor with whom they had contact. The eldest had been born into a two-mom family, and she continued to have regular contact with her other mom; the younger child was born when my ex was single. Despite the fact that I did most of the general homemaking during the years that we were together, I was never allowed to be "Mom"; my ex called me a coparent.

Due to fertility problems, I was not able to use my own eggs and used donor eggs to become pregnant. My ex therefore believed that she was as much a mother to my child as I was because, as she said, "You are only the gestational mother." Our relationship went downhill rapidly as soon as I became pregnant, although my ex had encouraged my efforts to become pregnant; however, once my daughter was born, it was clear that there was no room for two moms in our household.

I used a known donor primarily because my partner's children had a known donor, and we believed that it would create more consistency for our family. The donor and his partner were acquaintances but not close friends. Soon after I became pregnant, he and his partner drew up papers that explicitly stated that he (and his partner) would be noncustodial parents to this unborn child. They were present at the birth and became active dads caring for our daughter one to two nights each week when she was an infant.

When my daughter was about seven months old, it became clear to me that the relationship between my partner and I needed to be dissolved. From that point on, until we moved to our own home three months later, she refused to let me be with and care for her children, whom I had parented for the previous six plus years. However, she demanded to have time with my daughter, wanting to split our time four ways (between me, the donor and his partner, and her), leaving me as a quarter parent, something I could not agree to.

When we moved to our own home, my daughter continued to spend one to two nights each week at her donor dad's home. However, about two months later, when she was a bit over one year old, he brought a legal suit against me to establish his paternity and to request that he be granted sole legal and physical custody. He used various tactics in an attempt to show that I was an unfit mother as well as taking on the ex's cause that I was merely the owner of the uterus that carried his child. If I chose not to fight it, I would have lost custody of my daughter.

Family court established joint legal and physical custody shared by the donor/dad and me. In this state (California) and probably many others, it seems to be very easy for men who want to be considered fathers/parents to their children to gain paternity and shared custody. When the donor/dad was denied sole custody, he immediately went for a fifty/fifty "timeshare." (This really is the legal lingo; it always makes me think of that kind of thing where people buy one week a year in a resort.) Because of her age (one year at that time), the court maintained his two-nights-a-week visitation schedule. Over the years, however, he has continued to push for fifty/fifty custody, returning to family court two to four times a year until he finally succeeded when my daughter turned five and started kindergarten.

This custody battle has continued for the past seven years, and I expect it to continue until my daughter becomes of age. I have spent over $50K on legal costs; the emotional cost has been outrageous. Each time as "the boys" pushed for more and more of whatever they wanted—time, vacation, control, etc.—I pushed for more written clarity and specificity in the form of legal stipulations. Having it all written into a legal form as clearly as possible has helped me to cope, as there is now virtually nothing left to individual choice, and we have been able to avoid court time over the past year.

The legal system necessitated entering into a continuing relationship with a court-appointed psychologist who has been evaluating my daughter and the various persons in her family every one to one and one half years, as well as consulting with her infant-toddler center staff, pre-school director and teachers, and now her elementary school director and teachers. Fortunately, the psychologist is well-versed not only in the issues of lesbian and gay families but also in blended families; she also is a play therapist with an office full of wonderful miniatures that my daughter loves. We tried court-mandated mediation with a family court social worker that did not work; we tried family therapy that was a terrible disaster. We have been meeting monthly with a parenting consultant (a psychologist who consults with the court-ordered evaluator) with the focus on our child rather than the parents; this has been the most successful intervention thus far.

Almost eight years now after my daughter's birth, we are in a steady, albeit difficult and trying, parenting arrangement. We do not coparent; we parallel-parent. My daughter lives in two separate and disparate family households. She talks now about how hard it is for her to move between these two worlds. I feel sad that I am missing out on half of her life; I despair that my wonderful, bright, loving, creative, and sensitive child must hang in the balance between her two worlds. I hope that I am able to support her well through her childhood; I worry that she will be angry with me about her fractured family. The best thing that I have ever done is to become a mom; the hardest thing in my life now is to be the mom that I want to be to my daughter.

Rita Fahrner is mom to Kelly Fahrner-Scott, age eight, San Francisco, California.

lover, using the semen of a friend's friend, or having the semen delivered to you through a network of friends without ever meeting the donor who may live locally, the resulting legal situation can be immensely complicated regarding custodial rights to the child.

Sperm donor contracts are essential to establish the intentions of the bi-

Using Laws That Exist to Our Advantage
BY PAULA L. ETTELBRICK

The use of wills, health proxies, parenting agreements, and other legal documents for securing our family configurations are powerful vehicles for protecting the interests of our partners and children. Wills allow each of us to decide who gets our property, money, and even our cherished pets. They allow us to appoint guardians for our children, express our wishes for funeral and burial arrangements, make donations to our favorite charities, and set up trusts to secure the financial well-being of our children or elderly parents. Through a will we can appoint an executor, the person responsible for going through the treasures in our closets, knowing what to sell in the garage sale and what to keep, and making sure that every wish stated in our will is fulfilled. Wills, in short, allow every competent adult the chance to make her or his own decisions about events after our deaths that are vitally important to the interests and well-being of our partners and children. No need to wait for marriage laws to change when you can take action now. The alternative is letting the state decide who gets your money and who gets to rifle through your drawers. Hint: it won't be your partner!

Formal health proxy laws exist in most states allowing us to appoint another person to make health-related decisions for us in a crisis in which we are not able to decide for ourselves. In those states with health proxy laws, preprinted forms are also generally available. Again, failure to take this simple action will result in doctors and health providers turning to those other than your partner to help make critical decisions about your health or even your life. Many lawyers who serve the LGBT community would automatically include health proxy appointments into the deal as they are drafting your will. They can also advise about other legal arrangements that you may not have known were available in your state.

But, aside from the formal execution of these documents, it is equally important that we share the information in them with relevant people. My rule of thumb is, "No surprises." For instance, make sure that parents, adult children, or siblings know well ahead of an emergency that it is your partner who will be making all health care decisions and should be the one allowed into the emergency room. If you have a physician, make sure she has a copy of your health proxy in your file and speak to her about your wishes. Make sure extended family know that your partner will be the kids' legal guardian, and that you plan to be cremated, not buried as your mother's Catholicism would dictate. In other words, let them work out all of their disappointment and angst well in advance. It will not guarantee smooth sailing should a crisis arise, but it will help a lot.

Parenting agreements, whether with a donor or with a coparent, are a whole different ball game. Enforcement of them is generally disfavored in the law because of the court's traditional responsibility for ensuring that the interests of children are considered whenever a family separates or brings their conflict to the courts. But before you rip up that document you just paid some lawyer to draft, let me assure you that all is not lost. The world is changing rapidly, and judges, after years of advocacy by many of us, are slowly beginning to understand that our families are structured according to our agreements with others, not under the rules of biology and marriage. Thus, written agreements can serve a vital role in assuring the courts about what our parenting intentions were before and after the children were born. They can keep biological mothers honest about the fact that their ex-partners, whom they now hate, are nonetheless coparents and that known donors need to be accountable—being a biological father does not make one a legal daddy. In addition, the process of drafting such agreements adds some thoughtfulness to the decision to parent by forcing parents—and donors-to-be—to think through the range of thorny issues about their relationships with each other and to any children that may be born as a result of the agreement. With the increased use of second-parent adoptions to secure relationships between nonbio moms and the kids, the question of who are the legally recognized parents can be clarified in a growing number of states.

Just a brief word about known donors. There are many reasons that lesbians choose men they know to be the sperm donors, or often fathers, of their children. But the risk, legally, of using a known donor is still great for lesbian couples who distinctly do not want to have their donor considered a legal father. In a sexist world in which a family is still considered illegitimate if a man is not a part of it, (mostly male) judges simply cannot accept the idea that a donor who is known to the child and has even the barest relationship with the child should not be considered a father. So, if you really, really do not want the donor to be considered a father, go with an unknown donor. If you really, really want your child to be able to look a man in the face and know that half of her genes came from him, then make sure you select a man who you would consider including in your family for life and who will be a responsible and consistent presence in your child's life, according to the terms you want. Because, the fact is, as kids get older, we as parents cannot actually control the feelings and relationships they may develop for the man known as their "genetic donor." And it may not be in their interests to ban him from the child's life or to have created an expectation with a man who really has no interest in going with the flow of the child's needs. That is the beautiful thing about kids: they are actually real live people!

Paula L. Ettelbrick is a lawyer and law professor, and she has served as the family policy director for the Policy Institute of the National Gay and Lesbian Task Force and the legal director for Lambda Legal Defense and Education Fund. Paula and her partner of eleven years, Suzanne Goldberg, live in Manhattan with their two children, Adam, who is six, and Julia, who is three. She can be reached at pettelbrick@att.net.

ological mother, her significant other, and their relationship with the donor. Contracts specify whether or not the donor will give up all legal rights to the child, serve as an "uncle" or noncustodial parent, or whether the biological parents will share parenting. The relationship of the donor to the child can range from full paternal rights, to having no contact with the child until the age of eighteen, or only being available if there is a medical situation in which health and genetic information might be useful. The legal management of these differing family-building options is complex; donor agreements are necessary to make explicit the intentions of the family, although they are not often upheld in the courts when custody has been challenged. Some families have had incredibly positive experiences having a known donor, and others have been veritable nightmares.

Temporary Guardianship Temporary guardianship papers allow a nonlegal parent to be treated as a legal parent in medical emergencies. This means that if a child is hurt and in need of medical attention, or needs to be picked up from school, the paperwork allows a nonlegal parent to act for the legal parent, if the legal parent cannot be reached. These forms are easily attainable and can be used by a partner, a parent, a grandparent, or even a babysitter. They simply need to be filled out and notarized. If a parent does not have legal rights to their child, it is essential to carry legal paperwork at all times (some people laminate them so they remain readable even when wet), establishing the right to act as a legal parent.

Durable Power of Attorney A power of attorney document authorizes another person to act as your agent on your behalf and grants him or her access to your money and assets; it gives them power to make financial decisions for you should the time come when you are unable to make decisions for yourself. The durable power of attorney allows you to determine who will have the legal authority to act for you by paying your bills, depositing your checks, filing your taxes, selling your stocks, investing in securities, running your business, selling your property, and applying for insurance benefits for you—in short, everything that a legal spouse would be allowed to do.

Your legal agent has enormous power over your finances and business, and this person must be chosen carefully. If you do not assign a person the status, the decision will be made by the courts, who will most likely pick your next of legal (biological) kin.

Health Care Proxy A health proxy form is used exclusively for authorizing another person to make medical and health care decisions when you are no longer capable of making decisions for yourself. The designated person will be able to make all health care decisions, including the type of treatment, location of treatment, and in addition, the right to refuse or decline life-prolonging treatments. A health care proxy instructs medical personnel to follow the medical guidelines that the incapacitated person would have preferred; it is sometimes called a durable power of attorney for health care (versus finances).

A health care proxy will be allowed to visit you in the hospital, retrieve your personal property from a medical facility, and make important medical decisions for your continuing care, including surgical and pharmacological decisions. Like a durable power of attorney, if you do not have a health care proxy, the court will decide who should be your proxy, and they will most likely pick your next of legal (biological) kin. There is nothing more frightening than to find yourself unable to access a partner who has been hurt or may be dying because you are a legal nonentity. Trying to explain this to your children could be devastating.

Living Wills A living will insures that if you should become terminally ill or have a serious accident and do not want extraordinary measures used to prolong your life, that no lifesaving procedures will be performed, and it instructs your physician about your desires if you are in a life-threatening situation or facing a terminal illness. Without a living will, your life may be prolonged even if you are in a vegetative state, without any hope for recovery. It is best to have both a living will and a health care proxy, since one directs your agent regarding your ongoing needs, and the other directs your physician on how to address a life-threatening situation.

Last Will and Testament A will is a complex legal document that insures that your wishes once deceased will be carried out. If a person dies without a will, it is the state and not the person or his or her family that determines how the estate is distributed. The courts could make decisions regarding the distribution of money, belongings, property, and the guardianship of children that are in direct opposition of what the person may have wanted. Having a will is the only way to insure that family members are financially cared for and minor children remain in the custody of a parent who is not legally recognized. For an LGBT person, a last will and testament is an essential document to make sure that your family is well cared for in case of your sudden death. Having a competent attorney, who is aware of the pitfalls and complications of LGBT family issues, is essential.

Protection of LGBT families may involve an abundance of paperwork and detail that heterosexual partners do not need to prepare for. This can include having information about your partner's assets, knowing where the key to the safe-deposit box with all your important papers are, and making sure that grandparents are aware of your plans and intentions in case of crisis. It is also important if you are in a financial situation to afford life insurance to make sure that your spouse and children are properly recorded on the paperwork.

As long as LGB people are not allowed to legally marry, and the laws governing transgendered people's legal status remain vague, indiscriminate, random, and fluctuating, contracts that specify our intentions and responsibilities may go a long way in protecting our families.

PART THREE

WHEN THE AMERICAN DREAM BECOMES A NIGHTMARE

CHAPTER EIGHT

Divorcing till Death Do Us Part

WHEN LGBT PEOPLE complete the complex legal documentation in order to secure protection for our families, we are doing all we can to take charge of a system that does not have our best interests at heart. Our families are simply more fragile within the current legal structure. We are social misfits considered off the grid of those who believe in family values. Perhaps most of the heterosexual world does not recognize that we might want to reap the benefits of domestic security. Our relationships are assumed to be temporary by much of the straight world, and this is then structurally reinforced by the lack of social and legal supports that would assist us in building a solid foundation for our families.

In the last chapter, we talked about the fragility of families because we do not simply have available the same legal protections as heterosexually parented families. In this chapter, we are going to talk about ways that we ourselves—LGBT people—undermine our own familial commitments, using homophobic law to hurt our children and ex-partners. Blaming the outside world for the oppression we face is easy; surely there is plenty of it. Taking responsibility for how we collude with our own oppression is a harder task; it is always easier to look outside for someone to blame than it is to look within at our values, intentionality, and the ethics that guide our decision making. Sadly, as we have discovered in recent years, sometimes LGBT people do not ourselves recognize or honor the structures of our own families—the structures that we have insisted the courts socially and legally recognize—and then use the legal system to enforce homophobic precedents that dishonor our own relational bonds.

Often while our families are young, we are strongly committed to doing all we can to legally secure our families, although sometimes we are so caught up in the bliss of new love, we neglect to take care of these important matters; after all, many of us think, what could possibly happen to us? However, when things are not going well in our families, when we are breaking up, falling in love with someone else, or being left because our lover has fallen in love with someone else, the bonds that have secured our families can unexpectedly feel like nooses that entrap us. Suddenly, the fact that we don't have legal protections in place, or the precariousness of some LGBT legal precedents, becomes an easy out, severing established family relationships, harshly and with lightning speed, invalidating our children's families.

When couples divorce—and even using the word *divorce* in LGBT families is complicated, because we have not been able to legally marry, and therefore, we cannot legally divorce either—it is generally a painful time in family life, and people are frequently functioning at their lowest. They are sad, struggling with feelings of failure, or they are angry and feeling betrayed. There are financial fears, housing decisions to be made, and concerns about how to manage the daily life tasks, all this while grieving. Often the focal point of all these feelings is the custody of the children and their ongoing care.

Our families are often created, maintained, and structured outside of traditional legal parameters. Our separations and divorces are also therefore structured outside of traditional social systems. I've heard LGBT people complain that they saw an old friend who said, "Are you two still together?" as if their ten-year relationship was a weekend fling. Can you imagine someone saying that to a heterosexual married couple—"Oh, are you two still hanging out?" It is not only straight people who question our commitments to one another, or the homophobic right wing that perceives us all as sexually promiscuous bunnies, but even within our own communities we have often viewed our relationships as transient. It is a consistent complaint of LGBT people seeking therapy: Is it possible to have a long-term, stable, commitment?

And the answer, of course, is that it is very possible. Queer people have had stable, healthy, functioning, and enduring relationships, and we did it long before anyone outside had recognized that these were even relationships. Being queer has nothing to do with our staying power, our ability to commit, to love, to sustain deep, passionate, permanent partnerships. However, being queer does create some obstacles that heterosexual marriages can more easily evade.

First of all, there is the issue of marriage itself. Along with receiving new appliances and social recognition that comes from a public celebration, married couples (read: heterosexual couples) receive more than 1,000 federal protections that are denied LGBT people. This includes both rights and responsibilities to file joint tax returns and enjoy income and estate tax benefits; receive Social Security benefits, family and medical leave, and utilize military and health insurance benefits; inherit property and make medical decisions without filing special paperwork; have joint ownership of homes, cars, and other property (in many states), no matter who bought it; and, in case of a breakup, the sharing of assets and debts. These rights and responsibilities are endowed automatically by merely filing for a marriage license, which costs approximately $25. Additionally, legal marriage assures equal rights in parenting, including shared custody and equal responsibilities for the children's support.

At the time of this writing, it is unclear whether the legal marriages that took place since the winter of 2003 will be recognized by individual states, or how the federal government will respond, especially in the wake of President Bush's war on homosexual families. Although the constitutional amendment has been defeated, the status of gay marriage is still in flux. Will gay marriages remain legally sanctioned, or will this remain an act of outrageous civil disobedience, but without lasting impact?

I think we all recognize the kind of legal chaos that can ensue because we are not legally protected. Anyone who has been out more than a few hours, and perhaps these days anyone, gay or straight, who has read even the mainstream media, is aware of the kind of horrific situations that can impact our lives without these safeguards. Stories abound through the grapevine. For instance, there is the gay man who was denied access to his apartment that he shared with his lover of twenty years after his lover's untimely death, because he was never placed on the lease; if they were married, he would have been protected. There is the woman who was kept from visiting her deathly ill lover in the intensive care unit, because she was technically only a roommate; if they were married, she would've been escorted to the bedside immediately. These are, of course, not just stories, but painful real-life events.

We are at a disadvantage because of the homophobia and transphobia of the legal system even when everything is going well. When things are going poorly, it is a veritable nightmare. Legal precedents aside, there are huge emotional weights that come from having our relationships invisible. The divorce rate for heterosexuals, with all their legal protections and social recognition, hovers at about 50 percent, and the potential of divorce *increases* with each successive marriage. Although it would be great to imagine that queer people have a better handle on this than straight people, the truth is that we face far greater obstacles, both internalized and systemic homophobia, not to mention that we grew up believing that we were exempt from permanent partnerships. The bad news is that our relationships are fragile, like all relationships are, and perhaps increasingly so because of the ambiguity of our legal and social status. Because we lack basic rights, we also can more easily evade responsibilities. We can more easily "slip out the back, Jack," than our heterosexual counterparts, and sadly, many of us do exactly that. As repugnant as this may be for queer couples, when children are involved, it can become a tragedy.

When LGBT couples who are parenting together are facing a breakup, they are in a legal no-man's-land, and given the emotional difficulty of divorce under any circumstances, it can become tempting to use the system to redefine our families in a way that works for us, and disappears or invalidates our children's other parents. When faced with separation, many LGBT people invoke the homophobic laws of the legal system—the same laws we have otherwise opposed—to challenge nonbiological and nonadoptive parents from access to their children.

When we make a decision to parent a child, we need to remember that this decision is a forever decision. When we decide to share that parenting with a beloved, we need to remember that decision is also forever and should not be dependent on how well our adult intimate relationships are functioning. We cannot let our own pain (even when our exes behave in reprehensible ways) impede our ability to honor the familial bonds we'd already forged.

Wanting Out

My partner and I had been together for six years, had a wedding with all our family, and gone through three years of infertility before my partner quit trying and I had our first daughter through alternative insemination. She was a tough baby from day one. She had colic, she screamed from the second we entered air-conditioning until we left again, she screamed when she wanted to stand, she screamed if we put her in a crib, and most importantly, she screamed and wouldn't eat if we left her with anyone. She slept with us. When we tried to change that, she screamed for over three hours one night before we gave in. It was clear to us that she needed to be with us, and we provided that.

She was also delightful, and we parented together well, but we didn't have any time to be with each other, at least awake. After a year and a half of that, we separated. I left. I had absolutely no sense that we would ever be able to retrieve the good parts of that relationship. I didn't even remember what they were. I had all the power. I worked full-time, while my partner stayed home with our daughter. I was the birth mother, my partner only a guardian. We had just started the process of a second-parent adoption.

From that place of exhaustion and lack of hope, all I could see was a long road of shared custody and fighting, or taking advantage of laws not designed for us, and fantasized about leaving my partner behind. I had made a promise to work things out, to do therapy, to stay together through the difficult as well as the joyful. But the doing of it was much more difficult. Our friends were little help. The les-

bians expected serial monogamy, and did nothing to support our working things out. A few straight friends better understood the long-term commitment of children and tried to support us. We started therapy, allegedly to help bring us back together, but I thought more likely to reach an amicable separation. We did a pretty good job sharing custody during that time, with my partner providing the daytime care, and splitting nights and weekends. Interestingly, it gave each of us a break, to rediscover ourselves and begin to remember life before baby.

During this time, the coparent adoption was proceeding. My morals, and my promise, were clear. My partner had been a parent to this baby since the beginning. We dreamed of her, planned for her, and birthed her together. She had done years of infertility treatments, and but for fate, it would have been me with no legal ties. And yet, the pull to take advantage of laws designed not to help but to hurt us was incredible. I would not have believed before that I could have been so tempted to use the patriarchal, homophobic system against her, but I was. Oh, life would have been so easy if I could just walk away, sole parent, and never have to see her or think of her again. But I couldn't do it. It went against everything I believed, every promise that I had made. The vows made before friends and family at our wedding were invaluable in helping me keep focused. And I signed the papers to let her adopt, while sure we would never get back together. We hid the separation from our lawyer, certain she would interfere and stop the process if she knew.

We continued in therapy and actually managed to rediscover the good parts of our relationship. Our daughter got steadily easier as she got older and more able to communicate. She is still sensitive and intense, but now she can express it in other ways than by screaming. Now it is part of what makes her wonderful. We are back together and have two more children. Each infancy and toddlerhood has stressed our relationship, but now it comes back stronger, because we learned how to take care of ourselves as well as our children. We have children because we love each other, and that needs to stay central in our lives. We're still not great at it, but we keep getting better. We've certainly had practice.

Kate Patterson Neely, M.D., partner to Claudia for fourteen years, moms to two multiracial children by donor insemination: Bethan, age eight, and Webster, age four, and one biracial child, Icile, age two, adopted through a private adoption with ongoing contact with her birth family; all children are fully legally adopted now by both mothers. They live in Pittsburgh, Pennsylvania.

There is nothing more important in our battle for legal recognition of our families than our continued respect toward one another as joint parents of our children. Even when our committed relationships end, we must do all we can to secure the relationships our children have to both their parents.

Before we judge too harshly the kind of decisions couples make when breaking up, we need to honestly acknowledge how hard a decision it is to end a relationship and dissolve a family. Every time I sit with a family, queer or otherwise, struggling with separation and divorce, and a parent says to me (and they always do), "I can't bear to see my children's faces when I tell them we are breaking up," I find myself fighting back tears. As a feminist it has always been easy to encourage unhappy women to get the hell out of failing marriages, to seek more in terms of their own fulfillment, to encourage them to create lives that are meaningful and bring them contentment and joy. As a mother, I have come to have far more respect for women who say, "My marriage does not meet my needs, but I can sacrifice my needs for giving my children a good home." These are not easy decisions to make, and especially if our marriage is bad not because of violence or abuse, but just general malaise and dissatisfaction. As a single person, leaving might have been best; as a family member it evokes different challenges to consider.

When separating, it is tempting to want to take the kids and run. For heterosexual people, there are legal protections that stop most people from trying this. For LGBT people, there are often no legal protections, putting us in the complex position of having to defend a nonlegal parent's right to parent, when all we want to do is get as far away from them as we can. Before we talk about how one *should* behave—always easier to know from the outside of any situation—we need to examine the kinds of emotional turmoil someone might experience at the dissolution of a queer relationship, when children are involved.

Maintaining our commitments when faced with separation and divorce must come from carefully examining the kind of commitments we make to one another and recognizing that it is always easier to promise things when things are good than when things are not so good. Before you commit to forever parenting with someone, look carefully at your history of breakups, how you have behaved in the past during a breakup, the kind of contact you maintain with an ex, and imagine seriously what it would be like to have an ongoing committed, forever relationship with an ex, because that is what parenting together with a partner will mean.

The need for community ethics regarding custody disputes is obvious. As LGBT, we stand to a large extent outside of the law, and the courts rarely understand our families or recognize their unique configurations. Yet we are using the court system in increasing numbers to fight over child custody. Many activists and LGBT professionals believe that this is not in the best interests of the children of LGBT people; indeed, engaging with a homophobic system is usually a double-edged sword, even when the outcome is positive.

Due to the difficulty of maintaining cordial relationships following divorces and the reality that LGBT family law is a quagmire of confusion, a document outlining standards for community ethics has been developed. Called *Protecting Families: Standards for Child Custody in Same-Sex Relationships,* these guidelines are a powerful first step in setting a community-based ethic for divorce and separation in queer families with children. At the center of this powerful document is a philosophy that explicitly states that custody decisions are made on what is in the *best interests of the children;* it is assumed that children's interests are best served by respecting the intentions of the families we created and honoring the context of the actual relationship a child has with each parent, rather than the relationships between the parents or the legal or biological position of the parents. These community standards are not meant to replace having proper legal paperwork, nor as an alternative to fighting for the legal recognition of our fam-

The Ethics of Divorce
BY DALE ROSENBERG

I was truly shocked the first time I heard of a lesbian couple breaking up after having a child. Partly it was the shock of the particular situation, having known the couple for some time and thinking they were a happy family. My shock, though, was more than surprise that this particular couple was breaking up. It was an amazement that any lesbian or gay couple with kids would separate. There are so many obstacles for lesbians and gay men having children, and we are a self-selecting group. Generally, the daunting legal, financial, and social barriers weed out all but the most committed prospective parents, and it does not surprise me when couples give up or break up midway. Forming a new kind of family, outside of tradition and outside of the law, can put great stress on a relationship. Having come through all that, though, I had thought that a couple would have survived the big test. It was remarkable and disturbing to me that they would fall apart years later.

As time went on, I have gotten over my initial sense of shock, as I have seen more and more lesbian families going through divorces. In a society where half of all heterosexual marriages end in divorce, the same pressures and factors that cause stress for straight couples affect us, too. There is no denying the fact that having children is an additional stressor. Add to that the additional strain of living in a family that is largely unacknowledged by society at large, and it becomes clear that some of our families will inevitably experience separation and divorce.

So, I've become accustomed to the breakup news, sad as it is. What I can't get used to is what frequently follows. I remain alarmed and disheartened to see how couples decide on issues of child custody and visitation. The most common result seems to be the appalling picture of what Paula Ettelbrick calls "biological parents pulling rank." Couples who, when they plan for and have children, identify themselves as equal parents, suddenly become unequal in the face of divorce. In almost all the cases with which I'm familiar, the legal or birth mother becomes the custodial parent, and the nonbiological mother sees the children when the custodial mother allows it. Sometimes the birth mother allows little or no contact from the start. More often, the nonbirth mother starts off having frequent visitation, but frequency declines, and visits become less regular over time. As time goes on, the birth mother often stops referring to her ex-partner as the child's mother and insists that the child stop calling her "Mom." In any event, it is the birth mother who makes the choices, even when the couple had a clear, unambiguous agreement that they would both be parents to this child, regardless of what happened to their relationship. Birth mothers truly committed to coparenting after divorce exist, but they are the exception rather than the rule.

How can this happen? How can someone say at a child's birth that there are two parents, equally committed and equally responsible, but renege on that later?

Well, I have heard from a number of divorcing birth mothers, and they do not typically believe that they are reneging. In fact, they feel it is their ex-partner who reneged. I have so often heard divorcing birth mothers say, "She never really was a mother. She never truly committed to parenting together," along with a litany of the ways in which the ex failed as a parent.

Now, in many cases, it may well be true that the non-birth mother was an inadequate parent, but surely one's perceptions of the partner are somewhat colored during and after divorce. It's very easy to magnify a person's faults when you are breaking up with them. In fact, it's practically de rigueur. On the other hand, even if the non-birth mother was a really lousy parent, there is a big difference between being an inadequate parent and not being a real parent at all. We seem to accept the birth mother's right to determine whether or not her children have another parent and to change that determination over time. I don't see the lesbian parenting community saying that an inadequate parent is still a parent, that choosing to parent with somebody is a commitment that cannot be dissolved.

Our families are not families of blood ties, they are families of intention and of commitment. I believe we must honor those commitments, even when our feelings about our partners change. I believe children have a right to know who their parents are, and to know that the same people will always be their parents. I do feel enormous compassion for divorcing couples who must deal with these issues. There are few things in life more frustrat-ing than having a lifelong commitment to someone you can't stand. However, parenting *is* a lifelong commitment, and I think our community should support parents in dealing with that frustration, not in avoiding it.

There are those who say that the lack of legal protection is the problem, and that second-parent adoption is the answer. I disagree on both counts. It is absolutely true that we don't have legal protection for children of lesbian and gay couples and we should, but we in the gay community live outside the law in many respects. That doesn't prevent us from developing a sense of community ethics. And it is an overall sense of what is ethical that is missing in this whole dynamic. Family is a social construction at least as much as a legal one. If we are to truly have permanent parental relationships, we need a social ethic that says that they are permanent. There needs to be a consistent community value that says that a commitment to joint parenting is lifelong and nonnegotiable. I've gotten to the point where I feel we need to give this whole "love makes a family" thing a rest for a while. Love doesn't always last forever. A commitment to parenting must, or all of our children suffer.

Dale Rosenberg lives with her three children, Doran, age fourteen, Kendra, age ten, and Zara Miller-Rosenberg, age seven, in Brooklyn, New York. This article was originally published in a slightly different form, in Kids' Talk, a publication of the Lesbian, Gay, Bisexual, and Transgendered Community Services Center of New York.

Protecting Families: Standards for Child Custody in Same-Sex Relationships

These standards were developed by the Gay & Lesbian Advocates & Defenders in Boston, in collaboration with Lambda Legal Defense and Education Fund, National Center for Lesbian Rights, Family Pride Coalition, and the American Civil Liberties Union Lesbian and Gay Rights Project, and has been endorsed by Children of Lesbians and Gays Everywhere. The interpretations below are my own.

1. Be Honest About Existing Relationships Regardless of Legal Labels.

The reality about LGBT family-building is that each of our families is unique, both in terms of our creation and in how we identify our roles. It is essential that we talk about our family configurations and are honest with one another and ourselves about the nature of our relationships to one another and our children. This means that we must honor parental relationships that are neither biological nor legal; it also means that we need to recognize that not all intimate relationships between lovers automatically confer equal parental status (as every divorced and dating heterosexual person intuitively knows), but that situations need to be examined independently.

2. Consider the Dispute from the Perspective of the Child or Children.

The standards focus first and foremost on the needs of the child/ren and the belief that maintaining both parents' current relationships with their children is paramount and must remain the goal of any child custody resolution. They state, "Continuity of their relationships with significant adults is vital to children's well-being."

3. Try to Reach a Voluntary Resolution.

It is, of course, best to reach a satisfying resolution on your own, without involving attorneys. If you cannot resolve the issues, consider involving friends, family, or hire a therapist, mediator, or arbitrator.

4. Try to Maintain Continuity for the Child.

Regardless of the current relationship between the couple, the custody plan should create an ongoing arrangement that most closely resembles the child's current relationship with his or her family. This includes the parents maintaining the same involvement in the child's life, maintaining the same school and extracurricular activities, and sharing time on holidays and special events when possible. Both parents should continue to financially support the child. The standards take a strong stance about severing parental ties: "The abrupt departure of a loved adult simply because one parent has changed his or her view of that person can cause great harm to a child."

5. Remember That Breaking Up Is Hard to Do.

Although obvious, it is easy for people when ending a relationship to see their ex as a demon; remember that the pain of separation and divorce distort our views of our ex. Whether or not the relationship was healthy or ideal, and even if your hindsight is much clearer now that you are ready to leave, the home you shared is still the home in which your child/ren were raised. Demonizing your ex, or the lives you've lived, does harm to the child. Easy does it.

6. Seriously Investigate Allegations of Abuse in Determining What Is Best for the Child.

Allegations of abuse should always be taken seriously, and thoroughly investigated for accuracy. It is essential that professionals with expertise in the areas of domestic violence, LGBT families, and parenting issues are evaluating the situation, since domestic violence can so easily be denied and hidden. It may be difficult to find experts in all three areas, but this is what is necessary, or the evaluation may easily be distorted. It is rare for domestic violence experts to also be knowledgeable about LGBT issues; it is rare for those educated in LGBT issues to also be skilled in domestic violence assessments; and it is even more rare for experts in parenting and divorce to be experts in domestic violence and queer families.

When abuse is substantiated, the safety of both children and adults must be taken into consideration regarding all custody decisions. A caveat is important here: When couples are breaking up, allegations of abuse may be overstated or may be expression of feelings versus facts, (i.e., "I feel like you are cruel to me," versus, "Your behavior is psychologically or physically harmful to me or the children"). It

is, therefore, necessary to always substantiate abuse and never use just the accusation of abuse to deny another person's status as a parent.

7. Honor Your Agreements.

This includes agreements that are made verbally, as well as those that are written. Although circumstances can change, it is very important that commitments made to children are honored and respected.

8. The Absence of Legal Documents Is Not Determinative of the Issues.

For many complicated reasons, not all parents are able to take advantage of securing all legal documentation. This may be because a former spouse still has legal rights, or because it was financially prohibitive to do so; this should not be a determining factor of parental intentions, and should only be one aspect considered in the decision making regarding parental status and custody.

9. Treat Litigation as a Last Resort.

At the Pre-Conference Institute on Queer Parenthood at the In the Family Conference, held in San Francisco on June 1, 2001, Kate Kendall spoke eloquently and powerfully about the increasing frequency of lesbian moms trying to revoke parental rights from former lovers and coparents and the successful litigation attempts to protect the rights of nonbiological parents. Following a raucous round of applause, Jenifer Firestone stood up and, waiting for quiet in the room, deferentially and respectfully said, "We shouldn't be fighting our battles in the courtrooms." As important as it is to have the legal system recognize our families, and/or to fight for our rights, litigation attorneys should always remain a last resort for queer families.

10. Treat Homophobic Law and Sentiments as Off Limits.
It is very disturbing that LGBT people would use homophobic laws to disadvantage one another in a court of law. However, we have done precisely that, saying in essence that an ex-partner cannot have parental visitation because they are homosexual (!), or because there is no legal precedent to grant custody to a nonbiological related homosexual partner. LGBT affirmative attorneys should not be willing to take cases that use homophobic legal standing to invalidate our families.

ilies. It is meant to set a precedent for how we will treat one another, and our children, just in case our fantasies about our relationship or families do not work out as we intended. These guidelines are excerpted above.

Breaking up is obviously very stressful to everyone involved. If one reads the divorce literature, particularly the work of Judith Wallerstein, it is clear that the impact of divorce on children is profound and long-lasting. According to her research, children of divorce have little faith in adult relationships and fear intimacy. They have strained relationships with their families, particularly their noncustodial parent, and have a higher than average incidence of substance abuse and early teenage sexuality.

Wallerstein's research methodology, however, raises a number of important questions. First of all, her research was conducted on a small sample of families, all white, upper-middle-class, and well-educated. More importantly, one would assume that families who are divorcing are also families that are in trouble. In other words, parents don't commonly divorce on a whim; they are divorcing because there are problems in the relationship already—problems that might include everything from disagreements, lack of intimacy, and sexual betrayal, to more complex issues like domestic violence and substance abuse. Wallerstein's work does not compare the impact of how children fare in families that have remained intact but yet suffer from these sort of issues. To compare divorcing families to intact, functioning families begs the issue, which is: Do children being reared in families where the parents are in emotional trouble fare better if the parents separate or stay together? The problems Wallerstein identified might indeed be accurate, but it is possible that if the parents had remained together, the children would have done much worse. It is also true that the problems Wallerstein identified might not be related to divorces in general, but hostile divorces; a focus of research might be how to assist divorcing families in better divorces.

Of course, no one has yet studied how LGBT families cope following or during a divorce. Our research has still mostly focused on how to prove that the very nature of our families is not damaging to our children. We are defensive, and we have a right to be defensive, about any research where the implicit aim is to find dysfunction in our families, as it will surely be used against us. However, the bottom line is that LGBTs are simply people, trying to live as emotionally healthy lives as we can, given the human issues that plague all conscious beings. Our families are as healthy or dysfunctional as we are, which means our families are created with some mixture of the legacy from our own family of origins, plus the coping skills we've managed to accrue—and that's times two if there are two of us parenting together. Few of us are anything resembling perfection, most of us are works in process, all of us are doing the best that we can, and sadly, some of us are in big trouble.

No one likes to think of divorce when we are marrying. No one likes to imagine that we will be one of those couples that don't make it. Some of us LGBT people like to imagine we are better than heterosexuals with their 50 percent divorce rate. A few of us simply believe in serial monogamy and assume that permanent partnership is just a romantic illusion. Or perhaps some of us partner, without the same rules as traditional marriages, leaving more room for polyfidelity, open relationships, or simply moving on when the spark dies out. I've heard that a reporter once asked Margaret Mead, who had been involved in relationships with both men and women of long duration, why her recent marriage had failed. She said, "Oh, it didn't fail. It was glorious, and then it was over." Indeed, whether or not this story has historical veracity, it is a powerful reframing on "till death do us part." Perhaps not every relationship is meant to last forever.

The facts are that half of all children born after 1960 have experienced divorce. During this same time there have been numerous other major changes impacting family development including an obvious increase in women's legal rights and psychological, economic, and reproductive freedoms. For many children of divorce, this was a shameful, frightening experience that left lasting negative effects on their lives. However, we need to ask whether it was divorce per se that negatively impacted these people, or if it was a combination of society's judgment of these failing families, coupled with the dysfunction that was imbedded in an already troubled family.

Although the frequency of divorce might have been a shocking contemporary cultural phenomenon that feeds the religious right's zealous denouncements that the great empire was falling, in reality till death do us part *never* meant thirty to sixty years of togetherness. Two hundred years ago, the human life span was decidedly shorter, and women died in childbirth in higher numbers; a *long*-term marriage might have meant twenty years, or maybe even thirty, but commonly only meant a decade or so. Serial monogamy was as common then as it is now. What differed was the reasons for the dissolution of the first marriage—commonly death, not divorce. A bad marriage had a shorter duration; it certainly did not mean spending another forty years with the person!

Dr. William Pinsof, psychologist, educator, and family therapist, invites us to rethink our traditional assumptions about marriage and divorce; he suggests that, "Divorce and relational dissolution need to be viewed as normal social events in the life course of modern families." Now, before you all send me (or him) hate mail, let me say that I do not think he is minimizing the impact of divorce on individual human lives but rather is speaking to the levels of social policy and sociological theory. We can either continue to see 50 percent of our families as failed and flawed, or we can grow to understand that separation is a potentiality in all families, and something that all families can learn to grow and adapt to in a healthy and functioning manner.

Due to the growth and change that is inevitable during the human life span, it is a fact of modern life that some couples, despite their best intentions and fantasies of forever, will not be able to sustain that promise. It is true for heterosexuals as well as LGBT people. Numerous factors impact the decision to divorce: simple things like falling out of love, or more commonly falling in love with someone else, and complex things like substance abuse, domestic abuse, or mental health struggles. Additionally, people simply change; lifestyle changes can include things like increased religiosity, change of personal interests, following a creative, geographical, or career-oriented dream, or changes in sexual or gender identity. As furious as you may be if your partner leaves you for another woman (or man), or wants to move to Hollywood to pursue a career in the movies, or decides to join a religious community, these things do happen in life, and families need to

A Father's Rights
BY JAMISON GREEN

Our son, Michael, was born in 1989. I cut his umbilical cord and helped the nurse bathe him. He was very different from our daughter Katie, who was then age four. He was long and slender, big-boned yet almost frail in character, fussy and darting as if he were not sure he wanted to be here, while Katie had been solid, substantial, present, and observant, grounded like an old soul. I got a week of paternity leave, and being with both the children was deeply satisfying to me. Katie was a bit disappointed that she didn't have a sister, but she was still fascinated with the baby. She loved to sit in my lap and help me hold him. She loved to watch Robyn nurse him, loved to watch him get his diaper changed, and to talk about herself as a baby and as a big sister. Robyn was understandably tired and quiet during that first week. Friends came over to see Michael, and they often remarked, as I walked them to their cars, that Robyn seemed very distant, somewhat strange. At the end of the week Robyn told me our relationship was over.

I was devastated. We had been together over thirteen years. She had always supported my transsexual identity, but it seemed that once my body had started to change, she realized she did not want to be perceived as heterosexual. She promised to stay with me until after I had my chest reconstruction, the first surgical stage in the female-to-male transition. My transition to male was delayed for many years because of my own fear of losing relationships, the social privilege I had thus far attained in my female body, and the community I had developed in over twenty years among lesbians. She had thought she might be able to endure it, but within a few months she had made up her mind against staying with me.

My surgery was six weeks later. The weekend before I was to go back to work, after a two-week leave, Robyn moved out. The last thing she said to me was, "I'll never take the children away from you."

I maintained regular visitation with both children, although things were awkward and very difficult at first. I ached with loneliness when I would leave the children. And when I was with them I just wanted to hold their bodies close to me. Some people say testosterone takes away their tears, but I cried easily and often. The touch of their little hands around my neck when I carried them, their faces against mine, made me feel that I was real and connected to life.

One day, when Michael was nearly two years old, I received a subpoena and a restraining order. Robyn was suing me for nonpaternity and taking my name off Michael's birth certificate. She also informed me that if I ever tried to get him to call me Daddy, I would never see Katie again. Yes, she was taking Michael away from me. She told me she'd have taken Katie, too, but she acknowledged that Katie was too attached to me, and Robyn felt it would have been harmful to take me away from her. But Michael was not really attached to me, she said. She was in a new relationship, and she wanted her new lover, Linda, to be his coparent. He didn't need a father, too, she said. A child only needs two parents, she said. Katie was instructed not to call me Dad in front of her brother, and Michael was trained to ignore me from that time forward.

I had no legal rights. There was nothing I could do to stop this. There was nothing I could say that would convince Robyn that she didn't need to do this, that I could still be in Michael's life without threatening the new coparenting relationship she had. Five-year-old Katie asked me why I didn't want to be Michael's dad. I told her I did want to be Michael's dad, that as far as I was concerned I am his dad, that she and her brother are both the children their mom and I made together and I will always love them both the same.

"But," I told her, "your mommy and Linda are afraid that if Michael calls me Dad, it will mean he doesn't love them as much as he loves me."

"Well, that's silly," she declared. "There's enough love in the family for everyone."

"That's right, sweetheart. You know that, and I know that, but Mommy and Linda have forgotten it. I wish it could be different, but we have to do what your mommy wants, even though we know there's plenty of love."

As the kids have grown older, sometimes I see Michael when I pick Katie up. I always say hello to him if I can see him, because I don't want him to think I don't know he is there. He says hello to me sometimes. For most of her childhood, though, Katie has seemed to like having me to herself. She's appreciated having her own room at my house, and time

alone when she's with me. As she approached adolescence, I feared being rejected by her, but by the time she was twelve I realized that this was just a residual fear of Robyn on my part. My relationship with Katie is probably one of the healthiest and strongest relationships I will ever have. We grew together, and we respect each other. We love each other and don't think anything will ever change that.

For years I struggled with the shame of being an outcast from my own family. I was ashamed that I could not keep my family together, as if my lack of family unity invalidated me as a father, as a man. One of the worst aspects of being apart from my children was the feeling that I failed as a father because I was not present to do the things that my father did for me, that I wanted to do for my children. When I talk with other divorced men, men who are nontranssexual, who do not have primary custody of their children, I find that this feeling of not living up to the requirements of fatherhood because of lack of presence is common; for some men it is quite debilitating. This sense of failure can permeate every aspect of one's life, and occasionally I felt like I was hanging onto my self-esteem with every fiber of my being.

I still feel sad when I say good-bye to Katie in her mother's doorway. Until very recently she would hug me before her mother opened the door, as if she didn't want to offend her mother with affection for me. I remember how the door slowly swung shut and the lock engaged, leaving me to wonder what the neighbors thought as they watched me walk back to my car, watch me looking in vain at the windows for a child's face searching me out as I drive away after a visit with her. I want just one more look at them, and I wish they wanted to wave to me, the inverse of the way my own father always stood in the window and waved as he watched me drive away. It seems I am always driving away with no one watching now.

Katie is now eighteen and Michael is fourteen. Katie is poised, beautiful, talented, a straight-A student, and very loving with me, her mother, and her brother. The world belongs to her. Michael is not as strong as his sister, not as self-assured, but I hope he will weather his adolescence without too much damage. Linda and Robyn broke up two years ago, and Robyn has decided maybe it would be a good idea for Michael to get to know me now, but not too quickly lest I get the idea that I have any kind of parental relationship or authority over him. He and I have spent a few afternoons together trying to get to know each other. Robyn views herself as the sole parent of her children,

and I pay rent for one of them. I think the fact that Robyn had no incentive to be fair to me, to honor the agreement we had made to live as a family and bring two children into this world together, and that she had the power to control my relationships with our children, is a very sad result of the lack of legal rights for both gay and trans people. Nonetheless, I will persevere. I still accept the responsibility that I took on when we agreed to bring these two children into this world. I will be present for my children. I will be available if and when they need me, and they will always know I love them, no matter what.

Jamison Green, father of Katie, age eighteen, and Michael, age fourteen, is a writer and educator specializing in transsexual issues. He transitioned from female to male in 1988 and his book, Becoming a Visible Man, *is available from Vanderbilt University Press. He lives in the San Franciso Bay Area and can be reached through his Web site: http://www.jamisongreen.com.*

negotiate them in a way that preserves the children's relationship to both of their parents.

Many things impact a couple's decision to break up. For those of us who are very religious, our relationship to God may preclude any thoughts of divorce; for others it is not religious commitments, but moral or romantic commitments that disallow any thoughts of divorce. Sometimes financial dependence can impede thoughts of leaving, as well as questions about our rights to personal happiness. In our modern society, there are strong beliefs about coupling involving love, sex, romance, and passion; historically marriages were more economically based. Most of us believe that our intimate commitments *should* offer us intimacy and personal fulfillment, and we are deeply unhappy if they do not.

Although we've all heard that it is not good to stay together for the sake of the child, and certainly a couple that is in constant distress is not able to provide a loving home for children anyway, ending a relationship for those who are parents is a complex process. Accepting that divorce may be a natural social event in the life cycle of modern families does not mean that it is a trivial thing, or that it has no impact on the people involved. Nor does it mean that marriages are not worth working on, fixing up, healing, or committing oneself to. It simply means that after a person has done all they can to fix up a dysfunctional and unhappy partnership, divorce is an option that, if done respectfully and lovingly, can eventually make life better not only for the parents but also for the children.

One of the problems is that divorces most commonly follow misery and distress. By the time someone decides to leave an unhappy marriage, they rarely have any love or respect left for their partner. They are filled with so much anger and disappointment that it is all too easy to justify taking the kids and leaving, without considering the relationship the kids share with the other parent. Let's face it, heterosexual couples have not been good role models to LGBTs on how to divorce with grace, either. Our modern images of breakups are fraught with ugly legal battles, parents bad-mouthing each other to the kids, and custody battles that involve each parent trying to prove the other one bad; at its worst, parents kidnap their own children. This is not a healthy standard for our families. We must develop responsible ways of dissolving intimate lover relationships that allow for the continuation of coparental relationships.

It is this simple: If you plan on parenting with another person, you must understand that this is a forever relationship—regardless of whether this person betrays you, is a good parent, or whether you hate their guts. Intentional family-building must include permanency for the life cycle of our children. We cannot revoke parental rights on the whim of our passions changing or the fact that an ex-lover had different parenting values than those you agreed on together. We cannot abandon children whom we've agreed to parent based on lifestyle changes. Our commitment to our children must be the basis of all parental decisions that we make.

There are, of course, times when a parent is dangerous or so dysfunctional that responsible parenting is impossible, and in these situations outside authorities must be invoked who will ensure the protection of the children, as well as assist the parent in as much contact with the child as is possible. These situations are rare; in the majority of divorces the other parent is not truly evil or not really a bad parent, but the family is reeling from the shock of the dissolution, and parenting together *forever* truly feels like a nightmare that you can't wake up from. Sorry to say, but you should have thought of that when you decided to parent together with someone. *If you plan on parenting with another person, you must understand that this is a forever relationship.*

Now, I know many of you are reading this and thinking, *This has nothing to do with me, with us. We will never break up. We are not like those others. We have a special love, caring, and commitment.*

Who exactly do you think I am talking about? Where do you think those couples are who do think I am talking to them? Do you actually believe there are couples out there who think, *Well, we'll have babies together, but I don't really plan on being there forever,* or *I'll try this and we'll see if I like it, and if I don't, I'm out of here*? And even if you know a couple or two that is this cavalier, do you think this is really representative of the 50 percent of divorcing couples? We have to accept that couples who do not make it are no different from couples that do, in terms of commitment, desire for longevity, passion, or hope. The reason that some couples don't make it and others do is the subject of great debate and research today; this literature is well worth reading. If forever is your goal, it is good to learn what successful long-term couples *do* or have, so you can try to emulate it. (I recommend the books of John Gottman, Harville Hendrix, and Harriet Lerner for starters.) However, given the statistics we are facing, it is fair to entertain the thought that we *may* actually be one of the couples that don't make it. This is not putting a kibosh on our marriage; it is responsibly preparing for the potentialities. Nobody feels that you are willing a medical crisis or a house fire by buying health and fire insurance.

So what would preparation for potential breakup mean? The very first priority must be talking honestly with one another *before* we have children about the nature of our relationships and our intentionality. Too often we make assumptions about what marriage, coupling, shared parenting, and forever actually mean. Truly one of the great advantages of adoption is that couples are forced to look at these issues by the nature of the invasive adoption process. Couples must look at the impact of their childhoods, their opinions about discipline, their plans for child care, and their financial readiness *before* they are approved to be parents, and before the child/ren come home. It is a model, albeit without the need for Big Brother approval, that is worth emulating.

It is not enough to talk, however; we need to make explicit our intentions by writing them down and legalizing them whenever possible. Luckily, we have skilled professionals who are helping us create procedures and documentation for our intentionality. Jenifer Firestone outlines her personal experiences that have led her to develop a very powerful tool for assisting LGBT families to develop alternative solutions for disputes that arise in the context of our unique relationships. The Family Council, outlined below, pursues an alternative vision to ameliorate custody disagreements between partners following a breakup. Although Jenifer's work explicitly discusses lesbian and gay relationships, I believe the model would be equally successful for bisexual and transgendered people, as well as many heterosexual people in alternative family structures. It allows for creative problem solving, community support, and most important of all, forethought regarding a potential breakup that maintains the children's needs as the center of all decision making.

Jenifer Firestone brings a strong voice and great wisdom to this debate, and I wish that more LGBT families engaged in such conscious decision making while building their families. These guidelines also require professionals, attorneys, and therapists in particular to encourage families in crisis toward solutions that rest outside of the courtroom. Developing Family Councils infers that people have others in their lives that they can trust with this level of intensity and responsibility. It may be, as Jenifer suggests, "a recipe for family disaster" that so many families do not have this level of support; it is, however, an all too common recipe in American society. It seems that in order for Family Councils to become more popular, we need to reexamine how we begin family-building in the first place. We need to be entering building families with more conscious thought about the potential outcomes and the commitments we are making forever. Even if our marriages do not last forever, our relationships with our children must.

Reading this chapter might invoke feelings of angst, fury, or fear about the struggles that our families face if the partners divorce. The decision to honor our commitments to one another is vital, perhaps more important than any other decision we make as parents. It is too easy to dismiss bio-

Rethinking Baby-Making
BY JENIFER FIRESTONE, LCSW

From 1990 to 1996 I coordinated the Alternative Insemination Program at an LGBT-identified community health center in Boston, Massachusetts. During that time, I worked with over 500 women, 95 percent of whom were lesbian couples who wanted to have children by artificial insemination. My job there was largely administrative. I enrolled women in the program, taught them how and when to inseminate, ordered and received their sperm from the sperm banks every month, made sure there was enough dry ice and liquid nitrogen in which to store and transport the sperm, and was there to dispense it to them when they came to pick it up. I agonized with them over each of the hundreds of unsuccessful attempts and tore my hair out with them over the crazy-making quest of perfectly timing the next insemination.

It was never in my job description to talk to them about what it really meant to be coparents with each other forever, about how they knew that they were the right people for each other to do this with, or about how they might arrange their coparenting lives if they broke up when their child was fourteen months, two years, or six years old. I'm not sure I even knew how to talk with women about these issues ten years ago. And there was no question in my mind that they were not interested in taking even a tiny peek at these issues.

But, with every one of those 500-plus couples, I wondered about these issues. In the process of recovering from the devastating breakup of a seven-year

relationship that I adored and that nearly included parenthood, I personally could not fathom that level of confidence in a relationship of the magnitude of coparenting. I felt alone and somewhat ashamed of my skepticism about the nuclear family model I was facilitating every day in my work.

In the years since then, I have witnessed the deeply disturbing procession of breakups between at least 100 of the couples whose successful inseminations I assisted. I've seen a biological mother railroaded by her more dominant girlfriend into a second-parent adoption she didn't really want. I've seen nonbio moms who have second-parent adoptions wind up with visitation that is excruciatingly next to nothing. I've seen a nonbio mom abandon her former partner and their three children to pursue the youthful affair she never had, protracted custody disputes in the courts, and behavior between divorced moms in shared custody arrangements that is the equivalent of raising children on a toxic waste dump.

The Family Council
© *Jenifer Firestone, LCSW*

What is a Family Council? A Family Council is a creative problem-solving body of friends, family members, and/or professionals who help prevent and resolve family disputes between same-sex couples and between lesbians and gay men who have children together. Family council members are chosen by the individuals who agree to conceive or adopt a child together. The function of the Family Council is to help families in times of upheaval uphold the integrity of their mutual understanding for having and/or raising the child.

Inspired by the model of the Tribal Council, the supportive involvement of a Family Council provides a structure in which a family can dispense with shame and defensiveness and avail themselves of the creative and collective problem-solving capabilities of their selected body of close friends, colleagues, and/or professionals. The Family Council challenges the nuclear insularity and isolation common to many American families by creating an extended network of individuals who agree to look out for the internal welfare of that family.

Ideally, family members create their Family Council when they are in the process of planning how their family will look and function. These plans should be written down in the form of an agreement that are explicit written statements of understanding about the legal, logistical, financial, social, emotional, and interpersonal expectations, possible eventualities, and commitments involved in having and raising a child together. (If plans are not made before the child's birth or adoption, they can be initiated at a later date, preferably before a crisis occurs.)

In preparing such agreements, the parents examine assumptions that might otherwise go unspoken because of people's unconscious fear of jeopardizing the mutual pursuit of parenthood. Parents are encouraged to talk affirmatively and without judgment about the legal, emo-

tional, logistical, social, and interpersonal differences between biological and nonbiological lesbian mothers. Issues regarding the changes of heart, mind, and circumstance that must be acknowledged as part of the normal evolutionary possibilities of human relationships are discussed. Also discussed are the specific attitudes and actions that constitute cooperative and uncooperative ways of relating to one's coparent when they are no longer romantic partners.

Each parent agrees to choose one or two people to serve on the Family Council based on their ability to understand, appreciate, and support the family and their thorough agreement that the family has a viable model for raising a child. While each family member chooses members for the Family Council, they are not intended to represent any particular family member. Family Council members represent the family as a whole, the child in particular, and the intentions for the child's care and custody as described in the agreement. Given this responsibility, all parties must agree to and feel (relatively) comfortable with each Family Council member.

What must a Family Council member agree to do? Family Council members must:

- deeply understand the parenting agreement the couple has made and the intentions it represents;
- be enthusiastic about the child-rearing model it describes;
- appreciate the complexity of alternative family relationships;

- be interested and able to engage in creative problem solving;
- enjoy thinking outside the box;
- refrain from siding with the family member to whom s/he is most closely related;
- honestly and compassionately confront that family member if s/he thinks that person is being unreasonable;
- collaborate in good faith with the other Family Council members to hear all sides of the dispute;
- craft a thoughtful resolution; and
- advise the parties in the implementation of the recommended solution.

Over time, Family Council Members might need to be replaced if they no longer feel able to participate due to a change in their own circumstances or a significant change in their relationship with a family member.

Under what circumstances is the Family Council convened? Family members convene the Family Council when the parents have a problem that significantly impacts any of their respective relationships with the child, which they have been unable to resolve among themselves or in therapy or mediation, and one or both parents are threatening to go to court to resolve the dispute.

How does the Family Council operate? Members of the Family Council should respond to the request of the parents to convene, as they would come together for any serious family crisis. They should arrange with the parents to come together for several days so they can meet with each parent to hear their perspective and experience of the problem, as well as their suggested solu-

tion/s to the problem, and develop collective recommendations for resolving the conflict.

Their recommendations should include a description of concrete actions or arrangements; the logistics involved in those actions or arrangements; and the specific behaviors, attitudes, and sentiments required and forbidden in order to effectuate the recommendations and protect the child from the harm. Bringing Family Council members together could be costly and should be borne by all parents. However, the cost should be a fraction of the cost of litigation and should be recognized as such.

Why is a Family Council preferable to conventional courts of law? Litigation and the caustic behavior and sentiment it engenders leave children in an horrific position. Reliance on litigation as a default mechanism for resolving dispute cuts us off from people who could provide worthwhile perspectives and creative solutions. Litigation forces us to air our dirty laundry in the mainstream public that will not hesitate to use it against us in a larger context. Probate courts can issue orders but do not address the attitudes and behaviors that promote a climate of acrimony that undermines the effective implementation of postdivorce child-rearing arrangements. Probate courts do not recognize, much less appreciate, the complexities of alternative family relationships, nor do they seek alternative solutions to the disputes that arise in the context of those relationships.

Why are people skeptical of the concept or proposed use of a Family Council? Despite the financial expense, protracted procedures, and unreliable attitudes toward LGBT families, many in our community hold fast to the belief that existing mainstream courts will dispense justice to our families. People are often inclined to have more faith in an existing model, no matter how flawed, rather than a new, more appropriate model. LGBT family members who might benefit from homophobic laws and institutions will often resort to them in order to get what they want. These people would not be inclined toward an LGBT-specific model that does not ascribe to homophobic laws and sentiments.

LGBT people have not been permitted to engage in binding relationships and may be unaccustomed to having to answer to people outside the immediate family. Modern American culture is attached to a privatized, nuclear family arrangement. We often feel like we are the only ones we can trust to deal with family problems and view outside assistance as interference. Involving people outside the nuclear family in dispute prevention and resolution builds in a certain level of accountability.

Whether we like it or not, LGBT people are the essential creators of alternative family models. As such, we owe it to our children and our communities to evolve *a radically different community ethic and culture* for our families. Given the universality of family problems, it behooves us all to dispense with the pursuit of the picture-perfect family (not really attainable for queer families, anyway) and focus on managing our family problems in ways we and our children can be proud of. Alternative family planning must not *only* be about alternative ways of *getting* children, but about alternative ways of relating to those people with whom we conceive or adopt those children, particularly in times of adversity.

Jenifer Firestone, LCSW, is the founder of Alternative Family Matters in Cambridge, is the mother a nine-year-old daughter, whom she coparents with two gay men. She can be reached at 617-576-6788, or jenifer@alternativefamilies.org or www.alternativefamilies.org.

logical moms who sever ties with their ex-partner as selfish, cruel, stupid, or just plain evil. The truth is that power is a heady thing, and maintaining a relationship with an ex you despise is no easy thing.

During a breakup few people are rational. The nonbiological/nonlegal parent is terrified that the ex will use power, perhaps both partners are emotional wrecks, which then can be used as ammunition by the other (i.e., "*She* is in therapy, on medication, totally unfunctioning," etc.). Sometimes one or both partners are vicious to the other, and, of course, the children are witnessing this. It doesn't have to be like that.

Having a successful divorce may not have been part of the fantasy you imagined when you first fell in love and planned a family together. Yet having a successful divorce might be the greatest gift you can offer your children.

It Takes a Village of Exes

Any lesbian who denies her ex-partner parenting rights should be dragged in heavy wooden stocks through the local queer neighborhood wearing a dunce hat as she's pelted with rotten vegetables and cow dung. And any lesbian who takes her case against her ex-partner to court deserves to be sent to a Christian fundie homo-conversion program and forced to live out her days trapped in a show marriage to a closeted gay man in a small town in Oklahoma. If you're moronic enough to turn to a ruling body that doesn't recognize your relationship in the first place, you deserve everything Jerry Falwell wants for us.

Doesn't matter how much you hate your ex, doesn't matter how much you want her out of your life. If you do this to your children—rip them away from a parent, poison a loving relationship—I'll be the first in line with rotten tomatoes.

My ex and I broke up five years ago. We wanted to kill each other. I certainly couldn't imagine healing, moving forward, until she was erased from memory. Problem is, once you have children together, the parenting part of your relationship can never end unless one of you is willing to walk away from the kids, which was not going to happen here. So we set about doing what all couples with children need to do anyway: keeping the children first and pushing our own junk aside.

We went a few times to a couple counselor for what we thought was a last-ditch effort to stay together. The therapist quickly recognized, however, that this ten-year thing was *over*, and seeing that we were at times irrational, took strong, clear measures to ensure our sons' well-being. She very clearly put us second. It was sobering. She issued edicts: 1. no screaming/fighting in front of the children; 2. separate quickly, and avoid being in the same place around the kids any more than absolutely necessary; and 3. never say anything bad about the other mom in earshot of the kids. This gave us our first feeble sense of direction in the maelstrom.

My ex moved five blocks away. We worked out a schedule with equal custody, each keeping the boys half a week and every other weekend. Early on it was, of course, excruciating. The first time I watched my ex and her new girlfriend walk away with my sons on their shoulders—taking them for their first overnight in my ex's new home—I crumpled and cried so I thought my guts would rip. But time really does make a difference. Slowly, life began to take on order again. We settled into our new routine; still a family, but a family apart.

We had no choice but to communicate. Our sons were no fools. Almost immediately they learned to play one of us off the other in ways that made their pre-breakup efforts seem amateur. My ex and I quickly learned to compare notes and call the boys on their divide-and-conquer tactics. Like it or not, raising our boys demanded near-daily communication: music lessons, parent/teacher conferences, birthday parties, play dates, doctors' appointments, Little League, holidays—and it got easier. Gradually, the pain receded. A new relationship, a healthier one based on raising our children, replaced the poisoned one that died between us.

It's simple logic: if my ex suffers, so do my children. So even though every cell in me wanted revenge, I found myself doing things that, despite my venom, helped my ex, because it was good for my kids.

Where are we now? We are friends. We depend on each other. The bitterness is gone, and we're a team again, with a very clear purpose. No, it's not ideal. I still believe (as does my ex) that it would be best for our guys if we could have worked things out and stayed together. The separation was very rough on them. But we couldn't fix it, so we're giving them the best we can under the circumstances. Our boys need both of us. They were adopted at ages three and five respectively, and so both remember a time when they had no family. What would it have said to them if one of us had left their lives after promising to love them forever?

Successful coparenting apart is in part the result of a deceptively simple factor: putting our children first. If you've made the decision to become a parent, you should already have done that. If you now parent your children separately, you simply continue what you started. Golda Meir wrote, "We will have peace with the Arabs when they love their children more than they hate us." Same principle here. If you love your children more than you hate your ex, peace and healing will happen. Not overnight, but it will happen.

Julie Delaurier lives with her two sons Makara (Mak) and Vannarith (Van), five blocks away from her ex, Jenifer Levin, who also lives with her two sons Makara (Mak) and Vannarith (Van). Mak and Van are both twelve (no, they're not twins), and all live in New York City.

• • •

CHAPTER NINE

Nightmare on Elm Street

DESPITE HIGH HOPES, tenacity, and putting our nose to the grindstone, relationships and families do not always work out as planned. There, I said it. Sigh. No one really likes it when we talk about the underbelly of family life. But in reality there *is* an underbelly to family life, a soft, hidden vulnerable side of the American dream, a dream that is filled with terror, violence, drunkenness, and chaos. And it is something we need to talk about, even if we want to look the other way, turn the page, and deny the pain.

When I started doing work on lesbian battering in the mid-'80s, I was told over and again that violence didn't happen, didn't happen often, and didn't happen enough to make an issue out of it. I was told it was not a social problem but an aberration, nothing worth the time and attention of the queer community, and certainly not something we should let anyone outside the community know about. I was told numerous times that I was playing into the enemies' hands by exposing these facts, that the religious right would use the information that domestic violence happened in lesbian relationships as an excuse to push for homophobic laws. I was told, directly, and sometimes quite abusively, to *shut up,* that even if lesbian battering happened, it was best to keep it hush-hush, best to not tell, certainly not to publicize it in mainstream magazines.

There is a reason the first book written on lesbian battering was called *Naming the Violence*. Only a few of us were brave enough to continually speak out (the same few over and over again), but we did not make friends for doing this. I am still convinced that speaking out is what we need to do. It is true that some homophobes may use this information to hurt us, but they will use whatever they can find; it is their agenda to disqualify us from humanity, and although I do not want to purposely feed their goals, I will not live in a manner that dodges every anticipated move. More importantly, it is simply the truth: battering happens, and to avoid it or deny it would be a lie. Lying will not protect us from the homophobes, and it will hurt battered queer people and our children; thus the choice is obvious to me.

It is not just domestic violence that we often avoid talking about. It is addictions, and not just alcoholism, but hard-core addictions: crack cocaine, heroin, and designer drugs. It is mental illness: untreated bipolar disorder, post-traumatic stress disorder, panic disorders, and, of course, depression. And very sadly, it is child abuse, too. If we really care about making LGBT families safe and secure, we must start by looking at LGBT families that are the most in danger, unstable, and at risk.

DOMESTIC VIOLENCE, ADDICTIONS, AND MENTAL ILLNESS

We have spent the last decades convincing others (and ourselves) that LGBT people would make fine parents. We spent years advocating that our sexuality and our unique gender expressions did not impede our ability to be parents, and, of course, this is absolutely the truth. But what we haven't acknowledged is that although LGBT people can make fine parents, great parents, and wonderful parents, we are also simply humans and struggle with all the same issues that other human beings, other parents, struggle with. We are not immune from addictions or the ravages and legacies of our own dysfunctional families. LGBT people represent a cross-section of all humans, and therefore—although most of us are protective, conscientious, and skilled parents—there are also those among us who leave children alone in apartments while they go out drinking and using. Some of us are struggling with severe post-traumatic flashbacks and depression, which impede our ability to get our kids to school, or get bathed or fed; there are those of us who are enacting horrific violence and terrors on our same-sex partners in front of our children.

This is not easy to talk about. Perhaps you want me to be hush-hush, too. Perhaps you think I am exaggerating: this may happen, you are thinking, this may happen but not commonly, rarely, hardly ever; it's an aberration. Well, the truth is that I don't know how often it happens, and I'm not sure anyone else does either. We have some statistics about the frequency of domestic violence in lesbian and gay relationships, which is believed to be equal to the rates in heterosexual couples. How many of these people are parents is unknown. Whether domestic violence is more or less frequent in queer parents than in other LGBT people is also unknown. We do know that addictions, particularly alcoholism, are higher among lesbian and gay people; some statistics suggests it is as common as one out of three lesbians and gay men who struggle with addictions. How many of these people are parents is, again, unknown. What I do know for sure is that it does happen, and I have no reason to suspect it happens less often than it does among heterosexuals; I know that if any of these things are happening in one queer family, that it is all of our business to do something about it.

Mental illness is a subject rarely spoken about. Once upon a time all homosexuals were categorized as mentally ill, and were given our own label in the diagnostic textbooks. Transgendered and transsexual people still have this dubious honor; having a gender variant expression *is* a mental health disorder. The work of getting homosexuality out of the diagnostic manuals was an arduous task, and there are clinicians who still advocate for its inclusion; removing "gender identity disorder" out of the DSM, will be the work of the next decade. Most clinicians today feel comfortable admitting that lesbians, gay men, and bisexual people are not mentally ill, ipso facto, because of their sexual identity, and hopefully more and more clinicians are coming to understand that transgender and transsexual people are not mentally ill either, simply because of their variant gender identities. However, that does not infer that all LGBT people are mentally stable; some of us are struggling with mental illnesses or emotional dysfunctions, and that can impact our ability to function, including adequately parenting our children.

On one hand, this is a no-brainer. LGBT people can be as mentally or

emotionally challenged as can any other person. LGBT people can be addicted or living with domestic violence; they can be depressed or anxious or
agoraphobic. LGBT people can be good or bad parents just like any other
person. Sadly, in a homophobic and transphobic world, where the vast majority of child protective workers, addictions counselors, social workers,
psychologists, attorneys, and judges are poorly trained about the basic life
issues of LGBT people, their ability to discern queer issues from other issues is murky. When LGBT people are most vulnerable and most in need of
support, we are at the mercy of mental health systems that can be potentially traumatizing to our families.

Reaching out for help with an alcohol problem, having an emotional
breakdown in a public place due to a flashback about childhood sexual
abuse, getting caught dealing drugs, contacting an agency because you are
uncomfortable with how frequently you are spanking or yelling at your
kids, can, sadly, bring the wrath of homophobic authorities onto your family. Suddenly, instead of having helping professionals assisting in your healing and the maintenance of your family, you are additionally fighting foster
care systems for your right to maintain custody of your children. Often
families that are struggling with these kinds of issues are the least likely to
be financially solvent and are therefore dependent on public legal services
and mental health clinics versus private attorneys and psychotherapists
who may be better schooled in LGBT issues. Many of these families do not
know about, and may have never thought about, issues of legal protection;
some do not even know that there are specialized services for LGBT people,
i.e., therapists, attorneys, domestic violence services, and addiction treatment programs, who understand the unique issues of our families and, of
course, often these services are only available in larger cities.

Many LGBT people who are struggling with mental health issues are
also living in poverty, and some of them are parents. It is hard to confront
the reality that addictions, abuse, and mental illness exist in our communities; it is even harder to accept the consequences if we do not address it. The
greatest enemy for all of our families is not the addictions, violence, or
mental health struggles per se, but the isolation they can cause for loved
ones and the children who depend on us. In our efforts to prove to the outside world and to ourselves that we are just average families, we must not
avoid facing some of the ways that we really *are* just like other families. In
our mad rush out of the closets, and our insistence that we will not go back,

we must not forget that some of us are being haunted by skeletons we may wish we could leave back in the closet but that are following us around, loudly rattling their bones.

Addictions

Lauren was devastated when her lover of ten years left suddenly and without hardly any warning. They had parented Lauren's two children from a previous marriage together, sharing custody with the children's father, with whom they had an amicable and close relationship. Lauren was deeply in love with her partner, was shocked by her betrayal followed by her refusal to have any contact with the two children to whom she had been "Mommy" since their toddlerhood. The children were grieving and rageful, and she was thrown into severe financial debt, just as winter was coming to their rural homestead. Lauren began drinking and drinking and then drinking some more. She had never had any problem with alcohol before, although as the snow descended she was drinking on a daily basis, barely getting food on the table for dinner, ignoring the bills that piled up by the front door, and falling into a unconscious slumber on the couch each evening; the children began setting their own alarm clocks to make the school bus.

It was only when an old high school friend came to visit and, upon seeing the empty liquor bottles on the floor, the four days' worth of dishes in the sink, and the pallor of fear over the kids' faces, she took the risk of calling it as she saw it. She confronted Lauren on her alcoholism. Lauren's first reaction was to throw her friend out of the house, trash her living room, and then drink herself into oblivion. Her friend took the kids over to the dad's house, and over the next few days, slowly, as Lauren woke up from her alcoholic daze and heard the truth in her friend's words, she was shocked at how bad her drinking had become. Lauren agreed to an intake session with an addictions counselor, which began her long road to healing. It was not an easy time for the next few months, but Lauren did commit to getting sober, got active in AA and therapy, and continued parenting with her ex-husband but allowed him to take on the bulk of the parenting for a few months so she could focus on her recovery. Four years later, Lauren is still sober, has grieved the loss of her lover, and finally has become stable enough to help her children grieve that loss, too. She credits her friend's forcefulness as saving her life.

If you think that you, or somebody you love, have a problem with alcohol and/or substance abuse, do not hesitate to reach out for help. The truth is the addictions field is way ahead of most mental health professions in understanding and treating LGBTs who are chemically dependent. Many communities have AA and NA meetings specifically for LGBT people, and on-line resources are abundant. The common warning signs for addiction are listed below but, in short, if you think you might have a substance abuse problem, you probably do. And it is probably worse than you realize. Find a counselor or begin to attend an outpatient support group; if necessary, you can make arrangements for your children to stay with a friend or family member for a few weeks and treat yourself to an inpatient recovery program. Although it can be difficult to make the necessary arrangements, it can be done, and your children, although frightened at the time, will thank you for taking this step as they watch their lives improve.

If your partner is struggling with addiction and is in denial about how serious it is (which is likely), you must reach out for help for yourselves and your children. Interventions, whereby trained specialists assist the family in confronting the addict about their substance abuse, can be very effective in helping addicts see their problems and seek out help. There are few things more powerful than having your eight-year-old sit across a room and tell you the impact your drinking has on him and how it felt when you missed his baseball game, destroyed the Lego castle he'd spent the afternoon making, or how embarrassed he is to invite his friends over the house. Of course, these interventions are potentially volatile, and then the need for a trained professional is necessary.

Has Your Use Turned into Abuse?

Answer yes or no to the following questions.

1. Have you ever decided to stop drinking or taking drugs for a short period of time, but not been able to stick with it?

2. Have loved ones told you they are concerned about your drinking or drug use?

3. Do you find yourself drinking more than you said you would, or going to the bar when you promised that you wouldn't?

4. Do you ever wake up after a night of drinking or drugging unsure who you had sex with, or whether the sex you had was safe?

5. Do you ever wonder why other people seem to be able to drink without getting into trouble?

6. Have you had problems connected with drinking or drug use during the past year, whether legal, medical, financial, or social?

7. Has your drinking caused trouble with your personal relationships (parents, children, significant other)?

8. Do you tell yourself you can stop drinking or drugging any time you want to, even though you keep getting drunk or stoned when you don't mean to?

9. Have you missed days of work or school because of drinking or drug use? Do you spend money on drugs or drinking that should be used to pay the bills?

10. Do you have blackouts (times when you are drinking or using drugs and cannot remember what you've done after you are sober again)?

11. Do you find yourself using or trying drugs that you had sworn you would never use?

12. Do you drink or use on a daily basis? Do you get very drunk or stoned at least a few times a week?

Did you answer *yes* four or more times? If so, you probably have a drug and/or alcohol problem. Please take this seriously and seek out help for yourself and your children.

Abuse and Violence

Michael and Todd had been together for over eight years and had adopted two children from Guatemala. Todd had always been very controlling but became more so once they had children. Michael was a stay-at-home dad; although he would've preferred to continue working, Todd would not allow it. Todd would return home from work and berate Michael on a daily basis for the condition of the home, how bad dinner was, and blame him for the children's behavior. Occasionally, he would strike out, slapping Michael hard on his face, or pushing him against the wall while lecturing him about finances or housecleaning. He was very hard on the children, maintaining a near-military discipline that often left them fleeing and crying in their bedrooms. The older child began to pee his bed at night. Michael was frightened for his safety and for the children's.

The final straw came when Todd forced Michael to have sex. The next day, when Todd was at work and the kids were at school, Michael called a domestic violence hot line. He explained the situation, feeling embarrassed and concerned that the person would laugh at a man calling an abuse hot line. The counselor on the phone was supportive and outlined numerous options for Michael. She encouraged him to put together a safety plan—a friend he could call, emergency housing with his parents, contacting a lawyer to secure his parental rights and financial status, putting away a small amount of money and a suitcase with clothes for him and the kids that was hidden somewhere along with a car key. Most importantly, the counselor told Michael that the behavior was indeed abuse. Michael followed through on these suggestions over the next few days, and about a month later, when Todd came home yelling, slamming doors, and began hitting their youngest child, Michael knew he had had enough. After Todd fell asleep, he quietly woke the children, took the suitcase he'd hidden in the closet, and drove 300 miles to his parents' house, his hands shaking the entire way. The breakup was long and painful, but Michael was able to retain custody, Todd was granted supervised visitation, and Michael and the children began a new life, healing from the wounds that had been inflicted. Many years later, Todd was able to apologize for his behavior and admit that Michael had done the right thing for the children.

When domestic violence or child abuse is happening in a family, the level of powerlessness and terror can be overwhelming. Domestic violence is a pattern of verbally abusive, physically violent, psychologically threatening, or sexually inappropriate or forceful behavior. Resources, on-line or through a local agency, to help you identify violent behavior are easily ac-

Forms of Violence

- Psychological abuse/"gas lighting"
- Emotional abuse
- Threats/intimidation
- Destroying property, harming pets or animals
- Heterosexist control, outing partner without consent
- Financial abuse
- Sexual abuse
- Physical abuse
- Isolation
- AIDS-related battering
- Stalking/harassing

Myths of LGBT Domestic Violence and Sexual Assault

- Only heterosexual women are victims of domestic violence.
- Men are never victims, and women never abuse.
- Domestic violence is more common among heterosexuals than lesbians or gay men.
- It's not violence if same-sex partners fight—it's just a lovers' quarrel.
- It's easier for gay men or lesbians to leave abuse than heterosexuals.
- People who engage in violent behaviors more likely hang out in bars, are poor, or are people of color.
- People under the influence of alcohol or substance abuse can't be held accountable for their behavior.
- People who are victims of domestic violence suffer from codependency.
- Many people think that lesbians couldn't abuse one another since they are seen as nonviolent and peaceful.
- Only those who are in butch/femme relationships, or who practice S/M are thought to be violent, with the butch (or the top) assumed to be the batterer.
- Some people think that when gay men batter their partners, it is mutually abusive (mutual combat), because boys will be boys.
- Just as in heterosexual couples, many people think that victims of partner battering like the abuse, or that jealous rage is a form of love.

- The law or police will not protect LGBT victims of violence.
- Lesbians can't rape each other.
- Lesbian assault isn't as traumatizing for the victim.

- Gay men don't rape.
- Men always want sex.
- Male-on-male rape is gay sex.

cessible. If you feel threatened, feel like you are walking on eggshells, feel that you have no voice in your relationship, or if you are forced to engage in sexual behavior against your will, are repeatedly harassed, attacked, or isolated from loved ones, there is a problem in your relationship. Domestic violence is about power and control issues; it may involve physical or sexual violence but commonly involves a pattern of psychological control, jealousy, and assaults on the self-esteem and self-worth of the victim. Do not hesitate to reach out for help, although you may need to do so carefully so as not to invoke the increased anger of your perpetrator. Many domestic violence shelters have become educated about lesbian battering, although resources are still scant for gay men and transgendered people.

If you believe yourself to be a batterer, please do not hide behind shame and fear; your loved ones need you to help yourself. Eventually, they will seek out help, and then it may be too late for them to walk with you through your recovery process. Few things are harder than healing from domestic violence as a family, and it is rare that batterers will truly embrace the work they need to do to heal. It may be necessary for the partner and children to seek out safety by leaving the relationship.

If you are living in a family where children are being hurt—physically, psychologically, or certainly sexually—you must do everything you can to protect the children, even if you know the exposure will rip your family apart and put you under the scrutiny of a homophobic system. Placing the children first must be our highest priority. If you cannot do anything else, call an anonymous help line and let them walk you through the steps you can take. If you try to avoid dealing with the situation, eventually the abuse will be exposed, and the options available for your family will become far more limited, especially if the authorities discover the abuse, than if you make arrangements for your children's safety first, and then seek out help.

Depression and Other Mental Health Problems

Elsa knew that Matthew was depressed, but they both assumed that the depression would lift once he followed through on his gender transition. The process involved significant financial costs and emotional struggles over many years, while Elsa processed how Matthew's transition would impact her lesbian identity. During this time, Elsa had birthed two children through donor insemination, who had only known Matthew as their father. Matthew had everything he ever thought he'd wanted, after fearing for many years that he would lose Elsa if he transitioned. On the surface, their lives were perfect. But Matthew was still depressed; in fact, he was more severely depressed than ever before. He often couldn't get out of bed, was irritable to the children, demanding of Elsa, and not following through on work and social commitments. He resisted any suggestions that he seek help.

Elsa sought out therapy on her own. She was able to find a counselor that would help her develop coping strategies to deal with Matthew's depression while assisting her in understanding the serious nature of his depression and the impact it was having on the functioning of the family. Elsa became stronger in her awareness of Matthew's behavior and began to break away from the daily manipulations caused by the depression. She began to quietly insist that Matthew address these issues, or that she would need to consider ending the relationship. Angry and afraid, Matthew reached out for help. The first therapist he saw kept trying to analyze the depression as it related to Matthew's transition, particularly his often vulnerable fears about whether he was really a man. Although Matthew was able to identify his own struggles with his newly acquired manhood, he felt that the therapist was unable to see past the transsexual issue. Eventually Matthew found another therapist who was able to assist him in finding appropriate medication and working with him psychotherapeutically on acquiring daily skills to manage his depression, in addition to issues related to transition and adjusting to family life. Although the depression did not fully resolve, Matthew was able to continue to address the things he was struggling with, which made their home life less stressful. The family was able to refocus, for the most part, back onto the children's needs, now that the grown-ups were taking care of their own needs.

Mental illness, particularly depression, anxiety, and post-traumatic stress symptoms are common, in and out of the LGBT community. More people are currently receiving treatment for these problems than ever before, and thankfully the stigma of having a mental illness is somewhat lessening. There should be no shame for being depressed or anxious, or needing help to face issues from childhood sexual abuse. Panic attacks, obsessive-compulsive disorder, generalized anxiety, and serious mental health problems like bipolar disorder and schizophrenia are more common than most people realize. There are competent clinicians who can help you to receive a proper diagnosis. Advances in medicine are assisting people with biochemical mental disturbances to live healthier and productive lives. If someone you love is struggling with depression, flashbacks, or phobias, encourage them to seek out help, and if they refuse, seek out help anyway for yourself and your children. Most people with mental illnesses are capable of parenting their children, but they may need clinical and social supports to do so effectively. This may involve community involvement of social service agencies, family support, and resources within the LGBT community.

Depression is a serious mental health issue that affects thousands of people each year, sometimes to the point of complete disability, and more commonly where we feel a lack of interest in daily tasks and find ourselves exhausted and very sad. Depression is often accompanied by an overwhelming feeling of sadness, lethargy, and unhappiness, along with difficulties or changes in eating or sleeping patterns, and can include isolation and social withdrawal. Depressed people can be very irritable, angry, or anxious. Depression has biological and psychological components, and although some people are able to break out of depressions on their own, others find pharmaceutical medicine a literal lifesaver.

Depression is a common experience when dealing with unsuccessful attempts to get pregnant, following a miscarriage or ectopic pregnancy, or while waiting forever for an adoption to be completed. Although it is normal to feel depressed while coping with infertility, when it begins to impact your ability to work or enjoy the good things in your life, it can become potentially dangerous. Continuing infertility treatments can exacerbate the depression. Surprisingly, successful pregnancy might not alleviate it.

For those of us who longed for children and finally have them, we may be shocked to find ourselves unhappy, sad, isolated, and feeling very depressed. Postpartum depression is very common following the birth of a child, but it is also common to experience these symptoms postadoption. No matter how much you may desire children, no matter how happy you are to have a family, the shock and exhaustion of new parenting often throws us for a loop. This is not a gay thing. It happens to all parents, although we may feel protective and defensive talking about it if we are fearful that others will see our depression as proof that we are not capable parents. As LGBT parents, we are under greater scrutiny by the outside world—judgmental neighbors, adoption social workers, etc. It is important not to buy into the myth that our mental health difficulties are in any way associated with being LGBT parents. Postpartum blues happen to many new parents, not just LGBT ones.

As hard as it may be to admit that you are not taking to parenting like a duck to water, be patient and gentle with yourself. The reality of forever with a helpless, dependent child is enough to really frighten even the butchest among us. Becoming a parent is a huge transition and, especially for those of us who like things "just so," parenting brings with it a tremendous amount of indecision and worry. Be honest with what you are feeling, and seek support. When you speak with other parents, you will discover that you are not alone or unique in feeling depressed, blue, scared, overwhelmed, and fearful that you made the worst mistake of your life.

Parenting infants is often exhausting. The line between depression and exhaustion is a thin one, and postpartum depression, exhaustion, and any reactive depression can be hard to diagnostically differentiate. In addition to seeking therapeutic help, you might want to consider hiring child care or housecleaning help or leaning on your support system to assist you in getting more sleep. Ask your partner to get up in the middle of the night, even if it means pumping breast milk; ask your mom to come spend a week, even if you can't stand her. Find a way to get more sleep. If in a few days you notice that you are feeling better, your problem might not be depression but simply exhaustion. Don't minimize the impact exhaustion can have on your life, nor how dangerous it can be to care for an infant while you are that exhausted.

Commonly people also struggle with depression following the loss or death of a loved one. Perhaps you've had a terrible breakup or had a parent, a partner, or a child die suddenly. It is normal in these situations to feel extreme grief and even rage. Reactive depression can be an extreme grief reaction; the goal is to let yourself grieve without slipping so deep into depression that you can't lift yourself out. When depression becomes severe, people sometimes feel suicidal or even begin to fantasize about how they will kill themselves. Suicidal ideation should always be taken seriously, and you should not hesitate to call 911, or reach out to a suicide hot line (1-800-SUICIDE); that's why they are there!

If you find others are telling you that you are not yourself, that you are depressed, irritable, or difficult to get along with, it is easy to dismiss their concern or even blame them for creating your isolation and depression, but the truth is that if people who love you are that concerned, there may be something worth being concerned about. One of the complications of depression is that people are often unwilling or unable to seek help. If loved ones are expressing concern about you, you may be more depressed than you realize. You may be correct that they just don't understand, but they are correct that you are not coping well. Depression will not simply go away if ignored.

All mental health issues—depression, anxiety, PTSD, substance abuse recovery, eating disorders, and healing from abuse—respond well to self-care strategies. Some useful tools include getting exercise, sticking to a daily schedule, eating healthier foods, maintaining social contacts, and volunteering your time for a worthy cause. Exercise can include something as simple as a daily walk or as complex as working out, daily swimming, starting yoga, or taking a dance class. Movement can work wonders to alleviate depression. Eating healthier and not going long periods without food can bring further stability into your life. The tendency when depressed is to reach for particularly unhealthy foods—starches, sugar, salt, oily foods—or avoid food entirely, which fosters more illness and therefore increases mental and physical problems. Despite the desire to isolate, maintaining contact with friends and family can help to slow down the progression into deeper depression. Herbal, homeopathic, and natural medicines are often very effective for mild anxiety disorders or depression.

If you are unable to make lifestyle changes, or if the emotional difficulties are not lifting, no matter what you do, seek out a therapist. This can be a social worker, psychologist, psychotherapist, or counselor, preferably one who is trained in parenting issues and is comfortable with LGBT families. She or he may recommend a psychiatric evaluation and a possible course of antidepressants. It is a sign of strength to recognize that you need help or are feeling overwhelmed with parenting. The best thing you can do for your children is to be functioning at the highest level you can, and that may mean with support from a therapist, medication, or a support group.

For those of us who are not immediately impacted by any of these issues, let us not turn our backs on community members who may need our help. If you think a friend, neighbor, or colleague is drinking too much, if you are concerned about someone's black eye or intense social isolation, or if you find someone's behavior dangerous, unhealthy, or dysfunctional, do not assume it is none of your business. People rarely are happy to have you interfere with their drinking, abuse, or mental disturbances, but once they have gotten help, they usually will be very appreciative of your efforts. Let people know you care. Offer them and their children shelter. Tell them what you see in a nonjudgmental manner; tell them you are available to help, and let them know (concretely with phone numbers) where they can find help. Remember our first priority must be for the children, not about saving face in our community or what the outside world will think.

There are many things that we need to do as a community to address these issues. First and foremost, we must admit that they exist. We must acknowledge that some of us do have drinking and drug problems. We need to admit that some of us are abusive and violent to partners and children. We need to recognize that mental illness of all kinds impacts LGBT people. The first step is really breaking down this denial aspect of our community. Perhaps those of us who want children or have children work especially hard to separate ourselves from those who appear dysfunctional, since our families are fragile and vulnerable, but that creates a false distinction between them and us that is simply not realistic. They are us; some of our LGBT families are struggling with dysfunction, and if we don't care about them, I strongly suspect no one else will. Children growing up in homes with domestic violence, alcoholic parents, and parents with untreated mental disorders are all of our responsibility. Part of being a community is recognizing that we have responsibilities to one another; being a village means that we share in the care of all the villagers.

The second thing we need to do is insist upon nonhomophobic and sensitive care from those working in the social service system and from therapists working with families where addiction, domestic violence, or mental illness is extant. Understanding how to separate out the queer issues from the disorders is absolutely necessary. It is common for battering incidents to be noted as a roommate assaults, and that although the victim is given an order of protection, it is without any consideration of how this will impact her ability to continue parenting children that are not legally hers. Many times in legal and therapeutic situations, LGBT people who are entering recovery for addictions are encouraged to go into long-term treatment facilities, without any consideration for their children; the addictions counselor says, "Well, they are not really your children."

Professionals tend to err in either minimizing the issues (i.e., "They seemed like such a sweet lesbian couple, I never thought there was violence") or they tend to maximize the issue, evoking homophobic bias into an already chaotic situation (i.e., exaggerating cross-gender stereotypes in a police report). The need for extensive education in the helping professionals, way past homophobia 101, is essential. Sadly, we rarely have adequate resources, especially for those living in rural areas. For those people dealing with gender identity issues, finding competent mental health care can be a challenge. Nonetheless, we must move forward, honestly addressing our issues and seeking out support and help where we can find it.

Finally, we need to believe in the power of healing and recovery. Addicts really *do* get clean and sober, violence *can* end in intimate partnerships, and mental illnesses *can* be effectively treated both pharmacologically and therapeutically. Healing cannot begin unless individuals feel safe enough to reach out for help, knowing that friends, family, and their community will lend them support, and that the services available to them will be sensitive to their unique needs as LGBT people. Most of all, LGBT parents who are in trouble must know that their children will be safe and not taken away from them if they reach out for help.

PART FOUR

FAMILY LIFE

• • •

CHAPTER TEN

Coming Out and the Politics of Language

LET'S START WITH one simple truth about queer parenting: the closet is history. Even if you have somehow managed to not be very out during your child-getting process, having children makes remaining in the closet—or at least remaining securely in the closet—nearly impossible. I suppose you can manage it, although it would be a very constricted life. You would have to remain single, avoid same-sex affection both in public and in private, and live a very clandestine life, since children absorb everything in their environment and then repeat it at the most inopportune moments.

Perhaps in a funny way, an unintended consequence of the gay liberation movement and queer visibility is that it's harder to be closeted. Although there have always been queer parents, historically they remained below the radar, and this was not accidental. The closet was (and is), to a large extent, a socially agreed upon collusion about maintaining the secret of homosexuality. Often when people first come out, their friends and family say, "Yes, I always knew," or "I thought so." We agree, consciously or unconsciously, to don't ask and don't tell philosophies that have now become instituted into public policy. Now that so many same-sex couples live public and visible lives, it makes it much harder for those who still are closeted to remain invisible; two people of the same sex who live together, especially who actively parent together, will raise the eyebrows of neighbors, colleagues, and extended family.

In some parts of the world being closeted might be necessary, including rural areas of many progressive countries, or if you are in certain businesses where your homosexuality would mean immediate dismissal. Indeed, being in the closet in certain situations may be a life-and-death decision. One of the tenets of my Jewish faith is that you can break any religious proscription, at any time (even for those who are very observant), if you are saving a life. I suspect that includes one's own life. Although it is a good general rule that being out of the closet is better than being in the closet, it's okay to be in the closet if it is saving your life or protecting your family, for instance throughout a divorce process whereby knowledge of your homosexuality would surely mean loss of custody. For those pursuing international adoptions, closeting oneself is essential to successfully bringing a child home. Many transgendered people remain closeted about themselves for fear that if they tell their spouses they will lose custody and all contact with their children.

However, we should not minimize the impact of being closeted on the healthy development of family life. Years ago I knew a young lesbian woman who'd been raised by her mother and her mother's lover. She told me that they had never discussed that their family was lesbian-parented; it was a totally taboo subject. She never asked questions about their relationship and never brought friends over the house because she had no idea how to explain her family. When she was a teenager, her mother was diagnosed with breast cancer, and after a long, painful illness, died. It was only after her death, in the months of grieving that followed, that she and her mother's partner were able to sit down and discuss their family. For the first time they were able to name the parents' relationship as lesbian and talk about the years of secrecy. The woman was able to share with her mother's partner that she, too, was a lesbian, and their family was able to restructure itself as parent and child; their healing was, of course, bittersweet since her mother could not share in the joy that came from finally releasing the secret.

Years ago I wrote an article ("Lesbian and Gay Parenting," which was published in *Proud Parenting Magazine*) and mentioned a family that consisted of a divorced mother and her three children. The mother was involved in a long-term relationship with a lover who lived in a room in the basement of their suburban house. Although the family did everything together with the woman, she was viewed as a friend of the family. There was never any affection or touch in front of the children, and any intimacies they shared happened after the children were asleep, when the friend snuck up the stairs, returning to her room before the children woke up. The children, being bright and not easily fooled, were well aware of the situation, and continued to ply their mother with questions: "Are you lovers?" "Are you a lesbian?" but the mother denied any confrontation. The relationship did not survive. Indeed how could it? I have been surprised since the publishing of this article (available on the Internet and available from my Web site) how many E-mails I receive from women saying, "Wow, it was as if you were describing my family!" Many people in our queer communities are living very closeted lives.

In both of these families the parents were concerned that being part of a lesbian-parented family would be harmful for their children; in both cases the secrecy was far more damaging.

One of my many hats that I wear is as a columnist for LGBT parenting issues, including my Dear Ari column (available on www.ProudParenting. com and in *Transgender Tapestry*). By far the most common letters I receive involve issues of coming out. These often come from lesbians or gay men who have children from previous heterosexual relationships, but sometimes they come from single LGB people who have adopted and now that they are dating are unsure how to broach the subject with their children. Often the parent who is coming out feels so much confusion about their sexuality, fearful of how their ex will respond, and guilty regarding the impact on their children that their coming out process is filled with great tension. I suspect this tension impacts our children more than the actual information about sexual diversity. Here is one of my Dear Ari columns where I address the issue of coming out.

Our children can only name things once we give them the words. We are the ones who explain our relationships to our children, and can give them the language they need so that they can talk with ease to people outside our family who may have questions or be confused about our families. I was immensely proud of my older son when his teacher told me that on the first day of school, he walked up to her and said, "I just want you to know that I have two moms. One of my moms is kind of more like a dad.

Dear Ari,

My brother is gay and has lived with the same man for fifteen years. I have three kids, all girls, who dearly love their uncle. My brother is especially close to my oldest. The other day my oldest, who is eleven, asked, "Why does Uncle Scottie live with Uncle Tony?" I explained that sometimes people live together because they like each other and enjoy each other's company. When would it be appropriate to explain my brother's relationship? I wouldn't want to do anything that would compromise my daughter's relationship with her uncle. Thanks.

—Ryan W.

Dear Ryan,

It is encouraging to see heterosexual families grappling with issues related to the inclusion of their LGBT family members. Obviously, you care about your brother and have, in many ways, accepted his relationship and his partner into your extended family. As I am sure you know, LGBT siblings are often pushed out of their extended families, and their relationships with their nieces and nephews can be severely stymied.

It is not surprising that your daughter is beginning to ask about the nature of your brother's family; at her age she would be very sensitive to the meaning of interpersonal relationships as she tries to understand the world around her. I am sure that her younger siblings are just as curious, although they may not yet have the language to formulate their questions. I cannot help but wonder why you hesitate to simply say, "Uncle Scottie and Uncle Tony are partners—they are each other's love, just like Mommy and me."

It's important to examine why we struggle with naming the nature of the relationships (boyfriends, lovers, partners, spouses, husbands, etc.). What are the fears that arise if we say words like *love* when thinking about gay couples and families? Explore carefully what your concerns are in telling your daughter about your brother's family, and why you have not given her the language to understand the nature of their relationship, so that you are aware of your own internalized concerns. Our children can only name things once we give them the words.

Despite the rhetoric of antigay politicians, our children are not born into the world with a preconceived notion of what is a normal family. Like children all over the world, living in different cultures, tribes, nations, and societies, they learn what is right and socially acceptable by witnessing the world around them. They may notice what is common, as well as what is unusual, but we, as parents, are the ones who help them make sense of this in a nonjudgmental way that respects human diversity. The reason that your daughter asked the question is because she noticed that something was different about Uncle Scottie's family and needed to have that acknowledged as well as normalized.

Explain to your daughter that Uncle Scottie and Uncle Tony are a family, that they are partners who love each other and have decided to build a life together; this will give her a frame of understanding that relationship. She will be able to file it, so to speak, under the heading of Families, Lovers, Partners. If she then comments, as she is likely to, asking whether this makes them gay, the answer should be a simple "Yes." The words, *gay* and *lesbian* are words that children these days hear around them often, and although they may have heard it used in a derogatory way in the school yard, it should not be flinched away from in our responses.

If she has been exposed to homophobic ideologies, she may have many questions about homosexuality being a sickness or a sin, reflecting her concern for an uncle who she adores. Again, these questions can be answered directly, emphasizing the values and morals of your family; for example: "We believe that Uncle Scottie and Uncle Tony love each other, and that love is always a good thing." "We think being gay is a completely normal and healthy way to be, and many people do love, marry, and settle down with members of their own sex." Remember, you will be modeling your acceptance of gay relationships for them, and they are very sensitive to subtleties of your expressions, eye contact, and body language.

One way to avoid these awkward teaching moments is to discuss these ideas with your children from a much younger age. Do not wait until they are eleven and able to formulate a question. From the time they are toddlers, explain that there are all kinds of families, that some people love men and some people love women. As they get older, you can explain to them more about prejudice and bias, and oppression regarding issues of sexual identity, as well as race and ethnicity, in the world around us. The only reason that knowledge of her uncles' sexual orientation would "compromise her relationship with him" would be if she has internalized society's homophobia. The best way to ensure that this does not happen is through your modeling of your acceptance of your brother and combating outside bias by educating her about diversity, oppression, and tolerance.

This column was originally published by Alternative Family/Proud Parenting Magazine, *and this and other Dear Ari columns can be accessed at* www.ProudParenting.com.

I hope that is okay with you." She assured him it was just fine with her. My son would never have had the skills to talk about his family if he hadn't been given the words and the sense that his family was okay. Although we had been out to the school from the moment we arrived, my son's disclosure opened up a space for us to have a conversation about lesbian families and butch/femme identities with his teacher that would have been much harder to broach without his outing us.

The younger children are when you begin introducing these words and ideas, the easier it will be for them and the greater comfort and confidence they will have in talking about their family's makeup. Children who are born into or grow up in LGBT families will not initially find them different or alternative but will know them simply as home and family. Little kids are incredibly concrete. Their words are simple and direct; they don't understand metaphors or analogies; they need straightforward, clear facts. Gay is good; we are gay. The more we avoid the words *gay, lesbian, bisexual, or transgendered,* the more confused they will be about the very obvious differences they recognize in their families and see among their friends. The more words we give our children, the more words they will have to talk to their friends, and most of their conversations will happen far away from our eyes and ears.

The only language our children have to describe the world around them are the words we give them. We explain why they have two dads or two moms, what donor insemination or adoption mean. When one boy, age eleven, was trying to explain to his friend that his dads were taking a dance class with her mom, the girl was having a difficult time understanding how a boy could have two dads. She walked back over to her mom and said, "That boy over there says he has two dads. How can that be? You told me that kids come from inside moms. If he doesn't have a mom, where did he come from?" Luckily, in this situation the mother was able to explain how this could come to be to her daughter, who came back and said to the boy, "I get it now." However, sometimes grown-ups are the ones who suggest that it is not possible to have two parents of the same sex, or will say something like, "They are not really his parents." It is not easy being a child and having adults declare your family nonexistent. If we don't give our children the words to talk about donor dads or birth moms, they will be left with other people's words, "Who are your real parents?" "Where is your real father?"

Children are given words and concepts all the time that are baffling to them. Think about how a small child makes sense of concepts like "balancing the checkbook," "installing a furnace," "capping our teeth," or getting "fired from our job." They think of balancing the checkbook as something akin to balancing on a monkey bar, and clearly a checkbook is filled with check marks. A checkbook's relationship to actual money is very vague (and perhaps that is also true for many grown-ups who are reading this). The concept of heat coming from a furnace—a large machine in the basement filled with fire, and being regulated by small dials on the wall, well, that kind of still baffles me to be honest. After I got a cap on my tooth, my young son spent hours tapping at my mouth and asking, "Why did they file down your own tooth and put in another one?" I found him in the bathroom, tapping his own teeth. And indeed when children ask if you got burned when you were fired from your job, you can honestly answer, "Yes," while they put healing salve on your body to make you feel better. Indeed, children's worlds are full of confusing concepts and ideas. Our job is to give them words and help them to link the ideas together over time.

Early on in my parenting I was at a large party with many people I didn't know. Everyone was very interested in my new baby, and I was fielding a million questions about where he came from, and why his mother gave him up. I hadn't thought much about how to answer these questions before, and was mostly still caught up trying to learn how to change a diaper without dropping the baby or getting covered in poop. A wise friend pulled me aside and gave me the single best piece of advice I've ever been given about parenting an adopted child. She said, "The words you use now to describe his adoption, his family, and his life will always remain a part of his history. Even though he is only a few months old, if you say today to a ten-year-old child at this party, that his real mother is in Louisiana, or that she didn't want him, this will remain part of his legacy. The ten-year-old child will grow up, and she will remember him as the boy whose mother didn't want him."

We need to think carefully about the words we use to teach our children to describe their conception and their family configurations, and we need to acknowledge that the language we use might conflict with the messages they are receiving in the outside world. We need to prepare ourselves that a day may come when an adopted child yells, "You are not my real father," or a child says to his nonbiological mother, "I'm not really your child," or a child born from a donor egg or surrogacy, screams, "I want to know my real mother." In some way this is a defining moment for a family, and we need to know when that moment happens, that we are solid and secure in our parenting, our relationship to our children, and mostly in our own selves. Without flinching, we need to be able to say, "I am your parent. You are my child. Now please go clean your room." If we have any hesitancy about the realness of our role, the child will pick up that insecurity. For many of us it is startling that we are really grown-ups, we are still reeling that we were allowed to have children, and we are experiencing a daily heady rush that we really *are* parents. Having a child challenge your realness can throw you for a loop, a loop your children cannot afford to be caught in. Start practicing while they are young, practice in the mirror, and repeat daily with your vitamins, "I am really your parent, kiddo. This is as real as it gets." (Note: I am not saying that adopted children do not need to have information and access to information about their biological heritage. I am referring in this section to issues of language, and the kind of barbs children might throw at us in the heat of the moment.)

Children develop the coping skills they need to confront external prejudice by growing up in loving families that honestly address the issue of bias and teach their children survival strategies. After all, despite what we know about the difficulties of living within a racist and anti-Semitic culture, no one would suggest that people of color or Jews should refrain from having children (well, no one who would be taken seriously!). The more comfortable parents are with their sexuality and identity, the greater their ability to teach their children skills to cope with homophobia and bias. The problem is that kids who haven't been silenced and are comfortable with their families will out us at every moment.

At two, my son runs into the day care holiday party and up to a man I've never seen before in my life, but whom I assume is one of the day care parents, and yells, "I have two moms!" He does not recognize this as a decisive coming out moment; he is not revealing sexual secrets. He is simply excited to share something about his life, like a child might say, "My grandmother is coming from Brazil for Christmas," and another child says, "My mommy is having a baby."

Of course, by the time he turned six, he had become more cautious. We were leaving the synagogue one night, and while I was getting the kids in the car, my partner went off to talk with a couple, a lesbian couple, who were in their seventies. Rumor has it (well the rumor was from the lesbian rabbi, so it was likely a true rumor) that they met six years ago and fell in love and came out. My son wanted to know why Mommy has to talk with those women now. I explain, "Mommy is very excited to talk with them because they just came out as lesbians." "Why does that excite Mommy so much?" he asks. "Well," I explain, "sometimes it hasn't been so easy for people to come out, especially older people. Sometimes people can be mean to gay people, and Mommy wants to tell those women how great they are." At six I wanted to start introducing more complex ideas about homophobia to him, and I expected him to ask me why people are mean to gay people. He did not. Instead he says, "I know people can be mean. That's why I don't tell anyone that my moms are gay."

Out at the Lab

I was at the lab getting one of the umpteen thousand blood draws for fertility treatments, and on our way out, Matt, age four, turns to the phlebotomist and says, "I have two mommies!" She smiles at him, turns to me, and quietly, so her colleagues cannot hear, says, "When I have a family there will be two mommies in it, too!" I was so moved that we'd made this connection just by Matt being proud of his family.

Kelly McWilliams, partner to Lyne Landry for fifteen years, and parents of Matthew Landry-McWilliams and Kyle Landry-McWilliams, five-year-old twins, and Joseph Landry-McWilliams, age nine months. They live in Connecticut.

Long pause.

"Everyone at your school knows you have two moms, dear," I say gently.

"Yeah, but they don't know you are *gay!*" he says, and for the first time I realize that in his world, these ideas are not the same thing, not, if you will, synonyms. It never struck me before this shocking parenting moment that being proud of his two-mom family did not necessarily translate in his mind that this was a signal to most of the world that his parents were lesbians. At six he understood more about the world than when he was two and was proudly announcing our arrival as the most welcome guests of the king. He knows enough to let his teacher know about us, setting up careful parameters around his daily life. Although he is secure within his family, he also knows that his family needs explaining, but he is not always willing to take on the job of defending us. He told me recently that when people ask him questions about his adoption, or why his moms are white and he is black, that he changes the subject or says, "That's not what I want to talk about right now." That is, of course, his right, to determine when and where he discusses the circumstances of his family. My job is to make sure that he has the skills to do so when it becomes necessary.

Of course, when our children out us, it often opens the dialogue for other people to come out also. Our families are very visible, and our very presence challenges others, particularly other LGBT people, to decide whether or not to stay in the closet.

For those of us coming out later in life, we might need to spell it out more carefully for our children. Even though it may be obvious to you or

---

Out in the Restaurant

My kids had always known gay and bisexual people. After my marriage ended, I joined the local bisexual union and regularly brought my kids (the baby was then four and the twins six) to the meetings, which they loved. They became the mascots. I decided to make sure that I was out to them, that they understood, so after a meeting one evening, we went to dinner at a popular local restaurant. We talked about what the word *bisexual* meant. The kids then went on to ask about everyone in the group.

"Drew's bisexual?"

"Yes."

"And Ellen?"

"Yes."

"And Beth?"

"Yes."

"David, too?"

"Him, too."

After going through everyone in the list there was a pause, and I said, "And me, too."

My daughter started nudging her brothers, "Did you hear? Mom, too!"

At which point all three burst into that familiar childhood singsongy melody with the words loudly sung, "Mommy likes ladies! Mommy likes ladies!"

This very crowded restaurant was packed, and my face was very red. They definitely got it, and were fine with it, and went on to propose to my sweetie before I did, but that's another story.

Peg, partner for eleven years to Barb, parents of four teens, two of whom are gay, one adopted after the death of his mother, another dyke mom.

---

to other adults that you're hanging out with lots of gay people or attending gay events, these may not register as anything unusual or different to kids, any more than changing which malls you shop at or painting the living room—changes for sure, but not necessarily statements about sexual identity.

The thing about coming out is that it never ends. You don't come out once but over and over and over again. The new neighbors don't know, the new teachers don't know, the new coworker doesn't know, the new babysitter doesn't know, and even once the kids are long grown with lives of their own, the process begins again as our grandchildren grow up.

When parents have come out later in life, after the children have been born, it can often be very hard for the kids to deal with these changes in their lives. Especially teenagers, who worry about how they will be perceived, can be very protective of their families and fearful of anything that might make them appear different. Older children, particularly those in pu-

---

Out House-Hunting

It is not just older people who are moving to Florida. A few years ago, our daughter and son-in-law moved to southwest Florida with our two grandchildren. We decided to join them. While in the process of buying a condo, we brought our nine-year-old granddaughter, Samantha, to see it. We introduced her to the Realtor, who proceeded to ask Sam questions about where she lived, what school she attended, and how she liked Florida. They seemed to be harmless questions to make conversation. But then the Realtor asked Sam, "Which one of these ladies is your grandmother?"

We held our breath as Sam looked from one of us to the other and, without hesitation, replied, "They both are!" Sam has always had the picture.

Dana G. Finnegan, Ph.D., CAC, and Emily B. McNally, Ph.D., CAC, have been together for twenty-eight years and have three children, Tim, age forty-one, Steven, age thirty-nine, and Karen, age thirty-seven, and three grandchildren, Samantha, age twelve, Michael, age five, and Christine, age one, and a mother, Sylvia, age ninety-two, and live on the Gulf of Mexico in southwest Florida.

---

berty, may have greater difficulty accepting a parent coming out as they negotiate the white-water rapids of their own developing sexuality. For stepparents, being accepted into the family can be challenging.

Undoubtedly, children being raised in LGBT families face certain challenges. Since they will be raised within a primarily heterosexual (and heterosexist) culture, they will have to confront what it means to be different from their peers. They will not often see themselves or their families reflected on television, in books, or within their social circles. Other children might be astonished that they have two moms or two dads, and some adults may exhibit insensitivity by questioning whether a child is telling the truth about her family. When one little girl was asked which of her moms was her real mom, she looked at the grown-up, rolling her eyes, and said, "You're joking, right?!"

It can be frightening for children as they try to understand what it means that their parents cannot legally marry, or that their grandparents don't consider one of their parents really their parent, or that people can get hurt or arrested for being gay. One day, I was driving in a car with a lesbian mom and her two children. I said, "Slow down, there is a cop behind us." The five-year-old grew frightened. "Will they arrest you for being les-

Out Driving

Emily was sixteen years old and was still quite afraid of peer pressure. Even though I had been part of the family for two years, I mostly lived there under the pretense of attending school in Michigan. Emily had confided in her best friend that her mom was a lesbian and that I was her partner. Her friend thought that "So cool!" but Emily was still very afraid she would become the school reject if others found out, so we lived quietly to help protect her.

On the day of Emily's driving test for her license, Janet was unable to go because of work, so it was decided I would take her. Emily was so excited she was jumping around in the car. When we got to the counter, Emily proudly showed the woman the results of her test scores. After Emily signed the paperwork, the woman handed it to me and said, "Okay Mom, now I need your signature on it." Emily said, "Oh, this isn't my mom, this is my mom's friend." To which I quickly answered, "I have legal paperwork with me saying I can sign for her." The woman looked it over and said, "I need to talk to my manager."

I looked at Emily, and I could see the panic building in her face. I reached out and told her to calm down. The manager came to the counter and said, "I'm sorry, but this document says that you can sign legal paperwork if her mother is deceased." How could we have been so stupid not to have understood this? Emily absolutely flipped out, and before I could stop her, she started saying things like, "THIS IS MY MOTHER! I HAVE TWO MOMS. MY MOMS ARE LESBIANS!! WE HAVE A LESBIAN HOUSE!!" and then the ultimate, before I could stop her be-

cause she was so far out of control, she said, "YOU KNOW WHAT? WE—ALL—LESBIANS!!!!" I thought I was going to drop on the floor. The place had grown deadly silent. The manager leaned over the counter and quietly said to me, "Can you get in touch with her mother?" I said, "I sure can!" She told us to have Janet fax a signed consent, which she did immediately. When it arrived, we quickly signed the paperwork and left.

I drove us home, and then asked Emily if she would like to take the car and drive by herself; I threw her my keys. She ran over and gave me a big hug, and then ran out to the car. I got the camera and took pictures of her getting in the car and driving off for the first time on her own. That year, Emily gave me a Mother's Day gift—a silver-colored frame that said "Mom" all over it, and inside the frame was the picture of Emily as she got in the car the day she announced to everyone that I was her mother, too.

I still have that picture and treasure it. That day was another turning and growing point in our relationship as a same-sex stepparent. After that, Emily came out to more and more friends, all of whom were supportive. I never really felt much like a stepparent after that, and when people asked me how many kids I have, I always say, "I have three daughters," because I do, and we're just their moms.

Janeil E. Martin is partners with Janet Conners, and they have three daughters, Mary, age twenty-five, Erin, age twenty-two, and Emily, age twenty, in Chelsea, Michigan. Contact Janeil Martin by E-mail: JaneilMartin@aol.com.

bians?" he asked. Of course, children often misunderstand adult conversations, but we cannot underestimate the fears they may have concocted in their minds while they try to understand the unique status of queer people in a homophobic and transphobic system.

Children raised in LGBT families will need to develop coping skills to address heterosexism and homophobia, both real and imaginary. They might be faced with blatant hostility within school settings or ignorance from friends (or their friends' parents) about the nature or safety of their families. And sometimes the unthinkable happens. Homophobia, of course, is not just about discomfort or ignorance; it can be about violence and terror.

All children suffer in the face of bigotry, and all parents must be prepared to assist their children in facing school yard taunts. Whether they are teased for their weight, their religion, a disability, being the children of lesbians, or the kid whose father changed sex, all children must learn to develop self-esteem and pride when treated cruelly. Lesbian and gay parents, by virtue of having survived similar treatment, are often especially skilled at teaching children tolerance as well as self-respect. Our children are thriving despite societal homophobia and the taunts of their peers.

DO PARENTING AND GAY PRIDE MIX?

As issues of marriage and parenting take center stage in the lesbian and gay civil rights struggle, questions are being raised about the role of LGBT parents in the larger gay rights movement. Undeniably, as more LGBT people choose parenting, the community has needed to become more child-friendly, but what this ultimately means is a discussion still in its infancy. Certainly, the gay pride store in Provincetown sells T-shirts that say, I Love My Two Moms, right next to rainbow flags and his-and-his towel sets, but the lovely nelly waiter in the restaurant up the block still put a cup of hot coffee in front of my infant son and rolled his eyes when I jumped up to move it. The LGBT civil rights movement is not, of course, responsible for bad wait service, but questions of inclusivity and the safety of children need examining as more and more queers are becoming parents.

It is true, first of all, that parenting is time-consuming, and many parents who were once active grassroots organizers have retired (temporarily, it is hoped) to put their energy into raising their children. Some activists

Out Marching

"Mommy, why did they throw tear gas at us?" These were my three-year-old son's words to me after our family was attacked while marching in our city's Gay and Lesbian Pride.

We had begun the annual festivity with a group of seventy children, parents, and grandparents. Our contingent had been named this year's Outstanding Community Organization. We planned to follow the march route through downtown and spend the rest of the day at the Pride Festival in the city park. Gay Pride is our carnival, our old-home week, our family reunion. My family proudly wore matching shirts festooned with custom-made rainbow signs: mine read Queer by Nature (because I truly believe I am and always have been), John (my best friend and partner, who is heterosexual) wore Queer by Association, and our son Julian wore Queer by Heritage.

A few minutes into the march, the unthinkable happened: someone threw a tear gas canister that landed and exploded just beside the families. I saw the column of smoke and people racing away. I heard the screams. But my mind couldn't register what was happening until I tried to draw a breath and felt my throat on fire. John dashed down the street with Julian's stroller, and I followed as best I could. Having recently recovered from pneumonia, my lungs were already in a weakened condition—I couldn't keep up. John kept turning to look for me; I kept waving him on. "Run! Get Julian out of here!" I had to stop to cough and try to breathe, a futile effort. Two strangers grabbed my arms

and pulled me along with them, choking and hacking.

Finally, I met up with them blocks away. Julian was screaming in pain and terror. John didn't want to stop to pick him up and tried to comfort him with words as we ran. "You're okay, baby. Mommy and Daddy are right here. You'll be fine sweetheart." I grabbed John's arm, and we continued our escape as fast as we could manage. When we finally felt safely out of range of the smoke, John got him out of the stroller, and I poured the contents of my water bottle onto a tissue to wipe his face and eyes. He drank some juice and finally calmed. John was also okay once he washed his own face and eyes. I was still gasping. Snot and spit streamed from my nose and mouth. My face burned as tears made contact with my skin.

I wanted to go home, but John insisted, "We have to go back and finish the march." He was right. More than ever, our visibility was vital, particularly in the face of the terrorist who wanted us all to disappear.

So we marched to the bitter end: Julian clinging to John's neck, the two of us pushing the empty stroller, our tattered signs peeling off our bodies, me alternately sobbing and coughing, trying to acknowledge the crowds cheering us on. There was no triumphant celebration for us when we reached the end at Balboa Park. John pushed Julian on the swings while I sat on the grass retching and spitting.

We went home, put our son to bed, and watched the news. The hate crime received only a brief mention. None of the coverage noted that the attacker had targeted babies, children, and pregnant women, sending four to the hospital.

Two days later, I was still coughing, and the burns on my face were peeling. My son asked me repeatedly, "Why did they throw tear gas at us?" How can I explain hatred to my son when I don't understand it myself? The only answer I could give him was that some people do very mean things. I compared it to the bullies he's encountered at school. I did not tell him that this is what happens when bullies grow up and can buy deadly weapons. We will continue to encourage him to talk about it, even if I can't give him an answer that makes it all better.

What I can't shake is a deep feeling of sadness that my family's safety shield has been pierced. Everyone's got one—the protective fence you erect mentally that lets you operate day to day in spite of the frightening and violent world around us. But after Saturday's in-your-face incident, and someone scrawling FAG on our car the week before, I feel as though my shield has been ripped away, and all I want to do is hide. I've had flashbacks repeatedly since the incident, and find myself crying at my computer, my throat burning at the memory. I want my son to go to sleep at night still believing that his parents can keep him safe. My son, who has yet to touch a toy weapon or view a violent television program, now knows what a hate crime is.

Eve Diana, mom-writer-nerdgeek-queer-activist, partner to John for fifteen years, parents of Julian, age seven, live in southern California.

have expressed concern about this trend and see LGBT parenting as a conservative force in an increasingly conservative era. Lesbians, they say, are spending more time at their son's soccer games than at women's political caucuses, and gay men are advocating for safe playgrounds rather than safe sex. Most gay and lesbian parents admit that their priorities have changed since becoming parents, and that parenting duties compete for time and energy that might go into political meetings and demonstrations. However, as Eve Diana's piece suggests, LGBT people also put their children at risk by being out in the world, raising questions about how safe is it to participate, and what our community will do to protect our more vulnerable members.

As awful as it is to have tear gas thrown at any Gay Day Pride, the fact that pregnant women and children were targeted is particularly frightening, and the silence from both the mainstream media and the queer press regarding this act of terrorism was truly frightening.

Whether or not we are out marching, LGBT parents are visible in mainstream society in a way that other LGBT people are not. We are not only out holding hands in public, but we are out in areas long forbidden to known queers—areas where children congregate. As our children bring us face-to-face with day care programs, toy stores, pediatricians, and religious organizations, lesbian and gay parents are taking their politics into the mainstream. For example, lesbian and gay families are challenging business as usual in school systems as we confront gender stereotyping, and in courtrooms as we insist on the right to be recognized as the legal parents to our nonbiological children. Lesbian and gay parents are changing school curricula through their involvement with the PTA and challenging medical insurance reimbursement policies and hospital visiting rules to protect their children. We wear our ACT UP T-shirts to the school board meetings, and hold hands openly during our kids' school play, sending shock waves through institutions that are educating the next generation of children, including young LGBT kids. In all areas of society, lesbian and gay parents are in the forefront of social change movements, and we are doing this while changing diapers, wiping runny noses and singing the alphabet song one more time.

Lesbian and gay people are not selling out by becoming parents; rather we are reaping the benefits of thirty years of political struggle, and rearing the next generation who will continue the fight. COLAGE (Children of Lesbians and Gays Everywhere) is a national organization developed by children of LGBT people who are committed to not only supporting children growing up in LGBT homes, but also educating the public about the positive impact of growing up in queer families. These children (some of whom are now adults) who are gay and straight themselves, are testaments to not only the strengths of LGBT families but the legacy of being raised in homes where working toward social justice is a part of daily family values. COLAGE is proof that when LGBT people build families we are ultimately creating more energy for political change, even if the parents themselves are a bit preoccupied for a decade or more and unable to attend to politics in more obvious and structured ways.

When the children of LGBT people grow up, particularly those who are heterosexual, they represent a unique development within LGBT communities. Most LGBT individuals grew up in heterosexual homes and came out in the life; children of LGBT people grow up in families who are in the life and then move into their own adult lives, bringing community values into the mainstream. This is an unprecedented phenomenon, where children reared with respect for diversity and flexibility around gender roles are bringing these values into their own social milieus. Abigail Garner, author of *Families Like Mine* and the adult heterosexual daughter of a gay man, identifies as "culturally queer, but erotically straight," putting a new spin on the idea of a bicultural identity. I am not suggesting that children are our emissaries or that they should be encouraged to carry these torches, but that the benefits of growing up with good gay campy humor and strong progressive social values will impact American politics in ways that may or may not appear obvious on the first day of kindergarten.

Sometimes LGBT people say that they feel they are living in a fishbowl, with everyone watching their family as if the day-by-day experiences of our lives are reflective of their family's queer status. When my two-year-old lies down on the sidewalk in front of our house, screaming, "I don't want to go inside. I don't like you!" I imagine every neighbor peering out their windows thinking, "What do those damn dykes do to those boys anyway?" Of course, the fact that our neighbors are warm and friendly and bring us mums and banana bread only increases my fears. (Are they spying on us?)

The reality is that the children of LGBT people are under constant scrutiny to make sure that our kids are normal kids, not too nelly, not too butch, and that they don't have too many strange ideas. Of course, we fail again and again, in part because our children are ultimately themselves: nelly, butch, or none of the above. We fail also, though, precisely because our kids are often exposed to a wider range of experiences than many heterosexual families allow their children to see. The school psychologist calls up concerned because when an eight-year-old girl from a lesbian-parented family was asked what license plates were, she simply answered, "That's how the government keeps track of you." Now certainly many heterosexual families are equally distrustful of government policies, but when other socially uncommon lifestyles (Wiccan religion, vegetarianism, leftist politics) are coupled with queer families, they bring even greater scrutiny to our families.

Most of us have found that it is not being closeted that protects us from homophobia, but it is being completely out and going about our lives without asking anyone for permission or feeling a need to explain our lives. If you are uneasy about being queer, your kids will pick up on your discomfort, as will the intrusive strangers, so the more relaxed you are, the more you are modeling comfort for others. Practice saying, "Yes, I'm his mom, too," "We are both his dads," over and over again, until it sails easily out of your mouth.

Although the gayby boom has been given some media attention both within and outside of the queer community, the reality is that the relationship between the LGBT community and the queer parenting community is a tenuous one. Attitudes toward queer parenting in the LGBT community range from angry resistance to what is often perceived as heterosexual mimicry, to a bored disinterest in the vicissitudes of daily parenting. To be fair, many LGBT individuals embrace our families, but in terms of LGBT institutional life, LGBT parents have long been out on our own. There seems to be a perception that we are abandoning the queer cause on one hand, coupled with a lack of sensitivity to the amount of attention and care children need on the other. Being out as a parent involves risks that LGBT activists who are not parents do not seem to recognize or understand.

Despite the fact that mainstream America thinks that LGBT parenting is very radical, many LGBT people think parenting is one of the more conservative influences in our community. Personally, I do not subscribe to *Family Circle* magazine, and there is nothing remotely fiftiesish about this queer household; however, I respect the right of other LGBT families to engage in mainstream parenting rituals. There are plenty of apolitical child-free queers that are far more worried about how they look, how much money they make, and when they are going to get laid than they are worried about working for the passage of ENDA. LGBT parents should have the same freedom to be political or not as any other queer person. However, whether or not you are a political person, you must realize that LGBT parenting is still a political act.

Getting LGBT parents more involved in the larger political life of our communities means there needs to be a concerted effort to look at what parents need and how to accommodate those needs. A group of white political activists can't invite a group of black political activists to the table (their table) and expect the issues they discuss to remain the same. If you invite disabled people to join a meeting held in an unramped building, you may be disappointed at the turnout. LGBT parents are deeply committed to the state of queer life and policies that impact our lives, but in order to show up and do the work, we need to have quality child care providers so that we can be assured our children are safe. Child care needs are often an

Out of Danger
BY BEREN DEMOTIER

Being out of the closet is sort of like playing Russian roulette as a way of life. You forget you're playing the game, until something reminds you just how close you are to getting your head blown off. Like someone else getting theirs blown off.

As my wife put it, we're all one wrong outing away from mortality.

And who knows when that wrong outing might come up? Goodness knows, we try our best to enjoy an out-of-the-closet life, living honestly, giving people a chance to really know us, being open to the possibilities of acceptance and personal growth in those we meet, all while trying to assure we go on living. We all know the rules. If you: A. don't express affection in public, B. don't bring attention to your sexual orientation in other than gay-friendly environments, C. don't act exactly like your neighbors and appear to know each other when you're out sitting on your porch, you'll probably live to see another day and be invited to the neighborhood block party to boot.

Not that I think everyone is out to kill us (maim us, slander us, key our car, etc.), because they're not. Most people wouldn't harm a fly. But some are, and you've got to guess which ones. It used to be we had some control over who we came out to, but once we had children with the gift of gab, it was out of our hands.

It's not like we've been closeted ever, but there are times when discretion seems more than the better part of valor. Think survival tactic. But tell that to a three-year-old who announces joyfully to the mother next to you at the swings that he has two moms. Yes, you're happy he's proud of his family, and you don't want to stunt his budding sense of identity, but if the woman has spent the last half hour telling you about her work in the Christian fellowship, her husband's role as Boy Scout leader, and their collection of firearms, it's tempting to tell her he's going through a wish-fulfillment phase.

This is something prospective lesbian and gay parents have to think long and hard about before having kids. Being out comes with the territory. Children don't understand finesse, social appropriateness, or your fingers to your lips in desperation until they're thirty-five at least. Unless you want them thinking you're living a secret life (and want to pay for a therapist's Acapulco vacations for a decade), you're going to have to be honest whenever it comes up, wherever that may be.

Even when you're in over your head. I was in ten feet of water, taking swimming lessons with our eight-year-old son, trying to overcome three decades' worth of fear (and the hypocrisy of requiring him to take lessons when I couldn't put my face under water), when our son decided to tell the swim instructor all about the fund-raising party we were having at our house to raise money to fight the latest antigay legislation. Whether it was the swim teacher's professionalism or politics that kept me above water that day, I don't know, but I do know that from then on, I understood that coming out was literally a sink-or-swim activity, and that even if I sank, I'd have to push myself to the top and do it all over again.

Because I want our kids to be out about their lives, to be proud of who they are, and who we are. And if I'm not willing to take the risk, how can I expect them to?

Beren deMotier, is a stay-at-home mom and freelance writer. She and her partner of seven- *teen years, Jannine Setter (now legally married!), live in Portland, Oregon, along with their kids Duncan, age twelve, Anna, age nine, and Grae-mem, age one. Her humor and social commentary column, "I Kid You Not," is syndicated nationally. She can be reached at demotier@tele-port.com.*

afterthought and rarely do community centers have child care rooms or invest some of their funding into events that include and welcome children. LGBT parents would be more willing to pack the kids up, drink an extra cup of coffee to stay awake, and show up to do the hard work of changing the world if our children were not viewed as smelly, sticky annoyances that are disruptive to the real events of the day.

However, there is a reality to the limits of political involvement for LGBT parents of young children. All the child care availability in the world will never change this. I still attend political meetings, and I even organize them sometimes, but, and this is the big but, my children come first. They always come first, and any parent who places political work, social obligations, or work responsibilities before their children's well-being might do best to reevaluate their lives. The LGBT community often criticizes parents for isolating themselves or spending more time with heterosexual parents and our own families of origin, but yet the LGBT community often wants us to leave our children home while we come out and play, not understanding that although we sometimes like adult time away from our kids, we had kids because we actually like playing with them. Many of us had to explain to our own parents why they needed to treat our partners as family members; now many of us need to explain to our queer communities that our children are not appendages but our family. Some of us had to tell our parents that we wouldn't come home for Thanksgiving unless they invited our lover, too; now some of us are saying to our communities, we aren't showing up for the film festival unless you have some good-quality kid's programming, too.

Gay politics and parenting go together; they go together every day in the lives of LGBT parents. Our communities have a ways to go, however, to make LGBT families part of our larger institutions.

WHAT WILL THE CHILDREN CALL YOU?

This is one of those questions that everyone outside of the queer community seems to be very concerned about, as if babies are born programmed to have a mommy and daddy, and will be devastated to realize that they have two moms or two dads instead. When my son was an infant, his day care center made Mother's Day cards to send home (he was not even old enough to really hold a crayon yet). Very nervously, the teacher pulled me aside. "We didn't know what to put on the cards," she said, cocking her head to one side as if to say, *You know why*. I smiled gently. "Well," I said, "usually people write 'Happy Mother's Day,' but whatever you wrote will be fine." I told her that it was always okay to ask, and perhaps it was a good idea to always ask everyone, since some families have a stepmom, and others have a grandmother, and some people call their mom Lucy.

In our family, I'm Momma, and my partner is Mommy. Well, at least that was our plan. Our oldest son always referred to me as Momma, and my partner as Mommy Sundance. (Yes, that is actually her real name.) We never told him to do that, but he does. Our second son refers to *her* as Momma, and me as Mommy Arlene. Except of course, when our older boy calls out *Mommy*, very loudly and expects me to answer. Or when the younger child calls me Momma when he needs a diaper change, or when either child screams *Mom* and expects anyone in earshot to respond immediately.

Some parents chose the names they want their kids to call them and work diligently on instituting these names. They will correct the child if they use the wrong name and gently reinforce the correct sounds from babyhood on. One mom said she was insistent on using traditional maternal terms because she wanted to make sure at school and in public that it was clear that both of them are moms. She said, "I had this awful fantasy where Jess went to pick him up at school and they said, 'Oh you are not his mother. You have a different last name, and he doesn't even call you mommy.'" Other parents, however, say they couldn't care less what their kids call them, but will wait to see what names the kids choose. In yet other families, parents are addressed by their first names, although for other parents this is akin to blasphemy.

In most LGBT families, children utilize conventional Mommy or Daddy language, with some modification. The two moms are referred to as Mom, Mommy, Momma, Mother, or Ma, and the two dads are referred to as Daddy, Papa, Father, Pop, or Dad. Parents often want to be called what they called their own parents, and if you are lucky, this works out easily that you called your parents by different names than your partner did. Sometimes people use variations on their names as in Mommy Kathy and Mommy Sue, or Daddy B for Daddy Brian and Daddy M for Daddy Micky. This will not work if you both have the same first name.

I did some unofficial research once to see if biological mothers were more often called by the traditional nomenclature of Mommy, with their partners given less conventional names like, Mama, Ima, or Sally. Although there is some evidence that is a common practice, it did not seem to be of any statistical significance; anecdotes are, of course, not data.

Tania was pleasantly surprised to find that although she knew exactly what she wanted her daughter to call her, Sophia had her own ideas! Tania purposefully choose to teach her daughter the name chosen for her partner Beth, since Beth works outside the home and Tania wanted to give Beth the gift of being the first parent Sophia could call by name. Tania continually repeated the sound "Ma" to Sophia—as in "MaMaMaMaMaMaMaMa"— in Beth's presence or when referring to Beth. It worked like a charm, and soon Sophia was gleefully calling to Mama. Later, Tania started teaching her daughter to say "Mommy." Using the same technique she repeated "Mom-me-me-me." And you can guess the rest! The first time baby Sophia decided to say "Mommy" it came out as "MeMe," and Meme it is! For most of us, what our children call us is what we happily become.

As one father said, "Our son calls me Dad, and Chuck is Daddy. It's not something that is done consistently, but we honestly don't have a problem with anything he calls us—assuming it's not an unpleasant slang term." One child started calling his mom Pumba. One family refers to one of their moms as Gnu pronounced gutturally as *g'nuh*. Many parents attest to the fact that their small children referred to them as "Honey," picking up the sweet terms we refer to one another. "More banana, Honey," the little one says. My favorite name my son made up for me was Plum. "I love you, Plum," he'd say to my glee.

Sometimes parents use mom and pop terms from other languages and not only if they are from other countries, or speak these languages, but sometimes because they are borrowing the term. Common mommy terms are *ima* (Hebrew), or *mutti* (German), *mami* (Spanish), or *omma* (Korean). In much of the English-speaking world, outside of the U.S., *mummy* or *mum* is the most common referent for mothers; this includes England, Scotland, Wales, Ireland, Australia, New Zealand, and parts of Canada. Common daddy names are *babbo* (Italian), *baba* (throughout most of Asia), *pappi* (Spanish) and *abba* (Hebrew). *Oma* and *opa* mean grandma and grandpa in German, although some are using this for parents or stepparents.

Sometimes our children want to change what they call us, perhaps in an attempt to fit in better. Stephanie called her moms Mommy Ellen and Mommy Mary, but in second grade she decided she wanted to call one parent Mom and the other Mommy. They readily agreed, but the problem is that she never remembers that she changed the names, so they have remained Mommy Mary and Mommy Ellen.

In many black families, they retain the traditional use of Auntie or Miss. Rayna for the second mom. I have found that some white lesbian moms find this disrespectful of the second parent, but it is a very respectful way to acknowledge the difference between a birth mom and a second parent in families where this distinction may matter. Black culture has long honored numerous caregivers for children, particularly female caregivers, and aunties can be as important, and even more important in some situations, as biological mothers. Children learn to explain their families, in this case to both heterosexual people as well as lesbian families, and understand that their auntie is an intimate member of their family.

In families where a parent transitions their gender, names can become particularly problematic. When a child is referring to you as Daddy, and you've spent the last three years trying to do everything you can to present as a female to the world, it can really out you in a way you would perhaps prefer not to be outed. Sometimes the child's biological mother may be very resistant to sharing a female mommy name, and in some families, parents make up a new name for the transitioned parent. I have heard people express sadness that their child calls them by a first name rather than Mommy or Daddy because they long to have the child honor their gender change without feeling as if their parental status has been revoked. Some people, however, say that they have always been Daddy, and even though they are now living as a woman, they do not want to ask their children to change how they refer to them. It is undoubtedly socially awkward when a child is referring to a parent who looks like a male as Mommy. In some families children and parents work together for a viable solution, like Maddy, which rhymes with Daddy but is a female name that starts with an M for *mommy*.

There are, of course, no rules, no right way to do this. It depends on the family, what the members are most comfortable with, and finding ways to compromise with lovers, ex-spouses, and children to incorporate changes in gender identity within a family. In one family, they use the name Beda (*B-Da*) for *butch dad*. Although living as a man, it is important for this parent to acknowledge the fullness of his identity and history. When he was planting flowers with his daughter one day and a neighbor walked by and said, "Oh, are you and Daddy gardening?" his daughter was quick to educate her. "This is not my daddy," she said. "He's my Beda. He was born a woman." The neighbor nodded and quickly walked on.

In some lesbian-headed families with strong butch/femme identities, having two moms might not feel quite right. Some lesbians are a bit shocked that other lesbian-headed families are using traditional daddy names for one of the parents, like *abba*, which is Hebrew for father. Sometimes the names our children invent to call us sound like traditional *mommy* or *daddy* words but were not meant to be, for instance one child calls his mom Bapa, which sounds like *papa,* but is derived from the name Barbara. Some families want the names to sound similar and familiar, like *mommy* and *momma*, highlighting that they are a female-headed household. Other people want to downplay this, either because they find it linguistically confusing, or because they want to recognize clear differences in roles. One family uses Mommy and Boo—Boo being a traditional Chinese name small children call their father. Another family uses Momma and Ama—short for Amazon!

Children sometimes invent names for us that are particular to our families, like Leigh-Leigh for one mom named, er . . . Leigh. One little boy calls one dad Daddy and one Pappa, but if he wants either one, he calls out, "DaPa." One little girl calls one parent Daddy and her other parent Papi.

Boma and Wama

The other day at our Montessori school a little boy asked Elisa if she had a daddy. Elisa said, "No daddy—Papa!" She calls my father Papa. Then the little boy asked if she had a mommy. Elisa said, "No mommy." I'm thinking, why did she say she doesn't have a mommy when she's got two? She said, "No mommy—Boma and Wama!"

You see, Boma and Wama are the names she calls us. Boma (Boo-ma) is my partner's name. We came up with this when she was breast-feeding our oldest child Elisa. Kari didn't like being referred to as "the Boob," as in "Oh, good, Elisa, here comes the boob." So she became the boob mom or Boma instead. I always took baths with Elisa, so I became the water mom or Wama.

Catherine Bodine, partnered to Kari for seven years, parents of Elisa (Elisabetta Kathryn), age two and a half, and Frankie (Francis Eileen), age five months. They live in Sacramento, California.

But when she wants both she calls for Pop-Daddy. Beren deMotier says, "Our children call me Ber-Ber. When our son was born, he called us both Mama, but we could tell by his inflection which one of us he wanted, a linguistic subtlety we alone could discern. We referred to ourselves as Mama, and Mama Bear, because of my name. But Mama Bear evolved into Ber-Ber, and that's the only thing our daughter, born three years later, has ever called me." Sometimes the names our children invent for us are truly unique!

I know some of you are thinking that this is very confusing, but it's actually not as confusing as you might imagine. The most complicated thing that happens in our family is a parent says, "Oh, I didn't know you were talking to me." The kids learn young when someone outside of the family says, "Is your daddy there?" to say, "Which one?" And they also learn that if someone says, "Where is your mommy?" when you happen to be out with your momma, that this is because the person is just not wise enough to understand the difference between a mommy and a momma, and they simply say, "Over there," instead of explaining the language subtleties to a stranger.

LGBT families also need to make decisions about last names. Heterosexual families commonly use the last name of the father, a routine practice many feminist women find a bit deplorable. Many heterosexual women do keep their last names, and some hyphenate their last names. I have, however, never known a heterosexual man to take his wife's name, or hyphenate his name, if she hasn't hyphened hers (something women often do). LGBT people need to make conscious decisions about their family's last name and also to pay for a legal name change—one of the many extra costs of being queer in a society that does not allow the privilege of gay marriage.

In some couples, each partner will maintain their own names, and one family I know gave some of their children one last name and some the other's last name. Often if one parent can be a legal parent, the family will give the children the other parent's last name. Some families join their names with a hyphen. This might become cumbersome when our children decide to build families of their own. Yet others create a new family name, sometimes derived by mixing the two names (Weinstein and MacDougal, become MacWein or Dougalstein) and other times by using a word that has meaning for the family, either in English (Star) or in another language (Pais/Peace).

Having the same name can assist a family in feeling connected, when we live in a world that so often disregards our families. However, having the same name can be complicated when doing an international adoption, so you might consider waiting until after your family has been completed.

There is, of course, no doubt that our families are sometimes challenging for straight people to understand, but the problem is that they project their discomfort onto us. One mom received a call from the day care center; they were concerned that her son was having problems because he didn't have a father. Her son would put his hand on his hip and repeatedly say, "I am your father" and then yell, "Father!" The mom reassured the day care teacher that he was just acting out his favorite scene in *Star Wars,* and shared with her the proper theatrical response, which immediately lessened his need for repeat performances. She is not alone with fielding worried calls from school personnel who are, of course, only looking out for the best interests of our children.

Maybe it's just the children of lesbian therapists who create fathers when there are none, because one of my boys had a girl doll named, of course, Daddy. However, I suspect that our children simply have normal desires to have their families reflected around them, and they will often create moms (in dad-only families) and dads (in mom-only families), especially when they are very little. I mean everyone else had a daddy, so why shouldn't my son, even if his daddy was a dark brown baby doll with long black hair? I remember he once announced to me, while he was in the bath,

Two Moms and a Pig for a Dad

When our daughter Emma was born, we planned for her to call my partner, who had given birth to her, Momma and me Eema, the Hebrew word for mother. I am Jewish (my partner is a lapsed Catholic), and this made sense to us. Emma started in day care at six months, an in-home setting she shared with eight other children, all of whom had a mother and father. When fathers came to pick up their children, Emma would hear them shriek some variant of Daddy or Dada. She had figured out my partner was Mama, but was still struggling with what to call me. Not surprisingly, as she reached her first birthday, she began to babble and squeal with delight Dado (rhymes with glad dough) when I entered the room. It was tempting to let Emma decide and to embrace Dado as my name. After all, she expressed it with such intense delight. But we figured she would face enough challenges growing up being the daughter of two mothers without having to explain that she calls one of her moms Dado. Still, we felt we had to channel her exuberance in shrieking Dado somewhere. Around this time Emma became enamored of a pink stuffed pig she received for her first birthday. This pig went everywhere with her and was much beloved. Thus, we started to call the pig Dado. Emma embraced this with enthusiasm, and the pig has been Dado ever since.

As Emma got older, she has learned to call me Eema, and this should be the end of the story. However, when we gave the pig this name, we didn't anticipate the future well. Now, as Emma approaches three, we had her annual progress review from her day care provider, a straight woman.

"Emma is doing just fine," she said, "but I wonder if being raised by women has created some issues for her? She seems to think that all men are scary or pigs." I tried to explain that the "scary man" Emma talked about was a three-foot marionette we owned. This puppet was an older gentleman wearing a black trench coat, carrying a black violin case, and with a stern expression, which we had bought in Prague before she was born. He used to hang in our living room until Emma expressed her discomfort and he was stored in a closet. Still, she has continued to chat about the "scary black man" with some frequency and wants to ensure he is safely stored away from her. I also tried to tell her teacher that Dado was the name of her favorite stuffed animal, a pig, and if queried, Emma would tell you that Dado was her "baby girl."

What I have learned is that straight people, even those who are well-intentioned, seem to scan for problems they imagine the child of lesbians would have. The fact that Emma loves her one male day care teacher and talks warmly about many men that are part of her life didn't register. What stuck was that this poor fatherless child being raised by these man-hating lesbians thinks all men are pigs or scary. Sigh! And still I fear she will grow up, be in therapy someday, and have her therapist say to her, "Let me understand—you had two mothers, and Dado was a pig. . . . Very interesting."

M. Judith Block, Ph.D., partnered with Kathleen for five years, are parents to Emma Rose, age two, in Ann Arbor, Michigan.

that before he came to live with his two moms, he used to live with his two dads, in a big, rich, fancy house. I said, "Oh, I didn't think you remembered that," not wanting to disturb his fantasy. He assured me he did.

Our children will pretend that their families look like other families and will try to make sense of the roles they see fathers and mothers playing in the world around them. Sometimes their play gives us a lot of insight into the stereotypes of gender and family roles in the world around them. Rabbi Julie Greenberg writes that her daughter once announced that the family needed to "get a man." When asked why, she said because we "need a daddy?" Julie reminded her that in their family there is a single mom and asked her what a daddy would do. Her daughter suggested he could "read the paper."

Whatever our kids call us, the nature of our families means that they, too, have to be out, whether they like it or not. They will naturally fantasize about what life would be like in another family, a more normal family, and they will sometimes want us to hide ourselves, not be so out, and may even try to disappear one of their parents, especially as they enter adolescence. LGBT parents are often surprised that their children will play house with a mommy and daddy, wondering, "Where did they get *that* from?" The reality is that *that* is everywhere, and they pick it up, no matter what corner of the queer world you live in. It is worth remembering, however, that because there is a special name for "gay families," they may question what those other families are called. My son pondered this one day, asking me if his friend Jake's parents weren't gay, what were they? He wanted to know, who did they love? I explained that Jake's mom and dad loved one another, and that was a perfectly fine kind of family also. It also allowed me to introduce the words *straight* and *heterosexual* to his six-year-old vocabulary.

Most children are raised in homes where boy-girl couples are assumed to be the only kind of couples, and this is sometimes reinforced rather abusively. They need to be taught that there are different kinds of couples. One little girl walked up and down the hallway at a family wedding, announcing which family was staying in which hotel room. "Aunt Maria and Uncle Nelson are in this room; Aunt Claire and Uncle Tom are in this room; Aunt Francis and Uncle Mitch are in this room." She got stumped when she got to Uncle Paul and Uncle Ramon, though. She insisted, "It has to be boy-girl!" Children growing up in queer homes do not have boy-girl references as their base. You will receive notes home from day care that say, "Eleanor had a lot of fun playing today. She played house with Jacob, where she and Jacob were the moms." Personally, I think our influence on the world around us is a good thing, a very good thing.

When Lucas's moms came up to school to talk with his fourth-grade teacher, they overheard this conversation in the hallway.

"Who's that?"

"Lucas's mom."

"No, the other one."

"That's Lucas's mom, too."

Then he whispered, rather loudly, in the first kid's ear, "They're lesbians," followed in a normal, very matter-of-fact voice, "It *does* exist, you know."

Indeed, it does. We exist. We're here. We're queer. And we are out looking for a bathroom with a changing table.

CHAPTER ELEVEN

• • •

Sex Talk

IT WAS MY agent's idea to do a chapter on having a healthy sex life; it honestly never crossed my mind. When I read the book outline to my partner, she gently raised her eyebrows and said, "Oh, and what advice do you have to say about this, Dear Ari?" She kindly didn't mention anything about how experience is often helpful in giving other people advice.

I decided to do what I always do when I don't know what else to do. I send E-mails out into cyberspace. That is how I learned how to pick a contractor for my new kitchen, how I learned what foods I could and could not feed an infant (sadly too late for it to matter), and how I became educated about how to remove mold from clothes left in a flooded basement (vinegar one load, bleach the next, whatever survives can be worn two or three times without falling apart; ignore the white spots). I sent out numerous E-mails to many cyber lists: gay parenting lists, general LGBT lists, and even to Dan Savage, sex columnist expert. The E-mail said: "Seeking stories about sex after parenting—funny stories, sad stories, how-to stories, etc." Accustomed to having an exploding in box whenever I send out a one-to-two-sentence E-mail request, I was surprised by the silence. I received back a few one-liners, the most articulate written by one gay man, who said, "Duh!" I began to realize the seriousness of this issue.

Now, perhaps people were afraid to respond to a subject header that said: Parenting and Sex, so I clearly stated I was not recommending parenting and sex together, like peanut butter *and* jelly. In case that is not clear, let me say it directly. I am not talking about sex with your children. Despite the gory rumors and public confusion about homosexuality and pedophilia, LGBT people do not commonly couple thoughts about children with thoughts about sex. For that matter, most LGBT people don't even have sex to produce children. As Dan Savage joked, "It's ironic that the religious right opposes both gay sex and gay adoption because, in my experience, nothing puts a stop to gay sex faster than a gay adoption." This is one of the most paradoxical twists of life living under a foreign regime (read: heterosexual): that most queer people who are parents struggle to maintain any semblance of an active adult sex life (like, of course, most heterosexual parents), yet we are accused of acting out our sexual depravities on our children. They (you know, them) seem to assume that we are not only having inappropriate sex with one another all the time in front of our children but also dragging our kids into our scandalous sexual escapades. The reality is that our kids are dragging us to the park and the most licentious behavior we are enacting in front of our kids is making dinner and folding laundry, while our sex toys are dutifully locked up in the trunk at the foot of our bed—just like straight parents. One Christian-based Web site inferred that some (uncited) research found that 50 percent of children growing up in gay homes were incested; this kind of disinformation is extremely dangerous.

Since I know this chapter will be reviewed extensively by the conservative right-wing moral minority, I want to start by making one thing perfectly clear: countless homosexuals are still shtupping one another multiple times a day, and many of them are doing things that would clearly shock more conventional people. This group does not, however, seem to be parents. If, however, one's goal were to eliminate gay sex—this is just a suggestion of course—encouraging gay parenting would be an underutilized strategy with the greatest proven success rate. I want to encourage conservatives to seriously consider a campaign to support gay adoptions, lobby for increased visibility of gay parenting in the school systems, as well as promote free access to sperm banks for same-sex couples as a tactic in their war against homosexual behavior. This way we can be gay but not act gay. Those who are opposed to gay sex and think it is the devil's work should become far more supportive of gay parenting; it can often eliminate gay sex entirely.

MAINTAINING HEALTHY ADULT SEXUALITY (OR TRYING TO)

Everyone by now has at least heard that you shouldn't have a baby with the intention of saving a failing relationship, and hopefully everybody has followed those rules. With any luck, your new baby has entered a relationship that is basically healthy, of some duration, and that you have reasonable skills for taking care of each other and putting up with each other's foibles. If so, you've got about a 50 percent chance of having your relationship survive intact over the next few years, at least if our families have the same statistical odds as straight families. And only if you are very, very flexible about having your sexual needs met.

Romance, relationship development, intimacy, and hours of passionate sex are not the common buzzwords heard when children join a family. If you are single, it will probably not be the time when you start a new relationship (although there are always exceptions to this rule). Babies, as we've already determined, take up a tremendous amount of time. The majority of that time is stolen from your intimate adult relationships (sexual or companionate). Generally speaking, your interest in adult conversation will dwindle, in theory as well as practice. No matter how interested you previously were in international politics, geothermal warming, or the rise of agribusiness, world politics will seem like sound bites from another universe. The intimate details of your lover's/mother's/friend's workday rarely hold interest, and for some reason, people do not seem to find the details of your baby's gurgling facial expressions as interesting as you do. For many, many new parents the thought of sex after dozens of poopy diapers and sleepless nights seems like a feat of impossibility.

I know there are exceptions. Women who give birth on Monday and are doing it like bunnies by the next Friday. I know there are gay men who can't wait to bring the little one home, put him in his bassinet, and jump

Cuddling

Marco, who is two years old, crawls in between us every night. He loves the physical contact and throws a leg and arm over each of us. He wants/needs the contact, just like us grown-ups. He slept on the floor with the other kids in his orphanage in Cambodia.

We love having him there and all three cuddling together. He does not wake us, and he kind of fits perfectly. Waking up next to his kisses, hugs, and physical tenderness in the morning is something we look forward to. We occasionally talk of getting serious about getting him into his own bed in his room, but the few times we did the Ferberizing (sleep training), it wore us out and broke our hearts.

Ron and I have been together with an active sex life for thirty years. Of course, having our little one between us now limits our contact. We actually do fool around once he's asleep (against the experts' advice) but are always aware of his presence. Without much planning, our sex needs have diminished somewhat, and we can control our urges without much personal sacrifice.

We think of our past sex activities, inviting a third to bed with us, sleazing it up at a back room or moonlit beach, and know that was then, this is now. Marco gives us a new chapter and new energy on life. We do not miss the more frequent and spontaneous sex part—oh, maybe a little, but having a son more than makes up for it. This week we made some progress, and Marco fell asleep in his own bed for the first time. The sex was okay, and our bed was a bit empty.

Jeff, partner to Ron for thirty-one years, daddy to Marco, age two, lives in New York City.

each other with joy and pleasure ("each other," I said). I confess I haven't met these folks yet. Most parents will tell you that sex dwindles considerably in the early years of parenting, and I hear that it picks up as the kids age. I'll keep you posted.

Parenting can often change your interests and values. Although dancing till dawn and hot, steamy sex under the stars still sounds good after children—and still feels good when you can arrange for it—most parents find that other joys occupy them. Cuddling in bed with a ten-month-old, who seeks out your eyes, ears, and mouth with his pudgy little fingers, eyes filled with adoration, is often worth passing up a night or year of dancing in smoky clubs. Many parents find their interests have grown simpler: picnics in the park, a walk around the block, and watching your child use fingerpaints for the first time. A new kind of passion for your loved ones might develop. Watching your lover patiently and tenaciously burp a screaming infant, patting, rubbing, walking, soothing, until the big long *burrrp* is evicted, can open up a reservoir of love and delight for a life partner. Watching a friend visit your baby for the first time and scoop her up, carefully, lovingly, seeking eyes for connection, cooing, "Oh, you've come, you precious one. I've been waiting for you," might be worth passing up the endless phone conversations with college friends about the war on terrorism, however strong your convictions about world politics. This does not mean, of course, that you will become an apolitical blob, but that you might reprioritize your interests, and you may not be as much of an activist in the years that you have small babies at home.

Intimacy with your partner may change. It may not be about having passionate sex seven days a week, in exotic positions, but more about sweet cuddling together, loving gestures you do for one another, and planning for occasional weekends away when you can go back to loud, raucous, and intense sexual escapades. One man E-mailed me that sex has become "more routine (as in the timing) and also confined to the bedroom." Almost everyone commented that there is far more cuddling and less hard-core sex.

Be gentle with yourselves regarding your love lives during the early years adapting to children. Don't be surprised, though, if you find it is harder to leave the baby with a baby-sitter than you thought, if you are distracted easily during sex with the gurgling sounds coming from the baby monitor, or if the vision you had for sex is stymied by the complete exhaustion of your body. Lower your expectations about sex, and perhaps redefine your understanding of intimacy. By the time you have acclimated to life with kids, they will be heading out the door for lives of their own, and you can rediscover one another.

However, for some people, or some couples, the changes in their romantic life since having children are more than they can bear. Sex is an important and primal need for all people, but for some of us it is certainly a stronger desire or a greater part of our identity, and losing that special connection to someone during the incredibly stressful years of new parenting can impact our ability to remain connected to our lovers. The lessening of sexual frequency, desire, or connection is a common reason for couples to break up—not just LGBT couples—and we need to acknowledge that although some of us are willing to live with years of diminished sex and do feel fulfilled by cuddling and other intimacies, others are unable to maintain our commitments to our partners if the sexual and/or romantic expression is diminished.

Lack of Sex Can Destroy a Couple
BY PATRICK CALIFIA

Being a parent made it very difficult for me to keep sexual pleasure in my life. When my partner was pregnant, his pain and nausea took sex off of his agenda. Yes, his. Transsexuals are supposed to be too alienated from their genitals and reproductive anatomy to have kids, but some FTMs get pregnant and have children before or after transitioning to a male identity. Matt had always wanted to have children, and we thought our prospects for adopting or becoming foster parents were slim to none. So I called practically everybody I knew who had sperm and asked them to give us some. We decided to inseminate at home, using multiple donors, and on the third try, Matt became pregnant.

A handful of conservative and homophobic FTMs felt very strongly that it was wrong for him to do this, that it would invalidate the idea that FTMs were men. They also objected to our being parents because we were a gay couple and because of my work as an author and sex radical. I'm sure there are lots of nontransgendered people who would also be upset about our family as well. I feel very fortunate that we had a large group of family and friends (both gay and straight, transgendered and not) who surrounded us with love and approval.

Matt's pregnancy didn't erase his male identity in my eyes. I had more important things to think about during his pregnancy, like taking care of him, trying to locate an OB-GYN who would be supportive, and finding a safe place for Blake to be born. I think the fact that Matt had

a baby makes a lot of people question whether Matt is male or even transgendered. He says, "I don't understand why so many people are pissed off because I decided to use my uterus before I threw it away." The fact is that anybody, regardless of their gender identity or sexual orientation, can feel that call (which I liken to a spiritual vocation) to create a new life and become a parent. To deny that call is to do oneself a serious injury.

I get asked all the time how Blake deals with having such weird parents, and people try to scare me with horror stories about bigoted day care or schools. For the most part, our obstacles are much more mundane: Can I get the baby to eat lunch? Where has his other shoe gone? Is it time to buy him his own potty? How do you get wet and moldy Chee-tos out of car upholstery? Why is he crying? How long has this juice cup been under the couch? Will he ever take a nap? I don't know who pisses me off more, the people who believe Blake will grow up confused about his gender because he has parents who are transgendered, or the transactivists who harass me that I should be raising a child without gender. Blake was born with his own gender, thank you very much, and I think my job is to accept him on his own terms. No parent can change their child's gender identity; we can only decide to be on their side or shame them. Blake will grow up knowing there are a lot of different kinds of people in this world. He will be able to make important choices about his own identity without being afraid of our rejection.

Queer parents can bring tenacity, ingenuity, and a fierce commitment to our children that are unmatched by many nuclear families.

There are some people who think that all of Blake's present and future problems are caused by the fact that his biological parent is a tranny. Blake has severe gastric reflux, intermittent hearing problems, and delayed speech, so I usually feel that I have more in common with other parents of special-needs kids than I do with the queer community. Being a parent has, in many ways, superceded all my other affiliations and loyalties. Blake is a very bright, loving, curious, and active child, and he has to come first, ahead of politics, my pride, dignity, comfort, or sense of difference.

But my ability to provide for him, on a material or an emotional level, depends on my own quality of life. If I am constantly frustrated and deprived, I will feel more resentment for him than love. I grew up with parents who fought constantly and stayed together for the sake of the children, and I know that that isn't actually in the best interests of your offspring. Sexuality was not the only issue that caused our breakup, of course. But it was an important part of my dissatisfaction. I continue to believe, foolishly perhaps, that parenting need not eliminate desire. Sex is a key building block of a good relationship, and children benefit from having parents who have a satisfying sex life.

Granted, we were in an exceptionally challenging situation because of Blake's painful medical problems that made it almost impossible for him to sleep. The bed became a haven for napping and nothing more. (Well, occasionally I got myself off, but I always felt bad about it, because I really should have been washing bottles or doing laundry instead.) Matt and I were almost never together in the bed that we'd once been so reluctant to leave. We had to take turns holding Blake upright and giving him medication. It was very painful for me to feel that I was giving more and more to this relationship while my partner receded further and further away from me. He felt that having the baby ought to make up for any problems we were experiencing as a couple, while I had never anticipated the harsh fact that he would naturally choose a sick and suffering baby over me. I suspect that postpartum depression was a factor here, and I've also spoken to many people who've given birth who say their libidos went flat for a couple of years after that experience. Regardless of the cause, after two years, I just couldn't take the loneliness anymore.

I love Blake and I want to be in his life, but I also don't want to live with his other dad anymore. So I am struggling with the question of how to be a divorced parent. This is all complicated by my own health problems, which sometimes leave me with very little to give. I have to admit that at times I am angry about the fact that having a child means I need to remain connected to someone who has rejected me as a lover and a sex partner. I was never one of those people who made their ex-lovers into friends, and I worry about the stress that being a father places on my new relationship.

I still feel guilty about wanting romance and sexual pleasure in my life.

Does it mean I'm immature, a bad dad, wrong, or evil? But I think most parents do want the excitement and release of sexual tension, courtship, foreplay, and that alleviation of stress, that confirmation of being connected to one another. It's a major challenge to maintain desire or find the time to fulfill it, partly because capitalism is so punitive toward families. It's so easy to become alienated from one another, and resentful, to blame each other for things that can't be helped like financial problems, sleep deprivation, difficult in-laws, lack of space and cleanliness, isolation from friends, and loss of recreational activities, etc. I'm sharing my story partly to warn other couples that if you want to stay together, you have to be smarter or luckier than I was, and solve this problem, unless, of course, you are willing to have a relationship in name only.

Patrick Califia, M.A., is four years into a transition from female to male. He parents his son Blake, age three, with his former partner, Matt Rice, in southern California. Patrick is in private practice as a licensed marriage and family therapist and is the author of Sex Changes: The Politics of Transgenderism. *You can contact him by E-mail at: patrickcalifia@aol.com.*

My personal experience has been that I've been less at peace with my lack of a sex life than Jeff is, and less ready to leave than Patrick was—although to be honest, that would depend on the day you spoke with me. It has been challenging and frustrating to try to schedule in sex and romance around soccer, bill-paying, the piles of laundry, and working for a living. If I think about it, I know that Patrick is correct, that one should not trivialize how important our sexuality is to our well-being, but to be honest, I avoid thinking about it because of being so busy. Perhaps I shouldn't admit this in public, perhaps I should be some kind of role model for successfully balancing parenting with frequent queer sex, but the truth is that although I know exactly how to maintain a good sex life, and I really could help you to do it, today I've been too lazy to follow through on my own advice. It's a sad thing. It's one of those parenting experiences that gives me some unwelcome insight into the generation who raised me.

As I said, very few people were willing to write to me about their sex lives. I'd like to fantasize that's because they are so busy doing it. Interestingly enough, almost no lesbians offered at all, until I offered to kneel on my knees and beg. But I'll wait to tell you her story; think of it is as foreplay. First you have to hear mine, but don't worry, it's a short piece; there's not all that much to say.

It is worth noting that no one has told me that their sex life improved

It's Your Turn, Dear

BY ARLENE (ARI) ISTAR LEV

Sex is important to me. Despite coming out in the heyday of lesbian feminist politics when many women identified as "political lesbians" and being a political activist myself, I was always very clear that I was a lesbian for only one reason: I really like having sex with women. My desire for women has been no small thing in this life and has taken me down some very interesting paths. I have left long-term relationships because the sex wasn't good, wasn't frequent, or simply wasn't. Intimacy with my partner, sexual intimacy, has been a sacred expression of my love, and even as lesbians have gained so much social acceptance in these past decades, I have never lost sight of the fact that my sexual passion for women makes me a dangerous woman in this world. Yet it is something I would not compromise, not for my career, not for my family, and not even for my lovers.

Then I had babies. I swore when I had my first son—I was single at the time—that I would not give up my sexuality for parenting. When my son was just a few weeks old, I was dating women I met through a personal ad—women who mostly ran in the other direction when they heard I had a newborn. Or maybe it was the spit-up on my skirt that turned them off; it's hard to know for sure.

When my son was six months old, I fell madly and passionately in love with a woman (who I did not meet through the personal ad)—the butch of my dreams, who might prefer that I find a more neutral term than *woman*. Our entire relationship has developed woven around

the fabric of diapers, bottles, temper tantrums, and baby-sitters.

Early in our relationship, when having sex for hours at end was an indispensable priority, our son was very cooperative, sleeping long hours while we explored the depths of each other. We lived on very little sleep and were startled unexpectedly—sigh, often at very bad moments—by the sudden cry of a baby demanding a bottle, or a cuddle, or a soggy-diaper change. There were few illusions in our growing romance, since part of our courtship involved wiping poop off of each other's hands and soaking spit-up out of both lingerie and dress clothes.

I remember preparing for a hot date once, having a few moments of quiet in my house. I prepared a bath with bubbles and aromatherapy and planned on soaking and lathering my body with lotion, and doing all those girl things that I love. As I sank back into the bathtub, breathing a sigh of relief and relaxation, I felt a sudden piercing in the small of my back, as the rubber ducky jabbed into my kidney. I got used to the rhythm of our lives with one child, struggling to find time for our intimacy, but committed to finding it.

When we adopted a second child, also a son (surely a topic for another column, how my women-centered world has become a training academy for young boys), this one was not as cooperative as the first child, being a high-needs child who always wanted to be cuddled, held, fed, and spent hours screaming. We learned to live our lives with a child strapped to our bodies ("It's your turn, dear.") and to have conversations with wailing as the backdrop.

Sex is still important to me—theoretically. I mean, I still like sex, and we still have great sex—when we can get there. It is hard to find time to get there with *Rugrats* blasting on the tube, the dog whining to go out, and a baby screaming for another bottle. My honey looks at me over the children's heads and smiles a smile that tells me, *Sigh, yes, it would be nice to roll around for a while, wouldn't it.* The truth is that by the time we get the kids to bed, the lunches packed, the laundry moved from washer to dryer, and dog walked, we will be too tired to do anything besides fall into bed—baby between us—and, sigh, sleep.

We had plans for Mother's Day. My mother-in-law came to baby-sit; we made expensive dinner plans at a restaurant a block away from our house and went out on a lovely date. Sitting across from her, I remember romance and desire, though we both have to keep reminding each other to not talk about the baby's intestinal problems or the political problems in my older son's school.

We head home and upstairs. We light candles and incense, and move toward each other, just in time for our four-year-old to wake up screaming. He has developed some night terrors—normal, everyone tells me—and screams for fif-teen minutes before he finally falls into a deep sleep. Is it the thought of his parents having sex that frightens him?

I come back to bed, and reach out to her, just in time for the baby to start his frantic grunts that inevitably lead to another bottle, burping, farting, diaper changing, spitting up, clothes changing, before falling into another fitful sleep. We get up and feed, and burp, and clean up the baby, cuddling in bed, talking about how lucky we are to have such sweetness in our life, and looking at each other with hunger in our eyes . . . but I notice she is starting to yawn.

The baby is finally asleep, and as we roll over to each other, the sky crashes with thunder and lightning, and our twelve-year-old, seventy-five-pound dog jumps suddenly on the bed, on top of both of us, whining with fear. Shaking our heads, we fall asleep, reminiscing about the passion we have known, savoring its taste and smell in our centers. We know that soon our little one will sleep through the night, and all too soon they will not want to cuddle in bed with us, or share their night terrors. And we know that our bodies will still be here for each other, older, perhaps a bit fatter and hairier, longing with desire for one another.

This article was previously published on www. LesbiaNation.com, and in CommUnity, Albany, NY.

after having children. No one! As in not one person! One woman told me her sex life improved immensely while pregnant. Many queer people said their sex lives improved after they came out, which for some people happened long after having children. A few people said that their sex life lessened when the children were very little but resumed to its prechildren rate once the kids were out of diapers. A number of parents of teenagers said they had great sex lives, but being sexual with teens in the house often meant quieter sex than they preferred. For those who are into kinky or leather sexuality, it has often meant engaging in sex play in hotels or when the kids are visiting friends, or with their other parent for the weekend. Almost everyone agreed that this was the completely rational and acceptable solution, but that it was a major hindrance to the kind of sexuality they preferred having.

Finally someone wrote me about being able to maintain their sex life despite having kids. I am thrilled that it was from a woman, busting all the stereotypes that the boys are doing it, but the girls aren't. We now have proof that at least one lesbian parent is really having sex. She asked me to publish this anonymously, but it's such a landmark case, I thought she should be honored with a queer award of some kind, something better than a toaster oven. Maybe a gift certificate to a sex store like Babes in Toyland or Good Vibrations?

It is good to know that maintaining an active sex life is possible. I hope most people reading this take this to heart and go for it. One of the issues many couples have discussed is the question of cosleeping, whereby parents sleep with babies and small children. I will avoid all the controversies about this practice, except to say that human beings have been cosleeping with children for most of recorded history, and it is a natural and a safe way for families to sleep. The dangers for infants involve parents who are intoxicated, on medication, or sleeping in unsafe conditions (i.e., using a waterbed, having pillows near the baby's face). Just in case anyone who is reading this is thinking that cosleeping is some kind of weird, kinky, queer thing, one of the major cosleeping advocates are the Sears family, who are devout Christians. At any rate, since cosleeping can be a controversial issue, couples can wind up with each person on different sides of the debate. Sometimes one parent insists on keeping the baby close by, in the room, on the bed, and the other parent insists on putting the kid in a crib, in another room. This can cause conflict in terms of compromising, but the reality is that having a baby, or child, or gaggle of children, in the bed can interfere with the frequency of and desire for sex. Indeed, I almost want to say, it should! Of course, lots of people find solutions for this: including the fold-out bed in the living room, weekends away, putting the kids in their own rooms after they fall asleep, or simply living with less sex.

Still Crazy About Each Other After All These Years

We met in college and something sparked right away. Two years later, that spark caught fire, and we fanned it. While many of our friends thought that they knew what we saw in each other, only we knew: it's the sex. It was always that, and although we are well mated in every respect, sex is important. Our love is the happy marriage used as an example of how well a partnership can work by her therapist mom, but we still work at it. So when we decided to have a baby after five glorious years, the question of how we would keep the flame burning was an urgent concern for both of us.

Talking to our lesbian friends with kids, we were pretty gloomy about the future. One of my oldest friends (yes, that's dyke for *my first girlfriend*) is a researcher now, and she recently reported that in her interviews with coupled moms, many of them said sex was no longer important. One even said that cuddling in the kitchen while doing the dishes has become as satisfying as sex for her. I wondered whether she had never had the experience of getting laid on her kitchen counter, or whether she was replaying those memories during the cuddling! We talked about how we would keep the sexual element of our love alive, and decided to work and play at it until we could feel more confident about the adoption.

After our adoption journey, though, we had a drought of about eight weeks during our physical recovery from the various shocks to the system: tropical parasites, interrupted sleep, "helpful" visitors who never left. I felt as attracted to

her as ever, even more sometimes as she stumbled into our room with the baby, handing over the dry kid and full bottle before falling into her side of the bed. However, by the time we got to be alone each day, we were both too tired to care.

In the third month, we decided to leave the baby with my mom for the evening and step out to the movies. I chose something racy at the multiplex and only called home once, before the feature. When we got back to the car, the air was suddenly charged. We were giddy with delight at being alone together again, and as one we realized that nine weeks without sex had been intolerable. Mumbling between the kisses that this could never happen again, somehow I drove us home.

I knew that I had unlocked the back door, so I was confident that we could sneak straight to the bedroom from the car. I parked around the corner, and we tiptoed, giggling, up the back stairs to our bed. I didn't even look around the corner for the sleeping baby, just slipped past her door feeling pretty self-assured. I was definitely going to get some.

I undressed her quickly, and reached for the taut moist parts of her that had been so sadly neglected over the months since the adoption trip began. Still fully dressed, I carried her to the clean sheets, and we fell into bed, again, as alive as the night we had finally figured it out after two years of friendship. We were headed for the skin-to-skin contact I had been craving when I heard the most terrifying sound possible. Not the baby, who was sleeping comfortably; no, the sound I heard was my mother, stomping up our staircase from the living room saying, "Hello? Girls, is that you?"

I thought I would die laughing. We threw on some clothes, and I was sent to the hall with apologies. Mom walked to her car muttering about the strange things her younger daughter does, for no reason. "What kind of sense does that make, I ask you? They say they need an evening out, so I take care of the baby, put her in her own crib, but can they stay away for dinner and a movie? No, they come home and don't even say hello."

We're still doing it after nine years, which may be a record for lesbians, even without the added challenge of the kid. For us, raising this child together is one more tough set of circumstances that are not quite what we expected; our baby was an easy sleeper, it turns out, because her hearing impairment was untreated. Straight people raising children with disabilities have a 20 percent chance of coming through it married, and we figure we'll beat those odds like we've beaten the odds on everything else . . . one night at a time.

Sara and her partner Kate got married in May 1996, and have a two-year-old daughter named Jane. They live in New Mexico.

At least, when having children interferes with the sex life of couples, you can blame one another. For single people, you need to literally go out and find someone to have sex with, and then integrate a nonparenting sex partner into your lives. It's hard enough getting out at all, let alone getting out and looking good enough for meeting new people. For single people who cosleep with their children, a new lover who is not a parent might not understand why it is hard for you to put your child in a crib, or why the child refuses to stay in the crib, or why the child is sleeping in the double bed when you two are curled on an old pull-out sofa. One woman says she only dates other moms for that reason, but of course that is no assurance that you will agree on this issue.

Whether or not you cosleep with children, most parents are simply exhausted at the end of a long day parenting, and the energy for sexuality is often greatly diminished. Although mostly this is looked at as a problem, a disappointment, an inconvenience, a shame, there is another side to this. Nonsexual intimacy with a partner and finding other sources of joy and pleasure outside of sexuality can be a blessing in disguise for many people. It is no secret that sex for some of us can be addictive, and some have engaged in unhealthy and dangerous sexual practices. Although there is no guarantee that this will change when becoming parents, for some people parenting has served to reconfirm their commitment to healthy lifestyle choices. Indeed, we might unconsciously choose to parent as a way to honor the life force, our children's as well as our own.

As Joel describes, parenting encourages many to examine the sexual choices we are making with precision and care. A number of bisexual women mentioned that they avoid dating people of the opposite sex because of the need to use birth control. One woman says, "I was so ready to have my child, so ready to be pregnant, planned, hoped, wished, etc. . . . I can't imagine dealing now with accidentally getting pregnant and facing the decision of terminating a pregnancy." On the other hand, some bisexual men are drawn more to sexual relationships with women because of the potential ease of becoming parents together. For bisexual people in particular, parenting can render them more invisible as a queer person. Indeed, numerous bisexual friends in heterosexual relationships said they had nothing really to contribute to this book because they said their sexual identity was simply not an issue in their daily lives parenting children in heterosexual relationships. I can't help but wonder how their sex lives are.

So it seems that the issue of sex becomes increasingly more complex once we have children. The verdict seems to be that most people are having less of it, that some people have discovered other intimacies that fill their needs, and that for some of us there is simply no substitute for having an active sex life. If maintaining a sex life is important to you, put down this book right now and write a personal ad or go talk with your partner about it. Set up child care, go away for the weekend, wear something sexy, and most of all, put some distance between yourself and that Diaper Genie. *Go, now*; treat it seriously. Remember when you first discovered how absolutely wonderful queer sex was? You shouldn't have to remember; it's still that good. *Go!*

SEX EDUCATION: HOW TO TALK TO LITTLE PEOPLE ABOUT SEX (AND REPRODUCTION)

Talking with children about sex isn't really a queer discussion, of course. All parents need to be able to talk with their children about sex and sexuality. Some people might assume that LGBT parents have an easier time of this than heterosexual parents, and perhaps that is sometimes true (at least for those of us who also work as sex educators). Mostly, though, LGBT

Safer Sex—for the Sake of the Children

Is it okay to admit that my adoption of my son was not wholly motivated by altruistic reasons? Of course, I had a lot of love in my life to give. Of course, I always wanted to be a parent. Of course, I wanted to be a forever father to a child already on this planet as opposed to bringing another life into the world. All those statements are true, but also true is the fact that my personal life was less than rosy. I was a young gay man in the '90's with low self-esteem who romanticized sex and love to mean the same thing. It was only a matter of time until I became an HIV statistic. I didn't know how to emotionally protect my physical self. My partner's needs were always placed above my own, and if his needs were to have unprotected sex, then that's what happened.

I had been fortunate, though. I was twenty-five, and no one had yet to make that request of me, but it was only a matter of time. Now that the shocking information is out there, let me put it in perspective: 80 percent of my desire to adopt was for all the right reasons—my desire to raise a child with all the love I had to give. The other 20 percent? I needed to grow up in regard to my adult interpersonal relationships that I just couldn't handle. The confidence that I tried so hard to exude on the surface level was covering nothing more than insecurities, acting out behavior to gain attention, and a desire for approval from . . . anyone. So at twenty-five, when I adopted Josh (only hours old at the time) I took a dating, sexual, and relationship-seeking hiatus from the world. For six years, my center and my universe was Josh.

Let's set the record straight: adoptive parents do wonderful things for their children, as most parents do. Sometimes they are the knight in shining armor who rescues a child who no one else wanted, or wanted to love correctly. Mostly, though, we are parents who do the best we can in this manual-less endeavor called parenting. As with all parents, our children change us, and mine raised me in the early days just as much as I raised him. Josh protected me from a world that I wasn't ready for and kept me safe by keeping me home. That "who's the parent and who's the child" line starting to blur a little for you? Join the club. I was so committed to raising Josh that I vowed that I would do nothing that might take me away from my responsibility to him. I stopped social drinking, and I stopped social sex. I concentrated on building a support network that benefited Josh and my life. I took stock in my own merits and through introspection began to figure out why I felt a need to be a doormat in relationships. I took a time-out from a part of the world, and almost ten years later, Josh and I are the better for it.

When Josh was about six years old, we were beginning our Saturday morning errands, and our first stop was to the gym for daddy's workout. Josh sat with the receptionist and played with JumpStart 1st Grade on her computer while I worked on keeping my body fit enough to chase after him. Matt was a guy that I had seen on and off through the last year at the

gym. Disarmingly handsome and very social, there wasn't a person at the gym that
didn't know his name. When he came
over to me and started to make chitchat,
I wasn't surprised—he and Josh often
goofed around while I worked out. When
he started asking me if I was dating, I
wasn't surprised—simple yes/no questions aren't difficult to deal with. When
he asked me if he could take Josh and me
to the Indian restaurant after my workout
for lunch, I was surprised. Didn't he get
the memo? I don't date, I'm not a grown-
up. But we did have to eat, so certainly
lunch wouldn't hurt, right? The answer
was in fact correct. My lunch with Matt
opened my eyes. He talked about himself,
and he asked questions about Josh, and
then he asked about me.

Josh finished his lunch and went over
to the play area that the restaurant
owner kept for kids, and Matt told me
something that I don't think I had ever
heard. "You're a very handsome man." I
damn near choked. I had to set the record
straight, so to speak, so I explained to him
that I don't date—I was far too insecure
and immature to put myself on the line.
"How long ago was your last date?" he
asked. I told him it was over six years ago.
Then this stranger, this handsome
stranger with piercing brown eyes, said
the most amazing thing. "Do you think
you're that same insecure person you
were six years ago?"

Talk about your twenty-five thousand
dollar pyramid questions. I thought about
Josh, all we had been through, how much
I loved him, and the person I grew into so
that I would be the best parent he could
have. I realized that the answer was no, I
no longer was a person who would do
anything for the man I was involved with.
My first priority was my son, and no matter what relationship came my way, I
could never put myself in harm's way either emotionally, physically, or sexually. I
accepted another date from Matt for
later in that week, and things went okay—
but we never slept with each other. In the
end, Matt really didn't have enough to offer me to make me want to have sex with
him. I didn't become a prude, and have
had sex since, but I now have a balance in
my life. I have become a person who parents, dates, and interacts with the world
with equal determination. I am a person
of merit, I am a loving parent, and I am
worthy to be in a relationship.

There are other pieces I have written
about the successes and trials I have had
in parenting, but this is a testament to my
son, a thank-you, if you will. I thank my son
for giving me the gift of growing up, and I
thank the universe for letting me do so
before he had to.

*Joel Greenberg, father to Joshua Baruch Green-
berg, age eight, lives in West Palm Beach, Florida,
where Joel is finishing his degree in elementary
education and Joshua is finishing third grade.*

parents seem to stumble through these conversations with as much concern, nervousness, and lack of ease as every other parent does. You all
know the funny story about the kid who asks his mom where he came
from, and she, the ever-prepared mom, launches into a story about con-

Being BiSEXual

It's hard to be out to myself as bisexual sometimes. People keep calling Steve my husband. I don't remember people calling my ex-lover, Sandra, my wife. After nearly twenty years of being exclusively with women, I become involved with a guy I dated when I was a teenager. At work, when I started seeing him, people asked if I was still a dyke—like maybe bisexuality was a disease that could strike any other gay or lesbian clinic staff member next. Or maybe it was contagious? My ex told me if I was with a man now, it negated our entire eight-year relationship. I guess Steve's penis is so powerful it can change history retroactively?

If I want to pass as straight, it's certainly easy since that seems to be the default for woman with child. I get cruised by other dykes when I'm alone but not when I'm with my son Jason—it's like he converts me to straight by his presence. When I'm with Jason I don't really get cruised by anybody, although gay men in the Castro smile at me a lot. I have to put more effort into being out now that I'm a mother than I did before. Like if I go out in my Lesbian Avengers T-shirt, I feel like people are expecting I must have borrowed it from my gay sister.

I feel like if I were more butch, I wouldn't pass for straight, but that would mean I would have to present as butch, even though I identify as femme. Steve and I both cruise femme women, sometimes together, and I feel myself responding to feminine energy from him, yet he is a Kinsey 1 straight guy.

Sex is harder to come by than before Jason. He sleeps with us, so we have to go other places in the house—my office, the family room futon—to have sex while he's sleeping in our bed. We can never really be leisurely or elaborate, but it's still fun. I occasionally see a woman in another city, but she and I are both moms, so those times are nice but rare.

If something happened to our relationship and I ended up seeking another partner at some point in the future, I see myself looking for a woman. But I realize that how other women see me in the future might be very different from the way they saw me when I first came out and when I had been out as a lesbian with no boyfriends for such a long time. No longer a "real lesbian," would I still be in the running as a potential partner?

Beth Brown, M.D., has been partners with Steve for four years, and they are parents to Jason (the Giant Squid) age two, in Pacifica, California.

ception, and reproduction, and sperm and eggs. The child is wide-eyed, and when she is done says, "I was just asking what town we used to live in when I was young."

It is true that sometimes we are too zealous to give sexual information, and other times much too reticent; finding the balance is not easy. I think one of the errors generally made in all sex ed discussions with children is that we mix and confuse discussions about sexuality with discussions about reproduction. You'd think *we* would know better than that, but sadly I think we are as likely to do that as our next-door neighbors. The questions our children have about their bodies and sexuality rarely have anything to do with questions about where babies come from or their internal reproductive system. Both of these conversations are important, but when a girl is asking questions about menstruation, her concerns are more about embarrassment, cramps, mess, zits, and smell than about the journey her eggs are making through the fallopian tubes and whether or not she can get pregnant. And trust me, the questions boys ask about menstruation have nothing to do with fallopian tubes.

Children talk about their bodies very freely unless they have been silenced about it. They explore their genitals and ask for clarification about what their body parts can do and what to call them. Both of my sons at very young ages (under two) showed me proudly that their penises could get erect and asked me what you call it when it does that, and why it feels so funny. I simply explained that it's called being "hard" (although my older son told me it wasn't really "hard" but "tingly"), and that penises do that sometimes, and most people think the funny feeling is a good feeling. I had one interesting Freudian moment with my older son, who was about five at the time. As we were driving down a big hill, my son started laughing, and he said, "Oh, my penis feels *so* good going down this hill. You wouldn't know about that because you don't have a penis." I assured him that I had body parts that also felt good (although, to be honest, the hill didn't really impact me one way or the other). At which point he got quite animated, saying, "Penises are better. Boys have penises, and they feel great. You just don't know how great they feel. You don't have a penis, so you just wouldn't know." He kept repeating these words over and over again. It was one of those bizarre parenting moments where his words were so loaded with meaning in a hetero-patriarchal world where penises represent power, and yet it came from a simple place of his total joy in his body. At the stop sign, I turned around, smiling, and said in a mock stern voice, "Listen, buddy, I got a body that feels good, too, okay? Let's not say that either boy or girl bodies feel better or are better. I'm really glad you like your body, and I'm pretty happy with mine, all right?" He gave me that look kids do when grown-ups are kind of weird, and said, "Sure, Momma," but added quietly, "You just don't know how good my body feels."

Developing a healthy sexuality is about being in your body, although one of my editors says that's "therapy-speak." It is actually how I speak, so it stays. Children should learn that their bodies are sacred, that they feel good when touched, and that touch is a good thing, and that grown-ups like to touch one another. Of course, we need to also help them set boundaries on appropriate touch. I teach my boys that if they want to touch themselves they do it in the privacy of their bedrooms. (My little one squeaks as I go to change his diaper, "You can leave now. I need privacy.")

Children need to be taught about good and bad touch, and that nobody should be touching the private parts of their bodies at all, until they are much older, except themselves, a medical person, or their parents and caregivers if they are helping them wash or get dressed. They should know they can always come to you and tell you if anyone is trying to touch their body or making them feel uncomfortable because of how they are looking at them, or the things they are saying.

Children will, of course, talk to one another and get information that is less than accurate. Sometimes my son will insist, "Joey told me that boys can get pregnant," and generally I will correct him but not make a big deal if he argues with me. Over time they will come to realize that Mother is virtually always right. My partner recently found a pile of papers lying on the floor of my son's room after he had a friend visiting. They were filled with badly misspelled words suggesting that "Mary Alice kissed James," and that "Jason sat on Tara's butt," etc. She was appalled. I was thrilled. I would've been appalled if we'd found it hidden away. He feels safe enough in his home that he can talk about sex (albeit the seven-year-old version of sex) with his friends, and not need to hide it from his parents. He did tell me later that they had a "private conversation" in his room, but when I asked him where we should put those papers while we were cleaning up before bed, he shrugged and distractedly pointed his chin over to the bookcase.

I truly believe there is nothing more important we can do for our kids than create an atmosphere where they feel safe to explore their sexualities and ask questions without shame. They need to know that they will be given correct information. If they think that you are trying to withhold information from them, they will simply go elsewhere. This story dates me,

How the Sperm Gets to the Egg

As Dawn and I are preparing for our wedding, my nephew James, age five, is really excited about being part of the ceremony. He knows, as does everyone, that we are moving from our apartment to a house in a few days and planning to begin trying to conceive a baby. On the day before the ceremony, Dawn and James and I are alone in our kitchen, and James says, in this kind of offhand style of his, "Well, if you don't know, it takes a boy and a girl to get a baby."

Dawn is looking at me like, *Okay, you handle this one,* and I'm just thinking, *Please don't let me blow it!* So I say, "Well, you're right, James, it does take a boy and a girl. When the boy and the girl love each other, the boy can put the sperm right into the girl's body. But when the boy and the girl are just friends, the boy can give the sperm to the girl in a jar." And I look at him, and I wonder whether he even knows what sperm is when he gets this looks of deep understanding and nods his head. "Oh," he says, "I see. So you just swallow the whole jar, eh?"

Elizabeth Barbeau has been partnered to Dawn Barbeau for six years. They have been trying to conceive for the past four and a half years, and live in Vancouver, British Columbia, Canada.

but when I was in elementary school, the kids in my class were singing the Clementine song. . . . "There's a miner, forty-niner and his daughter, Clementine, Oh my darling, Oh my darling, Oh my darling Clementine . . ." except they kept changing "forty-niner" to "sixty-niner" and laughing up a storm. I asked my mother what was so funny about *sixty-niner.* She told me that they were ushering in the New Year—1969. Now I knew this was not true, although I didn't yet know what *sixty-nine* meant. When I realized a few years later what it actually meant and realized that my mother had known all along but didn't tell me, I was very angry. I didn't trust that she would tell me the truth about any other questions I might have had, so I stopped asking her. Consequently, I always answer my children honestly when they ask what a word or concept means, even if I'm not always 100 percent sure how to explain words like *sleeping together, leather dyke,* or why some women like to wear boxers.

Once while I was working on an article, my son came in the room and asked me what I was writing. "I'm writing about transsexuals," I said. "What is that?" he asked. "A transsexual is someone who isn't comfortable in their body, like a woman who'd rather be a man, or a man who'd rather be a woman, and so they decide to change their bodies so they are more comfortable," I said matter-of-factly. "Oh," he said thoughtfully, "I didn't know you could do that." "Well, you can," I said. "Great!" he said, "Now, can I please open the box of cookies? I've been waiting all day." The reality is that we live in a world where some people really do change their sex. My advocacy work in the transgendered community creates a bit more talk about that subject at our house than some, but any child living in the modern world will be faced with questions about this and a million other issues. Wouldn't you rather them hear the answers from you than anyone else?

Our children, like all children, will ask the "Where did I come from?" questions, and as hard as it is for most heterosexual parents to answer these questions, it is often very complex for LGBT parents. I was reading one of those "Where do babies come from?" books to my son. The opening line said, "All babies are born from a woman and a man." "Oh, no," my bright six-year-old says. "You can't believe everything you read," he tells me, proud to be mimicking his mother's words. He is quick to point out the bias toward lesbian families in the media. "Well, actually, that is true." I sigh. For an adopted son of lesbians to make the connection to an unknown birth father out there is quite a stretch. (I suspect the birth father would be equally stretched to discover where his son is now living.)

Parents need to explain to children who are born through donor insemination, with donor eggs, or surrogacy, the complexities of their conception. Parents need to explain to children who are adopted the differences between birth parents and adoptive ones. And all of us need to explain to our children the way that most of their friends were conceived, lest they grow not knowing that option exists. "I don't think Jacob's parents are lesbians, but what do you call it when a man and a woman love each other?" my son asks. Julie Greenberg's daughter tells a friend that she doesn't have a daddy; she has a donor. "Oh," the friend says. "Does he bring you donuts?" Trying to understand the vagaries of conception and donor insemination, our children, as well as our extended family, have many questions about exactly how we do it.

Most children take information about conception (any kind of conception) in stride, but other kids have many questions, confusions, and feelings about where babies come from, particularly where they came from. Commonly, the parents have underlying concerns about what they are sharing

In Search of a Tall Man with Glasses Who Likes to Dance

After my partner and I decided to use an unknown donor, I was referred by my doctor to a reproductive clinic. Living in the Deep South as an I-don't-shout-it-from-the-rooftops lesbian, I went alone and did not offer any explanation for my desire to have a baby. Not to worry. The woman who worked at the clinic reassured me, "Lots of middle-aged single women decide to do this." She showed me the rather short list of potential donors, saying, "You'll want to match your own coloring. Blonde hair and blue eyes . . ." I had to confess that the blonde was my hairdresser's idea.

We chose a donor with brown hair (my natural color) and blue eyes. We hit the jackpot—given the cost of semen—and I got pregnant with twins, two blue-eyed, blonde girls. (A few years later, I realized that living in a Southern climate, I could've picked a darker-complected donor, and their skin would have been less sensitive to the sun.)

When the girls reached an appropriate age, which turned out to be about eight, I explained the story of their conception. I tried to start with how conception works—egg meets sperm and so on—but they impatiently informed me that they knew all about that ("from

Charlie Brown's cyclopedia"). They wanted to know where I got the sperm to make them. They were especially intrigued by the fact that an actual husband was not required to make a baby. "So," they concluded, "you could do it again, and we could have a baby brother!" *Uh . . .*

Of course they were interested to learn what I might know about their donor. Since I couldn't tell them much, we tried to deduce some of his characteristics by things we know about ourselves. We know that the donor wears glasses, because the girls are myopic and I am not (myopia is a dominant genetic trait). Maybe he is tall, because the girls will be taller than I am. Maybe he can dance, because I can't (bad genetics here, but oh well). The next day, they reported back on how their story had been received on the playground. Their friends had decided that Steve, who is their friends' father, could possibly be the donor because he is tall, wears glasses, and is a good dancer. No word yet on how Steve's wife responded to that.

Carole is a single mom to ten-year-old identical twins, Rose and Louise, and drives a mommy van with a rainbow sticker in South Carolina.

and how it will be perceived, and our children (the little sponges) pick up on our discomfort. For families who adopt, there are always questions about where they came from, and who their birth parents are. Again, some children seek out answers with great persistence, and other children really don't care very much. My two-year-old repeatedly says, "I came from your belly, and I sucked at your breasts for milk." The reality is that he did neither, but he does see other babies doing this with their moms. I always tell him that he did not come from my belly, and I explain once again about his birth mother (giving him that word) and tell him her first name. Then, very animated, I tell the story about how I first met him (minutes after he was born), what he looked like, how happy I was, and how we all took care of him when he came home. I always tell him what his big brother, awestruck, said when he first saw him in the hospital a few hours old, "That's my baby brother?" Yep, kid, he is, for always and forever. Adoption stories are as important to children as birth stories are, and they need to be part of children's daily lives; children *love* stories about themselves.

The story of your child's conception, birth, adoption, or preadoption history may invoke difficult feelings for you, as you try to protect your child from the discomfort of being different. It is important, as a parent, that you develop language to tell your child their story, and become comfortable telling it, for this will become the story that they repeat, that they tell their friends, their future in-laws, and their own children.

Children with donors for dads, or who are adopted, may seek out information to try to understand parts of themselves. Here is one child's attempt to make sense of who he looks like.

Sometimes it is not just the children who are curious about the donor's influence. I, the committed sociologist, who make my living selling nurture over nature, am endlessly surprised when I spend time with my son's extended birth family, and they all gracefully move those large hands with long fingers past my face, with the exact same hand gestures as the child I tuck in at night. Biology matters little for some of us, parents as well as children, but for others it is a source of interest, fascination, and curiosity.

Whatever our curiosity about who our children will become, the reality is that our kids are growing up in different families than most of their friends. Just by having queer parents, they are exposed to same-sex couples, and often people who step out of traditional gender roles. They will naturally have a more open view of the world, especially regarding issues of gender and sexuality. My friend's daughter wakes up gleefully saying, "Oh, Mom, I had a dream that Barbie married Cinderella," and in her mind there is nothing remotely unusual about that wedding (except perhaps how many men were wearing rhinestones).

There has been a flurry of research on lesbian and gay parents (and a tiny bit of research on transsexual parents) over the past few years. As LGBT

Looking Good in Those Genes

We chose beauty over brains. Being the two unbelievers that we are, we thought only looks are inherited and were sure we could take care of developing the kid's personality ourselves. Our donor did not play piano and was not a published photographer. His favorite food was spaghetti. However, he seemed to have good looks, as he had done some modeling some years before, so he was a keeper. "Well," my mother said, "imagine if the child gets his looks and your brains." *Gosh,* thought I, *What if the child gets my looks and his brains!*

Manuel was born premature with a very low birth weight. As soon as that respirator was off and we could actually see his face, everyone wanted to know: "Who does he look like?" To Karine and me it was very obvious from the start that the kid did not look like me or anyone in my family, at least for the moment. My brother, however, decided immediately that the kid looked exactly like him. This absurd idea to try to find a family resemblance in a baby that has almost no flesh around his bones was quickly adopted by everyone else. "This kid is going to be blond," said the nurse.

"Is he?" said Karine and I on cue.

I was in the kitchen the other day when Karine asked me to come and see what Manuel was doing. She was taking pictures of him playing with a toy. As soon as he heard the click from the camera, Manuel would stop playing, raise his head in a cute angle, and smile. If Karine moved around him with the camera, he would turn his head to face the camera, eyes wide open, never stopping smiling for a second.

"He is acting like a model," said Karine. We looked at each other for a very long second.

"Do you think that . . . ?"

"Nah." I shook my head and went back to the kitchen.

Lucía Moreno Velo met Karine Hoffmann in Paris, and they now live with their one-year-old son, Manuel, in the mountains outside Madrid, Spain.

people parent in greater numbers, conservatives become vocal about their fear that we are harming our children. LGBT people and our allies have responded by conducting research on our families that has conclusively shown that our children have not exhibited any greater likelihood of being gay, nor of being gender-variant. "Phew," most people say, revealing their not so hidden feelings that gay parenting is somehow flawed and that being gay (regardless of your parents' sexual orientation) is not quite as good an outcome as being straight. I can't help but wonder if this research had shown that our kids did become gay in greater numbers, what would our reactions have been. Perhaps this is because we know a bit about how hard being different is, and we might want our kids to have an easier life. Black parents commonly have black children, too; most Jewish parents I know hope their kids will be Jewish, yet queer parents often cringe at the idea that our own kids might be gay. Perhaps we also fear that someone will blame us for our kids' queerness.

Judith Stacey and Timothy Biblarz reviewed the literature on children of lesbians and gay men, and they determined that although the research had accurately stated that our children were psychologically well-adjusted, there were other subtle findings. Our children, it seems, have a greater chance of being open to homosexual relationships themselves, although they are not necessarily gay-identified. Additionally, our daughters seem to be a bit more sexually adventurous, and our sons appear to be less traditionally masculine. Sadly, this information was presented in the media as if Stacey and Biblarz were trashing the previous research (and researchers), although nothing could be further from the truth. Additionally, this research has been used by numerous right-wing and fundamentalist Christian authors to back up their claims that our families are dangerous to children. In actuality, Stacey and Biblarz do not see these findings as negative statements about our families.

Why shouldn't children who grow up with positive gay role models not be more open to loving someone of the same sex? After all, they grew up witnessing loving gay relationships. Why would this not be considered a possibility, an option for them? And from a feminist perspective, I would think that having daughters who feel more empowered to explore their sexualities, as well as sons who are less caught up with patriarchal male modeling, are both very positive trends for the future. And hopefully, you will defend me for saying this by writing letters to your newspapers and congressperson when I am being publicly trashed and become unemployable.

Our children learn young how to juggle the values of their families with the values of the outside world. They do this naturally, organically, as all people who live biculturally learn to do. I was once looking at the homework assignment of a little girl in the first grade being raised in a lesbian family. She had to write a one-sentence description of a series of pictures. One picture showed two young children playing; they wore overalls and had short hair. She wrote, "The boys are playing." It was not clear to me how she knew those were boys, and she explained, "They don't have lesbians in school." Now certainly lesbians are not the only females with short hair and overalls (a short trip to the rural Midwest will cure that belief). And it is certainly sad that they don't have lesbians in school. And of course, small children are not yet expressing their sexual orientation by how they dress. But the point of this story is that she knew what was expected in school, and she also knew that the world was much more complicated than what is available within her school.

Our children are growing up in a much more complex world regarding gender—not just our kids, but all kids. My son attended a birthday party of a young girl, Alex. I asked him what she might like for a present. He said, "She likes footballs and action figures, that's all she likes." "Really?" I said, surprised because we've certainly bought enough of those Barbie-type toys for other girls in his class. "Those are not typical things that most of the girls in your class play with," I said. He looked surprised, "Most of the girls play football," he said. (He hates football, by the way.) "Anyway," he said, "you know there really aren't boy or girl toys. Kids can play with anything they want." "Yeah," my partner added in a mock-whining voice, "why were you thinking that, Momma? Sheesh!" I sigh. "When I was young," I say, "most girls weren't allowed to play with those kinds of toys, and they were teased if they did." He looks shocked and surprised by my small-town conventionalism. *That*, he assures me, was a long, long time ago.

Oh, course, it wasn't all that long ago. And of course there are plenty of places where it is just like it was a long time ago. But we really do not live in a very progressive community, and this following story was overheard in a small working-class neighborhood daycare. One little boy was talking to another little boy. He said, "What do you want to be when you grow up?" The other little boy said, "I want to be a mommy." A third child who was listening said, "Oh, like my daddy wanted to be a mommy, so he became one?" Without blinking, the second little boy said, "No, not like that. I want to be a mommy so I can use power tools." I love this story. This is not only about the ease with which small children accept gender transitions; it is also about the changing roles of women and men. For that child, being a woman meant that he could use power tools. Now perhaps it is stories like this that make the conservatives want to round us all up and ensure that we will never be near children, but to me it reflects the wonderful openness of our queer cultures. Our children grow up with expanded views of gender and possibilities for their own expression.

Many of us still cringe thinking our children might themselves be LGBT. Or at least we cringe when the day care teachers question how we are raising our kids, insinuating that something we are doing will make them gay. Sometimes the children of gay parents are more gender stereo-typed than other kids, and sometimes this is because their parents insist upon it. "I will not allow my son to wear nail polish or anything that is girly. I do not want anyone to have an excuse to make fun of him for hav-ing gay parents," one dad says. It is hard to cope with the judgments of out-siders when gay parents have gay kids, but I suspect that our reaction to others' reactions is a good indicator of our own internalized homophobia.

Perhaps some of us lean the other way and wish our kids will be queer themselves. Maybe we are not excited about the world of heterosexual dat-ing; maybe we think we will have more in common with them if they are gay? One bisexual mom says, "The only impact my sexuality has on my son is that he happens to be exposed to a whole lot of women and not so many men. I'm not very caught up in needing to expose him to male role models; I believe that gender is fluid and that by exposing him to people who represent the continuum of gender, he'll get enough role models. As it is, I think he's going to be gay; his actions and preferences follow the stereotypical gay model for now. I guess that's one way my sexuality does come into play: by being queer, I'm more aware and more open about his sexuality. If he's gay, so be it; but if he's not, then cool—maybe he'll be a gender-bender and turn those stereotypical views on their ear."

As LGBT parents we are constantly up against society's views that children need a mother and father (despite the fact that statistically few children grow up in homes with both a male and female parent for the du-ration of their childhoods). For gay men there is the ever-present mommy icon that they have to face. How can a man, or two men, ever replace the need for a real mommy, is the constant unspoken question facing gay men (and all actively parenting dads) as they take their kids to the park or go clothing shopping, especially if the gay dad is raising a daughter. Lesbian mothers are dealing with the opposite issue, which is that in a patriarchal system a family without a man is not a real family; it is a broken family, a damaged family, an incomplete family. And of course parents that are openly bisexual or transgendered are constantly facing the assumption that their sexual and gender expressions will completely confuse their chil-dren—as if June Cleaver vacuuming in her pearls, and Lucy and Ricky, who slept in separate beds, were less confusing for children of a previous generation.

Many people, including many LGBT people, fear that boy children growing up without a father or girl children growing up without a mother will lack role models of the sex that they are supposed to emulate. Although it certainly can be psychologically grounding to have role models of the same sex whom you feel close and intimate with, it is not necessary for healthy development. Many boys have been raised by single moms, and girls have been raised by their fathers, and have exhibited few problems in gender identity acquisition. First of all, unless children are being reared in a very rural area with little access to media, they are living in a world filled with children, teachers, neighbors, and television images. They see male and female role models all the time. Questions about finding quality role models raise different issues.

Families come in all different sizes and types. Children reared as only children have different life experiences than those reared in large families. Those who are raised with close relationships with grandparents and elders have different experiences than those reared without those connections. Although it is a good thing to have people of all ages, genders, and races in our lives, as long as children have a loving home with a family who cares for them, they will not grow up feeling deprived. They might, however, need to sometimes talk about the ways that their family is different or what it is they think they are missing because they do not have a mother/father/grandparent/sibling. When your daughter says, "I wish I had a mommy," it's okay to simply respond by saying, "Yes, that would be wonderful, wouldn't it," and honor her needs/fantasy/desire without silencing it, feeling guilty about it, or buying into the exaggerated romanticism of what-ifs.

Just to put our minds at ease, one black mom shared that her sixteen-year-old son came home from a friend's house, lay down on the foot of her bed, and looked up at her and said, "Ma, I'm glad that you were not with any men while I was growing up. I am glad that you had women in your life and that it was mostly just us." He shared with her how he felt watching his friends from intact heterosexual nuclear families go through problems with their fathers, stepfathers, and moms' boyfriends, and even though he would have liked to have had a relationship with his father, he felt better off with the void than with the problems.

Dads can still teach their daughters about menstruation, and moms can play catch or go fishing with their sons. Aunts, uncles, neighbors, teachers, and big brothers or sisters can fill in as role models as necessary, but the real secret is not to let anyone intimidate you (including your kids) into thinking that there is anything lacking in your family. Families come in all forms, and whatever form your family has taken offers your children all they need to develop solid gender and sexual identities.

My best advice: Don't assume anything about your children's sexuality. Don't worry about whether they will be straight, be typical boys or girls, and don't worry whether who they are has anything to do with who you are, whether you are a single-dad family, a four-parent same-sex family, a nelly queen, or a drag butch. Some of us were born to the Walton family and still look sharp in leather chaps, with or without stiletto heels. We of all people should know that you simply can't mold anyone's sexual orientation or gender expression; all you can do by trying to change others is make them feel bad about themselves. In my experience, most LGBTs really couldn't care less about whether or not our children turn out queer or not. Don't we know better than anyone how little control parents actually have over their children's future sexuality?

CHAPTER TWELVE

• • •

Godless Homosexuals and the Light of the Spirit

TYPING THE WORD *religion* and the word *gay* into my search engine did not immediately reveal the ancient and revered connections between queer people and the world of spirit. Instead, I was offered thousands of Web sites addressing the horrific sins of homosexuality and diatribes by religious leaders dedicated to eliminating this scourge from God's green earth. The fact is that people who have come to be known in modern parlance as gay, lesbian, bisexual, and transgender were historically seen as two-spirited, able to mediate between the worlds of men and women, and to have easy access to the world of the gods. Throughout the religious traditions of the world, queer people served their spiritual communities, often feeling particularly called to a life of spiritual service. Our unconventional sexual and gender expressions especially prepared us to be community leaders, medicine healers, monks, teachers, ministers, sadhus, mystics, and shamans. It is only in the modern civilized world that we have become godless heathens and depraved devil worshipers whose despicable perversions invoke God's punishment not only on ourselves but the rest of the world, as Jerry Falwell suggested following the fall of the World Trade Center. A sad fall from grace, in my opinion.

However, I must confess I do not enjoy the illusion of being seen as a saintly mystic any more than I appreciate being called a sinful pervert. Too much pressure either way. The sad truth is I have as little time for prayer and meditation as I do for sex. This homosexual will have to settle today for being no more reverent than I am horny. My spiritual life is, however, theoretically as important to me as is my sexual life, and being queer should not in any way limit our access to spiritual traditions and religious institutions. Many LGBT people have felt excluded from religious institutions and have difficulty maintaining contact with their spirituality due to the blatant homophobia and transphobia in most religious communities. It nonetheless appears that maintaining a spiritual life is important to many LGBT people (though certainly not all), and becoming parents for many of us reinforces the need to find a spiritual home.

LOVING THE SINNER OR WELCOMING HOME THE PRODIGAL SON

My initial Web search for information about LGBT spirituality yielded vitriolic, homophobic treatises, starting with Pastor Fred Phelps of the Westboro Baptist Church in Topeka, Kansas, who administers the God Hates Fags Web site. The Web site opens with biblical scripture and the statement, "Sodomy is an abominable sin, worthy of death." I felt immediately welcomed. He keeps track of the number of days since Matthew Shepard was brutally murdered and has a link to a Web page called, Matthew Shepard's Message from Hell, which is mostly selected scripture and dancing flames destroying a picture of Matthew, blessed be his memory. I guess Pastor Phelps has a special bat phone from the other side by which he receives these messages.

Another Web site called The Christian Truth shared this important bit of wisdom: "A child needs the influence of both male and female sexes in order to develop properly. Those who don't strive to give a child a 'balance' within their lives from both sides are depriving that child of the lessons learned through half of a complete family." I was relieved that my children are at least getting ample masculine modeling from their butch mom.

My search revealed numerous E-mail lists I could join in case I wanted to engage in heated debates with educated theologians like one gentleman who shared that being gay is a "sin like any other, [but] being gay does not preclude you from the Divine Word of God. Anyone should receive it and none should prevent it. If sinners weren't allowed into church, pews would be empty, pulpits vacant, choir lofts deserted and no one would be there to play the organ. Now, chances are homosexuality isn't a onetime occurrence, it's more of a lifestyle, like the arrogant, the depressed, the drunk, the adulterer, the repeat sexual offender, and the chronic liar, et al. any spectrum of sin can become habit." Addicted as I am to my drunk, depressed arrogance, I find this incredibly disheartening. Although I was not reared in a tradition that taught this sort of wisdom, and I was reading it purely as a student of the bizarre and unusual, I still found myself slipping into despair.

I was at least a bit assuaged when I read how Pastor Richard Rossi of the Immanuel Baptist Church in Long Beach, California, was locked out of his church after preaching. He said that ". . . we are commissioned to reach out to the lost gay person with unconditional love, grace, and compassion. We invite and welcome the gay community to our church to hear of Christ's gift of salvation and forgiveness upon sincere faith and repentance. . . . We hold the conviction that a person actively practicing the gay lifestyle cannot serve in leadership capacity in our church. . . . Simply put, our policy is, 'Welcome and transform.'" I guess this was not received well by the large gay population of Long Beach, who changed the locks on the doors of his church.

In 1975, the Vatican declared that there was a difference between having homosexual inclinations and engaging in homosexual acts, which many interpreted to be a positive sign of compassion for queer people. In 1986, the Pope issued a letter to the bishops of the Catholic Church titled the "Pastoral Care of Homosexual Persons," and in it he clarified that homosexuality should be considered an "objective disorder," and that although homosexual orientation was inborn, it was a sin to act on these feelings and that gay people should remain celibate. In 2000, Pope John Paul II expressed disapproval that Gay Pride celebrations took place in Rome during the Grand Jubilee year, saying, "Homosexual acts are against nature's laws. The Church cannot silence the truth, because this world could not help discern what is good from what is evil." Personally, I have higher requirements for compassion in my spiritual leaders.

For those who were raised in fundamentalist traditions, the position of the religious institutions, and particularly those of evangelical extremists, is not only cruel but can also serve to keep them away from all religious communities, as well as negatively impact their own personal relationship with God. Although by far the most outspoken antigay rhetoric comes from the conservative, Republican, born-again Christian wing of the Christian community, who have a strong presence on the Web, Orthodox Jewish and fundamentalist Muslims are equally disparaging, just not quite as techno-savvy (yet!). Although not as abundant or accessible, the hostile religious zeal among fundamentalist organizations of all kinds is equally belligerent and sometimes far more dangerous.

Al-Fatiha, which means "The Opening" in Arabic, is an international organization for LGBT Muslims that has largely formed because of the Internet; it took two years to build a community of 300 people across twenty-five countries. They are under careful scrutiny by the Islamic community, who has infiltrated their LISTSERV and distributed antigay leaflets in U.S. mosques. Al-Fatiha has also received a *fatwa,* or religious edict, that states, "The very existence of Al-Fatiha is illegitimate and the members of this organization are apostates. . . . Never will such an organization be tolerated in Islam and never will the disease which it calls for be affiliated with a true Islamic society or individual. The Islamic ruling for such acts is death."

Death threats, in general, are not on my personal list of redeemable spiritual acts. Thankfully, organizations like Al-Fatiha and the Gay and Lesbian Arabic Society (GLAS) continue to network and support LGBT Arabs in the U.S. and those living in Arab countries to educate their communities, end discrimination, and hopefully find a way to reconcile what may appear to be divergent realities. It is no accident, despite a thorough search, that I was unable to find anything about gay parenting or queer family-building emanating from the nascent community of Muslim and Arab queers. It will come in time, since Arab and Muslim cultures are very family centered, and hopefully the rest of us who are survivors of religious persecution will help them build a new community where queer families can live somewhat at peace among their religious brethren.

Within the Orthodox Jewish community, bare-bones dialogue has begun between some Orthodox rabbis and members of the gay community, although LGBT Jews have been mostly silenced and shunned among more observant Jews. When the book *Nice Jewish Girls: A Lesbian Anthology* came out in the 1980s, it was publicly denounced by the Orthodox rabbinate, but time is slowly fostering rudimentary connections between the queer community and Jewish establishment. A Web search will quickly reveal numerous Web sites for orthodox LGBT Jews, including a group called Orthodykes. Information and reviews of the movie *Trembling Before God,* released in 2002, which documents the very strained relationship between Orthodox Judaism and queer Jews, has brought greater depth to the dialogue. Those who are deeply religious are engaging with their holy books to find ways to make sense of the paradox of their lives, and slowly queer Jews—queer religious Jews—are building a home.

Spirituality and religion are profoundly important to many people; the rituals that we were raised with often remain important throughout our lives. For many LGBTs returning home to the spiritual lives of our families and religious institutions is returning, literally, to the fires of damnation. How do we make peace with deep spiritual values, traditions that we revere, and the venomous hatred espoused by religious leaders in the name of God, Allah, or Jesus?

Although some will stay and battle either their own sexual selves or the religious doctrines of their faith (truly a religious crusade in my book), others, of course, leave for less strict or more welcoming religious communities. We cannot minimize that for many, leaving orthodox communities means leaving a way of life that they love, that is embedded in their very souls; it is a painful and complex process that is perhaps too easily scorned by those of us who are less religious. Chris Hernandez is a lesbian mother who fought for custody of her daughter in the Alabama court system and was supported in her efforts by the Roman Catholic private school her children attend. She says, "My children attend a religious school because I made a conscious choice to educate them in a moral atmosphere. However, one should not always fear religion based solely on sexual orientation. My children are taught that we are all made in the image of our maker, and we will answer for our crimes against one another to the higher power. There is no right or wrong religion, there are simply differences in beliefs."

Despite the death threats, religious proclamations, and threats to burn in everlasting hell, religious institutions have begun to respond to LGBT concerns. Many religious communities have responded by developing "Welcoming Congregations," official policy decisions on the part of the church's hierarchy to actively welcome LGBT people; some churches hang the rainbow flag outside to identify themselves as welcoming. In February

The Minister's Blessing

I adopted my daughter when she was eight months old. My wife left me with full custody when my daughter was eleven months old. I came out when my daughter was sixteen months old. My partner moved in when my daughter was almost four. We have been together since then. My daughter is now nine.

It was interesting coming out at midlife. There I was with all the trappings of a middle-class existence: house, car, cats, a church, and a life. But it wasn't authentic, and I was living a lie. I was confused and in a great deal of pain at having overlooked something so basic to my entire being. When I started the coming out process, I met with my Unitarian Universalist minister, a wonderful woman named Craig Hirshberg. She knew me and had been to my house a few times. I invited her to lunch one day and told her I had something important to tell her. I then came out to her. She was very supportive during our conversation, and when I saw her later that day at a meeting, Craig handed me a package and told me to open it later. When I did I burst into tears, for the package was a book, entitled *Now*

That I'm Out What Do I Do? by Chris McNulty. My minister was also my supporter! It's this sort of support in my faith that has made all the difference. One of our songs/chants goes as follows:

Come, come whoever you are,
Wander worshiper, lover of leaving,
Ours is no caravan of despair,
Come, yet again come.

My faith, though still evolving in true Unitarian fashion, is strong, for we accept and affirm the inherent dignity and worth of all individuals, regardless of race, creed, or sexual orientation. These are not words but things we truly believe and act upon. My daughter has made many friends and learned so much about diversity and acceptance. The congregation has been amazingly supportive. My partner and I just celebrated our fifth anniversary. I stood up at church and announced it. The congregation applauded.

Alexander (Sandy) Lea, partner to Everett Lo and dad to Elizabeth Lea, age nine, lives in Somerville, New Jersey.

2004, some religious leaders openly defied the law by marrying lesbian and gay couples. Additionally, churches and synagogues that specifically serve LGBT people have proliferated in many cities; and many out gay religious leaders serve nongay congregations. Our families are finding homes within religious communities.

Sandy's experience has been echoed by many other people who came out to their pastors, their rabbis, and their priests, who have been warmly welcoming. The UU Church has been particularly welcoming of LGBT people, and has been a leader in the struggles to legalize gay marriage. Undoubtedly, some congregations and sects are more welcoming than others. Sometimes people have the experience of going to a welcoming congregation that is not so welcoming after all. Perhaps the minister is not supportive, or people in the congregation are aloof, so even though they are officially welcoming, you might not feel welcomed. If finding a safe place to worship is important to you, then continue to look until you find the right congregation. One woman in the process of gender transition left a fundamentalist church and sought refuge in a church community that professed to be welcoming and had many LGB members. Sadly, they were not as accommodating to a transsexual person. She later sought out a Unitarian Universalist (UU) church that warmly welcomed her and her daughter. She said, "They welcomed me into all the women's activities. My daughter is able to attend every other Sunday; on the alternating Sundays my ex takes her to a fundamentalist church. She is learning through the UU church that religion doesn't have to be hate-filled, exclusive, or negative. The congregation we attend has hundreds of LGBT members, is very affirming, making an explicit statement about inclusivity at the start of every service. They also incorporate far more ritual, including earth-based and feminist ritual into their activities and services. I love them, and they seem to love my daughter and me." The UU church is unique in its approach and inclusivity not only to all LGBT people, but to all people regardless of their religious affiliation.

In addition to UU, other Christian congregations have developed strong supportive welcoming policy positions to the LGBT community, including the Quakers (Religious Society of Friends) and the United Church of Christ. Some denominations have congregations that are welcoming as well as those who remain more conservative, such as the United Methodist Church, the Episcopal Church, which has ordained homosexual priests, and the Presbyterian Church. Surprising perhaps to some of us, even more conservative churches sometimes have welcoming factions like The Association of Welcoming & Affirming Baptists and The Brethren/Mennonite Council. Lutherans Concerned/North America started the Reconciling in Christ Program, which is an ecumenical movement of welcoming churches from ten faith traditions that now include over 1,500 congregations and ministries. Ironically, welcoming congregations may be the fastest-growing grassroots movement in mainline churches today.

Welcoming congregations are paving a way for people who have tradi-

Unitarian Universalism: A Welcoming Church

The living tradition of Unitarian Universalism (UU) extends love and acceptance to all people and recognizes the inherent good of all persons. At a time when some faith traditions are expressing deep ambivalence about whether to truly welcome LGBT persons, and others continue to express open hostility toward anyone who is of a minority in sexual orientation or gender identity, the UU Church is deepening its long-standing commitment to the full inclusion and affirmation of all persons, without regard to sexual orientation or gender identity.

With its historical roots in the Jewish and Christian traditions, UU is a liberal religion—that is, a religion that keeps an open mind to the religious questions people have struggled with in all times and places. We believe that personal experience, conscience, and reason should be the final authorities in religion, and that in the end religious authority lies not in a book or person or institution, but in ourselves. We are a noncreedal religion: we do not ask anyone to subscribe to a creed.

At a UU worship service or meeting, you are likely to find members whose positions on faith may be derived from a variety of religious beliefs: Jewish, Christian, Buddhist, naturist, atheist, or agnostic. All these people, and others who label their beliefs still differently, are faithful UUs committed to the practice of free religion. We worship, sing, play, study, teach, and work for social justice together as congregations, all the while remaining strong in our individual convictions.

There are many bisexual, gay, and lesbian ministers, and recently two transgender ministers in our churches. The first, Sean Parker Dennison, was the first openly transsexual minister called by any congregation in the U.S.A. UU presidents have spoken out against antigay foster care policies and other forms of institutionalized homophobia. UU has created and funded the Office of Bisexual, Gay, Lesbian and Transgender Concerns (OBGLTC), encouraged ministers and congregations to conduct services of union for same-gender couples, and supported Interweave (Unitarian Universalists for Lesbian, Gay, Bisexual, and Transgender Concerns). Is Unitarian Universalism totally free of homophobia? Of course not. But whenever the more than one thousand member congregations of UU are called on to take a position on bisexual, gay, lesbian, and transgender issues, the sentiment is always overwhelming: the human family is one, and the love that binds us is greater than the fears that divide us. Human loving and human sexuality are also sacred when shared between of the same gender.

UU has long had as its first guiding principle the commitment to "affirm and promote the inherent worth and dignity of every person," and yet the struggle against heterosexism and gender dualism in both the denomination and society at large continues. We are all spiritual beings, driven to find a pattern of meaning in our lives. UU is working hard to realize the dream of religious communities

where everyone is welcomed and cherished, just for who they are.

JoAnne Weber-Baligad, partner of ten years to
Mary Weber-Baligad, is the director of Religious

*Education at Orange Coast Unitarian Universalist
Church in Costa Mesa, California. After working
with children her whole life, she is working on
having one of our own.*

tionally felt excluded to connect to religious institutions. For many people, this is a gift that not only provides a greater spiritual connection to whatever Higher Power they believe in, but also a greater connection to community in general.

In addition to many churches becoming more welcoming to the LGBT community, other churches have developed whose ministry is exclusively focused on LGBT concerns. Dignity/USA is the largest, progressive organization for LGBT Catholics, which was started by Father Patrick Nidorf in1969, professing that gay people could express their sexuality in a manner that is consonant with Christ's teaching. The Metropolitan Community Churches were founded by Reverend Troy Perry in 1968 and states that their vision is to "embody the presence of the Divine in the world, as revealed through Jesus Christ; to challenge the conscience of the universal Christian Church; and to celebrate the inherent worth and dignity of each person." Clearly, from the worldview of orthodoxy, these are heretical ideas, yet these churches continue to grow in numbers as well as influence. MCC has more than 300 local congregations in eighteen countries and is one of the largest predominantly gay organizations in the world.

One very exciting new development is the organization Soulforce, founded by Reverend Mel White and his life partner of more than twenty years, Gary Nixon. Soulforce is an interfaith movement committed to ending spiritual violence perpetuated by religious policies and teachings against LGBT people. They base their philosophy in the teaching of Mahatma Gandhi and Dr. Martin Luther King. Below is an overview of their teachings and purpose.

Soulforce is doing important advocacy work of challenging mainstream homophobia that is disguised as religiosity. Despite these changes, and the proliferation of welcoming congregations, some people miss the traditional churches of their childhoods. Although not all people are interested in challenging the hierarchy of mainstream churches, some LGBT

Feels Good to Come Home

Going through the process of a gender transition in Republican, white-bread suburbia was a bit disconcerting, because we always felt so different. If there were other people who were also different, they weren't visible to us, and that was scary. We also were looking for a spiritual home, one that would allow us to find our own path and accept our own beliefs, but more importantly one that wouldn't just tolerate us but welcome us as a queer couple.

Well, we hit pay dirt ten minutes from our house! It is an Episcopal church but a very liberal one that is grounded in liberation theology. From the moment we walked into the church, we were blown away by how welcoming everyone was. The minister taught (I won't call it preaching) about finding your own path and using repentance as a framework for the future. The church emphasizes community and caring, not dogma, and I took communion that first day because I truly felt like I belonged.

What was even more amazing was in this bastion of Republican blandness, half the congregation was gay and lesbian, and not closet-case types. Many of the women are butches, and the men were not hiding anything. What really made us feel like this was the kind of place we were looking for was that the gay and lesbian members were active in the congregation (two of the wardens are a gay man and a butch dyke) and the fact that everyone really seemed to care about and love one another, almost as a kind of family. Talk about sticking your finger into the pie and pulling out a plum!

Since going regularly and joining, a big change has come over my whole family. We are having our eyes opened to the world out there, to the other injustices that are there, and are starting to try to help. More importantly, seeing people who are different, as we are, living and enjoying life outside the gay ghetto has caused us to open up as people. We have become active socially in the church, and a wall of fear between my spouse, myself, and the outside world seems to have melted quite a bit. We simply are learning through this church and its teachings that we are going to be loved and supported, no matter what we are.

Spiritually, it has opened my wife and me up a great deal. In effect, we have found what mainstream churches claim to give, finding something of a common spirit with other people. For our son it has been a really good experience. It has given him both a social outlet to be with other adults and kids and to share his own strong spiritual beliefs and has provided a safe environment for him to perform and share his musical abilities as well. I would also add that it has helped him a great deal dealing with our transition, since he is now regularly around people who are LGBT yet who have families and whom he loves a great deal. Church has come to be not an obligation or a burden but something that we look forward to each week.

Lauren lives with her spouse, Betty. They've been together seventeen years, and have a son, Eddie, who is seven years old. They live in northern New Jersey.

people have left gay churches and are seeking out spiritual homes in Catholic and Protestant churches. For people with strong roots in black churches, they miss not only the religious communities of their childhoods but the way the church is deeply integrated into their daily cultural lives; as parents they want their children to have this experience. For some LGBT parents the inclusion of their children and how they are treated within a religious community may be more important than whether the church is welcoming, or even having their own spiritual needs nurtured. One black bisexual dad who is single-parenting two adopted children says, "The boys and I have been attending the Messiah Episcopal Church for nearly a year now. The boys were baptized there this past May. They have a group of LGBT church members, but more importantly, there are plenty of activities designed to keep children involved in the church from infancy through adulthood. This was important to me, because I left a gay church, where I'd been a member for years, because I didn't feel children (especially foster and special-needs children) were valued there. Messiah is different. It more closely resembles the Catholic churches of my upbringing rather than the charismatic Christian churches I gravitated toward as a young adult. Still, I feel comfortable there. I can pray there, and in this church, my children have a place."

As churches within Christianity are becoming more welcoming and inclusive, Judaism, too, is adapting to a changing cultural environment. The return to a more Jewish-centered life for many LGBT people has been directly related to parenting. LGBT Jewish people are returning to synagogue precisely because they want a place for their children to learn to live a Jewish life.

My partner wrote the following piece. She gave it to me a few days before the manuscript was being sent off to the publisher. The last two pieces to come in, on the edge of the deadline, were both from butches, but I'm sure that was just a coincidence. Having my partner write something for this book is both incredibly sweet and incredibly intimate. It is sweet in that cute kind of way like when small children show you their artwork that is made up of green handprints. "Look, Mom, I made this for you!" It is no small task to offer your writing to a writer. But it is also very intimate, kind of like making a baby together, for words are to writers, well, the stuff the universe is made from. So, yes, sweet and intimate. So before she goes off thinking she can romance me (I don't *do* romance, okay?), I just have to tell

Soulforce

We believe that religion has become the primary source of false and inflammatory misinformation about lesbian, gay, bisexual, and transgendered people. Fundamentalist Christians teach that we are sick and sinful. Liberal Christian denominations teach that we are incompatible with Christian teaching. Most conservative and liberal denominations refuse to marry us or ordain us for ministry. The Roman Catholic Church teaches that our orientation is "objectively disordered" and our acts of intimacy "intrinsically evil."

They teach that we should not marry, adopt, coparent, teach children, coach youth, or serve in the military. Members of Dignity (the Catholic GLBT organization) are refused the use of Church property and the presence of a priest to conduct a Dignity Mass. We believe these teachings lead to discrimination, suffering, and death. Our goal is to confront and eventually replace these tragic untruths with the truth that we are God's children, too, created, loved, and accepted by God exactly as we are.

Six Soulforce Beliefs About Myself

1. I am a child of a loving Creator, a daughter or a son of the Soulforce at the center of the universe.

2. I am loved by my Creator exactly as I am. My sexual orientation is not a sickness to be healed nor a sin to be forgiven. My sexual orientation is a gift from my Creator to be accepted, celebrated, and lived with integrity.

3. I am not an accident. I have a purpose. I was shaped by my Creator to love God and to assist in God's eternal struggle to win justice for all Her children who suffer injustice.

4. I will not discover my purpose nor realize my power (my own soulforce) until I join my Creator in doing justice (making things fair for all).

5. When I join my Creator in doing justice, my own life will be renewed, empowered, and made more meaningful.

6. In serving others, it is as much my moral obligation to refuse to cooperate with evil as it is to cooperate with good.

Soulforce can be reached at www.soulforce.org.

you this: Although I completely trust her memory of Shabbat dinners, they are a bit more boisterous, a bit louder, and the prayers are punctuated with a lot of "Sit down," "Watch the juice," "Will you please stop standing on the chair," "Don't drop the challah," and "Please take your kippa (skull-cap) out of the rice." Amen.

Coming home to our traditions, reconnecting with our spiritual roots is very exciting for many LGBT people, and for LGBT families, being welcomed home is indeed a gift of the spirit. Like the prodigal son, we may find that if we travel half the distance, religious communities will journey out to meet us.

MAKING OUR OWN WAY

Not everyone has a spiritual life (including lots of straight people). Not everyone is seeking a spiritual life. There is no need to have one if you don't want one.

For those who do seek out spiritual paths, they often find them outside of mainstream religious institutions. LGBT people in Alcoholics Anonymous (AA) and Narcotics Anonymous (NA) identify the twelve steps as offering daily spiritual practices, but they are not necessarily linked to any formal religious institution. Attending meetings, reading AA books, and talking with a sponsor become the means for staying sober and also a way of connecting to God. Many people practice spiritual paths or seek connection with a Higher Power without necessarily following a particular path. One friend of mine just became the sole guardian of her four-year-old grandson—welcome back to daily parenting! She is committed to her spiritual path, which includes both Jewish rituals and frequent attendance at AA meetings. She says that if it wasn't for her AA family, she would never have been able to be such a healthy grandparent.

Many LGBT people have found spiritual solace in following Eastern religions—spiritual paths based in Hinduism and Buddhism—which tend to be the least blatantly homophobic of all the world's major religious paths. Buddhism, in particular, does not have much to say about homosexuality at all, negative or positive, and the spiritual qualities that are emphasized, such as compassion and awareness, are regarded as transcending such superficial distinctions as sex and gender. Buddhism, although a world

Be Fruitful and Multiply
BY RABBI DEBORA GORDON

Judaism has always been family-centered. The first mitzvah (Jewish obligation) recounted in the Torah is "Be fruitful and multiply." The earliest promises to our ancestors were of descendants who will be numerous "like the stars of the sky and sand on the seashore." Our foundation stories tell over and over about families who had trouble bringing children into the world, and then they recount the rejoicing when the next generation was finally born.

Family bonds are nurtured and supported by Jewish rituals in many ways. For two millennia, Jewish observance has revolved around the household, and home rituals (religious or secular) can delight, intrigue, and engage even very young children: gleaming candles, warm melodies, food of many textures and tastes. Questions and explanations are built into the Passover seder and ideally encouraged at any time.

Our foundation stories include quite a few families that in no way fit the mold of two-parent, heterosexual, single-ethnicity families. Consider Abraham and Sarah, the parents of the Jewish people, whose first child Ishmael is birthed by an Egyptian woman, Hagar, who lives in their household as a servant. Sarah adopts the infant, but birth mother and child are later banished; the two brothers reconcile after their father's death. Abraham and Sarah's grandson, Jacob, marries two sisters who are his cousins, and also has children with their maid-surrogates. Moses, the greatest Jewish prophet, was cared for by an extended family of women: His foster mother Batya, daughter of Pharaoh, who finds him floating in the Nile River; his biological mother Yocheved, whom Batya hires to nurse Moses; and his sister Miriam, who arranges the match between biological and foster mothers. When Moses grows up, he marries and has two children with Tzipporah of Midian, a woman whom Jewish tradition says is black-skinned. Finally, Ruth, the great-grandmother of King David, remained passionately committed to her mother-in-law Naomi after the death of both women's husbands, immigrating with Naomi to Israel; when Ruth married again, Naomi nursed the baby.

And yet despite all our ancient stories about Jews living in varied household arrangements (not all of which are worth emulating), the extended heterosexual nuclear family has come down to us as the Jewish ideal. Up until this generation, lesbians and gay men were simply not imagined as parents (and barely noticed as members of Jewish communities, for that matter). So there can be quite a sense of loss for Jews and others from highly child-centered cultures upon coming out, if the assumption is that being queer means that children won't be part of one's life. This longing and loss seem to be shared by Jewish men along with Jewish women.

But this generation is different. Once LGBT parenting became widespread, it was inevitable that Jews would be part of the LGBT baby boom. As two-mother or two-father Jewish families have proliferated, there has been tremendous growth and learning in the American Jewish community. The Reform and Reconstructionist movements have embraced LGBT families in many ways, on both synagogue and movement-wide levels. In particular, the role modeling provided by visible gay and lesbian rabbis—many of whom are raising children themselves—is undoubtedly helping communities putting welcoming resolutions and by-laws into real practice.

The Conservative movement currently has more widespread discomfort with LGBT issues, and lesbian and gay rabbis are more likely to be closeted. The attitude of the local rabbi often determines the extent to which LGBT families are welcomed, but certainly there are Conservative congregations with out LGBT families. The most astonishing growth recently has been the incremental changes occurring among American Orthodox Jews. The fact that our relationships and our families are being talked about at all, and spoken of with compassion and a degree of respect, is a great change. Ironically, the Orthodox community, with its strong emphasis on raising children, could theoretically be more supportive of LGBT parents than of gay men and lesbians who are not raising children.

In a profound way, our tradition recognized long ago that parent-child relationships are not determined by biology alone. Sanhedrin 19b: "One who teaches another's child Torah is regarded by the tradition as one who gave birth to the child." Given how often our prayers link the words "love" and "teaching," isn't that our tradition's way of saying, "Love makes a family?"

Rabbi Debora Gordon and her partner Judy Wienman were married in a Vermont civil union in 2000. They're trying to conceive and currently exploring foster-parenting and adoption; meanwhile they live with their dog and three parrots. They're blessed to be extremely welcomed and supported by the Jewish community of New York's Capital District, where Reb Deb is the rabbi of Congregation Berith Sholom in Troy.

religion with as many different branches and beliefs as Christianity or Judaism, is also a philosophy without a belief in a deity, based in meditation and following one's dharma, which is interpreted as teaching, truth, path, spiritual practices, and literally means "that which upholds." Dharma is the foundation, the ground one is standing on.

Followers of Eastern spiritual paths often have daily spiritual practices, reading scripture, meditating, doing physical exercises for grounding (like yoga or tai chi), chanting, or daily prayer sessions. Some seekers also attend ashrams, or satsanga, or meditation sessions with other seekers. When families are involved in Eastern spiritual practices, often children are also taught to meditate and follow the same practices as adults. The family might also have a spiritual teacher with whom they study. I once overheard a conversation between my older son and his friend. The friend said that in

Full Circle

Baruch ata adonai Elohenu melach ha olam, asher kid'shanu bemitzvotav vitzivanu lehadlik nir, shel Shabbat. Blesssed is thou O Lord our God, King of the universe, who commands us to kindle the Sabbath light.

This traditional blessing is said by Jews throughout the world as they light the candles welcoming Shabbat into their homes and their hearts. I recite these aged words marking the end of each week, every Friday evening, with my two boys and my partner. It is a momentous event each time, as I watch the candle flames leap into their eyes and tunnel down to my soul, bringing me the strength to drop my baggage and gather them up in their innocence. Thank God for Shabbat!

Not too long ago, prekids, although I embraced the intent of the prayer, I felt encumbered by the gendered Hebrew language. My dyke friends and I would wrestle with the masculine pronouns, the masculine images, and we would change words, add words, bend words, and remove words we found impeding our feminist (and mostly dyke) spirituality. "Of course," we would lament, "these prayers were written by men, and the women's voices were invisible." We loved the sacredness of the space we carved out as we gathered to honor Shabbat or each new moon, and it was real passion that

flowed for the divine presence, blessed be She, as we wrestled with the words and our tradition. We desired to make these words transcend time, to merge with our lived lives.

My discomfort with the language settled down a bit as I became more comfortable in my own masculine self. As a butch, I've learned to welcome and embrace my masculinity (without disparaging my dykeness) and this has allowed me to breathe more freely. The gendered language now flows more smoothly from my lips with less reticence, the masculine nouns and pronouns moving within me. I softly inhale—God, and slowly exhale—God. I can wear the language and my identity, as my friend Crow always says, "like a loose garment."

I am able to welcome Shabbat with my sons in this ancient language of my people, chanting both the traditional prayers as well as the more feminist revisions, free of resentment and full of sweetness. I welcome the Shabbat bride gliding into our home as she is reflected in the eyes of my children.

Sundance Lev has been partnered with Ari for eight years, and together they parent two boys, Shaiyah Ben, age eight, and Eliezer Ranon, age four, in upstate New York.

school they taught her how to meditate, and she showed him what posture he had to sit in order to meditate. My son corrected her. "You don't have to sit in any position to meditate. You just have to go inside yourself." And like all good spiritual teachings, that one is universal and applies to every religious and spiritual tradition on the planet—peace and serenity is what one finds within.

Now, in all fairness, although most Eastern spiritual paths are not homophobic in the hell and brimstone kind of way that orthodox Western paths can be, there certainly can be a subtle homophobia. Most of the bias is not based in scripture as it is in the West, but in cultural and ethnic mores that disregard LGBT people and our communities and make us invisible and silenced. Homosexuality is sometimes thought to be one of the evils of modern capitalism, and Indian and Asian religious institutions can sometimes be very leery of out LGBT people. More people in the world belong to Eastern spiritual traditions than to Western ones, but in most Western countries being Hindu, or Buddhist, or even Muslim (which many consider an Eastern path, not a Western one) is still off the grid of what is considered common and usual.

Ashrams, satsangas, temples, and meditation circles, like churches, mosques, and synagogues, often vary in how welcoming they are, depending on the community, the presiding teacher, and sometimes the day you show up. For some people, following traditional Asian spiritual paths is part of their cultural heritage, and they are trying to figure out how to bring their queer selves home; for others, they are seeking out a spiritual path, and Eastern traditions tend to be welcoming to outsiders. It is never simple balancing these parts of self, but through awareness and compassion, we can often find a home in Eastern-based spiritual traditions.

Native American spirituality has felt the ravages of colonialism, racism, and imperialism that have left a deep scar on Native American communities and impacted the ability of tribal elders to pass along their traditions to their progeny. Many Native Americans do not live on reservations, where traditionalists often reside, and although native cultures continue to survive and heal, it is hard for families to remain connected to the sacred hoop. Native American spirituality is often co-opted by well-meaning non–Native Americans; it is important to recognize that although many are drawn to the depth and vibrancy of traditional tribal spiritual traditions, outsiders are not always welcomed. If you are a non–Native American drawn to those spiritual traditions, be respectful in your quest.

For LGBT people who are Native American, seeking out connections with tribal elders can offer deep spiritual renewal. LGBT parents are often drawn back to their more traditional roots and seek ways to teach children

The Dharma of Devotion

Being a lesbian Hindu is a unique experience. I have made the choice to live in two very different worlds. My daughters are seven, five, and two years old. I strive to raise them with feminist ideals. Thus far, they are strong, vibrant, independent girls. They know they are intelligent, valuable beings, who deserve to be treated with respect. They are rough-and-tumble, vivacious girls who never hesitate to voice their thoughts and opinions.

I also strive to impart strong Vedic values to them. They are very involved in temple life and devotional service. In temple they wear saris and cover their heads. They offer obeisances to Krishna and Guru. They are discovering the joy that can come from submissive servitude. (Note that submission is taught because they are devotees, not due to gender!)

Are these two worlds incompatible? I don't think so. I certainly hope not. To me, being a lesbian Hindu is not a clash but a balancing act. The sect of Hinduism I belong to is fairly evenly divided on gay issues. I know many gays and lesbians within my faith; there are way more of us than one might guess. Some of these devotees are out, some are not. Some temples are very loving and accepting,

some are quite intolerant. A lot like society as a whole, I suppose.

Earlier this year a teenager, who was raised in our faith, hung himself. His suicide note stated his reason as being the pain of being a gay Hindu youth. I almost left when that happened . . . but I can't. There is work to be done. I love my religion. I owe it to myself, my children, and my religion to stay and work toward change. Maybe my choice to stay will make things easier for future generations. I have no idea how far I'll get. Maybe I will spearhead massive change. Maybe I will squeeze out some minuscule changes, but it will be a start.

My daughters are privileged to be a part of a wonderful religious tradition. They are gifted with both a beautiful history and a promising future. The world will be a richer place because of these three girls, raised by their lesbian, feminist, Hindu mother.

Radharani devi dasi currently resides in upstate New York, where she amicably coparents with her children's father. She is the mother of three children, Rohini, age seven, Vrindaban Lila, age five, and Gopi, age two.

traditional dances, rituals, language, and practices. Many Native Americans travel far distances to make sure their children attend annual pow-wows. It is too easy to lose this thread in our modern society, where traditional ways are not recognized or respected. It is hard for our children to understand and respect these ways without having the connection to elders.

There are many earth-based spiritual practices, including pagan and

Wiccan traditions that go back thousands of years to tribal religions of Europe. Those who practice paganism represent an eclectic group of people, some of whom have been practitioners for generations, and others who link earth-based spiritual practices with other more mainstream religious sources. New Age spiritual paths have embraced pagan, Wiccan, and goddess-worshiping rituals, often making practices more compatible with contemporary society. Women in particular have been drawn to goddess-based faiths, honoring the divine feminine. Despite societal oppression and cultural confusion about pagan traditions, circles continue to form, raising cones of power, and reconnecting to the earth as mother.

When an LGBT family practices a less common religious or spiritual practice—shamanism, Sufism, Yoruba—it is often these beliefs, values, and cultural traditions that mark the family's passage through time and are at the root of their understanding of the world. Although many people who are not LGBT have spiritual practices outside of the major world religions, it also often means that for children being reared in LGBT homes with less-than-usual spiritual faiths, that they are dealing with a double stigma. Although this can be serious in the sense that is deep and meaningful, and perhaps even sometimes burdensome, it is to be assumed that the reason a family is drawn to a particular spiritual practice is because it fills some deep need of the soul. It is always good to fill your soul, and to fill your children's souls. Hopefully, the spiritual tools you give them will also serve to assist them in dealing with the stigma of being different.

LET THE CHILDREN LEAD US

The great illusion for parents is the belief that we have to teach our children about spirituality and God and the meaning of life. In reality, children are deeply in tune with the life force rushing in their blood and the living energy that enlivens the birds flittering back and forth in the trees. They can spend hours watching the sunlight play on the lawn and rainbows that form on the oil spots in the driveway. They live in an immediate world, completely in the present—which is what all of us meditators are trying so desperately to accomplish. They are fully embodied and connected to the vibrations of human emotions, and experience the seasons changing in their bodies, although they cannot always verbalize what they feel.

The Earth Beneath Our Feet

Our family is headed by two women, and we practice Wicca, a form of nature-based religion. In reflecting on our lives together, I find that while belonging to two groups targeted by societal oppression, it is often more challenging to be out as a Wiccan than as a same-sex family. We've gotten more looks of discomfort and outright negativity for raising our children in a pagan household than in a lesbian-led one. People either think we are depriving our children by not celebrating Christmas or are teaching the kids evil ways through magic. Of course, both are misinformed points of view. A basic premise of Wicca is to treat all living things, including humans, with care. Devil worship and the like are Christian concepts mistakenly applied to pagan religions. Many also don't realize that the secular aspects of Christmas, which they feel our children are not able to enjoy, have their roots in pagan religions and were enjoyed by children long before the development of Christianity.

Our families of origin have had varying responses to the issue of my partner and me being out lesbians and Wiccan. Both sets of grandparents adore our daughters and consider them both to be their grandchildren. We are each birth mom to one girl and mamas of the heart to the other. Both of our sets of parents are Christian. My parents, in particular, have difficulty with the Wiccan aspects of our lives. They continue to ask us when we plan to baptize our daughters and don't acknowledge our holidays. We are helping our older daughter to understand why we don't celebrate Christmas, but rather we honor the Solstice. Grandma and Grandpa are no help, with their wonderings about what the girls would like for Christmas, thus reinforcing that one holiday holds more validity than the other.

Our family has been blessed with an outstanding home-based child care provider since their birth. She has fully acknowledged our family, educated other parents and children, and gently challenged assumptions about witches made by other children in her care. We are now entering the school scene with our oldest daughter, who is a preschooler. Her school already is affirming of lesbian and gay families, which helped influence our selection process. However, I think we're the first openly Wiccan family. Our daughter's teacher approached us early in the year to learn more about Wicca and how we celebrated various holidays, especially Halloween. It was an eye-opener for her to discover that Halloween is based on honoring those who have died and not fearing them!

Our older daughter is beginning to understand that the differences in her family go beyond having two moms. At Halloween, we point out to her the denigrating images of witches adorning shop windows and people's doorways. We've been explaining to her why these images disturb us and what messages they convey about Wicca, so that she doesn't simply take them at face value or see them as acceptable. A recent poignant story comes to mind that I think powerfully illustrates how our daughters will need to confront religious prejudice. My partner and I were leading a children's service on the origins of Halloween at our local Unitarian society, when a child, a close friend of our four-year-old daughter's, hid under the table upon finding out that Jani and I were witches. Upon witnessing her friend's reaction, our daughter became quite distressed, not sure what to do with such conflicting information and feelings. She was very aware of her friend's reaction and her own reality of knowing that witches aren't scary or mean. This incident became a profound lesson for Jani and me that we needed to start teaching our daughters from very early ages strategies for protecting their vulnerable psyches in such situations.

Denise Jess and her partner, Jani, have been partnered for twelve years. They have two daughters, Rowan, age four, and Gemma, fifteen months, and four spirit babies, Casey, Mandy, Keegan, and Molly. Their older daughter was conceived after six years of battling infertility, and their second daughter was conceived after four recurrent pregnancy losses. The family lives in Madison, Wisconsin.

For those of us not particularly drawn to spiritual life—traditional or contemporary—our children are still trying to make sense out of the world and will have a thing or two to teach us about God and the meaning of life.

Our children will wrestle with their own spiritual beliefs even if we are confirmed atheists, and sometimes the answers they will come up with are different from ours. They might have a different opinion about Jesus than the rabbi would like, or insist that the rocks are alive to their rationalist parents, or deny the existence of God to their deeply Christian parents. This is not a queer thing, it's a kid thing. Sometimes they just shock the muggles.

One last important point to make about spirituality and religion is that there is no guarantee, of course, that our partner will find the same fulfillment we do going to church or at the same church. There is also no guarantee that our children will be drawn to being part of a spiritual community, will believe in God (or the same God we believe in), or that they won't believe in God. For that matter, one of the few things you can count on is that you and your partner will have different levels of spiritual practice and belief, and that your children will probably disagree with both of you.

It can be challenging being in an interreligious relationship, particularly if religion is very important to one or both of you. It can also be just as challenging being in the same religion but having different levels of observance.

Who Is God Anyway?

My triplets were not quite four years old when they started preschool, which was run by a local Seventh-day Adventist church. Although one of us is an atheist and the other an agnostic, we were willing to ignore the churchlike atmosphere because it offered good, nutritious food, incredibly reasonable prices for day care, and a very kind and loving staff.

At the end of the first day, I took them to dinner at a local restaurant where they expect messes from kids, and the waitresses are kindly and sweet about it. I asked them how their first day in school was, and Risa replied quickly, "I don't like it, Mommy. They make me say a prayer before I can eat." Before I have any chance to process and respond, Sammy says: "Yeah! What is God anyway, Mom?"

I'm really befuddled by this time. How do you explain God to a three-year-old when you have no clue how to answer the question for yourself (if Gnostic means "to know," then I am a woman who knows that I don't know)? Again, before I can respond, Risa pipes up again, "God made everything—the trees and flowers and people and kittens." Sam looks to me with a mix of wonder and fear in his eyes and asks, "But Mom, you said Mother Nature made all those things. Didn't she?"

I'm really stumped now, and searching for words, when Gabriella, silent as can be to this point, very quietly says (between bites of pancakes), "Don't you guys get it? God and Mother Nature are sweethearts. They made it together."

Mimi Luther, mom to Sam, Risa, and Gabriella, eight-year-old triplets, coparents quite effectively with her ex, sharing the responsibilities and joys (and headaches) quite evenly; their family lives in Portland, Oregon.

Compromise and change: perhaps those are key issues in parenting, as well as in learning to live a spiritual life. In chapter 5, River told the story of the unexpected early delivery of her twin girls and their subsequent medical struggles. Here her partner, Rachel, tells another part of the story, the part that is not about doctors or medical facts but about the lessons of the spirit that come through parenting.

I'll end this chapter with a confession. Before I had children, I used to have a very active spiritual life. I sat for meditation and davaaned (Jewish daily prayers) daily. I attended sweat lodges and climbed mountains so that I could do yoga at the top. I read esoteric mystical books on the Kabbalah, and Kashmir Shaivism, and threw the tarot cards when I wanted answers. Although I'll save the details for another time, my babies truly came to me after engaging in deep spiritual practices (and letting go of the idea that

---

When I Grow Up . . .

My niece, Serena, who is now fourteen, was seven when she outed me to the nun at her school. The nun spoke at length to the class about what they might all do when they grew up, concentrating mainly on the probability, according to her, that they would grow up, marry a nice man, and have kids, etc.

"I don't think so," said Serena. "I'm thinking of becoming a Presbyterian like my aunty and live with a woman." My sister Fiona wasn't sure whether it was the lesbianism or the possibility of Protestantism in the family that shocked the old nun the most.

Erin, who successfully coparents Leon, age ten, Seamus, age ten, and Adrian, age eight, with her ex, lives in Wellington, New Zealand.

---

they had to come from *my* womb). My older son's name, in Hebrew, means god's gift, son of the heart; my younger son's name, also in Hebrew, means god has helped, song of the heart. I take this God stuff seriously.

After about five months of parenting, I called up my therapist, who has known me for nearly twenty years. I was hysterically crying. I was drowning in laundry, overwhelmed with work and single parenting, exhausted from no sleep, living on frozen food, watching television at all hours of the night, and I had just run out of diapers and there was five feet of snow and a sleeping baby. I said, sobbing and gasping for air, "I used to have a spiritual life." What she said shocked me, infuriated me, and changed my life. She first of all laughed. (Can you imagine?) And then she said, still laughing, "What do you think *this* is?"

Parenting children is simply the most profound spiritual task I have ever encountered. I do not sit to meditate (my altar is covered with books and papers and children's artwork). I do not read any books, let alone esoteric books on mysticism. I rarely do yoga, though I dream about it sometimes. But daily I get to practice compassion, patience, and gentleness. I get to contemplate suffering and have opportunities to live in a timeless space, in the present, where there is only the moment, the story, the boo-boo. Maintaining dispassion while changing a gross diaper, staying calm while watching the entire box of eggs crash to the floor, being awake and aware at 4 A.M. when I am woken by a screaming child with a nightmare and a peed bed, these are truly spiritual tests. As Rachel Donik said, it is growing

---

Compromise: Living Together in Spiritual Balance

Although we have been together for fourteen years, having children challenged us to compromise on very significant issues. Our biggest struggles so far have been around Jewish education and customs. Razel is Israeli with a very secular upbringing. I come from South Africa and had a religious upbringing. Razel came a long way over to my customs to make me happy, not out of conviction.

We go to a Chavura, where I pray and she goes for the social life. I agreed early in our marriage to travel on Shabbat. Although we keep kosher at home, we eat at nonkosher restaurants, too, and have occasional Friday night meals at Razel's parents', who do not keep kosher but agree not to serve us milk and meat together. Her parents will, however, serve ice cream following a meat meal, and make it very clear that I would be going too far withholding ice cream from Yossi. I would like to teach Yossi some prayers, have him wear a kippa at the Chavura, send him to a more religious school, have him sit with me in shul more, but Razel is fairly resistant. Since Yossi has autism, some of these issues are mitigated, as he needs special education; I suspect they will all be revisited if we have another child.

My parents are very Orthodox and live in a different country, so have distanced from our family. Razel's family is kind to us but took a long time to accept Yossi as their grandchild. Mostly Razel and I pretty much don't have anyone to rely on but each other.

Shulamit and her partner, Razel, are parents to Yossi, age four, and live in Tel Aviv, Israel.

---

and healing at the speed of light, with little time to reflect on the lessons of one day, when the next day comes flying toward you. Mysticism is defined as connecting to a Higher Power without any intermediary. That is the kind of spirituality that children invite, an intense mystical awareness of the divine present.

The Speed of Light

River and I are deeply spiritual and know these children have come to us as gifts and teachers. My first really big wake-up call to the spiritual nature of this journey with the girls came real early. I was at the time feeling uncomfortable with multiple unresolved issues and problems related to health, age, money, and creative dreams, and I was struggling with making the decision or commitment to participate in this life-altering process of parenting. River felt we were at a place in our discussion where there seemed to be no more think time left, as her biological clock was ticking.

River and I had always connected around eclectic and informal spiritual practices. So sitting on our bed after talking about making a decision to have children, we decided to honor and ask for help from the Sacred. At first the vagueness of it all almost made me think of this decision about parenting as if I had just put in a bid for a huge building project and was hoping for a little help from the almighty. I remember that in my prayer I asked that those souls that needed us to be their parents come to us, and I said that we would do our very best to honor their choice. It was in that moment that I really understood what I had heard described to me many, many times before when women would say to me, "I knew the moment I got pregnant." I just knew that I, the non–birth mother, had called these souls to us. My whole body knew it. This experience no longer seemed vague. It felt very specific, and I knew that I was a crucial part in this unfolding. I was surprised by an awareness of unbidden intimacy and divine certainty in our invitation, which resulted in me then finding myself perfectly grounded. In looking back, our decision was really for me a deep, full-hearted surrender to this plan to raise kids.

The second time I was aware of the extraordinary spiritual nature of this journey was in the NICU (neonatal intensive care unit). If I had to describe myself spiritually, I would say that I am a Jewish mystic at heart, and I tend to be an imagist—that is, I tend to think in images. Early on during the kids' stay in the NICU, I did what I call "looking inside" myself to search for hope, reassurance, guidance, anything that could help me deal with the lines, machines, and medical decisions that were supporting our daughters' lives at the moment. Call it meditation, visualized prayer, lucid dreaming, or just plain imagination, but this is what I experienced. I saw myself meet up with this really nice guy with a good sense of humor, and we went for a walk. I recognized the image to be Jesus, and He said with casual ease and kindness that everything was going to be all right and they were protected. It felt strange; being a skeptical (but open) Jewish kid from the Bronx, I was not accustomed to visits from Jesus. However, I took in what was said and was deeply comforted and renewed. I also knew that this would comfort River, a recovering Catholic.

The girls have so catalyzed my own spiritual growth. Whether directly or indirectly, absolutely everything—my work, my ideas, relationships, priorities, fears, the named and unnamed—has been impacted and changed as a result of this very present relationship with my children. The power of this kind of eye-opening love can only be viewed as divine in nature. Does it feel all good and warm like skipping and white fluffy clouds? Hell, no.

Joy is indeed deeper and comes so much more often, but then again, so does sorrow and the grip of living in a savage world. I am introduced daily to the chance and choice to be a better person than I thought I ever could be. I also just as easily come upon, up close and personal, an ugly awareness of my own prim-itive darkness that lies not so deeply buried in my psyche when I hurt. So many of my unresolved childhood issues that plague my adult life are bruised again and again as all of us in this family grow up together. I either struggle more or allow myself to heal. It is all happening so fast—it's like growing and healing at the speed of light.

Rachel Donik, and her partner of thirteen years, Barbara Rio (aka River), are both social workers living in upstate New York with their twin five-year-old daughters Sophie and Sasha.

All Good Books Must Go to Bed

All parents know that kids do best with a five-minute warning before changing from one activity to another (and if you didn't know this, then you are going to be very happy to have this information now). Consider this your five-minute warning. It is close to bedtime, and we are going to put this book to bed.

Putting a book to bed is not any easier than putting a child (or twelve) to bed. As a mom, I am always conscious at bedtime of my limitations. Forgot to remind the boys to straighten up their room because we ended up watching an extra show on television. Forgot to give them their vitamins this morning. Didn't wash a favorite shirt in time for the birthday party tomorrow. Oops, forgot to work on telling time again. I am usually more tired and cranky at reading time than I want to be, and it is often a bit later than I wish it was, meaning the kids will be more tried and cranky in the morning than I like.

As a writer, as I come to the end of a project, I am aware of all its limitations, too. Did I talk enough about gay men and how their experiences parenting are different from lesbians? Do I even know enough to say more? We (meaning academics) know so much more about lesbian-headed families than gay male-headed families. What important experiences did I miss? I tried to include the lives of both bisexual and transgendered parents, but there is so much more to say; I fear that it will leave these families feeling tokenized. Living as we do in a culture where white families are privileged, how do I, as a white woman, write about the lives of people of color that hold their experiences, not as an addendum, but at the center, as *the* model, of which everything becomes a comparison? Not very well, I suspect.

Like bedtime in my house, though, we have to end the day somewhere, and so it is time to end the book, and tuck in the little ones, aware constantly of all my shortcomings, all that is left unsaid, all that still needs to be done to honor the complexity and vitality of queer family-building.

I began this writing project because I was disappointed by many of the parenting books on the market. I felt completely invisible in mainstream books, and most lesbian—or lesbian *and* gay—parenting books felt incredibly middle-class and white. I felt invisible as a working-class-raised girl whose children were living a much more upscale life than the one I'd been brought up in, and I struggled with fitting in. I felt ethnically awkward; as a Jewish family, as a mixed-race family, I rarely saw myself in the descriptions of the families described. I was often offended by statements like, "No one would choose to be a single parent," which was absolutely how I planned my family (though not how it worked out), or, "Having children is expensive, so you may need to give up some of your vacations," as if we all have always had money to go on discretionary vacations.

As I have tackled this project, I realize how much bigger, broader, wider, and more complex we all really are. Talking about pagan families in one paragraph, or the meaning of mommy and daddy names in a family where a parent is transitioning in the next, does not do justice to all that needs to be said about the diversity of our families.

Years ago Joann Loulan, the stand-up lesbian sex therapist and educator, came to speak in my town. Joann was, as ever, irreverent, funny, and saying what others dared not say. My good friend Clove went with me. Clove is also irreverent, funny, and says what others dare not. She can also sometimes be just a tad critical. She thought that there were some things Joann hadn't said, and she honed her words carefully, artistically, and approached Joann with her well-worded critique. Joann smiled in her warm and welcoming way and said casually, "Those are great ideas. You should

Growing Out to Their Own Edges

We have four children. Max is nine, Henry and Rose are seven, and Sam is three. When we had the first one, like so many parents, we thought we had a lot more control over how our kid would behave and what he would be like than is actually the case. I spent much more time comparing Max to other kids and looking at the developmental charts and baby books than I do now. I often say that we all should have several kids so we realize that our kids are not about us, but about themselves.

If your kid is extremely well-behaved or quiet and shy or loud and physical, 90 percent of that is not because you are a great parent or a terrible parent. It's about your kid's general demeanor. We had a hard road learning this, because our first, Max, was and is very physical, very noisy, and very individualistic. As lesbians with a boy child, this was a big adjustment for us. Suddenly we found ourselves in the position of defending our wild little boy from judgmental women and girls. The worst are mothers of one well-behaved girl who is an only child. What they often don't understand is that they just happen to have a quiet kid who is a girl, not that they are doing a better job of parenting than people who have boisterous kids (boys or girls).

To this day, I feel the negativity toward boys by mothers of girls and more generally, toward the wilder kids by parents of the gentler kids. I didn't truly understand this until we had our twins, who are now in second grade. Henry and Rose were quiet, clingy, and shy as babies and preschoolers. They have reached out a lot now, but their demeanor is so very different from Max's. Henry is shy and gentle. Where Max is athletic and loves satire and comedy, Henry is serious and bookish and loves to make lists and play spy. It's not because he has gotten any better parenting, in fact he has received less attention and less quality time than Max because he's a twin. As I said, it's not about me but about him. Rose is outgoing, bubbly, sweet, and kind. She is very popular and loves everybody. She has a totally different personality than either of her brothers. Then there is Sam, who is calm, observant, relaxed, and happy to be wherever you take him. We always say you should have lots of kids to see what you will get next.

I remember when Max was in first grade I would look into the other kids' cubbies and see what kind of math homework they were taking home. Some of the kids were doing more advanced work than Max was, and it would feel like a stab to the stomach when I would see that. I felt like he was not keeping up. Now I realize how dumb that is. Max was in the lowest reading group in first grade. Rose was in the highest. It takes being at both ends to see that neither end matters, as long as you are there to support your kid. Rose wasn't in the highest group because I am so wonderful or even because she is so wonderful. Conversely, Max wasn't in the lowest because either of us has some failing. And now look—they can both read very well. What would hurt them would be instilling some competitive or self-judging attitude in them. That is one way we parents really can affect our kids' development.

I have to say that I think gay families are potentially really good at this skill. Most of us have suffered mightily because we couldn't fit into someone else's idea of what we ought to be. For us it goes beyond resolving not to do that to our kids. We just cannot do it to our kids. It would be beyond me to force my kids into a mold. It is incredibly freeing to me and feels like a cool drink of water on a hot day when I can encourage my kids to find and follow their own individual paths. I am so glad my kids are all so different. It is the most interesting thing in the world to me to figure them out and try to understand what they are about.

Laura Sky Brown has been partnered with Sue for fifteen years. They are parents to Max, age ten, Henry and Rose, age seven, and Sam, age three, and live in Ann Arbor, Michigan.

absolutely go out and talk about them. This is my work. This is what I do, you should go do your work."

My hope is that I have created a wider foundation for everyone else to do their work. We need a book on black lesbian parenthood, and a book written about bisexuals of all stripes and how they are building families, we need gay men and lesbians who are parenting together to talk more about their families, and we need leathermen who are parenting to please teach us all how to keep the sex alive. I wanted to say that our queer families are not all just like straight families, and I've now said it. Now it's your turn. Please, go do your work, and I will continue to do mine.

WORDS OF WISDOM

In the Jewish tradition, we have a concept called an ethical will. This is where a parent (historically a father) shares not their material wealth with their children, but their wisdom, experience, and values that they hope to pass on to the next generation. In some measure this book has been a contemplation regarding my wisdom that I want to pass on not to my children but to LGBT people who are building families. What was it that I wished someone had told me earlier on? How hard it might be to get pregnant. How easy it is to really really love an adopted child. How parenting together gives a whole new perspective to lesbian bed death and can make passion, let alone kink, far more complicated. How accepting and welcoming neighbors, physicians, religious institutions, and schoolteachers can actually be. How much room in one's heart parenting can completely capture. How it really does change *everything*.

In putting this book to bed, there is one thing I haven't fully shared, though, and I want to share it before we turn out the lights. It is simple, not so deep. But like much true wisdom, the more you contemplate it, the wiser it becomes. Ready?

Our children are each different. Wherever they came from—your womb, or another's—however they arrived—on a plane from the other side of the world, through invasive medical emergency intervention, or in a bathtub birth surrounded by loved ones—whatever their particular personalities or natures are, whatever challenges they present—*they are who they are, and all we can do is help them become themselves*. If I had to pick which side of the nature versus nurture debate I was on for most of my life, nurture was the winner by a long shot; after all, I'm a social worker! Parenting my two sons, I have come to see how so much of my parenting is filtered through the kinds of people they each are, and how, in essence, they have actually arrived here to teach me a thing or two about being the kind of person I am.

Listen:

Recognizing that our children have natures, perhaps even karmas, that we can have little impact on does not minimize the role we can play in helping our children become themselves. I can't help but wonder how my bright, inquisitive, curious, and rather intensely and assertive childhood self would've fared without having to be funneled through the social expectations of a 1960s perspective of women's proper role. How I wish everyone was less worried about how I would find a husband who would put up with me, and more interested in the love poetry I was writing to my best friend (bless her soul). For every sissy boy who was forced to play football, and every dykette who eschewed her first training bra, we need to respect that whether it is our little girls or our little boys who love their pink ballerina outfits, they are merely expressing themselves. Our job is to clap our hands, jump up and down, and exclaim, "Oh, lovely, lovely." We teach our children to feel good about themselves by how good we feel about them. *That* is a gift that goes on giving.

A friend shared this story with me. She said she once knew this man who had a teenage son who was interested in rock music and played in a garage band. The dad thought it was wonderful that his son would go play in East Village bars late at night without a hint of disappointment that his son wasn't going to college. He used to say, "The secret to being a good parent is to figure out what your kid wants to do and then encourage him to do it." This man is the father of Chris Barron of the Spin Doctors, but my friend insists that even if his son had done absolutely nothing financially successful with his music, he would still be thrilled for him because he would have done what he loved doing.

This means not feeling guilty, responsible, or proud because our children have punk hairdos, want to join the Special Forces, get pregnant at fifteen, read more comic books than they read Shakespeare, have no interest in volunteering at the food kitchen, or are off meditating in Tibet. Whether our kids are loners or social butterflies, it is good to teach them to wash their hair, as well as to be cautious with guns and value life. It is also good to teach your kids about birth control and encourage them to read. Civil responsibilities, as well as self-reflection, are both important skills. But most important of all is that they learn that, regardless of their hair color, reading tastes, professional interests, or personal styles, they absolutely know they can come home and tell you that they are joining the army, having a baby (or an abortion), or leaving for a Tibetan monastery, knowing that you will respect their choices, support their life decisions, and fully embrace the fascinating paths they choose to seek fulfillment.

It is nearing bedtime. Reading time is over, and we are past the groans of, "Can't we just read one more," after the two one mores we've already read. Teeth are brushed, clothes put in the laundry basket, and the dishes are still sitting in the sink. The kids are tucked into bed. The older boy, ever afraid of the dark and being alone, wants the same reassurance he does every night. "Where are you going to be? When are you going to bed?" and then promptly falls asleep before I turn to leave the room. My younger son has a few hours ahead of him yet. He is propped up in bed with his stuffed animals, an Elmo music tape, and numerous books and cards to look at. He will wander around his room for another hour, sometimes sitting in front of the "campfire" (his Winnie-the Pooh night-light) to read to his "babies." He will sing a few songs and try on some clothes from the dress-up box. When I go to check on him, he yells, "Leave the princess alone, please." We encourage him to go to bed. Okay, sometimes we yell at him to stay in the bed. Occasionally he falls right asleep. But mostly he is like me, a night-walker, and eventually he will fall asleep on his bed, on the floor, on his blanket, until "bweakfest time."

I try to let these boys just be themselves, to not punish them for having their own natures. One is a bold gladiator, one a gentle artist, and they adore each other like the sand loves the shore. I cannot make my more gentle son an athlete or my young warrior a monk. My job is to coax my gentle son to trust the wisdom of his own heart and help my warrior to become a chivalrous knight. They have arrived with all they need to become fine adults, and they arrived *here* because it is my responsibility to water, weed, and tend to that unfolding. And with those words of wisdom, I will tuck you all in and wish you sweet dreams.

· · ·

Bibliography on Lesbian, Gay, Bisexual, and Transgendered Parenting

The books listed below are a compilation of books on LGBT parenting, adoption and insemination resources, some of which are more scholarly and others are geared more toward parents themselves. Also included are a number of "advice" books on parenting that are not specifically LGBT focused, but address the daily issues of parenting from a psychological or spiritual perspective. Reading books on child development can be very helpful in assisting you in recognizing your child's emotional development and maturational milestones.

Abrams, N. (1999). *The Other Mother: A Lesbian's Fight for Her Daughter.* Madison: University of Wisconsin Press.

Alperson, M. (1997). *The International Adoption Handbook: How to Make an Overseas Adoption Work for You.* NY: Owl Press.

Barret, R. L., & Robinson, B. E. (1990). *Gay Fathers: Encouraging the Hearts of Gay Dads and their Families.* Lexington, MA: Lexington Books.

Benkov, L. (1994). *Reinventing the Family: The Emerging Story of Lesbian and Gay Parents.* New York: Crown.

Boenke, M. (ed.) (1999). *Trans Forming Families: Real Stories about Transgendered Loved Ones.* Imperial Beach, CA: Walter Trook Publishing.

Bozett, F. W. (1987). *Gay & Lesbian Parents.* Westport, CT: Praeger Publishers.

Brill, S. A. (2001). *The Queer Parent's Primer: A Lesbian and Gay Families Guide to Navigating the Straight World.*

Burke, P. (1993). *Family Values: Two Moms and Their Son.* New York: Random House.

Casper, V., and Schultz, S. B. (1999). *Gay Parents/Straight Schools*, New York: Teachers College Press.

Clunis, D. M, and Green, D. (1995). *The Lesbian Parenting Book: A Guide to Creating Families and Raising Children*. Seattle: Seal Press.

Cohen, K. M, and Savins-Williams, R. C. (eds.) (1995). *The Lives of Lesbians, Gays and Bisexuals: Children to Adults*. Fort Worth, TX: Harcourt Brace.

D'Augelli, A. R, and Patterson, O. J. (eds.). *Lesbian, Gay, Bisexual Identities Over the LifeSpan: Psychological Perspectives*. New York: Oxford Press.

Drucker, J. L. and Schulweis, H. (2001). *Lesbian and Gay Families Speak Out: Understanding the Joys and Challenges of Diverse Family Life*. Cambridge: Perseus.

Eldridge, S. (1999). *Twenty Things Adopted Kids Wish Their Adoptive Parents Knew*. New York: Dell.

Galluccio, J. and Galluccio, M., (2001). *An American Family*. New York: St. Martin's Press.

Gardner, A. (2004). *Families Like Mine*. New York: Harper/Collins.

Glazer, D. F., and Drescher, J. (2001). *Gay and Lesbian Parenting*. Binghamton, NY: Haworth Medical Press.

Green, J. (1999). *The Velveteen Father*. New York: Villard Press.

Howey, N. & Samuels, E. (2000) *Out of the Ordinary: Essays on Growing Up with Gay, Lesbian, and Transgender Parents*. New York: St. Martin's Press.

Johnson, S. M. and O'Conner, E. (2001) *For Lesbian Parents*. New York: Guildford Press.

Kabat-Zinn, J. and Kabat-Zinn, M. (1997). *Everyday Blessing: The Inner Work of Mindful Parenting*. New York: Hyperion.

Kaeser, G. (1999) *Love Makes a Family: Portraits of Lesbian, Gay, Bisexual and Transgender Parents and Their Families*. Amherst: University of Mass Press.

Karst, P. (2000). *The Single Mothers' Survival Guide*. Crossing Press.

Keefer, Betsy & Jayne E. Schooler. (2002). *Telling the Truth to Your Adopted or Foster Child: Making Sense of the Past*. Bergin & Garney: Greenwood.

Kurcinka, M. S. (1992). *Raising Your Spirited Child: A Guide for Parents Whose Child Is More Intense, Sensitive, Perceptive, Persistent, Energetic*. New York: Perennial.

Laird, J and Green, R. J., (eds.) *Lesbians and Gays in Couples and Families: A Handbook for Therapists*. San Francisco: Jossey-Bass Publishers.

Lamott, A. (1994). *Operating Instructions*. New York: Ballatine Books.

Martin, A. (1993). *The Lesbian and Gay Parenting Handbook*. New York: HarperCollins.

Mattes, J. (1994). *Single Mothers by Choice*. Three Rivers Press.

McGarry, K. (2003). *Fatherhood for Gay Men*. Binghamton, NY: Haworth Press.

Melina, L. R., (1998). *Raising Adopted Children Revised Edition: Practical Reassuring Advice for Every Adoptive Parent*. New York: Quill.

Mogel, W. (2001). *The Blessing of a Skinned Knee: Using Jewish Teachings to Raise Self-Reliant Children*. New York: Penguin Books.

Mohler, M. & Frazer, L. (2002). *A Donor Insemination Guide: Written By and For Lesbian Women*. New York: Harrington Park Press.

Moraga, C. (1997). *Waiting in the Wings: Portrait of a Queer Motherhood*. Ithaca, NY: Firebrand Books.

Morgan, K. B. *Getting Simon: Two Gay Doctors' Journey to Fatherhood*. Bearsville, NY: Bramble Books.

Noble, E. (1987). *Having Your Baby by Donor Insemination: A Complete Resource Guide*.

Pact's Multicultural Booksource: An opinionated guide to books that reflect, open and address issues for: adoptive families, blended families, families of color, foster families, interracial families, gay or lesbian families, kinship adoption, multiracial families, single-parent families, families with special-needs, transracial families. (second edition). San Francisco/Pact Press.

Patterson, C. (1995). "Lesbian Mothers, Gay Fathers and Their Children." *In* A. R. D'Augelli and C. Patterson (eds.). *Lesbian, Gay and Bisexual Identities over the Lifespan: Psychological Perspectives* (pp. 262–290). New York: Oxford University Press.

Pepper, R. (1999). *The Ultimate Guide to Pregnancy for Lesbians: Tips and Techniques from Conception to Birth*. San Francisco: Cleis Press.

Phelan, T. W. (1998). *1-2-3 Magic: Effective Discipline for Children 2–12*. Glen Ellyn, Ill: ParentMagic.

Pies, C. (1985). *Considering Parenthood: A Workbook for Lesbians*. San Francisco: Spinsters Ink.

Pollack, J. S. (1995). *Lesbian and Gay Families: Redefining Parenting in America*. New York: Franklin Watts.

Pollack, S. and Vaughn, J. (ed.) (1987). *Politics of the Heart: A Lesbian Parenting Anthology*, New York: Firebrand.

Savage, D. (2000). *The Kid: What Happened When My Boyfriend and I Decided to Get Pregnant: An Adoption Story*. New York: Plume.

Savins-Williams, R. C. and Cohen, K. M., and (eds.) *The Lives of Lesbians Gays and Bisexuals: Children to Adults*. Fort Worth, TX: Harcourt Brace.

Siegal, L., & Olson, N. L. (eds.) (2001). *Out of the Closets and Into Our Hearts: Celebrating our Gay/Lesbian Family Members.* San Francisco: Leyland Press.

Snow, J. E. (2004). *How It Feels to Have Gay and Lesbian Parents: A Book by Kids for Kids of All Ages.* Binghamton, NY: Harrington Park Press.

Steinberg, G. and Hall, Beth (2000). *Inside Transracial Adoption.* Indiana: Perspectives Press.

Strah, D., Margolis, S., Cozza, KL. (2003). *Gay Dads: A Celebration of Fatherhood.* New York: J. P. Tarcher.

Sullivan, M. (2003). *The Family of Woman. Lesbian Mothers, their Children, and the Undoing of Gender.* Berkeley: University of CA Press.

Sullivan, T. R. and Dawidoff (1999). *Queer Families, Common Agendas.* Binghamton, NY: Haworth.

Thompson, B. (2000). *Mothering Without a Compass: White Mother's Love, Black Son's Courage.* Minneapolis: University of Minnesota Press.

Thompson, J. M. (2002). *Mommy Queerest: Contemporary Rhetorics of Lesbian Maternal Identity.* Amherst: University of Mass.

Toevs, K. and Brill, S. (2002). *The Essential Guide to Lesbian Conception, Pregnancy, and Birth.* Los Angeles: Alyson Publications.

Verrier, N. N. (1993). *The Primal Wound: Understanding the Adopted Child.* Self Published.

Weeks, J., Heaphy, B., and Donovan C. (2001). *Same Sex Intimacies: Family of Choice and Other Life Experiments.* Routledge.

Wells, J. (ed) (2000) *HOMEFRONTS: Controversies in Nontraditional Parenting.* Los Angeles: Alyson Publications

Wells, J. (1997). *Lesbians Raising Sons.* Los Angeles: Alyson Books.

Weston, K. (1991). *Families We Choose: Lesbians, Gays, Kinship.* New York: Columbia University.

Are you seeking books specifically for children?

Check out the following resources:

Family Pride's online bookstore: http://www.familypride.org/store/
Tapestry Books: http://www.tapestrybooks.com/
Two Lives Books: http://www.twolives.com/

• • •

National and State Resources of Lesbian, Gay, Bisexual, and Transgendered Organizations

ACLU Lesbian and Gay Rights Project
The ACLU has been America's foremost advocate of individual rights and the Lesbian and Gay Rights Project puts lesbian and gay rights in context as part of a larger program to secure equal rights for all Americans, adding weight to arguments for lesbian and gay rights.
132 West 34rd St.
New York, NY 10036
212-944-9800
www.aclu.org/issues/gay/hmgl.html

Center Kids: Lesbian & Gay Community Services Center
Center Kids offers resources for gay men and lesbians interested in parenting. Lists adoption agencies, alternative insemination resources, attorneys, books and organizations. Mostly New York area.
208 West 13th Street
New York, NY 10011
212-620-7310 (messages)

COLAGE: Children of Lesbians and Gays Everywhere
3543 Eighteenth St. #17
San Francisco, CA 94110
415-861-5437
Fax: 415-255-8345
Box 165
San Francisco, CA 94114
(415) 861-KIDS
KIDSOFGAYS@aol.com
http://www.colage.org/
collage@colage.org

Family Pride Coalition
The only national not-for profit solely dedicated to promoting equality for lesbian, gay, bisexual and transgender parents and their families.
Family Pride Coalition
PO Box 65327
Washington, DC 20035
202-331-5015
info@familypride.org
http://www.familypride.org/

Family Services: L.A. Gay & Lesbian Center
Family Services supports the needs of lesbian, gay, bisexual and transgender families by coordinating a broad range of recreational activities, public forums, educational venues, workshops, and support groups.
The Village at Ed Gould Plaza
1125 North McCadden Place
Los Angeles, CA 90038
323-860-7397
Fax: 323-308-4004
familyservices@laglc.org
http://www.laglc.org

Fenway Community Health Center, Lesbian/Gay Family and Parenting Services
Fenway Community Health Center provides high quality medical and mental health care to Boston's lesbian, gay, bisexual and transgender community and offers home-based and Intra-Uterine Insemination (IUI), support groups for gay men and lesbians considering parenting and for children of gay and lesbian parents, and adoption consultation.
7 Haviland St.
Boston, MA 02115-2608
617-267-0900

888-242-0900 (in MA)
Spanish information—617-927-6460/TTY—617-859-1256
http://www.fenwayhealth.org

Gay & Lesbian Advocates & Defenders (GLAD)
GLAD is a legal rights organization dedicated to ending discrimination based on
sexual orientation, HIV status, gender identity and expression.
Phone: 800-455-GLAD or 617-426-1350
gladlaw@glad.org
www.glad.org

Gay, Lesbian, Straight, Education Network (GLSEN)
GLSEN is working to ensure safe and effective schools for all students.
121 West 27th Street
Suite 804
New York, New York 10001
212-727-0135
Fax: 212-727-0254
glsen@glsen.org
www.glsen.org

The Gender Public Advocacy Coalition (GenderPAC)
GenderPAC works to end discrimination and violence caused by gender stereotypes by changing public attitudes, educating elected officials and expanding legal
rights. GenderPAC also promotes understanding of the connection between discrimination based on gender stereotypes and sex, sexual orientation, age, race, and
class.
1743 Connecticut Ave. NW
4th Floor
Washington, DC 20009
202-462-6610
Fax: 202-262-6744
gpac@gpac.org
http://www.gpac.org/

Human Rights Campaign—Family Net
The Human Rights Campaign is America's largest gay and lesbian organization,
that lobbies Congress; mobilizes grassroots action in diverse communities; invests
strategically to elect a fair-minded Congress; and increases public understanding
through innovative education and communication strategies.
919 18th St., N.W.
Suite 800
Washington, DC 20006

202-628-4160
TTY: 202-216-1572
Fax: 202-347-5323
hrc@hrc.org
www.hrc.org/familynet

Lambda Legal Defense and Education Fund
Lambda Legal is a national organization committed to achieving full recognition of
the civil rights of lesbians, gay men, bisexuals, the transgendered, and people with
HIV or AIDS through impact litigation, education, and public policy work.
120 Wall Street
Suite 1500
New York, NY 10005-3904
212-809-8585
Fax: 212-809-0055
legalhelpdesk@lambdalegal.org
www.lambdalegal.org

The Lesbian and Gay Family Building Project
A Project of the Ferre Institute, Inc.
The Lesbian and Gay Family Building Project is located in central New York and is
dedicated to helping LGBT people build and strengthen their families. The Project
offers educational programs for LGBT parents, prospective parents and their
providers, including information and referral services; the Lesbian and Gay Family
Building Conference; the Directory of Family Building Services for LGBT People,
which lists gay-affirming health and human service providers; and supports Pride
and Joy Families, a social and support group for LGBT-headed families in Binghamton, NY.
124 Front Street
Binghamton, NY 13905
(607) 724-4308
Fax: (607) 724-8290
LesGayFamBldg@aol.com
http://www.ferre.org/newbrow/family.html
http://www.prideandjoyfamilies.org/

National Center for Lesbian Rights (NCLR)
NCLR is a national legal resource center with a primary commitment to advancing
the rights and safety of lesbians and their families through a program of litigation,
public policy advocacy, free legal advice and counseling, and public education. In
addition, NCLR provides representation and resources to gay men, and bisexual
and transgender individuals on key issues that also significantly advance lesbian
rights.

870 Market St., #570
San Francisco, CA 94102-3012
415-392-6257 (NCLR)
Fax: 415-392-8442
info@nclrights.org
www.nclrights.org

National Gay and Lesbian Task Force (NGLTF)
NGLTF is the national progressive organization working for the civil rights of gay,
lesbian, bisexual and transgender people, with the vision and commitment to
building a powerful political movement.
1325 Massachusetts Ave. NW
Suite 600
Washington, DC 20005
202-393-5177
Fax: 202-393-2241
TTY: 202-393-2284
E-mail: ngltf@ngltf.org
http://www.thetaskforce.org/

National Transgender Advocacy Coalition (NTAC)
NTAC works for the advancement of understanding and the attainment of full civil
rights for all transgendered, intersexed and gender variant people in every aspect of
society and actively opposes discriminatory acts by all means legally available.
PO Box 76027
Washington, DC 20013
info@ntac.org
http://www.ntac.org/

Transgender Law and Policy Institute
TLPI is a nonprofit organization dedicated to engaging in effective advocacy for
transgender people in our society. The TLPI brings experts and advocates together
to work on law and policy initiatives designed to advance transgender equality.
info@transgenderlaw.org
http://www.transgenderlaw.org

On-Line Internet Resources for LGBT Parents and Wanna-Bes

Adoption.com
http://www.adoption.com

adoption.com
http://www.transracialadoption.com
Transracial and transcultural adoptions.

AdoptionSites.com
http://www.adoptionsites.com
Very comprehensive resource for adoption-related Web sites.

Alternatives to Marriage Project (AtMP)
PO Box 1922
Albany, NY 12201
518-462-5600
http://www.unmarried.org/index.html
A national nonprofit organization advocating for equality and fairness for unmarried people, including people who choose not to marry, cannot marry, or live together before marriage.

The American Surrogacy Center, Inc.
Kennesaw, GA
TASC@surrogacy.com
http://www.surrogacy.com
The most complete source of surrogacy and egg donation information on the Web!

Camp Lavender Hill
16420 Cutten Dr.
Guerneville, CA 95446
707-544-8150
Fax: 707-869-2884
staff@camplavenderhill.org
http://www.camplavenderhill.org
Camp Lavender Hill offers a weeklong summer camp for children of lesbian, gay, bisexual, and transgender families.

Dads at Home
Dadsathome.com
c/o Alpine Summit Group, Inc.
7800 Metro Parkway, Suite 210
Bloomington, MN 55425
info@dadsathome.com
http://www.dadsathome.com
Dadsathome.com was developed by and for gay fathers and gay stay-at-home dads in the hope to bring aid and assistance to gay fathers in the day-to-day trials and tribulations of raising children. Access is free; however, registration is necessary.

Donor Sibling Registry
P.O. Box 1571
Nederland, CO 80466
burlwindow741@yahoo.com
http://www.donorsiblingregistry.com

"Empirical Studies on Lesbian and Gay Parenting" by J. Ainslie et al.
http://www.apa.org/pi/l&gbib.html
APA research on LGB parenting.

EverythingSurrogacy.com
alex@everythingsurrogacy.com
http://www.everythingsurrogacy.com
Great surrogacy site: articles, lists of books of interest to the surrogacy community, message boards, free classifieds, and more.

Fairfax Cryobank
3015 Williams Drive, Suite 110
Fairfax, VA 22031
1-800-338-8407 or 703-698-3976
Fax: 703-698-3933
cryobank@givf.com
http://www.fairfaxcryobank.com
Fairfax Cryobank, a division of the Genetics & IVF Institute, is one of the world's largest human sperm banks. The cryobank provides a large selection of the most up-to-date genetic and infectious disease tested donor semen, as well as freezing and storage services to patients desiring to have their own semen specimens preserved for future use.

Family Pride Canada
c/o UWO Pride Library
University College, Rm. 355
UWO
London, ON
N6A 5B8
519-661-2111, ext. 85828
familypride@uwo.ca
http://familypride.uwo.ca/

FTL (Faster Than Life)
http://www.geocities.com/fasterthanlife_2000/family.html
Advice for single dads, straight, gay, lesbian, transgender parents, and FTMs about parenting toddlers and babies, hormones, and fertility issues.

Gay Family Options
info@gayfamilyoptions.org
http://www.GayFamilyOptions.org
Gay Family Options is a great Web site to find sperm donors, surrogates, or parenting partners. Place your own ad!

Gay Parent magazine
PO Box 750852
Forest Hills, NY 11375-0852
718-997-0392
acain@gis.net
http://www.gayparentingmag.com

Growing Generations
5757 Wilshire Blvd., Suite 601
Los Angeles, CA 90036
323-965-7500
Fax: 323-965-0900
family@GrowingGenerations.com
http://www.growinggenerations.com
The first and only gay and lesbian owned surrogacy firm exclusively serving the gay community worldwide. Their expertise and personal experiences enable them to assist their community in realizing the dream of parenting through surrogacy.

HRC FamilyNet
Human Rights Campaign
1640 Rhode Island Ave. NW
Washington, DC 20036-3278
202-628-4160 or 800-777-4723
http://www.hrc.org/familynet/chapter.asp?chapter=75
Comprehensive and up-to-date resource on gay, lesbian, bisexual, and transgendered families.

Internet Health Resources (IHR.com)
http://www.ihr.com/infertility
This Web site provides extensive information about IVF, ICSI, infertility clinics, donor egg and surrogacy services (e.g., surrogate mothers), male infertility services, sperm banks, pharmacies, infertility books and videotapes, sperm testing, infertility newsgroups and support organizations, and drugs and medications, such as Metrodin, Pergonal, Clomid.

"Lesbian and Gay Parenting" by Arlene Istar Lev
http://www.members.aol.com/tjfronczak/lesgayparenting.htm

"Lesbian and Gay Parenting" by Charlotte J. Patterson
APA on parenting.
http://www.apa.org/pi/parent.html

Lesbian Mother Support
c/o Calgary Gay & Lesbian Community Services Association
205a-223-12 Avenue SW
Calgary, AB T2R 0G9
403-265-6433
lesbianmothers@shaw.ca
http://www.lesbian.org/lesbian-moms/

Let Him Stay
The Lofton family.
http://www.lethimstay.com/index.html

Mid-Atlantic Center for Surrogacy
100 Springdale Rd., A3-#353
Cherry Hill, NJ 08003
856-629-0529
Fax: 856-629-9542
http://www.midatlanticsurrogacy.com
MACs was founded to help people like you create the family of your dreams
through surrogacy. Every member of their staff has been personally involved in the
surrogacy process and is dedicated to the success of their program. With over
twenty years' combined experience, their staff fully understands the issues that surround surrogacy, and are able to provide the highest quality of service to clients.

Mothers Who Think
http://www.salon.com/mwt/feature/1997/12/
cov_15feature.html?CP=SAL&DN=110
"Confessions of a Lesbian Sperm Donor" by Hank Pellissier

New England Cryogenic Center
665 Beacon St., Suite 302
Boston, MA 02215
617-262-3311 or 1-800-991-4999
Fax: 617-262-1234
info@necryogenic.com
http://www.necrogenic.com
New England Cryogenic Center, Inc., is North America's largest, full-service cryobank and second-largest facility of its kind in the world. They have been proudly
serving the reproductive community since 1982, when they were one of the first pioneers in cryogenic storage of human cells and an early provider of donor specimens. Although their name is regional, they are an international company, shipping
specimens to over twenty-eight different countries. If you are looking for donor
specimens, sperm bank, embryo storage, or cryogenic transportation, NECC is here
to help. No one does it better than NECC.

Ova the Rainbow
PO Box 187
Stevinson, CA 95374
209-669-8556
Fax: 775-307-9948
info@ovatherainbow.com

http://www.ovatherainbow.com/index.html
A hands-on egg donation and surrogacy agency that matches diverse egg donors and responsible surrogates with hopeful prospective parents.

Pact, An Adoption Alliance
4179 Piedmont Ave., Suite 330
Oakland, CA 94611
510-243-9460
Fax: 510-243-9970
info@pactadopt.org
http://www.pactadopt.org/
At Pact, we believe that in making an adoption plan, birth parents and adoptive parents enter into an agreement to recognize and protect the best interests of the child. Essential to that agreement is a lifelong commitment to recognize, respect, and address the dual heritages—both personal and cultural—that are the child's birthright. Our goal is for every child to feel wanted, honored, and loved, a cherished member of a strong family with proud connection to his or her rich heritages.

Parenting Articles
http://www.lesbian.org/lesbian-moms/articles.html
Gay and lesbian parenting articles.

PlanetOut's Families
Corporate Headquarters
PlanetOut Inc.
PO Box 500
San Francisco, CA 94104-0500
415-834-6500
Fax: 415-834-6502
http://www.planetout.com/families/
PlanetOut's on-line family community for gay, lesbian, and alternative lifestyles. Chat rooms, message boards, and more . . .

Prosepctive Queer Parents
http://www.queerparents.org/

ProudParenting.com
http://www.proudparenting.com/
Proud Parenting magazine.

R Family Vacations
2 Washington Avenue
Nyack, NY 10960
1-866-r-fam-vac
845-348-0397 (International Guests)
Fax: 845-348-0396
info@rFamilyVacations.com
http://www.rfamilyvacations.com
An LGBT family vacation guide run by Gregg Kaminsky and Rosie and Kelli O'Donnell.

Rainbowkids.com
letters@rainbowkids.com
http://www.rainbowkids.com
On-line international adoption.

Sample Parenting Contracts
http://www.queerparents.org/contracts.html

Soulforce
http://www.soulforce.org
An interfaith movement committed to ending spiritual violence perpetuated by religious policies and teachings against gay, lesbian, bisexual, and transgender (GLBT) people.

Surrogate Mothers, Inc.
PO Box 216
Monrovia, IN 46157
1-888-SURROGATE or 317-996-2000
scl@surrogatemothers.com
http://www.surrogatemothers.com
Their surrogate program is a full-service agency, coordinating all medical, travel, and legal procedures. It is the only recognized surrogacy program in the world that also openly works with gay and lesbian couples/individuals.

Surrogate Parenting Consultants
PO Box 1502
Highland, CA 92346
909-862-8228 or 1-800-500-7122
Fax: 909-864-7751
staff@spcsurrogates.com

http://www.spcsurrogates.com
Surrogate Parenting Consultants has been around since 1996 and words with alternative families and the gay and lesbian community. Their goal is to help make
the surrogacy and egg donor process go as smoothly as possible. Surrogate Parenting Consultants are here to help you build a family. Please visit their site—they are
an affordable option for surrogacy and egg donors.

Thegaybyboom.com, Inc.
6520 Platt Ave., #577
West Hills, CA 91307-3218
818-883-4753
Fax: 818-883-4755
info@thegaybyboom.com
http://www.thegaybyboom.com
Offers all the resources you need from the planning stage of having a baby to family living. Their network includes doctors, adoption and surrogacy resources, attorneys, health insurance providers, and the list goes on. This network has been
created to help you find the professionals you need to make your dream of having
children a reality in an open and comfortable environment.

Tiny Treasures, LLC
PO Box 45278
Somerville, MA 02145
1-866-357-6868
info@tinytreasuresagency.com
http://www.tinytreasuresagency.com/
An egg donation facilitation agency that helps guide prospective parents and egg
donors through the egg donation process.

Two Lives Publishing
PO Box 736
Ridley Park, PA 19078
http://www.twolives.com/
The on-line home of Two Lives Publishing and a complete resource center for lesbian, gay, bisexual, and transgendered parents and their children. Our mission is to
publish quality books for children in alternative families and to provide information to the LGBT family community through our Web site.

LGBT Family Magazines

And Baby Magazine
Out of the Box Publishing
499 Van Brunt Street
Brooklyn, NY 11231
http://www.andbabymag.com/frameset.cfm

Gay Parent Magazine
PO Box 750852
Forest Hills, NY 11375-0852
718-997-0392
acain@gis.net
http://www.gayparentmag.com

In the Family
Laura Markowitz, publisher
7850 N. Silverbell, #114-188
Tucson, AZ 85743
520-579-8043
lmarkowitz@aol.com
http://www.inthefamily.com/

In the Family is the only magaziane that focuses exclusively on lesbian, gay, bisexual, and transgender families, posing challenging questions and drawing on the wisdom of mental health experts who have been offering concrete advice and creative solutions to les-bi-gay families for years.

ProudParenting.com
Kelly Taylor, publisher/editor
Box 8272
Van Nuys, CA 91409-8272
323-512-2922
Fax: 818-909-3792
info@proudparenting.com
http://www.proudparenting.com
ProudParenting.com serves as an on-line portal for gay, lesbian, bisexual, and transgender parents and their families worldwide. Kelly previously published *Proud Parenting* and *Alternative Family* magazines.

INDEX